The Economic Geography of Innovation

This critical addition to the growing literature on innovation contains extensive analyses of the institutional and spatial aspects of innovation. Written by leading scholars in the fields of economic geography, innovation studies, planning, and technology policy, the fourteen chapters cover conceptual and measurement issues in innovation and relevant technology policies. The contributors examine how different institutional factors facilitate or hamper the flows of information and knowledge within and across firms, regions, and nations. In particular, they provide insights into the roles of important institutions, such as gender and culture, which are often neglected in the innovation literature, and demonstrate the key role that geography plays in the innovation process. They also discuss institutions and policy measures that support entrepreneurship and cluster development. The result is an excellent comparative picture of the institutional factors underlying innovation systems across the globe.

KAREN R. POLENSKE is Professor of Regional Political Economy and Planning in the Department of Urban Studies and Planning at Massachusetts Institute of Technology.

D1557078

The Economic Geography of Innovation

Edited by

Karen R. Polenske

CAMBRIDGE UNIVERSITY PRESS
Cambridge, New York, Melbourne, Madrid, Cape Town, Singapore, São Paulo

Cambridge University Press
The Edinburgh Building, Cambridge CB2 8RU, UK

Published in the United States of America by Cambridge University Press, New York

www.cambridge.org
Information on this title: www.cambridge.org/9780521689533

© Cambridge University Press 2007

First published 2007

Printed in the United Kingdom at the University Press, Cambridge

A catalogue record for this publication is available from the British Library

ISBN 978-0-521-86528-9 hardback
ISBN 978-0-521-68953-3 paperback

Contents

Figures

Tables

Notes on contributors

ESBEN S. ANDERSEN is Associate Professor at the Department of Business Studies, Aalborg University, Denmark. His PhD is in evolutionary economics, and his research interests range from development of agent-based simulation models of multi-sectoral economic evolution to the history of the economic analyses of evolutionary processes. He is engaged in the Danish Research Unit for Industrial Dynamics (DRUID) and in the development of the European Doctoral Training Program on the Economics of Technological and Institutional Change, in both cases since their start in 1995. He has written the book *Evolutionary Economics: Post-Schumpeterian Contributions*, as well as articles on economic organization, innovation theory, evolutionary modeling, and the history of economic thought.

CHRISTIE BAXTER is Principal Research Scientist, Department of Urban Studies and Planning, Massachusetts Institute of Technology (MIT). In her research and consultancies, she explores how governments and nonprofit institutions participate in major real estate projects. She directed, with Bernard J. Frieden, a nationwide study of how local communities use former military bases to achieve economic development goals. From 1992 to 1998 she directed the MIT Project on Social Investing, which sought to increase private and nonprofit investment in beneficial capital and business projects. Previous research has examined major infrastructure initiatives, downtown redevelopment, and innovative contracts for public building development. She has authored *Program-Related Investing: A Technical Manual for Foundations* (1996) and a number of studies, papers, and book chapters about public-purpose real estate development.

ANNE P. CARTER is Fred C. Hecht Professor of Economics Emerita at Brandeis University. She is a former Dean of the Faculty at Brandeis, Founding President of the International Input-Output Association, and a Fellow of the American Association for the Advancement of Science. Her research continues to focus on structural change in an input-output context and the broad challenge of measuring economic variables in the evolving economy.

BENT DALUM is Associate Professor in Economics at Aalborg University, and Head of the Socio-Economic Implications of Telecommunications (SEIT) research group at the Center for TeleInFrastruktur at Aalborg University. His research focuses on regional innovation systems and industrial economics; technology; structural competitiveness and international trade; and national systems of innovation and industrial policy.

MARYANN P. FELDMAN is Jeffrey S. Skoll Chair, Innovation and Entrepreneurship, and Professor of Business Economics at Rotman School of Management, University of Toronto. She is the author of some thirty-five articles on economic geography in related academic journals, and of books including the *Geography of Innovation and Innovation Policy for the Knowledge-Based Economy* (with Al Link). Her current research focuses on the issues of innovation and technological change: in particular, the process of innovation and the determinants of technological change and economic growth.

BERNARD FINGLETON is Reader in Geographical Economics at Cambridge University. He holds PhDs in Geography and in Economics, with research interests in spatial econometrics, regional productivity growth, the "new economic geography," urban economics, cluster analysis, simulation and dynamics, and urban, regional, and spatial economic development. He is Director of Postgraduate Studies in the Department of Land Economy, and Editor of *Spatial Economic Analysis*. He has been a consultant and research proposal evaluator for the European Commission and UK government departments.

MERIC S. GERTLER is Professor of Geography and Planning, Goldring Chair in Canadian Studies, and co-director of the Program on Globalization and Regional Innovation Systems at the University of Toronto. He also co-directs the Innovation Systems Research Network (ISRN), a national network of scholars in Canada funded by a $2.5 million grant (2005–2010) from the Social Sciences and Humanities Research Council to study "The Social Dynamics of Economic Performance: Innovation and Creativity in City-Regions." His publications include *Manufacturing Culture: The Institutional Geography of Industrial Practice, Innovation and Social Learning* (with David Wolfe), and *The Oxford Handbook of Economic Geography* (with Gordon Clark and Maryann P. Feldman).

AMY GLASMEIER is E. Willard Miller Professor of Economic Geography in the Department of Geography, Pennsylvania State University. She is also Editor of *Economic Geography* and Director of the Penn State Environmental Inquiry Minor. She has published three books on international industrial and economic development, including *High-Tech America, High-Tech Potential: Economic Development in Rural America*, and *From Combines to Computers: Rural Services Development in the Age of Information Technology*, and more than forty scholarly articles. Her poverty research website is http://www.povertyinamerica.psu.edu/.

MIA GRAY is University Lecturer in the Department of Geography and Fellow of Girton College at the University of Cambridge. Her current work includes a socially oriented analysis of occupational and job segregation; research on skill formation, diffusion of knowledge, and innovation in high-tech labor markets; and investigation of new types of labor organizing in low-paid service sector occupations.

DANILO C. IGLIORI is Affiliated Lecturer in the Department of Land Economy, University of Cambridge and Assistant Professor in the Department of Economics, University of São Paulo. His interests are in applied economics, with focus on spatial models. His research topics include spatial clustering, innovation, economic development, urban economics, land use, environmental problems, and spatial econometrics.

AL JAMES is an Assistant Lecturer in the Department of Geography at the University of Cambridge, and a Fellow of Fitzwilliam College. He is an economic geographer with ongoing research interests in cultural economy, the geographical foundations of regional economic development, and geographies of work and workers in the New Economy.

BJÖRN JOHNSON is an Associate Professor and Reader in Economics and connected to the economic studies program, Aalborg University, Aalborg Øst, Denmark. His earlier research dealt with regional aspects of consumer behavior, planned economies, comparative economic systems, and comparative analysis of contemporary strategies in economic policy. His current research is in the field of institutional economics and focuses on the relations between technical and institutional change.

ALICE LAM is Professor of Organization Studies at the School of Management, Royal Holloway University of London. Her current research covers the relationship between organizational forms, knowledge creation, and societal institutions. She has published in a wide range of academic journals including *Organization Studies*, *Journal of Management Studies*, and *Industrial Relations*.

LENA LAVINAS is Professor, Institute of Economics, Federal University of Rio de Janeiro. She specializes in Social Policies at the International Labor Organization (ILO) in Geneva (Switzerland) and teaches about labor, poverty, and other social issues at the Universidade Federal do Rio de Janeiro – Rio de Janeiro Federal University (UFRJ). She also has published on social policies with the Instituto de Pesquisa Econômica Aplicada – Applied Economic Research Institute (IPEA) in Brazil.

BENGT-ÅKE LUNDVALL is Professor of Economics in the Department of Business Studies at Aalborg Uiversity, and Special Term Professor in the School of Economics and Management at Tsinghua University. His current research is on the economics of knowledge and innovation in relation to economic development. He is former Deputy Director of the OECD Directorate for Science, Technology, and Industry and initiator and co-ordinator of the global network of innovation scholars Globelics (www.globelics.org).

ALEJANDRO MERCADO-CELIS has a PhD in Urban Planning from the University of California in Los Angeles and a masters degree in regional development from Colegio de la Frontera Norte, Tijuana, Baja California. He is a Professor at the Center for North America Research in the Universidad Nacional Autónoma de México, México City, DF, México. He conducts research on comparative studies of Canadian, US, and Mexican regional restructuring.

BARRY MOORE is a Fellow in Economics in Downing College at the University of Cambridge, University Reader in Economics in the Department of Land Economy, and Senior Research Associate in the Centre of Business Research, Judge Business School, at the University of Cambridge. He has been a special advisor to the OECD, and consultant to the European Commission and different government departments in the United Kingdom. His current research interests include regional economic development and policy evaluation, the competitiveness of cities and the city system, high-technology clusters and collective learning, including the role of research institutes and universities.

RAAKHI ODEDRA has a BA in Economics from the University of Cambridge and an MSc in Economics for Development from the University of Oxford. She has completed research for the Scottish Executive on the social care labor market. Currently, she is posted in the Ministry of Education, Rwanda, on an Overseas Development Institute fellowship.

KAREN R. POLENSKE is Professor of Regional Political Economy and Planning and Head of the International Development and Regional Planning (IDRP) group in the Department of Urban Studies and Planning at the Massachusetts Institute of Technology (MIT). She is the author or the editor of seven books including the *Technology – Energy – Environment – Health (TEEH) Chain in China: A Case Study of Coke-making in Shanxi Province*, and *Chinese Economic Planning and Input-Output Analysis* (co-edited with Chen Xikang). She has also published numerous articles in key economic, energy, environmental, and planning journals. Her current research includes an analysis of cokemaking and steelmaking technology options in the People's Republic of China (PRC, China); socioeconomic impacts of the silent aircraft initiative in the United Kingdom; economic growth in distressed counties in Appalachia; spatial dispersion of innovation; and land recycling in China.

APIWAT RATANAWARAHA is a doctoral candidate in the International Development and Regional Planning (IDRP) group at the Massachusetts Institute of Technology (MIT), in the Department of Urban Studies and Planning. He is also a Doctoral Fellow at the MIT Industrial Performance Center and a Research Fellow in the Science, Technology, and Globalization Group of the Science, Technology, and Public Policy Program at Harvard University's Belfer Center for Science and International Affairs. His current research covers topics on technical standards, international trade, and technological catch-up by latecomer countries.

ANNALEE SAXENIAN is Dean and Professor in the School of Information Management and Systems (SIMS) and Professor in the Department of City and Regional Planning at the University of California, Berkeley. As an expert on economic development in information technology, she has written extensively on the social and economic organization of production in technology regions such as Silicon Valley. Her current research explores how immigrant engineers and scientists have transferred technology entrepreneurship to regions in China, India, and Taiwan. Her publications include *Regional Advantage: Culture and Competition in Silicon Valley and Route 128*, *Silicon Valley's New Immigrant Entrepreneurs*, and *Local and Global Networks of Immigrant Professionals in Silicon Valley*.

EDWARD S. STEINFELD is Associate Professor of Political Science at the Massachusetts Institute of Technology (MIT). Professor Steinfeld, a China specialist, focuses on the political economy of reform in socialist and post-socialist systems. Much of his research has focused on the reform of state-owned industry and the transformation of the financial sector in China. His current work focuses on decisionmaking in the Chinese energy sector. Steinfeld's publications include the book *Forging Reform in China* and *Financial Sector Reform in China* (co-edited with Yasheng Huang and Anthony Saich).

MICHAEL STORPER is Professor of Regional and International Development in the School of Public Affairs at the University of California – Los Angeles, Professor of Economic Sociology at Institut d'Etudes Politiques de Paris, and Professor of Economic Geography at the London School of Economics and Political Science (LSE). His most recent books are *Worlds of Production: The Action Frameworks of the Economy* (with Robert Salais), *The Regional World: Territorial Development in a Global Economy*, and *Latecomers in the Global Economy*. He has been a consultant with the OECD, the European Union, and the Brazilian government.

PETER TYLER is University Professor of Urban and Regional Economics in the Department of Land Economy at the University of Cambridge. He has been working on issues of local labor markets; evaluation of government policies; economic restructuring; and business performance – small and medium-sized enterprises (SMEs). His recent publications include *Enterprising Places: Sustaining Competitive Locations for Knowledge-Based Business* (with several co-authors), and *Developing the Rural Dimension of Business Support Policy* (with two co-authors).

Acknowledgments

Working with such distinguished scholars from many parts of the world has been an exciting and challenging experience. The basic conception for a seminar that enabled me to have the contributors to this book prepare their papers arose from a graduate seminar I gave to a few students the two years previous to the official "Geography of Innovation" Special Program on Urban and Regional Studies (SPURS) seminar. At the initial graduate seminar, a small group of talented students helped me decide on what was missing from the innovation literature and who might be invited to give a talk to help fill the gap. The graduate students in the initial seminar included Genevieve Connors, who worked with me as an RA/TA, Criseida Navarro-Diaz, Smita Srinivas, and Christine Erickson. I thank each of them for the intellectual challenges they posed throughout the year. In the Fall of 2003, I gave the seminar as part of the SPURS seminar series. I thank Christine Erickson, the teaching assistant, Nimfa deLeon, SPURS administration, and especially John deMonchaux, SPURS director, and Lawrence S. Vale, department head, for their support during the summer as I prepared for the seminar as well as during the seminar itself.

When I moderated the Fall semester SPURS seminar, I had most of the speakers not only give a talk to the SPURS fellows, but also meet with a group of ten graduate students, most of whom were PhDs. Just when I thought I knew most of the current literature, one of these bright energetic students would find still another book or article that would shed new light on our discussions. The students were so motivated that I never had to assign anyone to do the reading for a specific day, because all of them did it and were prepared to discuss the issues covered in a critical, insightful way. I can truly say that this is the best seminar I ever taught at the MIT since coming in 1972. That exuberant feeling was evidently shared by the students who gave the seminar unusually high ratings in the end-of-term evaluation, and they requested that we continue to explore the topic of spatial concentration/dispersion in the following Spring term. Several of the students have used the papers they did for this seminar to jump-start them on dissertation research. I am eternally grateful for the unique contribution each and every graduate participant made, including: Alberto Blanco, Liou Cao, Christine Erickson, Myoung-gu Kang, Criseida Navarro-Dias, Apiwat Ratanawarada, Elizabeth Reynolds, Michael Sable, Ryan Tam, and Christopher Zegras.

When the Cambridge-MIT Institute (CMI) agreed to fund the seminar series and the subsequent publication of this book of papers compiled from the lectures, I decided to hire a graduate student to help me review and edit the papers given by the speakers. I selected Apiwat Ratanawarada, and we soon became more like colleagues than professor – student. He is highly sought after to work with faculty in MIT, so that I was delighted that he agreed to work with me for a year on the reading and editing of the papers. He helped me provide the authors with an excellent critique of their papers and suggestions for revising them. The work we put into this stage of manuscript preparation paid off when Cambridge University Press agreed to publish the manuscript as a book. I deeply thank Apiwat for all his efforts in relation to the editing of the chapters, but also for the intellectually demanding questions he kept asking.

I deeply thank each of the authors who presented interesting lectures and have written exciting chapters. I had each do several rounds of revisions, but each person kept his/her sense of humor as I asked for one more change, often on the eve of a major holiday. You were a wonderful, supportive set of colleagues who have helped expand my own knowledge of innovation greatly. This book is indeed a fascinating contribution to the literature because of the knowledge you have shared with the world.

After Cambridge University Press agreed to publish the book, I needed to get the papers into a form that followed their guidelines, which is not an inconsequential task. Since October 2005, I have been assisted by three skilled people. Francis Diaz did all the reference checks and rearranging the references into the style required by the Press. This was a challenging job, partly because authors each initially used their own style, so that, in reality, we had fourteen different ways of doing the references. Jacob Wegmann assisted me in formatting the papers to the Press guidelines- and, in the process, he also did some excellent editing of each paper. Li Xin did an outstanding job of putting all the papers into a single document and doing final checks, with some assistance by Chen Zhiyu on the final day. I especially appreciate their willingness to take time during the busy winter holiday season to do this work.

Funding for the SPURS seminar, the travel and honoraria for the speakers, and for supporting for the student assistants, came from CMI and from the Department of Urban Studies and Planning (DUSP). I thank John deMonchaux (SPURS), Scott Shurtleff and James H. Keller (CMI), and Bish Sanyal and Larry J. Vale (DUSP) for seeing that sufficient funding was provided to me from the three academic divisions that they represent. Finally, I am required to say the following, but I do appreciate the support from the UK government for the CMI project. In this case, I believe they have received real value for the funds, thanks perhaps to all the people mentioned above, plus all the talented authors. I especially thank the staff at Cambridge University Press for their careful work on this manuscript. Chris Harrison, Publishing Director (Social Sciences), kindly gave me strong encouragement and important information on the publication protocols during the initial stages of the review and editing; Dr. Lynn Dunlop, then Assistant Editor, Economics and Business, Joanna Breeze, Production Editor, and her colleague Jodie Barnes responded quickly to my e-mails and kept their sense of humor as I had to delay longer than anticipated in sending the final product, Barbara Docherty, copy-editor, did an excellent job of editing. Overall, these and other CUP employees helped make this a superb publication.

This publication is an output from a research project funded by CMI. CMI is funded in part by the UK government. The research was carried out for CMI by the MIT. CMI can accept no responsibility for any information provided or views expressed.

Abstracts

Part I Concepts and measurements in innovation

1 Introduction

Karen R. Polenske

Innovation occurs in a particular place at a particular time. One recurring theme throughout this book is how technology, innovation, and alternative means of transferring knowledge are changing spatial relationships among firms, hence the title of the book, *The Economic Geography of Innovation*. I discuss in this chapter some of the reasons this book is unique among the many publications on innovation. My main reason for collecting this set of contributions is to highlight the fact that innovation is done in space, whereas most innovation studies are aspatial, with the analyst focusing on the type of innovation done, not where it is done and on how knowledge is transferred depending upon whether it is codified or tacit knowledge. I end the chapter with a review of the remaining thirteen chapters.

2 Measurement of the clustering and dispersion of innovation

Anne P. Carter

In modern economics, we try to explain levels of output and of input, prices, and incomes in quantitative terms. Measurement is thus prerequisite to scientific progress in this field. Innovation generally involves qualitative change, and therefore complicates the problem of measuring economic variables. In this chapter, I explain the obstacles that innovation poses to measurement, and therefore to quantification, in economics. I review the "double-inversion" strategy proposed by Leontief to represent the most rapidly changing sectoral outputs in terms of their more standard inputs. Because change affects virtually all inputs and outputs, this strategy proved impractical, and Leontief recognized that input-output analysis, and indeed most analysis implemented with the national accounts, could be valid only in the short or medium term.

Contemporary economists have used proxies and other creative strategies to study innovation, circumventing the essential difficulties of measuring qualitative change. In this chapter, I provide an overview of these strategies and their contribution to our understanding of how a rapidly evolving economy works. However, the problem of measuring the standard economic variables in the face of rapid innovation remains unsolved. Is it possible that today's quantitative economic variables are themselves becoming obsolete?

3   *Measuring the geography of innovation: a literature review*

Apiwat Ratanawaraha and Karen R. Polenske

We focus in this chapter on the measurement issues arising from analysts using diverse definitions and approaches to study the distributive patterns of innovation, none of which is ideal. Through a review of innovation literature, we identify the data and indicators commonly used to assess innovation and its distribution, as well as the strengths and weaknesses of such measures. We conclude that the available measures are inadequate not only because of limited data availability, but also because analysts have not sufficiently defined and conceptualized theoretical methods to conduct the measurements, nor have they considered the trade-offs between relatively simple indicators and more comprehensive means of conducting measurements of innovation.

4   *Employment growth and clusters dynamics of creative industries in Great Britain*

Bernard Fingleton, Danilo C. Igliori, Barry Moore, and Raakhi Odedra

In this chapter, we test some of the main hypotheses about the importance of horizontal clusters for employment growth in small firms. We adopt a simple concept of clustering to examine its impact on SME's employment growth in creative industries, using evidence for Great Britain, 1991–2000. In the main section of the chapter, we estimate spatial econometric models, controlling for supply- and demand-side conditions in order to isolate the effect of initial cluster intensity. One important aspect of the chapter is the existence of a declustering mechanism due to congestion effects. The estimated spatial econometric model provides evidence supporting the presence of positive and negative externalities associated with different levels of cluster intensity, with respect to employment growth in the creative industries. It is also apparent that external effects spill over across area boundaries. These effects point to the importance of local spin-offs and knowledge flows creating technological externalities that transgress area boundaries. These findings reinforce the claim by other analysts that agglomerations play an important role in economic performance. However, they also indicate that the positive effects of cluster intensity have upper thresholds, and we can have the opposite situation where negative externalities predominate and employment is destroyed.

Part II Institutional and spatial aspects of information and knowledge flows

5   *Tacit knowledge in production systems: how important is geography?*

Meric S. Gertler

Within economic geography and industrial economics, interest in the concept of tacit knowledge has grown steadily in recent years. Nelson and Winter stimulated this interest in the work of Michael Polanyi by using the concept of tacit knowledge to inform their analysis of the routines and evolutionary dynamics of technological change. Recently, the concept has received even closer scrutiny. Analysts argue whether or not geographical proximity is a precondition for the effective transmission of tacit knowledge between economic actors. In this chapter, I seek to bring clarity to this debate by exploring an important, but hitherto neglected, aspect of tacit knowledge in the workplace – namely, its institutional underpinnings. While much of the innovation literature focuses on a single question: can tacit knowledge be effectively shared over long distances?, I argue that this issue cannot be properly analyzed without considering a prior question: how is tacit knowledge produced, and what role do institutional frameworks play in this process? I explore these arguments through the use of a case study examining attempts to transfer tacit production knowledge between geographically distant partners.

I revisit Michael Polanyi's original conception of tacit knowledge, showing it to be limited by its experiential and cognitive emphasis, with insufficient attention devoted to the role and institutional foundations of social context. Alternatively, I argue that analysts cannot sort out the geography of tacit knowledge (i.e. whether, or under what conditions, it can be transmitted over long distances) without inquiring into the foundations of context and culture and the institutional underpinnings of economic activity, taking the work of another Polanyi (Karl Polanyi) as the logical starting point.

6   *The self-aware firm: information needs, acquisition strategies, and utilization prospects*

Amy Glasmeier

Debates about the extent to which regions are differentially conditioned to foster innovation move in two divergent directions. The first set of analysts takes a normative approach in suggesting what is required of regions and firms to be competitive, innovative, and resilient. Their perspective draws largely on case studies of "successful" regions or of firms where learning either occurs or is in some way suboptimal. The second set of analysts takes a perspective with a positive approach to firm learning and investigates the practice of information acquisition, knowledge creation, and behavioral change in firms. While the first analysts suggest that firms can and do act deliberately and with forethought, the second, survey-based, analysts suggest that firms are fallible, narrowly focused, and myopic. How do we reconcile these two apparently divergent perspectives?

In this chapter, I affirm the ways in which firms acquire information and the degree to which they act on it. These results demonstrate that firms by and large minimize their search processes for information. Further, having acquired it, they fail to act on this information in a deliberate fashion. These findings appear invariant across locations, suggesting that decisionmakers who design policies to enhance firm-level innovation and regional competitiveness should be mindful of the actual behavior of firms as they design public-sector programs. I provide a broad representative assessment of the capabilities of SMEs to acquire and utilize strategic business and technical information and speculate about the stages of being firms can and do reflect that coincide with a heightened ability to acquire, translate, and internalize strategic information.

7   *Theorizing the gendered institutional bases of innovative regional economies*

Mia Gray and Al James

Although social institutions are widely regarded as key determinants of success in high-growth regional economies, the regional learning and innovation literature remains largely premised on a series of assumptions regarding work patterns and social interactions among entrepreneurs and science oriented employees that are gender-blind. Focusing on the industrial agglomeration of ICT firms in Cambridge, England, we examine the role that gender plays in constructing distinctive patterns of work and sociocultural interaction among male and female workers within this so-called "blueprint" regional economy, and how female workers' abilities to contribute to key processes widely theorized to positively underpin learning and innovation at the levels of the firm and the region are constrained relative to their male colleagues. We also discuss the wider implications of these findings for socially inclusive regional economic development strategies.

8   *Multinationals and transnational social space for learning: knowledge creation and transfer through global R&D networks*

      Alice Lam

In this chapter, I contrast the experiences of four MNCs, headquartered in two countries, Japan and the United States, in order to evaluate the influence of national patterns of organization and innovation on global R&D networks. I consider the comparative effectiveness of the different models of R&D organization in co-ordinating globally dispersed knowledge creation. I find a substantial amount of variation in the degree to which the firms succeed in attaining a high degree of "embeddedness" in the innovation networks of the host country, in this case the United Kingdom, where their overseas research facilities are located. Among other factors, I find that the degree to which a corporation's R&D network is distributed rather than hierarchical bears significantly upon the degree to which it successfully achieves the goal of fostering transnational learning.

9   *Brain circulation and regional innovation: The Silicon Valley–Hsinchu–Shanghai triangle*

      AnnaLee Saxenian

A highly mobile community of Chinese engineers and entrepreneurs with work experience and connections in Silicon Valley is transferring know-how and skill between distant regional economies faster and more flexibly than most MNCs and transforming the geography of IT production. The focus of the chapter is on the relocation of semiconductor design and manufacturing from its original concentration in the United States and Japan, first to Taiwan and subsequently to Shanghai, in the last two decades. A similar process of "brain circulation" has reshaped the spatial distribution of other IT sectors.

Part III   Institutions and innovation systems

10   National systems of production, innovation, and competence building

Bengt-Åke Lundvall, Björn Johnson, Esben S. Andersen, and Bent Dalum

The authors have worked on innovation systems for almost two decades, and this chapter is an attempt to take stock. Section 10.1 reflects on the innovation system concept in the light of economic geography and it has been authored specifically for this volume, while the following sections form a shortened and slightly revised version of a paper published in *Research Policy* (Lundvall *et al.* 2002). In section 10.2, we reflect upon the emergence and fairly rapid diffusion of the concept of "national system of innovation," as well as related concepts. In section 10.3, we describe how the Aalborg version of the concept evolved by a combination of ideas that moved from production structure towards including all elements and relationships contributing to innovation and competence building. In section 10.4, we discuss the challenges involved in both a theoretical deepening of the concept and in moving toward a broader approach.

11   Perspectives on entrepreneurship and cluster formation: biotechnology in the US Capitol region

Maryann P. Feldman

The US Capitol region ranks as one of the important biotechnology (biotech) clusters in the United States. This chapter documents the highlights of the historical development of the cluster. The Capitol region biotech cluster, in essence, is the result of three reinforcing sets of factors: pre-existing resources, entrepreneurship, and the incentives and infrastructure provided by government. Because of significant investments in science and technology (S&T), the region was prepared to capitalize on technological opportunities in biotechnology as well as institutional policy changes that facilitated technology-based entrepreneurship, which partially contributed to its rise in the United States from twelfth place in 1975 to fourth place in 1999 in the number of biotech patent applications.

12   *Facilitating enterprising places: the role of intermediaries in the United States and United Kingdom*

Christie Baxter and Peter Tyler

Regions around the world want the economic benefits associated with high-technology companies. But creating and nurturing such centers, what we call "enterprising places," is a complex process. Even when a place has the essential resources – an excellent university or research center, facilities for companies, and an educated workforce – it is not clear how to sustain a center from them. The efforts of policymakers to do just that comprise a rich source of experimental evidence. We examine that evidence here, focusing on the kinds of organizations regional leaders have used to facilitate the development of enterprising places in Eastern Massachusetts and Scotland's Central Belt.

We find that intermediaries, organizations whose structure and mission was to connect different sectors, were central in the design and implementation of development policies and programs in the two regions. In addition to their programmatic missions, intermediaries enabled entrepreneurship, leadership, innovation, and a continuity of purpose during periods of political and economic change. These intermediaries also changed over time, reflecting evolving theories of economic development and the geographic, cultural, and political environment of the regions in which they were embedded. We find that the differences between intermediaries in Massachusetts and Scotland, which reflect national differences in institutional structure, have affected the kinds of partnerships and outcomes these intermediaries have achieved. Such differences could contribute to the greater vitality of centers in the United States relative to those in the United Kingdom.

13   *Innovation, integration, and technology upgrading in contemporary Chinese industry*

Edward S. Steinfeld

China's extraordinary economic transformation over the past two decades has been linked inextricably with the interaction between the depth of the domestic institutional reform and the degree of Chinese producers' engagement in the global economy. Even so, the competitiveness and sustainability of China's firms in the global market are still under debate. I argue that Chinese firms are structured in a fashion that allows them to compete extremely effectively on the basis of low cost in relatively low-value manufacturing activities, although this structure does not easily allow them to move upward in the production chain into more innovative, higher-return activities. In this chapter, I examine the limits and sustainability of the "virtuous interaction" between Chinese firms' engagement in the global competition and governmental reform style, state capacity, as well as industrial policy. I examine both whether Chinese firms can develop organizationally the sort of innovative capacities that lead to long-term competitiveness, and what the obstacles to date have been.

14   Society, community, and development: a tale of two regions

Michael Storper, Lena Lavinas, and Alejandro Mercado-Célis

Contemporary social science remains quite divided about the type of co-ordination that allows some groups of agents to carry out successful economic development and which distinguishes them from cases of failure. In some cases, it is said to be traditional or nonmarket forms of co-ordination, such as family, networks, or shared traditions: these are "communitarian" sources of organization. In most mainstream economics, however, the opposite is said to be necessary: anonymous and transparent rules of the market, property rights, and contracts. These are "societal" forces. For example, for some analysts, Silicon Valley is a case of community, while for others it is due to appropriate societal forces. The same cleavage can be found in rival interpretations of the success of the "Asian Tigers," the industrial clusters of the "Third Italy," or any of a host of other cases. A more robust explanation shows how both communitarian and societal forces act as checks and balances on one another, all the while each creating specific, but different, sources of efficiency in the economy. We illustrate this view via a study in contrasts, between a failed case of low-technology economic development in the Brazilian Northeast, and a success story in the state of Jalisco, Mexico.

REFERENCE

Lundvall, B.-Å., B. Johnson, E. S. Andersen, and B. Dalum, 2002. "National Systems of Production, Innovation, and Competence Building," *Research Policy*, 31: 213–231

Abbreviations and acronyms

2S LS	Two-Stage Least Squares
ABPI	Association of the British Pharmaceutical Industry
ADV	Advertising
AGCI	Adjusted Geographic Concentration Index
AGS	Alliance for Global Sustainability
AMRICD	Army Medical Research Institute of Chemical Defense
AMRIID	Army Medical Research Institute of Infections Disease
ARC	Architectural/engineering Activities
ART	Artistic and Literary Creation
ASE	Advanced Semiconductor Engineering
B2B	Business-to-business
BANCOMEXT	Banco Nacional de Comercio Exterior
BNDES	Banco Nacional de Desenvolvimento Economico e Social
BRIMS	Basic Research Institute in Mathematical Science
BSI	BioSpace International
CAD	Computer-aided design
CAPES	Coordenação de Aperfeiçoamento de Pessoal de Nível Superior
CASPA	Chinese American Semiconductor Association
CEO	Client executive officer
CESPRI	Centre for Research on Innovation and Internationalization
cGMP	Current Good Manufacturing Procedures
CIE	Chinese Institute of Engineers
CINA	Chinese Internet and Networking Association
CIS	Community Innovation Survey
CMI	Cambridge–MIT Institute
CORDIS	Community R&D Information Service

CORDIS–RTD	Community R&D Information Service – Research and Technology
CQI	Continuous Quality Improvement
CR4	Concentration 4 ratio
CRADAs	Cooperative Research and Development Agreements
CSISS	Center for Spatially Integrated Social Science
DBED	Department of Business and Economic Development
DCCS	Dynamically Controlled Crystallization System
DCMS	Department for Culture, Media and Sport
DRUID	Danish Research Unity for Industrial Dynamics
DTI	Department of Trade and Industry
DUI	Doing, Using, and Interacting
DUSP	Department of Urban Studies and Planning
EGGCI	Ellison–Glaeser Geographic Concentration Index
EPAT	European Patents Database
EPO	European Patent Office
ERI	Edinburgh Research and Innovation Ltd.
ERSO	Elections Research and Service Organization
EU	European Union
FDA	Food and Drug Administration
FDI	Foreign direct investment
FMS	Flexible manufacturing systems
FRB	Federal Reserve Bank
FT	*Financial Times*
FY	Fiscal Year
GCI	Geographic Coincidence (Concentration) Index
GDP	Gross domestic product
GERD	Gross expenditures on R&D
GR	Gene-Related
GREMI	Groupe de Recherche Européen sur les Millieux Innovateurs
GSMC	Grace Semiconductor Manufacturing Corp
GTDN	Group for the Development of the Northeast
HC	Horizontal Clustering
HCLQ	Horizontal Clustering Location Quotient
HGS	Human Genome Sciences
HHI	Herfindahl – Hirschman index
HP	Hewlett-Packard
HPAEs	Highly-performing Asian economies
IA	Interfirm Alliance
IBGE	Instituto Brasileiro de Geografia e Estatística
ICs	Integrated circuits

ICSI	Integrated Circuit Solution, Inc.
ICT	Information and communication technology
IDRP	International Development and Regional Planning
IKE	Innovation, Knowledge, and Economic
ILO	International Labor Organization
IMF	International Monetary Fund
INEGI	Instituto Nacional de Estadística Geografia e Informática
INPI	Institut National de la Propriété Industrielle
INSEE	Institut National de la Statistique et des Etudes Economiques
IPEA	Instituto de Pequisa Econômica Aplicadae
IPRs	Intellectual property rights
ISI	Institute for Scientific Information
ISLI	Institute for System Level Integration
ISSI	Integrated Silicon Solutions, Inc.
ISRN	Innovation Systems Research Networks
ISTAT	Instituto Nazionale di Statistica
IT	Information technology
ITIs	Intermediary Technology Institutes
IUL	Institut für Umweltschutz und Landwirtschaft
IV	Instrumental Variables
JCL	J-ICT Cambridge Laboratory
J-ICT	Japanese Information and Communication Technology
JLL	Japan London Laboratory
J-Pharma	Japanese Pharmaceutical
JPO	Japanese Patent Office
JV	Joint venture
KM	Knowledge management
LECs	Local enterprise companies
LGC	Locational Gini Coefficient
LQ	Location Quotient
LSE	London School of Economics and Political Science
M&As	Mergers and acquisitions
MAED	Mass Alliance for Economic Development
MBI	Massachusetts Biomedical Initiatives
MERIT	Maastricht Economic Research Institute on Innovation and Technology
MERIT-CATI	Maastricht Economic Research Institute on Innovation and Technology – Co-operative Agreements and Technology Indicators

MIT	Massachusetts Institute of Technology
MNCs	Multinational corporations
MNE	Multinational enterprise
MOT	Motion Pictures and Video Production
MRC	Microelectronics Research Centre
MTC	Massachusetts Technology Collaborative
NAFTA	North American Free Trade Agreement
NAICS	North American Industrial Classification System
NASA	National Aeronautics and Space Administration
NBER	National Bureau of Economic Research
NCEQW	National Center on the Education Quality of the Workforce
NIH	National Institutes of Health
NIS	National and regional innovation systems
NIST	National Institute of Standards and Technology
NOMIS	Nomis Official Labor Market Statistics
NSB	National Science Board
NSI	National System of Innovation
NSF	National Science Foundation
OECD	Organization for Economic Co-operation and Development
OEM	Original equipment manufacturer
ONS	Office for National Statistics
PACEC	Public and Corporate Economic Consultants
PC	Personal computer
PCTPAT	Patent Convention Treaty Patents Applications Database
PHT	Photographic Activities
PRC	People's Republic of China
R&D	Research and development
RBS	Royal Bank of Scotland
RDAs	Regional Development Agencies
RIP	Registro de la Propriedad Industrial
RISESI	Regional Impact of the Information Society on Employment and Integration
RTD	Research and Technology Development
RTV	Radio and Television
S&E	Science and engineering
S&T	Science and technology
SBA	Small Business Administration
SBIR	Small Business Innovation Research

SCI	Science Citation Index
SCNM	Sistema de Cuentas Nacionales de México
SE	Scottish Enterprise
SEIJAL	Sistema Estatal de Información Jalisco
SEIT	Socio-Economic Implications of Telecommunications
SEZ	Special Economic Zone
SFT	Software Consultancy and Supply
SIC	Standard Industrial Classification
SIE	Scottish Institute for Enterprise
SIMS	School of Information Management and System
SKU	Stock keeping unit
SMEs	Small and medium-sized enterprises
SMIC	Semiconductor Manufacturing International Corp
SOEs	State-owned enterprises
SPRU	Science Policy Research Unit
SPURS	Special Program on Urban and Regional Studies
SRAMs	Static Random Access Memory
STI	Science, technology, and innovation
STTR	Small Business Technology Transfer
SUDENE	Superintendency for the Development of the Northeast
T&T	Tlaquepaque and Tonalá
TEDCO	Technology Development Corporation
TEEH	Technology–Energy–Environment–Health
TLO	Technology Licensing Office
TPO	Technology Patent Office
TSER	Targeted Socio-Economic Research
TSMC	Taiwan Semiconductor Manufacturing Corp
TVE	Township and Village Enterprises
UALAD	Unitary and Local Authority Districts
UCL	University College London
UFRJ	Universidade Federal do Rio de Janeiro
UK	United Kingdom
UNCTAD	United Nations Commission for Trade and Development
UNIVIMP	University Impact Variable
USA	United States
USPTO	US Patent and Trademark Office
VAT	Value-added tax
VINNOVA	Systems of Innovation Authority

WBDC	Worcester Business Development Corporation
WIIG	Walden International Investment Group
WPI	Worcester Polytechnic Institute
WRAIR	Walter Reed Army Institute for Research
WTO	World Trade Organization

Part I

Concepts and measurements in innovation

1   Introduction

Karen R. Polenske

1.1   Introduction

Every day people talk about innovation on the radio and television, as well as in newspapers, books, and popular and academic articles. In May 2004, for example, Alan Greenspan, then head of the US Federal Reserve Bank (FRB) spoke at an FRB conference of the Federal Reserve Board of Chicago on "Globalization and Innovation" (Greenspan 2004). *The Boston Globe* each Monday since February 7, 2000 has devoted an entire section of the newspaper to the topic of innovation, covering a wide spectrum of sectors, such as biology, information technology, and e-commerce. Even so, these leading conveyors of information, for the most part, neglect the fact that the innovation occurs *in space*. The product may be conceived in an office, a garage, or on an airplane, but to begin the process of developing the product to bring it to the market, a production facility must be built or located, or a part of another production area taken. The influential authors from the economics, industrial organization, planning, and political science fields I selected to write chapters for this book all help fill this "spatial gap" in the literature. They summarize and critique previous innovation theories and concepts, and provide insights into the spatial concentration and dispersion of innovation. They provide an interesting comparative picture of the institutional factors that underlie innovation systems in East Asia, Latin America, the United Kingdom, and the United States, indicating the vast geography over which innovation occurs.

1.2   Background to the book

The chapters in this book are mainly based on talks the authors gave at a seminar I organized for the attendees at the weekly Special Program on Urban and Regional Studies (SPURS) seminar at the MIT in the Fall of 2003, entitled Geography of Innovation. Speakers covered a number of topics related to innovation, its origins, concentration, and dispersal, and how industries, communities, and regional economic-development planners have succeeded in developing knowledge-intensive industries. These different groups often form partnerships with universities and business, which is one of the aims of the Cambridge–MIT Institute (CMI), which helped to fund the seminar.

Recent success stories of cluster-based economic development emerging from cases such as Silicon Valley (California), Research Triangle Park (North Carolina), Bangalore (India), and the Ouli Region (Finland) suggest that the nature of innovation and economic development is changing. Regions all over the world are now attempting to follow these role models. Several years ago I began to question whether or not these economic-development strategies focused on innovation were effective and/or universally applicable. Too many of my colleagues have been concentrating their research and teaching on industrial clusters, whereas in my own work in China on cokemaking (Polenske 2006) and in the United States on the auto sector (Polenske 2004), I find many examples of industrial dispersion, sometimes along supply chains and sometimes not (Li and Polenske 2004).

Analysts and professional planners disagree on many aspects of innovation, including whether or not space or location matter in the new global economy, and whether or not some new forms of innovation could be the drivers of economic development for all regions. These are important issues for regional analysts to consider.

For this book, the authors draw on the perspectives in the literature of a wide variety of policymakers, bureaucrats, corporate innovators, and academics about innovation and its relationship to space and the process of economic development. One recurring theme is how technology, innovation, and alternative means of transferring knowledge are changing spatial relationships among firms – hence the title of the book, *The Economic Geography of Innovation*.

1.3   Issues concerning innovation

Those writing about innovation have stressed at least three main issues. First, the main theme of many of the studies is the attempt to define innovation. For those of us who are economists, we often refer to Schumpeter (1926) and his extensive discussion of technological change during the course of economic development. Actually, Schumpeter defined three phases of technological change: invention, innovation, and dispersion of innovation. Carter (2006, chapter 2 in this volume) clearly delineates how Schumpeter interprets these three phases and the importance this distinction has for research on innovation as the second stage of technological change. Some analysts in other theoretical disciplines who write about technological change, such as geographers, planners, and management analysts, may or may not refer to Schumpeter as the foundation of their understanding. Although they may use the terms "innovation," "technological change," and "entrepreneur," many will use one or more of the three terms without providing a theoretical structure or definition underlying the term, nor explain how either of the first two terms can be measured. In fact, Schumpeter probably wrote more about the entrepreneur – i.e. *who* innovates – than about innovation – i.e. *what* is innovated.

Second, as researchers discuss their concerns about how to define innovation. I am struck by the many different interpretations of innovation, the lack of consensus on a framework both to define the theory of innovation and the ways to measure it, and by the vast number of empirical studies that are done, but using relatively simplistic measures. Most of the studies are aspatial, with the analyst focusing on the *type* of innovation done, not where it is done and on how knowledge is transferred depending upon whether it is codified or tacit knowledge. The researchers often measure the amount of innovation being done in a region/country by examining patents, funds allocated for innovation research, and other unidimensional measures, often not even determining the location where the person applying for a patent is located or in which region, city, or country the innovation research expenditures are made. Basically, for many innovation analysts, it seems that location is not an important variable.

Third, one of the key themes in this book is innovation diffusion across space, and the related topic of knowledge dispersal, which are also major themes in much of the innovation literature. To study the question of innovation diffusion, analysts must not consider something after it has been innovated, but where, i.e. – the geographical place – the innovation occurs, and under what conditions. If all innovators and people using the innovation were clustered in the same location, those who write about tacit versus codified knowledge would have far less to say. The transmission of tacit knowledge would blend with the transmission of codified knowledge. It is precisely because the geographical places where innovation occurs are often widely dispersed that many analysts have written about the creation, acquisition, and sharing of tacit versus codified knowledge.

As Lundvall (2006, chapter 10 in this volume) maintains in chapter 10, to understand how knowledge is transferred, analysts need to distinguish that knowledge that is local from that which is global, and to understand that the process of learning is an interactive, socially embedded, localized one.

Schumpeter discussed ways in which the entrepreneur was a key to pushing technological change, with progress being the result of creative destruction. In a different, but related vein, Dahmén (1970) and Hirschman (1958) both looked at the backward and forward vertical linkages in the production system, emphasizing that the backward linkages were especially important to ensure that development occurred.

One of Leontief's major contributions to economics was his elegant, but simple, input-output model to show quantitatively the interactions among sectors in an economy (Leontief 1936). The fact that sometimes indirect effects of any given investment, say, in air transportation, may outweigh the direct effects is still not well known among economists. Lundvall and his colleagues (2006) are some of a growing group of analysts who examine the underlying institutions (e.g. laws, codes of behavior, norms) within which such quantitative interactions occur. As analysts examine innovation across countries, the differences in such institutions become critical for understanding the nature of the development process. In this volume, Gertler (2006, chapter 5) and Lam (2006, chapter 8) illustrate how conditions may appear identical in a firm operating in two countries, but these underlying institutions, especially the way workers obtain the knowledge they bring to the workplace, may play a critical role in determining whether the knowledge can be or is transferred successfully from one worker to another.

1.4   General focus of the book

The contributors in this volume explore the spatial elements of innovation and their economic, organizational, and social impacts. How do these impacts affect regional development and public policy? How can a region begin to build a labor force that can sustain innovation? The authors discuss flows of knowledge, regional asset-based economic development, and sustainability, and they therefore differentiate the perspective of a national from that of a regional planner. Some authors discuss the concept of a "learning region," a concept used by a growing number of communities in Europe. The chapters enrich our discussions of the academic and professional-practice literature as they provide answers to the following types of questions:

- First, what innovation concepts have important spatial implications, and how have analysts measured these concepts? How applicable are the concepts and the measurements to developing as well as developed countries?

- Second, what are the institutional and social factors – such as education, gender, income, and laws – that affect the flows of knowledge and information within and across firms, regions, and countries?
- Third, which national patterns of organization and innovation affect the global research and development (R&D) networks and transnational learning in multinational enterprises (MNEs) in different countries?
- Fourth, are networks of skilled engineers becoming increasingly important mechanisms for transferring skill and know-how across long distances?
- Fifth, how do local and national institutional arrangements affect the development of entrepreneurship and technological capability in different regions and countries?
- Sixth, do companies in different countries have similar or different criteria for locating and growing where they do? What are the key factors affecting their initial location decision, as well as any later decisions to move or expand?
- Seventh, what types of co-ordination allow some groups of agents to carry out successful economic development, and what distinguishes these groups from cases of failure?

Obviously, no one contributor attempts to answer all these questions but, in combination, they provide interesting insights into these and related questions. They explore the innovative ways in which new developments in different industry sectors affect the clustering of firms, the development of global supply chains, and the ability to develop and sustain learning regions. They examine some of the new-economy developments in terms of the ability of a region to be or to become sustainable.

We are not the first to look at the issue of innovation and its spatial dispersion, but our discussions are differentiated in a number of ways from most others who write about the general topic of innovation. First, like some others before us, we are interested in the historical development of the concepts of national systems of innovation, learning economies, tacit and codified knowledge. In each case, however, we try to show how these and related concepts affect analysts' understanding about innovation concentration/dispersal over space and time; thus, many of the contributors take an economic-geography perspective as they write. Second, in this volume, the contributors present evidence from a wide number of countries, such as Brazil, Canada, Japan, Mexico, PRC, Taiwan, the United Kingdom, and, of course, the United States. In most of the currently available books, the focus is primarily on Europe (e.g. Fisher and Fröhlich 2001; Acs, Groot, and Nijkamp 2002; Asheim 2003; Brocker, Dohse, and Soltwedel 2003; and Fornahl and Brenner 2003). Third, some contributors in this book use quantitative measures, others use qualitative measures, and some use both types of measures to emphasize the points they make about the economic geographies of innovation. The reason is obvious. An analyst should approach a complex issue such as innovation and its concentration/dispersal with the means to examine the issue from many different sides, which must, of necessity, include the use of quantitative as well as qualitative methods.

1.5   Specifics of the book

For each chapter, the author has provided a detailed abstract (pp. xix–xxvi), so that here I only summarize briefly the different contributions, starting with those on measurement of innovation, in order to understand the full diversity of this volume. The three major parts of the book are (I) Concepts and measurements in innovation, (II) Institutional and spatial aspects of information and knowledge flows, and (III) Institutions and innovation systems.

Part I of the book contains three chapters concerning concepts and measurements of innovation. In chapter 2, Anne P. Carter makes a thorough and fascinating exploration of whether or not innovation limits the effective measurement of standard economic variables – and, if it does, in what way – and examines current strategies for studying innovation itself. Based upon her unique personal knowledge of Joseph Schumpeter and extensive work for many years with Wassily Leontief, she discusses the historical and institutional roots of the concept of innovation. Apiwat Ratanawaraha and Karen R. Polenske, in chapter 3, build upon the more general treatment of innovation by Carter to review the existing innovation literature from a spatial perspective and identify many types of innovation concentration/dispersion measurements and their strengths and weaknesses – a first-ever summary of such measurements. Bernard Fingleton, Danilo C. Igliori, Barrry Moore, and Raakhi Odreda in chapter 4 emphasize realism by focusing on how the clustering of SMEs in Great Britain affects employment growth in so-called "creative industries" from 1991 to 2000.

Part II of the book concerns institutional and spatial aspects of information and knowledge flows. Meric S. Gertler, in chapter 5, eloquently introduces the reader to the nuances and the institutional foundations of workers' tacit knowledge, how it is produced, and how it is distinguished from codified knowledge. If they are distinct types of knowledge, is geographical proximity a precondition for the effective transmission of tacit knowledge between economic actors? Gertler explores how it affects the geographical structure of production and innovation systems, especially in terms of the effective transmission of tacit technical knowledge, showing that culture plays an important role.

In Chapter 6, Amy Glasmeier builds upon the learning-economy concept by discussing organizational learning. She asks two critical, interrelated questions. First, how do firms acquire strategic information, what are their sources and uses, and what actions do they take based on the information acquired? Second, what characterizes firms that actually act in a self-aware manner; at an existential level are there multiple stages of being? Her answers are partially based upon an extensive firm survey she conducted with colleagues. Mia Gray and Al James, in chapter 7, successfully make the reader consider some real situations within organizations, namely the role that gender plays in information and communication technology (ICT) firms in Cambridge, England, in constructing distinctive patterns of sociocultural interactions, and, specifically, what of those gendered patterns of social interaction the material impacts are on firms' abilities to innovate.

In chapter 8, Alice Lam continues the examination of clustering, but she uses empirical evidence from case studies she conducted in the R&D laboratories of US and Japanese MNEs in the United Kingdom. She examines how these MNEs establish collaborative linkages with higher-education institutions in order to obtain access to the foreign academic knowledge base and scientific labor. She finds that US firms co-ordinate dispersed learning more globally and embed themselves in more local innovation networks than the Japanese MNEs. In chapter 9, AnnaLee Saxenian brings new and exciting insights into the role Taiwan is playing in supplying networks of skilled engineers and entrepreneurs to Shanghai who first returned to Taiwan from Silicon Valley and elsewhere and now are setting up firms in Shanghai. These networks allow entrepreneurship and innovation to continue to occur away from the established technology regions.

Part III of the book concerns institutions and innovation systems. The last part of chapter 10, by Bengt-Åke Lundvall, Björn Johnson, Esben S. Andersen, and Bent Dalum, has been previously published. The chapter is particularly relevant for this volume, partly because Lundvall and Johnson's concept (1994) of a learning economy was one of the exciting concepts discussed by many participants throughout the 2003 innovation seminar at MIT, and it initially drew me into an in-depth examination of spatial aspects of innovation. Lundvall writes an extensive preface to their already-published paper (Lundvall *et al.* 2002) in which they extended the theoretical concept of a learning economy, partially in order to make it applicable to the analysis of poor countries. In chapter 11, Maryann P. Feldman examines the Capitol region in the United States, arguing that it is one of the most important US biotechnology centers because of three interrelated factors: pre-existing resources, entrepreneurship, and the incentives and infrastructure provided by government. Christie Baxter and Peter Tyler, in chapter 12, compare how high-technology centers in the United States and the United Kingdom originated and developed and the roles that government and public policy played. Whereas the quality of the workers and the availability of a critical network infrastructure were the dominant factors facilitating their origin, public policy played the most important role as development and expansion occurred. This "policy context" permitted different organizations from different sectors to share a collective role in facilitating business development. The organizations functioned within and across academic, government, high-tech industry, and nonprofit sectors.

No book on innovation would be complete without a discussion of the PRC. Edward S. Steinfeld, in chapter 13, forcefully argues that Chinese firms, on the one hand, can compete well in producing relatively low-value manufacturing goods because of their low production cost, especially low wages. On the other hand, he argues that they have limited innovative capacity and ability to work within global supply chains of high-technology goods, primarily because of their historical Chinese traditions, bottlenecks in the institutional reform process, and inconsistencies in governmental industrial policy. In the final chapter 14, Michael Storper, Lena Lavinas, and Alejandro Mercado-Célis compare a success story from Jalisco, Mexico, with a failure story of low-technology economic development in Northeast Brazil. They show that the type of coordination of family and social networks, as well as property rights and other rules and regulations, are some of the key factors explaining the difference.

So much is being written about innovation by so many different authors that one can question whether another book is needed. I believe it is, because the spatial distribution of innovation is not well researched, and the contributors to this book are important analysts in the field of innovation and have made a tremendous contribution to thinking about spatial distribution issues. Innovation itself is important, for a number of reasons. According to Debresson (1996, p. 10), "innovation can contribute to the creation of wealth and induce growth, structural change, and development." Some people, and some regions, are poor and others are rich. If innovation does contribute to the creation of wealth, then its spatial distribution may help some of the poor people and regions to rise out of the poverty in which they live, or it may be one of the factors leading to a widening of the gap between the rich and the poor. Although this aspect of innovation is not an explicit part of what the authors of these chapters cover, I am certain that those interested in these and related topics can gain from reading their fascinating contributions.

REFERENCES

Acs, Z. J., H. L. F. Groot, and P. Nijkamp, 2002. *The Emergence of the Knowledge Economy*, New York: Springer

Asheim, B. T. (ed.), 2003. *Regional Innovation Policy for Small-Medium Enterprises*, Cheltenham: Edward Elgar

Brocker, J., D. Dohse, and R. Soltwedel, 2003. *Innovation Clusters and Interregional Competition*, New York: Springer

Carter, A. P., 2006. Measurement of the clustering and dispersion of innovation, chapter 2 in this volume

Dahmén, E., 1950/1970. *Svensk industriell foretagarverksamhet (Entrepreneurial Activity in Swedish Industry, 1919–39)*, Stockholm: Institut für Umweltschutz und Landwirtschaft (IUL), also published in 1970 by the American Economic Association Translation Series under the title *Entrepreneurial Activity and the Development of Swedish Industry, 1919–1939*, vols. 1–2, Homewood: R. D. Irwin.

Debresson, C., 1996. *Economic Interdependence and Innovative Activity: An Input-Output Analysis*, Cheltenham: Edward Elgar

Fischer, M. M. and J. Fröhlich (eds), 2001. *Knowledge, Complexity, and Innovation Systems*, New York: Springer

Fornahl, D. and T. Brenner, 2003. *Cooperation, Networks, and Institutions in Regional Innovation Systems*, Cheltenham: Edward Elgar

Gertler, M. S., 2006. "Tacit Knowledge in Production Systems: How Important is Geography?," chapter 5 in this volume

Greenspan, A., 2004. "Remarks by Chairman Alan Greenspan: Globalization and Innovation," *Conference on Bank Structure and Competition, sponsored by the Federal Reserve Bank of Chicago*, Chicago, Illinois, May 6

Hirschman, A. O., 1958. *The Strategy of Economic Development*, New Haven, CT: Yale University Press

Lam, A., 2006. "Multinationals and Transnational Social Space for Learning: Knowledge Creation and Transfer through Global R&D Networks," chapter 8 in this volume

Leontief, W. W., 1936. "Quantitative Input-Output Relations in the Economic System of the United States," *The Review of Economics and Statistics* 18(3): 105–125

Li, Y. and K. R. Polenske, 2004. "Measuring Dispersal Economics," in *Entrepreneurship, Spatial Industrial Clusters and Inter-Firm Networks*, Trollhättan, Sweden: Universities of Trollhätten/Uddevalla (Papers from Symposium 2003) pp: 615–633

Lundvall, B.-Å, and B. Johnson, 1994. "The Learning Economy," *Journal of Industry Studies*, 1(2): 23–42

Lundvall, B.-Å., B. Johnson, E. S. Andersen, and B. Dalum, 2002. "National Systems of Production, Innovation and Competence Building," *Research Policy*, 31: 213–231

Lundvall, B.-Å., B. Johnson, E. S. Andersen, and B. Dalum, 2006. "National Systems of Production, Innovation, and Competence Building," chapter 10 in this volume

Polenske, K. R., 2004. "Competition, Collaboration and Cooperation: An Uneasy Triangle in Networks of Firms and Regions," *Regional Studies*, 38(9): 1029–1043

2006. *The Technology–Energy–Environmental–Health (TEEH) Chain in China: A Case Study of Cokemaking*, Dordrecht: Springer

Schumpeter, J., 1926. *The Theory of Economic Development*, Cambridge, MA: Harvard University Press

2 Measurement of the clustering and dispersion of innovation

Anne P. Carter

2.1 Introduction

The chapters in this volume deal with the interplay of two characteristic features of today's global economy: rapid technological change and shifts in the loci of economic activity. As might be expected, no two authors interpret the terms "location" and "innovation" identically. Both domains are very broad and complex and authors single out particular facets for separate study. It is striking that most of them focus on research and the creation, acquisition, and sharing of knowledge, rather than dealing directly with changes in the production process and in the kinds of products on the market. Perhaps this should be taken as a reminder that we have indeed entered the era of the "knowledge economy."

Economists might see this emphasis on information and communication as a focus on the first of Schumpeter's three major phases of technological change, namely invention. Seeing technological change as the primary focus of capitalism, Schumpeter draws sharp distinctions among invention, creating the idea behind a change in the production process; innovation, implementing that idea in the market environment for the first time; and diffusion, the spread of implementation to sites beyond the original one.

Schumpeter saw the innovator as the visionary and the primary risk-taker in the chain of individuals responsible for technological change (Schumpeter 1926). His inventor was an inspired individual with a new idea, but was not an economic actor. Today, invention is likely to be purposive economic activity involving significant investment and risk. Pharmaceutical firms use routine screening and synthesis techniques to "invent" some new drugs; other "inventions" require significant venture capital during the R&D (i.e. invention) phase. For Schumpeter, the innovator was the hero, the primary risktaker who first implemented a new process or product technology. Today, the implementation (innovation) stage sometimes involves less capital at risk than invention because, in some sectors (such as pharmaceuticals) research now absorbs enormous

13

investment. Would-be entrepreneurs may think they are innovating and later find that others have preceded them. In Schumpeter's classification they are really "diffusors." In practice, it is difficult to draw the lines between innovation and diffusion: how can an entrepreneur anticipate the recent plans and/or actions of competitors in a global market? Sometimes novelty is a matter of judgment or convention: why should changes in the design of babies' diapers count as innovation while changes in women's fashions do not?

In the economist's scholarly world, as in that of business, innovation has come to stand for "doing something new," leaving unanswered the questions of "new in what sense?," "new to whom?," or "how new is new?" Von Hippel's "user innovation" is generally "user invention" in Schumpeter's terminology (Von Hippel 1986). The frequent use of patents or expenditures on R&D as proxies for innovation and the common use of the phrase "very innovative," as though innovation were a matter of degree, suggest that the stages of the Schumpeterian trilogy are no longer seen as discrete.

Geographical concepts seem to rest on firmer ground, but they are still subject to interpretation. Location can involve coarse or fine grids – focus on local, intermediate, or global interchange. The choice of an appropriate grid depends, in part, on whether the study focuses on the exchange of ideas, of commodities, or both. Technology broadens the range of options with respect to transportation of goods as well as to human communication. In turn, the significance of geographical proximity in the exchange of ideas, as well as in linking the stages of manufacturing, keeps changing.

This chapter's main focus is on a fundamental problem that plagues studies of technological change regardless of whether they focus on ideas or on goods, on invention, innovation, or diffusion, and regardless of the chosen geographical grid. Although thinkers make an informal distinction between big and small ideas, they have no metric for comparing their sizes. To the extent that change in the technology involves new kinds of inputs and outputs, analysts cannot count on standard units to measure production. Although I have no remedy for the problem, its recognition should provide a background for interpreting the range of findings about geography and innovation in this and in other chapters.

Although there is now a growing interest in institutional economics, modern economics continues to emphasize logical precision and quantitative methods where measurement is a fundamental prerequisite. Thus far, economists have searched in vain for measures to convert innovation into a quantitative variable, tractable by modern economic techniques. There are a number of recognized proxies: patent applications, expenditure on R&D, employment of engineers and scientists, number of non-production workers, etc. These make it possible to proceed with established econometric techniques as if innovation could be measured. But each of these proxies measures only a very special aspect of innovation, as is generally acknowledged.

Innovation is not simply an exotic variable of interest to a few specialists. The fact that it resists measurement while still growing in importance threatens to undermine economics' impressive progress toward quantification since the Second World War. Actually, respected scholars, including several contributors to this volume, see economists' emphasis on quantification as misdirected. To the extent that this emphasis tends to mask the disruptive role of technological change, it does indeed lead to distortions.

In this chapter, I explore how technological change limits the effective measurement of standard economic variables, and then examine current strategies for studying the process of change. As noted above, Schumpeter used the term "innovation" to denote only one of three aspects of technological change, but the distinctions are now unclear. In accord with more recent usage, I use the terms "technological change," "change," and "innovation" interchangeably in the text that follows.

2.2   Innovation and measurement: are they at odds?

Juxtaposing the concepts of "measurement" and "innovation" dramatizes a dilemma central to economics today: measurement is essential if economics claims to be a science. It involves quantifying, establishing a standard "unit," and comparing an observed variable to that standard. In economics, our variables are commonly commodities, industries, resources, and prices. Except in special cases, innovation involves change in what we mean by a unit of such variables.

Without measurement, we cannot use the powerful tools of mathematics and statistics to answer our questions. In the 1930s, founders of the Cowles Commission, the research arm of the Econometric Society, adopted the motto "Science is Measurement" (Cowles Commission 1947). This presumably signified a commitment to operational definition of economic phenomena as a basis for explaining how an economy functions. In response to pressure from members, the motto was diluted to "Theory and Measurement" in 1952 (Christ 1953). In practice, however, the economics profession in general and the Society, whose members have always constituted a talented elite subset, have given relatively little attention to measurement itself, concentrating, rather, on mathematical and statistical methods of analysis. The collection of meaningful quantitative data and the development of quantitative measures are left to administrative agencies and "applied" economists, who supposedly rank lower in the intellectual hierarchy. Thus, the link between conceptualization and the stubborn realities of implementation is weaker than it otherwise might be.

The dangers of this division of labor have generated concern for some years. Prominent economists have pointed out an imbalance between our appetite for sophisticated theoretical apparatus and our scant attention to the measurement problems that limit our data (Leontief 1971; Griliches 1994). Alan Greenspan, then the widely esteemed chairman of the Board of Governors of the Federal Reserve System, joined the chorus of those who recognize the importance of measurement: "more important than building ever-more-complex computer models that try to predict where the economy is headed . . . I suspect greater payoffs will come from more data than from more techniques . . .We soon learned that the economic structure did not hold still long enough to capture its key relationship" (Greenspan 2001).

To say that the profession tends to ignore measurement difficulties is not to deny the fundamental contributions of Fisher, Mitchell, Kuznets, Leontief, and other early giants in developing quantitative economics. Sophisticated national income accounts, price indices, input-output tables, user-friendly regional and national Census information and financial databases are rooted in the systematic measures that they designed. These pioneers tackled the important problems of classification and aggregation essential to national accounting. An economy encompasses countless transactions. They vary, for example, with respect to product, process, location, price, and time. To explain how an economy works, someone had to sort these transactions into meaningful categories. For the most part, they measured the size of each sector and of the whole economy as the dollar value of its output.

Over the past half-century, economists and statisticians have created elaborate systems for classifying and measuring commodity groups, industries, natural and human resources, financial transactions, national income and product accounts, international trade, and more. They have measured prices and quantities for these categories and traced them over time. Many of these series were not available prior to the Second World War. Such progress merits far greater appreciation than it receives at present. Although much of our analytic effort seems blithely detached from measurement issues we can now take for granted a serious and comprehensive data system. Today, the problem of change complicates – and, indeed, overshadows – that of aggregation. As the economy evolves, new elements must be incorporated and old ones phased out. Those responsible for measurement must run faster and faster. The growing importance of innovation accelerates the pace of the treadmill.

Schumpeter, Leontief, and the measurement of innovation

I first became aware of the tension between economic measurement and innovation as a graduate student with two powerful mentors, Schumpeter and Leontief. Both were highly regarded; both were innovators. Their approaches to measurement, however, were antithetical. Schumpeter (1926, 1942) had a really bold idea: capitalism was first and foremost an engine for change, rather than just a system for efficient allocation of resources. He saw economic growth as an evolutionary process where entrepreneurs planted the seeds of creative destruction of old capacities by creating and implementing more efficient new ones. The recognition that the free market fosters change, rather than simply efficiency, was a fundamental insight that was very radical fifty or sixty years ago. In a sense, Schumpeter substituted Darwin's metaphor of "survival of the fittest" for Adam Smith's sunnier view of the effects of specialization. Even today, many do not recognize the pervasive significance of change in the market system.

Leontief did not deny the importance of change, but he concentrated on interindustry interdependence at a given time. He set out to map the interdependence of sectors by building an input-output table. His breakthrough insight was to measure interdependence by the volume of transactions between each pair of sectors in a multi-sectoral grid. These transactions could be measured in physical or in value units. Both kinds of information were readily available in the economic censuses for many of the sectors specified in an input-output table. The rest could be approximated by combining fragments of data and/or applying industrial and commercial rules of thumb. Leontief's measures of structural change (Leontief 1953) were based on the assumption that product quality remained constant. He was aware of the problem of qualitative change, but made no attempt to take account of it.

Leontief's major contribution was path-breaking. He measured interindustry interdependence by the volume of transactions among the various sectors to launch the first detailed operational general equilibrium system (Leontief 1941). As might be expected, his great innovation was met with immediate skepticism. He used to tell a story that dramatized his position as an innovator in economics. When the economics department offered him a post at Harvard, he accepted with a condition: he asked for $1,500 in research money to support his work toward the first input-output table. They granted his request, but made him promise to report his (presumed) failure at the end of the grant year. (No one now remembers whether the department considered his table evidence of success or failure!)

Schumpeter envied his younger colleague's mathematical proficiency – this was just before mathematics became the standard language of economics – but expressed little awareness of the measurement problems that innovation would pose. By the mid-1940s, he had joined the newly formed Econometric Society and had hired a math tutor. He may not have recognized that Leontief's major achievement went beyond simply representing sectoral economic interdependence as a system of equations. The magic leap was to measure economic interdependence by intersectoral transactions.

Schumpeter died in 1950 and thus missed the chance to see his ideas about innovation commonly accepted. In the post-Second World War period, we have witnessed a surge in the pace of change, to the point where no model that ignores, or "abstracts from," change can hope to mirror the world it purports to explain. Praise, in today's business world, is given to an organization that is "innovative" rather than simply "efficient." This development is highlighted by the major antitrust case launched against Microsoft in 1998. The antitrust laws were enacted in the nineteenth century to protect the public from the high prices associated with concentrated market power. However, the government's case against Microsoft hinged not on price fixing or output restriction, but rather on the idea that market power enabled Microsoft to limit the pace of innovation. Did anyone question the shift in objective from that of the original legislation?

Schumpeter, in his later work, had claimed that large firms tended to be more innovative than small ones. "Monopolies" could assemble the vast amounts of capital required for R&D and, in contrast to small firms, could capture the surplus earnings associated with innovation before competition could gobble them up. Although Schumpeter might have disapproved of the case against Microsoft, the government's charges reinforce his claims about the centrality of innovation.

Measuring output when products change

Change prompts us to question our previous economic understanding. What does it mean to say that the economy grew at 3 percent per year since 1800 when the gross domestic product (GDP) subsumes no output whose units are identical in the two terminal years? When inputs and outputs are changing qualitatively, long-range quantitative comparisons or projections become ambiguous. Leontief believed that the problem is insoluble. I remember many searching conversations with him about ways to incorporate change into the quantitative input-output system. They always ended up with agreement that input-output analysis, or any quantitative study of production, would be valid only so long as the major variables did not undergo "significant qualitative change." How long is that?

Leontief tried hard to maintain the integrity of his system while acknowledging that change brings inexorable erosion. An inveterate pragmatist, he invented a practical and yet elegant method for increasing the period over which comparisons would be valid by "netting out" the products that changed rapidly. Instead of trying to compare the successive outputs of fast-changing commodities, such as plastics or automobiles, he would represent them by their input-contents, such as energy and steel, whose qualitative nature was relatively constant (Leontief 1967). This was the so-called "double inversion." To measure the net output of an economy in fixed units he would divide products into two categories: products that changed qualitatively and those that did not. To measure the economy's final output, he proposed to sum the final deliveries of unchanging products and the outputs of unchanging products that would be required to produce final deliveries of changing products. Products that changed qualitatively would then be represented by their (unchanging) inputs that did not. Unfortunately, it proved virtually impossible to partition an eighty-sector US matrix into sectors that did and did not undergo qualitative change. The latter set was empty! Even forty years ago, there was significant qualitative change in the outputs of the energy and the steel sectors over a decade. Quality change in those sectors is even more rapid now. Leontief recognized that qualitative change, an essential feature of Schumpeter's innovation, limits the significance of our current system of prices and quantities to the short run. As change accelerates, the short run becomes shorter.

Do the problems of comparing individual outputs over time vanish at the aggregate level? Analysts might hope that ambiguities in measurement of individual products would "cancel out" in the aggregate, but there is no explicit basis for such a belief. Why, then, do the public, the business community, and the economics profession take seriously the official (or unofficial) news reports of small changes in national growth or inflation rates? Is our faith in these measures based on an old and now invalid notion of fixed composition and quality?

Most economists have been trained to look upon the economy as a system that grows (and sometimes shrinks) subject to fixed technological constraints. Our measures and categories (industry outputs and prices, GDP, etc.) fit that system. If "productivity" and its growth are to be measured then, strictly speaking, the qualities of inputs and outputs must remain the same. As Schumpeter and Leontief knew all too well, they do not. Like the industrial innovations he celebrated, Schumpeter's concept of innovation disrupts the economics "industry."

Research strategies going forward

Although innovation places a significant roadblock in the route to unambiguous quantitative input-output and national accounts, it has not blocked all traffic. Economists who study change have found clever ways to advance understanding of the change process while bypassing the challenge of comparing heterogeneous outputs. Solow's "residual" measure of technological change (Solow 1957) can be seen as his attempt to measure innovation indirectly within the national accounts framework. Although many raised an eyebrow at representing so important a variable as innovation by a residual, the strategy seems a clever and direct response to the measurement problem (or perhaps a tongue-in-cheek reminder of its difficulty).

Despite the fundamental impossibility of translating qualitative into quantitative change, economists have contributed insights into important aspects of the process: how the market encourages, sorts, and incorporates change; how technological ideas spread; externalities associated with networks and information; and much more. Mansfield (1968), Nelson and Winter (1982), Griliches (1994), and DeBresson (1996) are only a few of a long list of major contributors in this area of economics. Essentially they sidestep the problem of measuring change in aggregate or sectoral output by choosing problems with variables that are easier to measure. They avoid direct confrontation with the measurement problem using three major detours:

- Pure theorizing – i.e. putting forward general ideas without empirical evidence. This postpones measurement problems or delegates them to others. The high-profile literature on endogenous growth models (Romer 1994; Aghion and Howitt 1998) provides examples.
- Relying on "proxies," which are measurable variables associated with technological change, such as patent applications or expenditures on R&D, to represent change itself. In testing Schumpeter's hypothesis about the role of innovation in business cycles, Jacob Schmookler (1961) focused on patent applications rather than proposing to measure "innovation" itself. Patenting is only sometimes associated with innovation, and some patents affect a broader range of economic activities than others. Still, Schmookler's findings led the economics community to question Schumpeter's hypothesis.
- Investigating particular innovations or classes of innovations where change is quantifiable in terms of recognized technical parameters.

Perhaps the best-known example of this is "Moore's law," the notion that the circuit density of semiconductors doubles every two or three years (Moore 1965). We can learn some things from studying the output of the semiconductor industry with a convenient metric like circuit density, but chips have other important qualities, such as reliability, effective life, and programmability, that also matter to this industry's customers and suppliers. These other qualities may change at different paces; some may not change at all. Measuring the economic output of semiconductors as they change over time involves combining many component qualities with appropriate weights.

Griliches (1957, 1994) partially solved this problem in designing his "hedonic" price indices. Essentially, he used a hedonic-price index to assign separate prices to several attributes of a product and combine them with appropriate weights. Hedonic-price indices can thus reflect changes in the relative importance of individual product features, as well as their prices. As Griliches certainly recognized, hedonic-price indices do not eliminate the problem of new product attributes or of the changing relative importance of those already recognized. Still, hedonic-price indices do extend the "useful life" of conventional price statistics.

Researchers can learn a lot about technological change without attempting to measure change in output at all. Edwin Mansfield, a pioneer in empirical research on technological change, relied heavily on this strategy. Thus, he answers questions such as: "What is the relation between firm size and R&D expenditure?," "How long does it take to bring individual inventions to market?," "How do distributions of returns on R&D investment and of diffusion rates vary among firms?" (Mansfield 1968).

DeBresson (1996) maps innovation "counts," the frequency of innovation, rather than attempting to distinguish small from large instances. This strategy involves surveys, either interviews or questionnaires, inquiring directly about innovative activity at the plant or enterprise level. This seems particularly promising because it motivates collection of information not accessible through administrative reporting. Survey design, in turn, narrows the gap between analysts and data gatherers, while interviews bring the investigator into close contact with the phenomenon being studied.

2.3   Identifying innovation

Innovation surveys, clustering, and dispersal: back to square one?

Right now, information about innovation is not reported directly either in our economic censuses or in other broad tax and administrative data systems. Starting in the early 1980s, DeBresson and his associates in Canada, China, France, Greece, and Italy, undertook to fill the void by conducting primary economywide surveys of establishments. They attempted to map the loci of innovation by directly questioning individuals involved and "counting" affirmative responses (DeBresson 1996). These early academic initiatives paved the way for more ambitious and comprehensive data gathering on the part of governments, particularly those of Canada, Denmark, and Italy. The OECD endorsed this approach and encouraged governments to sponsor innovation surveys. Their *Oslo Manual* (OECD 1997) codifies a comprehensive methodology for such work.

At first, innovation surveys struck some old-timers, including myself, as retrograde. Innovation "counts" do not distinguish between major and minor, between path-breaking and incremental changes; they do not really "measure" innovation. Furthermore, because innovation is self-reported in these surveys, it is difficult to make a distinction between invention, innovation, and diffusion. The innovator has, in fact, no way of knowing in advance whether, when, or how his/her innovation will succeed and/or spread – nor, in fact, does anyone else. Realistically it is impossible to gauge the importance of an "innovation" until long after it has ceased to be new. Because the innovator's knowledge is generally local, he/she also may not know whether the change in question is really invention, innovation, or diffusion. How important will this distinction be in understanding the process of economic change as we go forward?

Although innovation counts bypass, rather than solve, the measurement problem, they do provide a significant new source of information for studying the change process across geographical and industrial lines. Innovation counts are essentially qualitative; they do not blend into or enhance the national accounts. Nevertheless they represent a significant breakthrough – recognition that new primary information must be gathered for serious research on innovation, and that new information is an essential basis for new insights. Analysis of clustering, facilitated by graphics, is a straightforward and, at the same time, powerful and flexible way to explore the spatial variation of innovation. I note some special features of this approach below.

Invention, innovation, and diffusion

The term "innovation" currently used in economics, in general conversation and in the press actually subsumes all three activities distinguished by Schumpeter. His original distinction has lapsed and almost any kind of change in the production process is now classed as "innovation." The tripartite distinction is especially difficult to maintain in surveys where innovation is self-reported. If I install a computerized system for broiling steaks in my restaurant, I am inclined to announce it as an innovation. It is new for me, after all. If competitors already use computers for this purpose, Schumpeter might call it diffusion, but responders in a survey may not know about others who introduced the technology elsewhere. Often the distinction between innovation and diffusion is a matter of discretion: what if I use my computerized oven to broil fish? The *Oslo Manual* specifies that, to be counted as an innovation, a technological or process innovation should be new (or significantly improved) to the firm (it does not have to be new to the world) (OECD 1997: 31).

Clustering as a heuristic device

Because empirical research on innovation is still exploratory, it is understandable that much of it relies on clustering. Searching for and mapping clusters is not generally regarded as the final product of research: it is a time-honored and effective strategy for seeking to form a hypothesis. A police department looks for locations or neighborhoods where crimes have clustered in the past. A teacher needs to know at what questions the errors clustered on the last exam. If the clustering of grades indicates that men in the class did poorly as compared with women on certain questions, how can the discrepancy be explained? Remedied? Did a particular error occur only among those students seated in the left rear of the room? Did respiratory infections strike third-graders more frequently than the rest of the school?

The search for clusters begins with choosing a grid and locating observations with respect to that grid. In the case of errors in an exam, analysts look for clustering with respect to questions, to location in the room, possibly to gender, age, or other personal characteristics of the students. When trying to understand crime, they might look at clustering with respect to place, time of day, weather, or deployment of the police force.

Students of innovation have looked for clusters with respect to a variety of economic grids, and they have found significant clustering in some of them. The better-known grids are:

Phase of the business cycle (i.e. time) Schumpeter believed that innovations clustered because technical and market linkages fostered a kind of chain reaction among them. This clustering, in turn, drives the business cycle. If he was right, then we would expect to find innovations clustered just prior to, or early in, the recovery phase of the cycle. Jacob Schmookler (1961) conducted detailed studies of four industries and concluded that waves of investment preceded, rather than followed, clusters of innovation.

Schmookler used patent applications as a measure of innovative activity. His findings suggest that the business cycle – and investment in particular – drives innovation, rather than the reverse. However, patent applications may be an inappropriate proxy here. If, in fact, patent applications precede innovation significantly, or if a significant portion of innovations is not patented, the timing of patent applications misrepresents the timing of innovation. With a different proxy for innovation (yet to be specified!), Schumpeter's hunch might be confirmed.

Geographical location   This kind of grid is of particular interest to regional planners and other policy-oriented individuals focused on building technological capabilities. A better understanding of the conditions under which innovation clusters would provide guidance to policymakers eager to promote innovation. In the 1980s Japan tried, with limited success, to replicate the conditions of Silicon Valley in the hope of building a similarly powerful engine for innovation. Harold Varmus, six major medical schools and four universities are trying to foster a biotechnology cluster in New York City (Smaglik 2002). Varmus argues that New York already has the academic, business, and investment resources to generate a major stream of innovation in biotechnology. Many industrial research parks have been planted near to large research universities in the hope of fostering profitable innovation. Some flourish; others languish. Will this one succeed?

Can innovation surveys give a clue as to why some clusters succeed and others do not? The success of regional "incubators," such as Silicon Valley (Saxenian 1991), Route 128 in Massachusetts (Dorfman 1987), and the very successful textile complex in northern Italy (DeBresson 1996) suggest that there are lessons to be learned about the role of geographical proximity in supporting rapid innovation. Clustering can also be instructive at the micro level of the individual plant. For example, the proximity of automobile assemblers and their suppliers may be a key factor in the innovation process. Witness, for example, Volkswagen's novel organization in Brazil, housing independent suppliers and assemblers under a single roof (Schemo 1996). How important is physical proximity? Will the internet alter this tendency to cluster geographically?

Intersectoral linkages   To the extent that industries "take in each others' washing," innovation in one sector is likely to require or induce innovation among its suppliers and customers: new designs call for changes in the properties of components and materials, and vice versa. My own early simulations (Carter 1970) indicated that changes in input vectors were adaptive: a sector's input-output structure required less total factor input per unit of its output when embedded in the context of current, rather than earlier, input-output structures for other sectors. Scherer (1982) assumed that the benefits of innovation are transferred among sectors in proportion to their purchases from the innovating sector. Was he right? DeBresson and his associates (1996) studied the clustering of innovation in the input-output grid in many countries and found a high degree of clustering at certain sectoral and geographical nodes. Eric Von Hippel (1986) counted and mapped innovation in a functional grid of supplier–manufacturer–user, demonstrating the prevalence and importance of users in generating innovative ideas. In his model, innovations cluster primarily at the user–manufacturer node of the grid.

Organizational structure   At the firm level, successful managers are aware that integration and outsourcing affect the level and quality of innovation. Similarly, the goal of innovation often motivates mergers and acquisitions (M&As), divestitures, and joint ventures (JVs). The popularity of Japanese management styles in the 1980s and 1990s rested on Japanese success in mobilizing innovative ideas from workers at many levels of the production process. Thus far, analysts have studied these matters at the level of individual cases rather than whole sectors.

Several years ago Carr (1999) reported in the *Harvard Business Review* that a group of business consultants developed a tool for "visualizing innovation" by mapping the number of innovations into each of ten categories: (1) business models, (2) networking, (3) enabling processes, (4) core processes, (5) product performance, (6) product systems, (7) service, (8) channel, (9) brand, and (10) customer experience. Inspecting the profile of innovations in a sector or in an individual firm can identify bottlenecks and suggest priorities for innovation strategy.

Thus, some analysts have shown that innovation clusters in the context of several important grids; many other grids remain to be explored. Furthermore, grids often overlap – for example, processes that are linked technologically are likely to be linked economically; processes that are related economically are likely to be close geographically (or at least they used to be!). Clustering is primarily a heuristic device. Like shadows on an X-ray, clusters indicate an association, but it may be something trivial, something very important, or an artifact of the search process.

Special problems in the study of diffusion or "dispersal" of innovation

The economic significance of an innovation is heavily dependent on the degree to which it will spread. Thus, it is not possible to rate the importance of an innovation *ex ante*. In the 1960s, the laser, which represented a scientific breakthrough, had only few and tentative industrial applications. Many worried about whether there would be significant commercial applications, and how to promote them. Thus, diffusion, which lacks the romantic connotations of invention (associated with creativity) and innovation (associated with courage), determines whether any given change will, in retrospect, be judged significant.

Many economists favor a "vintage" model for explaining the distribution of techniques in use at a given time. The prototype for this is an industry where the technique in use at any given time is dictated by (the economists' term is "embodied in") the kinds of machinery installed in its plants. Until quite recently, economists assumed that many layers of technology would co-exist in most sectors. Diffusion of new technologies was tied to investment in new equipment and scrapping of old. The process was seen as "sedimentary," with old layers being removed slowly as new ones were added. It took more than twenty-five years for diesel engines to replace steam in American railroads (Rochester and Genesee Valley Museum 2002), during which period diesel engines improved gradually, and steam engines were retired as they wore out.

With the acceleration of change and the competition associated with globalization, it seems unlikely that old equipment and technology will continue to serve alongside new as long as it once did. The age range of computers and mobile phones in service at any given time is small. Disposal, rather than maintenance, is the major challenge. Competition from new firms, new technologies, and new countries coming on line results in a situation where equipment is retired long before it wears out.

Studies of diffusion have always been hampered by the dearth of information on retirements of old equipment. We still need such information to understand the diffusion process. Now, however, equipment vintage is dwarfed by the growing importance of know-how and human capital. How is diffusion related to education, labor turnover, professional organizations, "user groups," internet connections, international travel, espionage, and foreign direct investment (FDI)? If we cannot keep track of obsolete machines, how will we track the obsolescence of human beings?

2.4   Conclusion

At this point, the pervasiveness of innovation limits the relevance of the standard models and measures in economics. Like creative destruction in the economy itself, the pervasiveness of innovation disrupts the intellectual traditions of economic research.

Measures of innovation

A strategy for measuring innovation would certainly ease its incorporation into the traditional intellectual stream of economics and national accounting. Although Griliches' hedonics can extend the period over which outputs are comparable, there is no solution for the long run. Analysts using surveys tend to focus on counting instances of innovation; they cannot gauge their economic importance *a priori*, nor can they maintain the classic distinctions among invention, innovation, and diffusion.

In addition to the use of standard proxies (patent applications, expenditures on R&D, etc.) new research on innovation involves original surveys of innovative activity in establishments. These data lend themselves to analysis of clustering with respect to criteria such as location, industry, size, etc. Analysis of clusters is important as an exploratory tool.

Directions for future research

Innovation is a heterogeneous phenomenon, still loosely defined. What all innovations have in common is that they are "new," but "new" is a vague and general term and measurement is a distant goal. It is unlikely that we can measure innovation in the context of our current methods of economic accounting. Darwin, after all, did not quantify, compare, or aggregate the evolution of all the different species.

To raise doubts about the measurement of change is not to discourage research in this area, but rather to acknowledge the serious analytical challenge it poses. I believe, for example, that creative destruction involves important externalities that affect the entire system. When the innovator does not bear the entire financial burden of induced obsolescence, systemic inefficiencies are generated. Although the "degree of novelty" defies measurement, the financial implications of a given change can be traced. We can learn more about the costs and benefits of a given change without "measuring" the change itself.

To find out what conditions foster innovation and/or diffusion, we must continue to track clustering and dispersion in particular areas. What are the innovation experiences in business alliances as compared with those in integrated firms? How do multinationals implement change in different locations? How do university–business partnerships affect the innovation process? What are the spillovers when financial institutions outsource back-office functions to developing countries?

I believe that attempts to answer such specific questions will bring us closer to whatever broad generalizations are possible. If we find, as well we might, that broad generalizations remain elusive in this area, then that, too, will be an important lesson.

REFERENCES

Aghion, P. and P. Howitt, 1998. *Endogenous Growth Theory*, Cambridge, MA: MIT Press
Carr, N., 1999. "Visualizing Innovation," *Harvard Business Review*, 17(5)
Carter, A., 1970. *Structural Change in the American Economy*, Cambridge, MA: Harvard University Press
Christ, C., 1953. *History of the Cowles Commission, 1932–52*, at http://cowles. econ.yale.edu/P/reports/1932-52b.htm
Cowles Commission for Research in Economics, 1947. *Report for 1947*, Chicago, see also at http://209.41.24.153/rmt/rmt114k.htm
DeBresson, C., 1996. *Economic Interdependence and Innovative Activity*, Cheltenham: Edward Elgar
Dorfman, N., 1987. *Innovation and Market Structure*, Cambridge, MA: Ballinger
Greenspan, A., 2001. "The Challenge of Measuring and Modeling a Dynamic Economy," Presented at the Washington Economic Policy Conference of the National Association for Business Economics, Washington, DC, March 27, 2001, at http://www.federalreserve.gov/boarddocs/speeches/ 2001/20010327.default.htm
Griliches, Z., 1957. "Hybrid Corn: An Exploration in the Economics of Technical Change," *Econometrica*, 25(4): 501–523
    1994. "Productivity, R&D, and the Data Constraint," *American Economic Review*, 84(1): 1–23
Leontief, W., 1941. *The Structure of American Economy*, Cambridge, MA: Harvard University Press
    1953. "Structural Change," in W. Leontief et al., *Studies in the Structure of the American Economy*, New York: Oxford University Press
    1967. "An Alternative to Aggregation in Input-Output Analysis and National Accounts," *Review of Economics and Statistics*, 49(3): 412–419
    1971. "Theoretical Assumptions and Nonobserved Facts," *American Economic Review*, 61(2): 1–7
Mansfield, E., 1968. *Industrial Research and Technological Innovation*. New York: W.W. Norton
Moore, G., 1965. "Cramming More Components onto Integrated Circuits," *Electronics*, 38(8): 114–117
Nelson, R. and S. Winter, 1982. *An Evolutionary Theory of Economic Change*, Cambridge, MA: Harvard University Press
Organization for Economic Cooperation and Development (OECD), 1997. *Oslo Manual (revised)*, at http://www1.oecd.org/dsti/sti/stat-ana/prod/ eas_oslo.htm
Rochester and Genesee Valley Museum, 2002. "Statement," at http://www1. rgvrrm.mus.ny.us/diesels.htm
Romer, P., 1994. "The Origins of Endogenous Growth," *Journal of Economic Perspectives*, 8(1): 3–22

Saxenian, A., 1991. "The Origins and Dynamics of Production Networks in Silicon Valley," *Research Policy*, 20: 423–437

Schemo, D. J., 1996. "Is VW's New Plant Lean or Just Mean?," *New York Times*, December 19

Scherer, F. M., 1982. "Inter-industry Technology Flows and Productivity Growth," *Review of Economics and Statistics*, 64(4): 627–634

Schmookler, J., 1961. "Changes in Industry and in the State of Knowledge as Determinants of Industrial Invention," in R. Nelson (ed.), *The Rate and Direction of Change in Economic Activity*, New York: Universities-NBER: 195–228

Schumpeter, J., 1926. *The Theory of Economic Development*, Cambridge, MA: Harvard University Press

  1942. *Capitalism, Socialism and Democracy*, Cambridge, MA: Harvard University Press

Smaglik, P., 2002. "New York: Building Cooperation," *Nature*, 419: 4–5

Solow, R. M., 1957. "Technological Change and the Aggregate Production Function." *Review of Economics and Statistics*, 39(3): 312–320

Von Hippel, E., 1986. *The Sources of Innovation*, New York: Oxford University Press

3   Measuring the geography of innovation: a literature review

Apiwat Ratanawaraha and Karen R. Polenske

3.1   Introduction

Innovation has a spatial distribution. Many researchers, including those we review in this chapter, have recently studied the spatial distribution and concentration of innovation, or "innovation geography" for short, and the underlying mechanisms by which innovation occurs and spreads/concentrates. Any empirical study of innovation geography requires measurement. However, as Carter discusses (2006, chapter 2 this volume), measuring innovation and its geography is difficult both conceptually and empirically. Indeed, measurement continues to be one of the most challenging issues in the studies of innovation geography. As Zvi Griliches (1994) pointed out, many unresolved empirical issues in economics are just measurement problems. The same is true for studies of innovation geography. Although limited data availability is a major obstacle to studying innovation geography, inadequate theoretical models and conceptual precision also weaken the ability of analysts to determine appropriate data and to devise robust empirical indicators, indices, tests, and analyses of innovation. In other words, precise measurement of innovation geography requires precise concepts and definitions.[1]

Nevertheless, innovation-geography analysts have found data and attempted ingenious ways to measure innovation and its distributive patterns, mainly using indicators and indices, often by adopting and adjusting various available indicators of regional growth. First, we discuss the different data they use to measure different aspects of innovation, in general, to illustrate that innovation is still a broad and poorly defined concept. Of the several extensive reviews of measurement issues in science, technology, and innovation (STI) studies, we have found some to be especially relevant. These include classic survey articles by Griliches

[1] We thank Anne P. Carter and two anonymous referees for their comments on the original draft of this chapter.

(1990) and Archibugi and Pianta (1996), who focus on the use of patent statistics as indicators of innovation, and the more comprehensive compendia, such as *Handbook of Quantitative Studies of Science Policy*, edited by van Raan (1988) and, more recently, *Handbook of Quantitative Science and Technology Research*, edited by Moed, Schmoch, and Glanzel (2004), both of which contain extensive details. We do not attempt to match the comprehensiveness of those works; however, these and most other existing reviews do not focus on how economic geographers and regional planners have determined the appropriate data and the underlying mechanisms for attracting innovation, nor on the indicators used in measuring the spatial distribution of innovation. Thus, one of our goals is to guide the reader to those data and indicators being used by innovation-geography analysts who are studying innovations and their spatial concentration/dispersion.

Second, we critically examine methods to measure the spatial distribution of innovation, focusing on indicators that innovation geography analysts have adapted mainly from location theory to measure the agglomeration/dispersion of innovation. We find that not only do they inadequately define and conceptualize theoretical methods to conduct the measurement of innovation and its diffusion, but they also rarely consider the trade-offs between relatively simple indices and more comprehensive means of conducting measurements of innovation. We also discuss the geographic levels of the units of analysis and how they affect the studies of innovation geography.

Finally, we conclude by explaining that the available measures of innovation are inadequate partly because of limited data availability and partly because of poorly defined and conceptualized comprehensive theoretical methods to conduct the measurements. The indicators are unidimensional – usually representing a single set of data – whereas innovation affects economies in multi-dimensional ways, requiring more comprehensive means than most analysts currently use to conduct measurements of innovation.

3.2   Innovation data for studies of innovation geography

Innovation-geography analysts have primarily used the innovation data already available in the field of STI studies. Sirilli (1998) and Godin (2002a, 2002b) do a thorough review of the most relevant data, which we categorize into three groups, representing the traditional concept of the innovation production process: namely, innovative inputs, innovative outputs, and innovative agents. As shown in table 3.1, we add a fourth group, namely, innovative networks, to reflect the growing number of

Table 3.1 *Data used in measuring spatial concentration/dispersion of innovation*

General data		Specific data	Examples of empirical work	Geographical scale and location	Time frame	Industries	Data sources
Innovative inputs	R&D expenditures	Funding for research projects	Feldman and Lichtenberg (1998)	Country (EU)	1962–1996	All	CORDIS–RTD database
		Laboratory R&D budget	Adams (2002)	Distance from laboratory location (200 miles) (US)	1991–1996	All	Survey of Industrial Laboratory Technologies (1996)
	R&D personnel	Number of scientists and engineers engaged in R&D	Porter and Stern (1999)	Country (OECD)	Various years	All	OECD Science and Technology Indicators
		Number of "star" scientists and collaborators	Zucker, Darby, and Brewer (1994)	Zip-code, County, and Functional Economic Area (US)	1975–1989	Biotechnology	GenBank database
	Employment	Employment in "creative sectors"	Fingleton, Igliori, and Moore (2003)	UALAD (UK)	2000	7 "creative industries"	Annual Business Enquiry of the Office for National Statistics
		High-tech manufacturing employment	Malecki (1985)	Metropolitan Area (US)	1983, 1993	4 high-tech	Dun & Bradstreet Corporate Market Identifiers File

		Study	Spatial unit	Period	Sector	Data source
		Alecke et al. (2003)	County, Labor Market Area, and Planning Region (Germany)	1996	9 high-tech	NA
		Maggioni (2002)	State, Census divisions (US), County, Region (UK), Departement, Region (France), Provincia, Regione (Italy)	1991–1995	5 high-tech	County Business Patterns (US), ONS (UK), Institut National de la Statistique et des Etudes Economiques (INSEE) (France), ISTAT) (Italy)
Innovative outputs	Patent counts	Number of applied patents — Guerrero and Sero (1997)	Province (Spain)	1989–1992	16 productive sectors	RIP data
		Number of granted patents — Thompson (1962)	Standard Metropolitan Area (US)	1947	16 patent classes	Official Gazette of the Patent Office
		Patent families — Criscuolo (2005)	Countries (EU, Japan, US)	1989–2000	All	EPO, USPTO, and Japanese Patent Office (JPO)
	Innovation counts	Number of new products introduced to market — Feldman (1994)	State (US)	1982	All	SBA database
		Innovative outputs (direct innovation surveys) — Hinloopen (2003)	Country (EU)	1992, 1996	All	Eurostat CIS I and II databases

(cont.)

Table 3.1 (cont.)

General data	Specific data	Examples of empirical work	Geographical scale and location	Time frame	Industries	Data sources
Potential innovations	Publications on R&D outcomes	Feldman and Lichtenberg (1998)	Country (EU)	1962–1996	All	CORDIS–RTD database
	Awards in the SBIR Program	Wallsten (2001)	State and Metropolitan Statistical Area (US)	1993–1996	7 technology areas	SBIR database
Innovative agents	Innovation-related establishments: Universities, R&D institutes, and new firms, Venture capital firms	Zucker, Darby, and Brewer (1994)	Zip-code, County, and Functional Economic Area (US)	1976–1989	Bio-technology	GenBank database
	Formation of new firms: Number of single-location firms	Malecki (1985)	Metropolitan Area, State, Region (US)	1986–1993	4 high-tech	Dun & Bradstreet Corporate Market Identifiers File
Innovative networks	Innovation networks: Research and technology partnerships	Vonortas (2002)	Country	1980–1998	All	MERIT–CATI database
	Knowledge spillovers: Patent citations	Jaffe, Trajtenberg, and Henderson (1993)	State, Standard Metropolitan Statistical Area (US)	1975, 1980	All industries	USPTO

Note: NA, Not available.
Source: The authors.

empirical studies on that topic. We now briefly review each of the four groups.

Innovative inputs

As in other areas of STI studies, the most widely used innovative input data pertain to R&D personnel and R&D expenditures, such as gross expenditures on R&D (GERD) and number of scientists and engineers, which analysts (e.g. Porter and Stern 1999) use for international comparisons of resources devoted to STI efforts. Analysts often use innovative input data as independent variables within, for example, the framework of a knowledge production function to examine the extent of knowledge spillovers across locations.

R&D expenditures Innovation-geography researchers use different general sources of R&D expenditures data to examine various distribution issues, such as the geography of high-technology industries (Malecki 1985, 1986), industry R&D expenditures and university R&D expenditures (Jaffe 1989), and university R&D and industrial R&D expenditures (Feldman 1994). They also use more specific types of R&D expenditures data, such as program funding and number of projects in the Community R&D Information Service (CORDIS) databases to examine the distribution of R&D activities in Europe (Feldman and Lichtenberg 1998) and a survey of laboratory R&D budget allocated to learning activities and its proportion to total R&D to indicate the extent of such activities in certain locations (Adams 2002).

R&D personnel Innovation-geography analysts conducting empirical studies commonly use R&D personnel to compare innovative capabilities and their economic effects across nations and regions. For instance, Adams (1990) uses data on the distribution of an industry's scientists by academic discipline to examine the relationship between fundamental stocks of knowledge and industry productivity growth. Unfortunately, in most countries, innovation-geography data for R&D personnel are generally not available at the regional and city levels. Partially to overcome this problem, Fingleton *et al.* (chapter 4 in this volume) use employment data in creative industries – i.e. activities that originate from individual creativity, skill, and talent – as a measure of innovation in the regions under investigation. Regional innovation-geography analysts often use employment data as proxies for innovation in high-technology (high-tech) sectors. One good source for US state-level data on distribution of R&D personnel and expenditures is the *Science and*

Engineering State Profiles Database, published annually by the US National Science Foundation (NSF). The NSF database includes state-specific data obtained from numerous surveys conducted by the NSF and other federal government agencies. The NSF survey databases include: doctoral scientists and engineers; doctorates awarded, including by major fields; graduate students and postdoctorates; federal R&D obligations, by agency and performer; total and industrial R&D expenditures; and academic R&D expenditures, including by major fields.

Innovative outputs

Another important group of innovation data is innovative outputs, which range from those for intermediate outputs, such as patented inventions, to those for final innovative outputs, which are, or are embodied in, commercialized products. Many analysts use one of two groups of innovative-output data, namely, patent counts and/or citation indicators and direct-innovation counts.

Patent counts and citations   Patents are arguably the most widely used data among researchers in STI studies, in general, and in innovation geography, in particular, since they are the first data to be used in the history of STI measurement (Godin 2002). Several factors explain their popularity among researchers. First, patent data are readily available in most countries, especially in industrialized economies where governments have collected the data for many decades. Second, the extensiveness of patent data enables researchers to conduct both cross-sectional and longitudinal analyses. Third, patent data contain detailed information such as the technological fields, the assignees, the inventors, and some other market characteristics that can be useful for STI studies. Fourth, many patent offices and commercial entities have developed databases that facilitate the use of patent data for empirical research. Some patent offices, such as the US Patent and Trademark Office (USPTO) and the European Patent Office (EPO), have online databases from which users can easily download necessary information.[2]

---

[2] Examples of patent databases include: (1) the WPI(L) database developed by Derwent, Inc. for the Worcester Polytechnic Institute, which covers patents from thirty national patent offices since 1963; (2) the European Patents Database (EPAT) and the Patent Convention Treaty Patents Application Database (PCTPAT) produced by the Institut National de la Propriété Industrielle (INPI) for European patents since 1978; and (3) for US patents, the US PATENTS database by developed Derwent, Inc. for 1970 onwards, and the CLAIMS database developed by the IFI/Plenum Data Corp. (US) for 1950 onwards.

Patent data include patent counts and patent citations. Patent counts are the number of patents either applied or granted during certain periods. Most analysts (e.g. Guerrero and Sero 1997) conducting empirical studies use patent-application data, because they reflect the timing and the intention of the firms/individuals that seek protection for their intellectual property. Analysts may use data on patents granted, if the data come from one patent office, or from patent offices that share similar procedures. If they wish to compare patent data across countries, they encounter problems in terms of different procedures and criteria for granting patents. Despite their many shortcomings, analysts still use them widely even in recent empirical work.[3]

As in STI studies in general, analysts conducting empirical work on innovation geography have also relied primarily on patents to measure innovation. For instance, Thompson (1962) classifies patent grants according to patent classes and locations in the United States. Similarly, in a study of knowledge spillovers, Jaffe (1989) links the patent activity to knowledge inputs located within the same states. Specifically, he uses patent counts available from the USPTO as the output of innovation, and he links those data with the expenditures on R&D. It is important to note that the USPTO publishes a filing only when a patent is granted. Furthermore, patents filed with the USPTO are not necessarily granted within eighteen months after the application, as in many countries. Analysts need to keep these unique features in mind when interpreting the US patent data.

Many other analysts use patents counts from the EPO to study innovation geography. For instance, in cross-industry analysis of innovation activity in Europe, Breschi (2000) uses the EPO–CESPRI (Centre for Research on Innovation and Internationalization) database, which refers to patent applications made in four European countries: France, Germany, Italy, and the United Kingdom. Similarly, Verspagen and Schoenmakers (2004) use a database from the EPO to examine the innovative patterns of multinational firms in Europe.

Although patents continue to be used by many analysts to measure innovation, they also use information on patents to measure technological specialization. By organizing patents into patent classes and subclasses according to technical areas, they can identify the technical areas in which firms and/or other entities in certain geographical areas are specialized to study knowledge spillovers across locations (Jaffe 1989; Jaffe, Trajtenberg, and Henderson 1993; Jaffe and Trajtenberg 2002). Narin

---

[3] For further discussion on the advantages and disadvantages of using patents, see Griliches (1990) and OECD (1994).

and Olivastro (1998), Maurseth and Verspagen (1999), and others use patent citations to indicate technological linkages between firms, between technological areas, and between technology and science. STI analysts, for example, use two types of citations of earlier patents: (1) citations by inventors, which are included in the text of patent applications, and (2) citations by patent examiners in their search reports.

Several analysts have used patent citations in empirical work on innovation geography. In his pioneering study of geographic spillovers, Jaffe (1989) uses state-level times-series data on corporate patents, together with data on corporate R&D and university research. In another study, Jaffe, Trajtenberg, and Henderson (1993) test the extent of localization of knowledge spillovers by comparing the locations of the citations with the "originating" patents that they cite. The researchers select the patents granted to US firms and universities in 1975 and 1980 as the "originating" patents. They also control for the US patents granted to foreigners and for the existing spatial distribution of technological activity.

In addition to patent citations, STI analysts also use other variations of patent data, including renewal fees, patent families, and patent claims (Archibugi and Pianta 1996). To the best of our knowledge, however, innovation-geography analysts have only used information on patent families – i.e. a set of patents in various countries that protect a single invention – in examining internationalization of innovation (e.g. Schmoch and Kirsch 1993; Criscuolo 2005).

Innovation counts/citations   As we noted earlier, patents are only intermediate outputs of innovation production processes, covering only certain parts of the innovation process. The final innovative outputs are, by definition, innovations that are introduced into the economic system. Final innovative outputs could be new commercialized products or innovations embodied in existing products sold in the market. Researchers have used alternative data to represent the final outputs of the innovation process.

One such data set is innovation counts, obtained from direct innovation surveys or censuses. European analysts started using innovation surveys on an experimental basis in a few countries. Later, they standardized the surveys within the framework of the *Oslo Manual* of the OECD (OECD 1992). During 1993–4, the European Union sponsored a Community Innovation Survey (CIS), during which they standardized the procedures and methodologies for innovation surveys in Europe (Sirilli 1998).

In contrast to patent statistics, analysts have developed innovation surveys for the specific purpose of gathering information on innovative activities in firms. From such surveys, they obtain innovation counts, which are comprehensive lists of innovations made by various firms and institutions. For the innovation surveys, analysts use two different approaches: the "object" approach, in which they collect information on individual innovations, and the "subject" approach, in which they collect data on firms that produce or adopt innovations. The object approach is generally literature-based, in that analysts collect data from publications, such as technical and trade journals and magazines. Literature-based output data originated from the work of Edwards and Gordon (1984) and were later developed by Acs and Audretsch (1990) and Kleinknecht and Bain (1993).

Several databases for innovation counts are available. For instance, the Science Policy Research Unit (SPRU) innovation database, developed at the University of Sussex, contains information on major innovations in the United Kingdom since 1945. The information includes sources and types of innovation, industry innovation patterns, cross-industry linkages, as well as geographic aspects of the innovations. Another useful database on innovation counts is available from an extensive survey by the US Small Business Administration (SBA), discussed by Edwards and Gordon (1984). The database covers 8,074 innovations introduced to the US market in 1982, of which 4,200 are from manufacturing products. The SBA used more than one hundred trade, engineering, and technology journals to construct the database. More recent, but smaller, literature-based surveys have also been constructed, such as the database on British innovations constructed by Coombs, Narandren, and Richards (1995).

The subject approach, on the other hand, is based on surveys of firms. The CIS is one example. One of the advantages of the subject approach is that the surveyor can gather information not only on innovations, but also on other characteristics of the firms and their innovative activities.

Innovation counts obtained from innovation surveys are supposedly more representative of innovative output than patents, as they directly measure the final output from the innovation process. Surveyors can also standardize the ways data are collected from various firms and institutions. This makes the dataset more reliable and usable for interfirm comparison.

Analysts have increasingly used the results from innovation surveys in STI studies. In the area of innovation geography, for example, Feldman (1994) pioneered the use of the SBA database in her study of spatial aspects of innovative activity in the United States. Similarly, Audretsch and Feldman (1996) used the database to examine the extent of industrial clustering and to test whether knowledge spillovers are the cause of the geographic distribution. Recently, as part of a study that compares innovation counts from the SBA database with the patent counts from the USPTO, Acs, Anselin, and Varga (2002) find a close similarity between the spatial distribution of innovation counts and patents.

Analysts in Europe have also increasingly used the results from the CIS, for instance, Hinloopen (2003), to examine innovation performance at the firm level across Europe. Analysts in other parts of the world (e.g. Quadros *et al.* 2001 for innovation surveys in Brazil) have also found innovation surveys to be an important source of information.

Researchers (e.g. Wallsten 2001; Black 2004) have more recently started using a novel measure of innovative outputs to examine the geography of small-firm innovations in the United States. Specifically, they use a measure based on the awards made by the US Small Business Innovation Research (SBIR) Program. The so-called SBIR Phase II awards are given to firms that have feasible research projects with the goal of commercialization. These projects have already undergone the review in Phase I, which means their commercial potential is higher than in Phase I. Strictly speaking, SBIR awards are similar to patents in that they are not final innovative outputs but intermediate outputs. However, because the selection criteria are based on the commercial potential of the projects, the awards measure innovative outputs that are close to final innovations. In addition to their novelty, the awards data have the advantages of being available for 1983 onwards, making it possible for analysts to conduct time-series studies, and of providing extensive information on research topics, firm characteristics, and locations.

Innovative agents

Innovative agents are the third category of innovation data and are ones that make the studies of innovation geography distinct from other areas of STI studies. They differ from the innovative input and output data in that they focus on the geographical locations of agents that produce innovations. They are also distinct from the R&D personnel data, which are considered as an input into the innovation production process. Innovation-geography analysts, such as Adams (2002), most commonly use firms or their R&D laboratories as a proxy for innovation agents to study the localization of knowledge spillovers. This is naturally expected, as firms are more likely to implement new ideas and introduce them to the market than are other innovative agents, such as universities, research institutes, and individual innovators. Although there are now close links between corporate and university labs, firms remain as the main agent that introduces innovations to the market, but geographical units, such as cities and states, can also be the unit of analysis.

Innovative networks and other indicators of innovation

Innovation-geography analysts use many types of innovation data available in the STI literature to examine innovative networks. They have used patent citations, for example, to investigate networks of knowledge (Breschi, Lissoni, and Malerba 2003), knowledge sourcing (Almeida 1996), and technological overlap and interfirm co-operation (Mowery, Oxley, and Silverman 1998), whereas Almeida and Kogut (1997) use patent citations as a means of identifying the importance of inventions and innovations. Although these analysts have not explicitly investigated the geography of innovative activities, the empirical results of their studies have implicit spatial implications.

There are many more data available for us to explore, including bibliometric data, technometric data, and interfirm-collaboration data. Bibliometric data are scientific publications and citation data from the Science Citation Index (SCI) and the Institute for Scientific Information (ISI) database. As shown by Narin, Hamilton, and Olivastro (1997) and Narin and Olivastro (Narin and Olivastro 1998), analysts can use bibliometric data to examine the linkage between science and innovation. In fact, using bibliometric data together with patent data, Branstetter (2000) finds the localization effects in measured knowledge flows from academic scientists to industrial innovations. Technometric data, which analysts use to explore the technical performance characteristics of products through expert interviews, are another group of data available for researchers to explore (e.g. Grupp 1994).

Feldman and Lichtenberg (1998) use information on published or announced outcomes of R&D programs to derive data for the "articulability of knowledge," which indicates the extent to which tacit knowledge becomes explicit or codified. They construct the distribution of each country's knowledge base by scientific field and type of organization, such as universities and educational organizations, and manufacturers. The CORDIS databases provide references on bibliographic details and abstracts of publications and other documents from the Research and Technology Development (RTD) programs. Information on inter-firm collaboration could also be useful for researchers interested in the spatial aspects of innovation networks. Such analyses have been conducted in Europe to show the links among innovations with the use of input-output tables for some of the OECD countries. DeBresson (1996) discusses the techniques and offers examples of how the input-output analysts have combined an analysis of innovation interaction matrices with traditional production-flow input-output matrices. They derive the innovation interaction matrices from surveys (e.g. the CIS of Eurostat) to describe flows of innovations between innovation producers and innovation users, thus focusing on actual innovation interdependencies and actual inter-actions among innovating industry groups (Roelandt and den Hertog 1999: 5). Analysts can combine graphical network analyses made with the survey data with descriptive data on regional industries to show both the interdependence among innovating industries and regional industry growth. Such innovation-flow surveys are difficult to design and costly to implement; as far as we know, they have not been conducted in the United States.

Different analysts cover a number of data-measurement issues. Prior to discussing indicators, we list nine of these issues, because many of the indicators are based upon one or more of these innovation datasets.

1. Available data and indicators do not show the nature of the innovation process in which innovative inputs are transformed into innovative outputs.
2. They do not convey any information on the economic efficiency of the process.
3. They do not show the technical complexity and economic significance of the innovative inputs, outputs, or agents.
4. Innovative activities are not limited to R&D. Firms invest in a wide range of non-R&D activities, resulting in both tangible and intangible assets that contribute to innovations, as reflected in the *Oslo Manual* (OECD 1992) and as part of the CIS by the European Union in 1993–4, in which expenditures on categories of innovation activity other than R&D were included.
5. In most countries, innovation-geography data for many of the indicators are not available at the regional and city levels. Patents are probably the most commonly used set of data and are relatively widely available, but they are imperfect proxies for innovations. Patents represent inventions, rather than innovations, as defined by Schumpeter. At the same time, not all inventions and technological advances are patented or patentable. In addition, different firms and institutions have different policies and strategies in patenting, while legal and institutional systems for patenting vary across countries. It is important to note that the USPTO publishes a filing only when a patent is granted. Furthermore, patents filed with the USPTO are not necessarily granted within eighteen months after the application, as in many countries. Patents are only intermediate outputs of innovation production processes, covering only certain parts of the innovation process.
6. R&D personnel data have at least one major disadvantage. Analysts using this employment indicator assume uniform employment patterns across all plants and establishments in an industry, which places

more weight on employment at branch plants than at R&D labs where most R&D personnel are employed (Feldman 1994). Locations with many branch plants will therefore appear to be relatively innovative even though their main activity is production.

7. Innovation counts also have a few shortcomings, such as the following: because surveyors are the ones who decide what an innovation is, the survey result could be subjective and arbitrary. Large surveys are also expensive and time-consuming. As a result, innovation counts are now available at the firm level for limited years and only in a few countries (Sellenthin and Hommen 2002). Archibugi and Pianta (1996) and the *Oslo Manual* (OECD 1992) provide a detailed account of innovation surveys.

8. As Black (2004) notes, some shortcomings of the SBIR awards, one of the latest measures of innovative outputs developed, include the lack of industrial classification of participating firms, the small number of awards compared with other innovation indicators, and the limitation to only small-firm innovations.

9. Especially problematic is the fact that many R&D projects are now carried out and funded by alliances of firms and institutes in various locations. In multinational firms, R&D is not limited to a single facility in a single country, but may range from the R&D headquarters where the R&D is centralized in the home office, to a flexible R&D network where managers assign the R&D on a project-by-project basis to different R&D facilities. Globalization of R&D activities thus makes it even more difficult to use R&D expenditures, personnel, patents, or any other single type of data to measure firms' innovative activities in specific locations, and these data certainly do not provide insights into innovation as a process.

As we noted earlier, strategic alliances may affect the results of using different innovation concentration/dispersion data. We believe that considerable research is still needed to develop new types of data and ways of measuring innovation concentration/dispersion.

Other types of analyses are being done in geostatistics, a discipline created by Matheron at the Ecole des Mines, who developed the theory of regionalized variables, which treats variables distributed in space (or time). As Syed Abdul Rahman Shibli (2004) states, "The theory says any measurement can be viewed as a realization of a random function (or random process, or random field, or stochastic process)." Still another approach is to use equivalence analysis to show the correlation between technical knowledge networks and an underlying attribute of people in the population, under the assumption that innovation is done by people, and people pass the tacit and codified knowledge to others either within the same facility, to others in other facilities, or even across the globe through knowledge networks. Greve and Salaff (2001) and Lazer (2001), for example, look for common attributes of individuals, such as those with similar knowledge network positions. A group with these common attributes should have a higher equivalence score than the population at large.

In the future, analysts will undoubtedly be able to locate these data and other measures of innovation on the website that was created by the Center for Spatially Integrated Social Science (CSISS) at the University of Santa Barbara as part of a five-year US National Science Foundation project (http://www.csiss.org/search/tools.html).

3.3   Measuring innovation geography with spatial indicators

Analysts interested in innovation geography have predominantly been concerned with three main issues. The first issue concerns the question of whether innovation, however defined, is spatially concentrated or dispersed in certain areas. Once analysts confirm that an innovation is spatially concentrated/dispersed, the second issue they investigate concerns the various mechanisms and factors that underlie such a distribution and concentration/dispersion, such as regional resource endowments, knowledge spillovers, and industrial organization. The third issue is how the spatial concentration/dispersion affects other variables, such as regional and national economic growth. To examine these issues empirically, analysts often have to devise proxy indicators to represent the variables in the study. In this chapter, we focus only on the first issue – namely, the ways in which researchers measure the concentration and dispersion of innovation and the indicators they use.

Innovations may be concentrated in certain regions, such as Silicon Valley in California and Route 128 in Massachusetts, or they may be dispersed along supply chains, or located globally in random patterns. Analysts have not devised/used specific measures of innovation geography to test their intuition and hypotheses about the distribution. Many researchers, such as Oakey (1984) and Saxenian (1985), have adopted the case-study approach to investigate innovation geography in specific regions; however, researchers have difficulty generalizing from case studies. Only in the late 1980s did innovation-geography analysts start to use quantitative research methodologies with larger data sets to explore spatial aspects of innovation, mainly using indicators of geographic concentration that are already available in the economic-geography, economic-development, and regional-science literature. For the most part, they have not devised new methods.

These researchers use basic methods, such as simple aggregation of innovation-related data by geographical area. They may also represent the distributive patterns graphically by plotting the data on a map of the world, a country, or a region. They also use two distinct types of more sophisticated concentration indicators, which we group depending upon whether the indicator can be used to measure spillover effects or not. The first set, which does not measure spillover effects includes (1) the Location Quotient (LQ), (2) the Horizontal Clustering Location Quotient (HCLQ), (3) the Locational Gini coefficient (LGC), and (4) the Herfindahl–Hirschman index (HHI). The second set, which does measure spillover effects to some extent, includes (5) the Ellison–Glaeser Geographic Concentration Index (EGGCI), (6) the Geographic Coincidence (Concentration) Index (GCI), and (7) the Gene-Related (GR) indicator. Although analysts do not use the GCI to measure geographic concentration *per se*, they widely use it to control for size differences across units of observation. Science analysts use the GR indicator, which is similar to the GCI, to take alliances among firms into consideration, an important issue with the proliferation of intellectual property rights (IPRs). In table 3.2, we provide the mathematical formulae, information that we do not repeat in the text.

Geographic concentration index without spillover effects

The following four indicators are widely used by analysts to identify the absolute concentration of economic activities.

LQ   Analysts widely use the LQ indicator to measure the relative concentration of, say, employment/innovation, based upon a calculated ratio between the local economy and the economy of some reference unit. An LQ greater than one indicates that there is an above-average proportion of employment/innovation in a given industry in a given area. Feldman (1994) and other analysts have used the LQ technique in empirical studies on innovation geography. Although the LQ indicates whether an area has a higher or lower share of a particular industry's employment/innovation than the national share, it does not provide information regarding the absolute size of the industry in that area. This lack of scale sensitivity of the LQ led Fingleton, Igliori, and Moore (2003) to develop what we call the horizontal cluster location quotient (HCLQ).

HCLQ   Fingleton, Igliori, and Moore (2003) and Fingleton *et al.* (2006, chapter 4 in this volume) weight LQ values with an indicator of size, such as the local share of the national industry or number of jobs in

Table 3.2 *Geographic Concentration indicators*

	Indicator	Formula	Description
GCIs without spillover effects	LQ	$(LQ = (E_{ig}/E_{in})/(E_{og}/E_{on}))$	E_{ig} is employment in sector i in region g E_{og} is total employment in region g E_{in} is national employment in sector i E_{on} is total national employment
	HCLQ	$HCLQ = E_{ig} - \hat{E}_{ig}$	E_{ig} is actual employment in sector i in region g $\hat{E}_{ig}$ is estimated employment in sector i in region g when LQ equals one
	LGC	$LGC = \dfrac{\sum\limits_{i=1}^{n}\sum\limits_{j=1}^{n}|x_i - x_j|}{2n(n-1)\mu}$	x are LQs in each region, μ is the mean of LQ of the study area, n is the number of regions.
	HHI	$HHI = \sum\limits_{i=1}^{n}(s_i - x_i)^2$	s is the industrial employment share in region i, x is the total employment share in region i
GCIs with spillover effects	EGGCI	$EGGCI =$ $\sum\limits_{i=1}^{n}(s_i - x_i)^2 - \left(1 - \sum\limits_{i=1}^{n}x_i^2\right)\sum\limits_{j=1}^{m}z_j^2$ $\left(1 - \sum\limits_{i=1}^{n}x_i^2\right)\left(1 - \sum\limits_{j=1}^{m}z_j^2\right)$	s and x are the same as in HHI, z is the market share of each individual firm in region i
	GCI	$GCI_t = \dfrac{\sum\limits_{s}U_{ts}TP_{ts}}{\left[\sum\limits_{s}TP_{ts}^2\right]^{1/2}\left[\sum\limits_{s}TP_{ts}^2\right]^{1/2}}$	TP_{ts} is the total number of R&D lab workers in a city or an region, U_{ts} is the university research, GCI_t is the uncentered correlation of the vectors U_{ts} and TP_t across cities or regions within a state
	GR ratio	$\text{GR ratio} = \sum\limits_{j=1}^{4}C_j \Big/ \sum\limits_{j=1}^{4}C_i$	C_j is the count of field trials of the top four frequently used gene constructs C_i is the count of field trials of each type of gene construct

Source: The authors.

the local industry to take into consideration the relative local importance of an industry and the size of the agglomeration in terms of number of jobs. They define HCLQ (referred to as HC* by Fingleton *et al.*) as the number of jobs in the local industry that exceeds its expected number. They further define the expected number by the number of jobs in the industry that would correspond to the area having the national share of the industry and therefore produce an LQ equal to one. Finally, they obtain the measure of horizontal clustering as the difference between the actual and expected number of jobs, hence $HCLQ = E_{ig} - \hat{E}_{ig}$.

Alternatively, taking into account the size of the spatial unit of observation while including information about geographical proximity of firms, they use cluster intensity as a measure for employment per unit area. They then calculate cluster intensity as $HC = Eig/A$, where A is area of region g. We believe that this indicator could also be used to measure concentration/dispersion of innovation.

Both the LQ and HCLQ possess similar weaknesses. First, the results from both measures may vary, depending on what industrial classification level an analyst uses. The more disaggregated the number of sectors, the more accurate the results will be. If the analyst, for example, conducts a study using the 3-digit North American Industrial Classification System (NAICS) codes, he/she may not detect some detailed clusters of innovation, because subsectors offset each other at the aggregate level; however, at a 4-digit level of analysis, one or two subsectors of innovation may occur. This is a phenomenon technically called "aggregation bias." Second, with both measures, an analyst fails to explain to what degree the industry is dispersed over the region. Hence an analyst using the two measures is unable to answer questions concerning whether there is an agglomeration or dispersion trend for the industry and whether innovative clusters have spillover effects on firms' location decision. We cover the spillover effect issue later but, first, we discuss two other indicators of concentration/dispersion, namely, the LGC and the HHI.

LGC Krugman (1991) proposed the so-called LGC to indicate regional income disparities. An analyst can construct it by calculating both the share of total national employment and the share of national employment in the industry for each of the geographic units in the study. Then, he/she can rank the units by the ratios of the two numbers. Finally, he/she plots the values according to the ranking, while keeping a cumulative total of both the sum of total employment share and the sum of employment share in the industry.

The LGC thus indicates the distribution of employment, or other measures of innovation, in an industry relative to the distribution of total employment. The LGC takes a value of zero if the industry's employment/innovation is located in each geographic unit in the same proportion as the total employment/innovation. The LGC becomes closer to one, as the industry employment/innovation relative to the total employment/innovation becomes greater.

Note that Krugman uses the LGC to measure the spatial distribution of manufacturing employment, not innovation *per se*. However, several analysts (e.g. Audretsh and Feldman 1996; Agarwal and Cockburn 2002; Suzigan *et al.* 2003) have used the indicator to examine the geographic concentration of innovative activity although the measure actually indicates geographic disparity, which is conceptually distinct from geographic concentration. Geographic concentration, on the one hand, refers to the extent to which a region accounts for a large proportion of industrial and innovative activity. Geographic disparity, on the other hand, indicates the degree to which the intensity of the activity in question differs among regions. This confusion perhaps arises because the Gini coefficient is based on the Lorenz curve, which analysts sometimes refer to as the "concentration" curve (Arbia 1989; Wolfson 1997; Spiezia 2002), thus confusing inequality and concentration.

HHI Analysts use HHI as another geographic indicator for innovative activity to measure market concentration. The original HHI is defined as the sum of the squares of the market shares of each individual firm. The index, therefore, can range from zero to one. An analyst obtains the highest number one, when the market has only one firm, which thus controls 100 percent of the market. Thus, a large HHI index indicates a high concentration of firms in the market for the industry. By squaring the market shares, an analyst gives more weight to large firms, thereby providing a contrast to the simple concentration ratio, which is the percentage of market output generated by the N largest firms in the industry. When the market shares of small players are widely dispersed, they do not add to the HHI value. Such a situation indicates intense competition. The usefulness of the HHI is therefore partly dependent upon an appropriate definition of a particular market.

In a study of patenting patterns of multinational firms in Europe, Verspagen and Schoenmakers (2004) calculate a "Herfindahl-equivalent-number-of-regions" indicator to measure the geographic distribution, based on a procedure similar to that of the HHI. They first calculate the share of each region in total patenting of a firm, then the sum of the squares of this share over all regions. Finally, they calculate the inverse of this result. The result can be interpreted as the number of regions that would generate the same value as the indicator if there were equal shares of patents in all regions. The larger (smaller) this value is, the more (less) widely distributed are the innovative activities of the particular firm.

Although more complex measures than LQ and HCLQ, analysts who use LGC and HHI fail to distinguish whether firms choose a specific location randomly or on the basis of certain considerations, such as spillover effects and natural advantages. They do not take into account the sources of externalities that contribute to the geographic concentration of innovation. Although internal economies of scale may arise when firms locate their plants or R&D labs in proximity to one another, external economies of scale occur when independent firms locate their plants in the same area or when they benefit from natural advantages, such as local pools of scientists and engineers. In addition, both indices are "sensitive to the number of establishments" (Kim, Barkley, and Henry 2000: 239), so that they become incomparable across industries and across regions. Thus, these indicators, which are widely used in empirical studies of manufacturing and other sectors, share the major disadvantage that they do not distinguish whether the concentration of innovation activity is due to internal or external economies of scale.

Geographic concentration indices with spillover effects

Partially in response to the disadvantages of the indicators just discussed, analysts have recently developed three indices to reflect spillover effects in the geographic concentration of industries/innovations.

EGGCI In order to distinguish between the concentration caused by internal or external economies, Ellison and Glaeser (1997) developed the EGGCI, which is derived from an explicit location-decision model. Using the EGGCI, an analyst takes into consideration the effect of the randomness of firms' location decisions by comparing the estimated spatial concentration index

$$\sum_{i=1}^{n} (s_i - x_i)^2$$

and the expected value of the spatial distribution,

$$\left(1 - \sum_{i=1}^{n} x_i^2\right) \sum_{j=1}^{m} z_j^2.$$

The spillover effect is reflected by the difference between the two.

Because the sum of x squared and the sum of z squared lies between zero and one, the sign of EGGCI is determined solely by the numerator. A negative value implies that spillover effects or natural advantages do not have a strong influence on establishments' location decisions/innovations, while a large value indicates that the industry/innovation is concentrated in the study area. According to Ellison and Glaeser (1997: 900), this index has two distinct properties. First, an analyst can easily compute the index without help of any advanced statistical package. Second, the index is not sensitive to the number of establishments, geographic size, and number of geographic areas, so that the indices are comparable across industries, across regions, and across time.

Ellison and Glaeser originally developed the EGGCI index to examine the geographic concentration of manufacturing industries, not innovation or innovative activities *per se*. An analyst can easily adapt the index to an empirical study of innovation geography. The EGGCI, however, does not correctly depict the reality of a firm's location-decision process, as indicated by Alecke *et al.* (2003), who applied it to the United States, while Devereux, Griffith, and Simpson (1999) applied it to the United Kingdom, Maurel and Sédillot (1999) to France, Callejón (1997) to Spain, and Mayerhofer and Palme (2001) to Austria.

One drawback of the EGGCI is that it is not internationally comparable when regional sizes differ systematically between countries. To overcome this problem, Spiezia (2002) proposed the Adjusted Geographic Concentration Index (AGCI), defined as

$$AGCI = GCI/GCI^{MAX}$$

where *GCI* is the EGGCI reformulated to correct for aggregation bias:

$$GCI = \sum_{i=1}^{N} |y_i - a_i|.$$

The AGCI index lies between zero (no concentration) and one (maximum concentration) in all study areas. It thus appears to be suitable for international comparisons of geographic concentration.

GCI The GCI, first devised by Jaffe (1989), does not measure the spatial distribution of innovation *per se*, but it may be useful as an indicator for investigating knowledge spillovers within certain areas. In his study of spillovers of R&D and university research, Jaffe constructs the index to deal with the problem that state-level data may not capture the right geographic scope of knowledge spillovers. GCI_t is the uncentered correlation of the vectors U_{ts} and TP_t across cities or regions within a state. Varga (1998) and Anselin, Varga, and Acs (2000) provide more discussion on the choice of the unit of observation.

Although the EGGCI and GCI are more advanced than the HHI and LGC indicators in the way that they can distinguish the existence of spillover effects of current innovation clusters, without sophisticated modeling, no analyst can use these indices to solve such problems as how much the spillover effect is, or how it happens.

Interfirm Alliance (IA) ratio   We discuss the IA ratio that is called the GR ratio in agricultural biotechnology sciences, although conducting a review of the science and engineering literature is beyond our scope for this chapter. We include it both because it is closely related to the measures mentioned above and because interfirm alliances are becoming more common than before in regional analyses. Rather than using R&D as the indicator, Oehmke and Wolf (2003) devise a GR ratio to account for strategic interfirm alliances, which are common within biotechnology. They state that previous analysts studying innovation in that industry have looked at the pace of innovation, the distribution of benefits, the role of the public sector, and appropriate policy, but no one previously looked at the strategic alliances – i.e. cases in which "one biotechnology firm grants another firm access to its proprietary plant gene constructs" (Oehmke and Wolf 2003: 134).

They construct the ratio as follows:

1. Count the number of trials of each type of gene construct, oriented towards the specified varietal characteristic.
2. Sum to obtain the total number of trials for that variety (use as the denominator).
3. Sum the number of field trials oriented towards the specified varietal characteristics of the four most frequently used gene constructs (use as the numerator).
4. Divide the denominator into the numerator to give a ratio from zero to 100 percent that is interpreted analogously to the concentration 4 ratio. (CR4 ratio, see below) with a value of 100 percent indicating a pure monopoly, and with a value of 0 percent indicating a purely competitive market structure.

Oehmke and Wolf found that the GR ratio was always higher and less volatile than the CR4 ratio, which is the aggregate market share of the four largest firms in an industry. Their work also could be important for regional analysts studying alliances and networks, so that we have renamed it the IA ratio. In fact, analysts may find the use of the IA ratio important for any industry in which IPRs play a critical role in the expansion and location of firms.

Summary

Although analysts have devised several ways of measuring innovation geography, systemic measurement of innovation networks is still in its incipient stage. Some analysts use a case-study approach to analyze networks of innovation (e.g. Saxenian 1990). Others rely on existing data sets or specialized surveys. One of the most comprehensive data sets is the database on alliances for the exchange and development of technology compiled by the Maastricht Economic Research Institute on Innovation and Technology (MERIT) (e.g. Powell, Koput, and Smith-Doerr 1996; Knoke, Yang, and Granados 2002).

Economic geographers have used a number of different indicators for networks, a few of which include a beta index to compare the number of links with the number of nodes in a network; the Shimbel index to indicate the minimum number of links necessary to connect one node with all nodes in the network; and the Koenig number to indicate the accessibility (or centrality) of a node by the number of links needed to connect this node with the (topologically) most distant node in the network. For these and other indicators, refer to Krumme (2004).

Similarly, DeBresson and Amesse (1991) propose the use of graph analysis, a branch of mathematics in which dots and arrows are the fundamental building blocks. Although a high number of arrows can make the analysis very complex when used to represent networks, the structure of the graph can be summarized in some simple forms. In fact, this measurement technique has already been used by Czepiel (1975) to analyze the diffusion of technological innovation. Overall, as Alecke *et al.* (2003) indicate, any indicator of the concentration of innovation should allow an analyst to do at least the following: (1) compare across industries; (2) control for overall agglomeration; (3) control for industrial concentration; (4) make unbiased measures with respect to geographic scale and aggregation; and (5) obtain a measure of the statistical significance.

Regional analysts are continuing their interest in innovation and its spatial concentration/dispersion. We therefore anticipate that they will continue to use the data and indicators we have reviewed here, most of which provide a single number, but that they will also do considerable work to get less finite data and indicators that may provide policymakers with an insight into the types of policies that will help attract innovative activities into a region or an industrial sector.

3.4   Geographic units of observation

Another important issue in measuring the geography of innovation is the choice of geographic units of observation. For analysts conducting empirical studies to investigate national innovation systems and efforts, nations are the appropriate unit of analysis. National data on innovation are available in most countries, even though the quality of the data varies.

Just in terms of data availability, analysts perhaps find it easier to conduct a cross-national comparison than a cross-regional one.

The choice of spatial units affects the research results and implications. Most analysts have to rely on the use of jurisdictional units, as data are often collected according to the jurisdictional boundaries. Choices are mostly limited by the availability of data. Some analysts do their own surveys to overcome the limitation of using existing data. Their studies, however, tend to cover only specific areas.

Analysts conducting empirical studies on innovation geography use various spatial units of analysis, ranging from relatively broad geographic units, such as states, to much smaller levels, such as cities, counties, or zip codes. Most analysts agree that in the United States states are too large for use as an appropriate geographic unit of observation, especially for research on knowledge spillovers. Instead of using fixed geographic units, some analysts (e.g. Wallsten 2001; Adams 2002; Adams and Jaffe 2002) have used the concept of distance decay. Others (e.g. Feldman 1994, 2002; Branstetter 2000) contend that geography is more a platform for organizing economic activity and that the measures of distance do not capture complex social relationships.

3.5   Conclusion

From our review of indicators of innovation and their concentration/dispersal, we have found several major gaps in the literature. So far, researchers have developed indicators of innovation production, including innovative inputs and outputs, but they could also develop indicators of innovation consumption. Economic geographers may be able to develop some additional measures based upon science and engineering studies, much as the GR ratio was developed by agricultural biotechnology analysts modifying the CR4 ratio from industrial studies. Also, no analyst has yet looked at different economic, political, and social systems to see if innovation is more likely to occur under capitalism, socialism, or communism, or under a federal system of government, or under a dictator, or under a patriarchical or matriarchical society. Each of us thinks we know the answer, but we might be surprised if a study were to be done.

From our review of the literature, we learned that whereas we started our review assuming that we could separate product from process innovation, the OECD researchers and others have found from their survey that the majority of firms engage in both types of innovation. The lack of precise definition and measurement of innovation processes makes it difficult to conduct empirical studies on the geography of innovation processes. Researchers also need to devise new indicators that take into account the fact that innovative activities by firms and research institutes are increasingly globalized and interconnected through alliances and consortia. For instance, the location where innovation actually takes place may not necessarily be the same as the location where firms apply for patents.

In reviewing the innovation literature, not surprisingly, we have not found a single innovation data measure or indicator that is ideal. As we noted earlier, we maintain that the available data and indicators are too unidimensional, in general; specifically, for a concept as complex as innovation, analysts need to consider the multi-dimensional economic, social, and political context within which innovation occurs. This probably involves incorporating the relatively new literature on learning regions and learning economies into these measurements. In Europe, analysts have helped form an important theoretical framework for use in national and regional policy decisions with the concepts of learning economies, learning regions, and national and regional innovation systems (NIS), as covered by Lundvall (1996) and Lundvall *et al.* 2006, (chapter 10 in this volume). Lundvall and Johnson (1994, p. 26) define the learning economy as extending to not only "science and technology systems – universities, research organization, in-house R&D departments and so on – but also to the learning implications of the economic structure, the organizational forms and the institutional set-up . . . Firms start to learn to learn." Asheim (1996) has been instrumental in extending the concept spatially for regional applications in Norway and elsewhere in Europe.

Where does this leave an analyst? Basically, all innovation data and indicators lack the detail we desire in order to conduct excellent studies of innovation. As we noted earlier, strategic alliances may affect the results of using different indicators of innovation concentration/dispersion. To study innovation and the process by which it occurs and is disseminated, an analyst needs to look not only at those alliances, but also at the institutional codes of behavior, laws, etc. that may enable/restrict an innovation from being dispersed, the interindustrial relations among sectors, and the locational advantages/disadvantages that may aid/hinder the dissemination.

REFERENCES

Acs, Z. J., L. Anselin, and A. Varga, 2002. "Patents and Innovation Counts as Measures of Regional Production of New Knowledge," *Research Policy*, 31(7): 1069–1085
Acs, Z. J. and D. B. Audretsch, 1990. *Innovation and the Small Firm*, Cambridge, MA: MIT Press
Adams, J. D., 1990. "Fundamental Stocks of Knowledge and Productivity Growth," *Journal of Political Economy*, 98(4): 673–702

2002. "Comparative Localization of Academic and Industrial Spillovers," *Journal of Economic Geography*, 2: 253–278

Adams, J. D. and A. B. Jaffe, 2002. "Bounding the Effects of R&D: An Investigation Using Matched Firm and Establishment Data," *Rand Journal of Economics*, 27: 700–721

Agrawal A. and I. M. Cockburn, 2002. "University Research, Industrial R&D, and the Anchor Tenant Hypothesis," NBER Working Paper, 9212, Cambridge, MA

Alecke, B., C. Alsleben, F. Scharr, and G. Untiedt, 2003. "New Evidence on the Geographic Concentration of German Industries: Do High-Tech Clusters Really Matter?," Presented at the Uddevalla Symposium on Entrepreneurship, Spatial Industrial Clusters and Inter-Firm Networks, Uddevalla

Almeida, P., 1996. "Knowledge Sourcing by Foreign Multinationals: Patent Citation Analysis in the US Semiconductor Industry," *Strategic Management Journal*, 17: 155–165

Almeida, P. and B. Kogut, 1997. "The Exploration of Technological Diversity and the Geographic Localization of Innovation," *Small Business Economics*, 9(1): 21–31

Anselin, L., A. Varga, and Z. Acs, 2000. "Geographical Spillovers and University Research: A Spatial Econometric Approach," *Growth and Change*, 31: 501–516

Arbia, G., 1989. *Spatial Data Configuration in the Statistical Analysis of Regional Economics and Related Problems*, Dordrecht: Kluwer

Archibugi, D. and M. Pianta, 1996. "Measuring Technological Change through Patents and Innovation Surveys," *Technovation*, 16(9): 451–468

Asheim, B. T., 1996. "Industrial Districts as 'Learning Regions': A Condition for Prosperity?," *European Planning Studies*, 4(4): 379–400

Audretsch, D. B. and M. P. Feldman, 1996. "R&D Spillovers and the Geography of Innovation and Production," *American Economic Review*, 86(3): 630–640

Black, G., 2004. *The Geography of Small Firm Innovation*, Norwell, MA: Kluwer

Branstetter, L. G., 2000. "Measuring the Link between Academic Science and Industrial Innovation: The Case of California's Research Universities," Presented at the 2000 NBER Summer Institute, Cambridge, MA

Breschi, S., 2000. "The Geography of Innovation: A Cross-Industry Analysis," *Regional Studies*, 34: 213–229

Breschi, S., F. Lissoni, and F. Malerba, 2003. "Knowledge Networks from Patent Citations? Methodological Issues and Preliminary Results," Presented at the DRUID Summer Conference 2003 on Creating, Sharing, and Transferring Knowledge: The Role of Geography, Institutions and Organizations, Copenhagen, June 12–14

Callejón, M., 1997. "Concentración geográfica de la industria y economías de aglomeración," *Economía Industrial*, 317: 61–68

Carter, A. P., 2006. "Measurement of the Clustering and Dispersion of Innovation," chapter 2 in this volume

Coombs, R., P. Narandren, and A. Richards, 1996. "A Literature-Based Innovation Output Indicator," *Research Policy*, 25: 403–413

Criscuolo, P., 2005. "The 'Home Advantage' Effect and Patent Families: A Comparison of OECD Triadic Patents, the USPTO and the EPO," Paper presented at the EPIP Conference, Copenhagen, March 10–11

Czepiel, J. A., 1975. "Patterns of Interorganizational Communications and Diffusion of a Major Technological Innovation in a Competitive Industrial Community," *Academy of Management Journal*, 18(1): 6–24

DeBresson, C., 1996. *Economic Interdependence and Innovative Activity*, Cheltenham: Edward Elgar

DeBresson, C. and F. Amesse, 1991. "Networks of Innovators: A Review and Introduction to the Issue," *Research Policy*, 20(5): 363–379

Devereux, M. P., R. Griffith, and H. Simpson, 1999. "The Geographic Distribution of Production Activity in the UK," The Institute for Fiscal Studies, Working Paper, 26/99

Edwards, K. L. and T. J. Gordon, 1984. *"Characteristics of Innovations Introduced on the US Market in 1982,"* Washington, DC: Future Groups for the US Small Business Administration

Ellison, G. and E. L. Glaeser, 1997. "Geographic Concentration in US Manufacturing Industries: A Dartboard Approach," *Journal of Political Economy*, 105(5): 879–927

Feldman, M. P., 1994. *The Geography of Innovation*, Boston, MA: Kluwer
      2002. "The Internet Revolution and the Geography of Innovation," *International Social Science Journal*, 54: 47–56

Feldman, M. P. and F. R. Lichtenberg, 1998. "The Interaction between Public and Private R&D Investment: Cross-Country Evidence from European Community's R&D Information Service," *Annales d'Economie et de Statistique*, 49–50: 199–222

Fingleton, B., D. Igliori, and B. Moore, 2003. "Employment Growth of Small Computing Services Firms and the Role of Horizontal Clusters: Evidence from Great Britain 1991–2000," in B. Fingleton (ed.), *Regional Growth in Europe*, Berlin: Springer Verlag: 267–291

Godin, B., 2002a. "Measuring Output: When Economics Drives Science and Technology Measurements," Project on the History and Sociology of S&T Statistics, Paper 14
      2002b. "Outline for a History of Science Measurement," *Science, Technology and Human Values*, 27(1): 3–27

Greve, A. and J. W. Salaff, 2001. "The Development of Corporate Social Capital in Complex Innovation Processes," in S. M. Gabbay and R. T. A. J. Leenders (eds.), *Research in the Sociology of Organizations: Social Capital of Organizations*, 18: 107–134

Griliches, Z., 1990. "Patent Statistics as Economic Indicators: A Survey," *Journal of Economic Literature*, 28: 1661–1707
      1994. "Productivity, R&D, and the Data Constraint," *American Economic Review*, 84(1): 1–23

Grupp, H., 1994. "The Measurement of Technical Performance of Innovations by Technometrics and its Impact on Established Technology Indicators," *Research Policy*, 23(2): 175–193

Guerrero D. C. and M.A. Sero, 1997. "Spatial Distribution of Patents in Spain: Determining Factors and Consequences on Regional Development," *Regional Studies*, 31(4): 381–390

Hinloopen, J., 2003. "Innovation Performance Across Europe," *Economics of Innovation and New Technology*, 12(2): 145–161

Jaffe, A. 1989. "The Real Effects of Academic Research," *American Economic Review*, 79: 957–970

Jaffe, A. and M. Trajtenberg. 2002. *Patents, Citations, and Innovations: A Window on the Knowledge Economy*, Cambridge, MA: MIT Press

Jaffe, A. B., M. Trajtenberg, and R. Henderson, 1993. "Geographic Localization of Knowledge Spillovers as Evidenced by Patent Citations," *Quarterly Journal of Economics*, 108(3): 577–598

Kim, Y., D. L. Barkley, and M. S. Henry, 2000. Industry Characteristics Linked to Establishment Concentrations in Nonmetropolitan Areas," *Journal of Regional Science*, 40(2): 231–259

Kleinknecht, A. and D. Bain, 1993. *New Concepts in Innovation Output Measurement*, New York: St. Martin's Press

Knoke, D., S. Yang, and F. J. Granados, 2002. "Dynamics of Strategic Alliance Networks in the Global Information Sector, 1989–2000," Presented at the Standing Working Group for Business Network Research "The Dynamics of Networks," 18th EGOS Colloquium, Barcelona, July 4–6

Krugman, P., 1991. *Geography and Trade*, Cambridge, MA: MIT Press

Krumme, G., 2004. *Analysis of Interdependence Structures: Networks*, at http://faculty.washington.edu/krumme/lot/networks.html, accessed on July 25, 2004

Lazer, D. M. J., 2001. "The Co-Evolution of Individual and Network," *Journal of Mathematical Sociology*, January: 69–108

Lundvall, B. Å., 1996. "National Systems of Innovation and Input-Output Analysis," in C. DeBresson *et al.* (eds.), *Economic Interdependence and Innovative Activity*, Cheltenham: Edward Elgar: 356–363

Lundvall, B.-Å. and B. Johnson, 1994. "The Learning Economy," *Journal of Industry Studies*, 1(2): 23–42

Lundvall, B.-Å., B. Johnson, E. S. Andersen, and B. Dalum, 2006. "National Systems of Production, Innovation, and Competence Building," chapter 10 in this volume

Maggioni, M.A., 2002. *Clustering Dynamics and the Location of High-Tech Firms*, New York: Physica-Verlag

Malecki, E. J., 1985. "Industrial Location and Corporate Organization of High-Technology Industries," *Economic Geography*, 61: 345–369

1986. "Research and Development and the Geography of High-Technology Complexes," in J. Rees (ed.), *Technology, Regions, and Policy*, Totowa, NJ: Rowman & Littlefield

Maurel, F. and B. Sédillot, 1999. "A Measure of the Geographic Concentration in French Manufacturing Industries," *Regional Science and Urban Economics*, 29(5): 575–604

Maurseth, P. B. and B. Verspagen, 1999. "Knowledge Spillovers in Europe. A Patent Citation Analysis," Presented at the CRENOS conference on Technological Externalities and Spatial Localization, University of Cagliari

Mayerhofer, P. and G. Palme, 2001. "Strukturpolitik und Raumplaung in den Regionen an der mitteleuropäischen EU-Außengrenze zur Vorbereitung auf die EU-Osterweiterung," Teilprojekt 6/1: Sachgüterproduktion und

Dienstleistungen: Sektorale Wettbewerbsfähigkeit und regionale Integrationsfolgen, at http://www.preparity.wsr.ac.at/public/veroeffentlichungen/at/veroeffentlichungen_a6.htm

Moed, H. F., U. Schmoch, and W. Glanzel (eds.), 2004. *Handbook of Quantitative Science and Technology Research: The Use of Publication and Patent Statistics in Studies of S&T Systems*, Dordrecht: Kluwer

Mowery, D. C., J. E. Oxley, and B. S. Silverman, 1998. "Technological Overlap and Interfirm Cooperation: Implications for the Resource-Based View of the Firm," *Research Policy*, 27(5): 507–523

Narin, F., K. S. Hamilton, and D. Olivastro, 1997. "The Increasing Linkage Between US Technology and Public Science," *Research Policy*, 26(3): 317–330

Narin, F. and D. Olivastro. 1998. "Linkage between Patents and Papers: An Interim EPO/US Comparison," *Scientometrics*, 41(1–2): 51–59

Oakey, R., 1984. *High Technology Small Firms: Regional Development in Britain and the United States*, New York: St. Martin's Press

Oehmke, J. F. and C. A. Wolf, 2003. "Measuring Concentration in the Biotechnology R&D Industry: Adjusting for Interfirm Transfer of Genetic Materials," *AgBioForum*, 6(3): 134–140

Organization for Economic Co-Operation and Development (OECD), 1992. *Proposed Standard Practice for Collecting and Interpreting Technological Innovation Data – Oslo Manual*, Paris: OECD

1994. *The Measurement of Scientific and Technological Activities: Using Patent Data as Science and Technology Indicators – Patent Manual*, Paris: OECD

Porter, M. and S. Stern, 1999. *The New Challenge to America's Prosperity: Findings from the Innovation Index*, Washington, DC: Council on Competitiveness

Powell, W. W., K. W. Koput, and L. Smith-Doerr, 1996. "Interorganizational Collaboration and the Locus of Innovation: Networks of Learning in Biotechnology," *Administrative Science Quarterly*, 41: 116–145

Quadros, R., A. Furtado, R. Bernardes, and E. Franco, 2001. "Technological Innovation in Brazilian Industry: An Assessment Based on the São Paulo Innovation Survey," *Technological Forecasting and Social Change*, 67(2–3): 203–219

Roelandt, T. J. A. and P. den Hertog, 1999. "Cluster Analysis and Cluster-Based Policy Making in OECD Countries: Introduction to the Theme," in OECD, *Boosting Innovation: The Cluster Approach, OECD Proceedings*, Paris: OECD: 9–23.

Saxenian, A., 1985. "Silicon Valley and Route 128: Regional Prototypes of Historical Exceptions?," in M. Castells (ed.), *High-Technology, Space, and Society*, Beverly Hills, CA: Sage

1990. "Regional Networks and the Resurgence of Silicon Valley," *California Management Review*, 33(1): 89–112

Schmoch, U. and N. Kirsch, 1993. "Analysis of International Patent Flows," Final Report to the OECD, Karlsruhe: FhG-ISI

Sellenthin, M. O. and L. Hommen, 2002. "How Innovative is Swedish Industry? A Factor and Cluster Analysis of CIS II," *International Review of Applied Economics*, 16(3): 319–331

Shibli, S. A. R., 2004. "The Big Picture: issues and problems," *AI-GEOSTATS FAQ*, at www.ai-geostats.org/geostats_faq/Syed/bigpicture.html, accessed on October 10, 2005

Sirilli, G., 1998. "Old and New Paradigms in the Measurement of R&D," *Science and Public Policy*, 25(5): 305–311

Spiezia, V., 2002. *Geographic Concentration of Production and Unemployment in OECD Countries*, Paris: OECD

Suzigan, W., J. Furtado, R. Garcia, and S. Sampaio, 2003. "Local Production and Innovation Systems in the State of São Paulo, Brazil," The 43rd European Congress of the Regional Science Association – ERSA 2003, Jyvaskyla, August 27–30

Thompson, W. R., 1962. "Locational Differences in Inventive Effort and Their Determinants," in R. R. Nelson (ed.), *The Rate and Direction of Inventive Activity*, Princeton, NJ: Princeton University Press

van Raan, F. J. (ed.), 1988. *Handbook of Quantitative Studies of Science Policy*, Amsterdam: Elsevier Science Publishers

Varga, A., 1998. *University Research and Regional Innovation: A Spatial Econometric Analysis of Academic Technology Transfers*, Amsterdam: Kluwer

Verspagen, B. and W. Schoenmakers, 2004. "The Spatial Dimension of Patenting by Multinational Firms in Europe," *Journal of Economic Geography*, 4(1): 23–42

Vonortas, N., 2002. *Partnerships and Networking in Science and Technology for Development*, New York: United Nations

Wallsten, S. J., 2001. "An Empirical Test of Geographic Knowledge Spillovers Using Geographic Information Systems and Firm-Level Data," *Regional Science and Urban Economics*, 31(5): 571–599

Wolfson. M. C., 1997. "Divergent Inequalities: Theory and Empirical Results," *Review of Income and Wealth*, 43: 401–421

Zucker, L. G., M. R. Darby, and M. B. Brewer, 1994. "Intellectual Human Capital and the Birth of US Biotechnology," NBER Working Paper 4653, Cambridge, MA

4 Employment growth and clusters dynamics of creative industries in Great Britain

Bernard Fingleton, Danilo C. Igliori, Barry Moore, and Raakhi Odedra

4.1   Introduction

The definition of creative industries has been outlined by Britain's Creative Task Force as "those activities which have their origin in individual creativity, skill and talent, and which have the potential for wealth and job creation through the generation and exploitation of intellectual property" (Department for Culture, Media and Sport – DCMS 2001)

Creative industries have been identified as contributing to over 5 percent of GDP (DCMS 2001). A selection of some of these industries, for which data are available, generates £112.5 billion a year in revenues, of which £10.3 billion is through exports. Output growth in this set between 1997 and 1998 was a strong 16 percent, compared to 6 percent for the economy as a whole (Freeman 2002).

These industries are likely to be characterized by differentiated products, niche markets, vertical disintegration, and consumer externalities. Location also has the potential to act as a brand or image. It is estimated that 50 percent of all employees in the sector are clustered in London and in the South East of England. In addition, an important share of these jobs is to be found in SMEs. Creative industries have in particular received a fresh wave of attention as "London's Core Business" (Freeman 2002). Between 1995 and 2000, they produced the second largest source of job growth, the second largest source of output, and were the third largest source of jobs in the city.

The authors wish to thank Public and Corporate Economic Consultants (PACEC) for data provision. Especial acknowledgements go to Nic Boyns for his suggestions and efficiency in preparing the variables, and to Matt Rooke for preparing the map in figure 4.1. We are also grateful to Professor Karen R. Polenske, Apiwat Ratanawaraha, and the participants at the SPURS International Development Seminar (MIT November 4, 2002) for very useful comments on earlier versions of this research. Igliori acknowledges support from the Ministry of Education in Brazil under his scholarship program (CAPES). The usual disclaimer applies.

The remarkable concentration of employment in creative industries jointly with the potential role of intellectual property, human capital, and the flow of knowledge and ideas in explaining performance in these sectors, provides the motivation for this research. In this chapter, we adopt a simple concept of clustering to examine its impact on SMEs' employment growth in creative industries, using evidence over the period from 1991 to 2000. Here, we define a "cluster" as an agglomeration of firms and therefore employment in a particular industry. We call this type of agglomeration a *horizontal cluster*. The analysis is based on appropriate econometric methods, focussing on employment growth and levels in 408 of the unitary and local authority districts (UALAD) of Great Britain.

After an initial summary of theoretical considerations (section 4.2), we analyze the structure of the sector with regard to spatial distribution and employment performance over the 1990s (section 4.3). We then turn to the problems of measuring clusters and variable construction (sections 4.4–4.6). In section 4.7, we estimate spatial econometric models of employment growth in SMEs, controlling for levels of horizontal clustering and a set of other initial conditions. The models also capture the spillover effects across area boundaries. The regression results indicate that there is a significant association between the intensity of horizontal clustering and employment change. Section 4.8 examines the dynamic implications of the model, highlighting one aspect of the chapter, the presence of a declustering mechanism due to congestion effects. Section 4.9 concludes.

4.2   Cluster externalities

In recent times, some regions have demonstrated a remarkable ability to sustain an above-average economic performance, based mainly on the birth and growth of a large number of SMEs. As famous examples, one could mention Silicon Valley and Route 128 in the United States, the industrial districts in Italy and Germany, and the high-technology clusters in Cambridge and Oxford in the United Kingdom. These regions are far from representing a homogeneous phenomenon regarding sectors, technologies, and institutional environments. Nevertheless, they reveal some similarities, which have attracted the interests of many researchers. Among them is the existence of different kinds of relationships between the firms, from the traditional input-output supply-chain linkages to a wide range of collaborative relationships, and the capacity to maintain considerable knowledge flows and innovation between organizations. Antonelli (1999), in analyzing the emergence of the new knowledge industry, identifies this mode of knowledge production as "scientific entrepreneurship." A fundamental idea of the "cluster" literature is a shift in focus from the firm to productive systems and an understanding of the phenomena of competitiveness as a collective result rather than the outcome of individual processes.

An early recognition of this phenomenon is of course to be found in the work of Alfred Marshall (1920). Marshall identified three main factors related to external economies, which could stimulate industrial concentration:

1. The existence of "thick markets" for specialized labor,[1]
2. The occurrence of knowledge and technology spillovers
3. The emergence of subsidiary trades.

Following the approach suggested by Marshall, there have been attempts – for example, Krugman (1991a, 1991b, 1995) and Fujita and Thisse (1996) – to explain the existence of industrial clustering through formal models, which associate increasing returns in the firm's production function with pecuniary external economies in the context of monopolistic competition. Two basic ideas characterize these approaches. The first states that if internal increasing returns to scale exist at the firm level, then geographical concentration may occur purely as a result of the presence of pecuniary external economies together with the effect of transport costs. The second states that a cumulative process of concentration can be initiated by a particular combination of the market structure assumptions, transport costs, and production under internal increasing returns. One element that is absent from these models is the consideration of technological externalities, which include spillovers due to information flows. Although these may detract from the theoretical elegance of formal models, they are nevertheless accepted as necessary elements of a more complete explanation. We cannot explicitly map from these formal models to our econometric model, but technological externalities have influenced our thinking on some of the underlying processes leading to and reinforcing agglomeration. However, the lack of emphasis given to technological externalities has reinforced our perception of their necessity. Without them, our empirical estimates would undoubtedly be biased.

A different perspective is offered by Porter (1990). Based on an extensive set of case studies, he developed a theory of competitive advantage ("the diamond") founded on the interaction of factor conditions; demand

---

[1] The definition of "thick market" is not precise. A labor market is said to be "thick" where there is a high probability of a firm finding workers and vice versa after a relatively small search: in other words, where the period of frictional unemployment is likely to be low, and firms have no difficulties in fulfilling their labor requirements.

conditions; related and supporting industries; and firm strategy, structure, and rivalry. The idea is that the components of the "diamond" form a system which determines the competitive environment of firms. According to Porter, this system is rooted nationally where the supporting facilities for the firm's performance, such as information flows, institutions, infrastructure, and competence formation, are localized. However, Porter's later works emphasized subnational concentrations, as the following cluster definition (Porter 1998: 197) reveals: "Geographic concentrations of interconnected companies, specialized suppliers, service providers, firms in related industries, and associated institutions (for example, universities, standard agencies, and trade associations) in particular fields that compete but also co-operate."

Another relevant approach to the cluster literature is represented by the work of the *Groupe de Recherche Européen sur les Milieux Innovateurs* (GREMI), with their concept of "innovative milieu" (Camagni, 1991) that place innovative SMEs center stage. A milieu becomes innovative as a result of the processes of interaction and learning carried out by its agents through a set of networks. Networking is a crucial feature of the local productive system, which contains an innovative milieu and can be internal to the milieu or involve external partners. On the one hand, besides the firms, many different institutions can take part in the networks, – such as universities, centers of research, associations, and government agencies. On the other hand, spin-offs of new firms emerge as a side result of networking, information exchange, and innovation flows. The GREMI researchers who rely on the concept of innovative milieux, emphasize that the interaction between agents does not happen only through formal relations or material transfers. They argue that the informal links present in a local environment must be taken into account. Similarly, Storper (1997) highlights the whole of tacit knowledge flows and untraded interdependencies as key features of knowledge-based clusters.

Different co-operative links between firms can emerge from these interactions. Combinations of elements can explain the networking outcomes – such as the same industry, cultural and social identity, location, business relations, and technological similarity. However, the crucial element is the presence of "trust" among the agents involved. In this context, economic clusters and SMEs become relevant to our understanding of interfirm co-operation.

Two main types of co-operative relationships can be identified. The first relates to sharing related to particular assets, or activities related to productive activity, such as the common use of equipment, or the sharing of a large order or joint marketing efforts. The second concerns information exchange. Here, information flows can include technical or economic information and can derive from a variety of informal or formal links. The rationale for the existence of co-operation is therefore based on the collective gains to related individuals in terms of their operational efficiency. What seems to be important for the firm's competitiveness is the combination of the stimulus due to competition together with adequate levels of interfirm co-operation.

The endogenous process of innovation promoted at the regional level through formal and informal networking can be summarized by the concept of "collective learning," which was first adopted by the GREMI's researchers and which has been exploited in research on the Cambridge and Oxford high-technology concentrations (Keeble *et al.* 1999) and by the Targeted Socio-Economic Research (TSER) European Network (Keeble and Wilkinson 2000). Collective learning connotes a broad notion of the capacity of a particular regional innovative milieu to generate or facilitate innovative behavior by its firms (Keeble 2000: 200). A particular aspect emphasized by Keeble is that collective learning processes can be seen as mechanisms for reducing uncertainty in a rapidly changing technology context.

The capacity of a local environment to enhance innovation flows is also emphasized by the approach based on the notion of systems of innovation (Freeman 1995). Inspired by the neo-Schumpeterian tradition, this approach states that the features of the institutions present in a region can positively impact on the innovative performance of firms, providing scientific, technical, and organizational knowledge. The systems of innovation are therefore the results of the interaction between the firms and the respective set of institutions, including supplier/customer relationships, governmental incentive mechanisms, and educational systems. Notwithstanding the importance of growing international integration, it is recognized that national and regional systems of innovation remain as essential domains for the economic analysis of technical change.

Two additional points must be mentioned when discussing the systems of innovation approach: the role of multinational companies and the links between technical and organizational changes. Related to the former, it is recognized that large corporations can be crucial in maintaining the technological dynamism in regional systems. Their ability to transfer equipment and to organize training programmes and technical co-operation agreements may be an important aspect of the functioning of the system which helps avoid lock-in effects. Regarding the second point, interdependence between technical and organizational change means that the latter acts as a constraint on the former and therefore if organizational development is slow, technical progress may be impeded.

Although it is recognized that many other factors can influence the performance of SMEs, the specific features of clusters discussed above would seem to create an environment supporting their competitiveness. In addition to the possibilities of cost reduction through external economies, clusters and networks of SMEs can reduce uncertainty and foster innovation. These factors can be crucial in maintaining competitive advantage if one considers recent trends concerning forms of competition that are not based on price.

In this chapter, we aim to contribute to the literature reviewed, by empirically testing the hypothesis that the clustering of high-technology SMEs impacts positively their economic performance, in terms of employment growth, through the existence of positive externalities. To reiterate our earlier point, we follow Krugman's approach here, defining a "cluster" as simply an agglomeration of firms in a particular industry. We call this type of agglomeration a *horizontal cluster*. However, we are not so rigid in our treatment as the formal modeling literature and, depending on its particular characteristics, a horizontal cluster may or may not imply some sort of relationship or interconnection between firms and institutions. Neither is the presence of positive externalities (pecuniary or technological) listed by the literature discussed above taken for granted, rather the presence and impact of such externalities is the subject of our empirical analysis.

Our objective is to test whether part of the employment growth experienced by creative industries' SMEs in a particular area can be attributed exclusively to the agglomeration of firms – in other words to examine whether the level of horizontal clustering is a significant factor for employment growth, controlling for other variables. In order to do that, we structure our econometric modeling approach by selecting a set of control variables and initial conditions, which could have direct or indirect impacts on SMEs employment performance in a particular location.

In the discussion, we provide some of the key economic foundations linking clustering with the increase of competitiveness and economic dynamism. Different sources of externalities may be present in localities where those clusters exist and can explain above-normal economic performance. However, one may also imagine that excessive clustering can generate negative externalities. Because of sector-specific congestion effects, a high geographical concentration of firms is likely to face more difficulties in creating employment in a sustainable fashion. For instance, local competition for sector-specific factors may intensify, creating shortages of key skills, specialized inputs, and appropriate office space. In addition, more general congestion effects can occur as a result of high

Table 4.1 *Creative industries*

SIC code	Creative industries	Abbreviation
7220	Software Consultancy and Supply	SFT
7420	Architectural /Engineering Activities	ARC
7440	Advertising	ADV
7481	Photographic Activities	PHT
9211	Motion Pictures and Video Production	MOT
9220	Radio and Television	RTV
9231	Artistic and Literary Creation	ART

Source: 1992 SIC.

Table 4.2 *Employees per firm size, 2000*

Firm size	SFT[a]	ARC	ADV	PHT	MOT	RTV	ART
Tiny (1–10)	110,034	129,732	29,442	21,112	9,129	6,571	44,138
Small (11–49)	50,353	71,545	19,046	6,793	3,046	6,240	6,543
Medium (50–199)	60,283	55,943	17,706	5,611	2,725	11,412	8,814
Large (200+)	51,929	46,295	28,610	3,951	876	44,057	4,320
Total	**272,599**	**303,515**	**94,804**	**37,467**	**15,776**	**68,280**	**63,815**

Note: [a] For abbreviations, see table 4.1.
Source: Annual Business Enquiry, ONS.

population density. In this chapter, we provide some insight as to where and when these effects will be felt in the creative industries.

4.3   Empirical evidence of growth and clustering of SMEs in creative industries

The main data we analyze are extracted from the Annual Business Enquiry of the Office for National Statistics (ONS). They include employees in employment and number of establishments in Great Britain from 1991 to 2000. The spatial breakdown covers regions, counties, and UALAD. The SME classification adopted here is defined as firms with up to 199 employees. The industry classification follows the 4-digit 1992 Standard Industrial Classification (SIC) provided in table 4.1.

Looking at the distribution of employment according to firm size in 2000 from table 4.2, we find that apart from in Radio and Television

Table 4.3 *Employment growth rates, 1991–2000 (%)*

Firm size	SFT[a]	ARC[b]	ADV	PHT	MOT	RTV	ART
Tiny (1–10)	195	–	127	130	51	259	968
Small (11–49)	62	−29	−2	−5	−41	21	67
Medium (50–199)	95	−39	49	−6	1	46	94
Large (200+)	178	−58	156	1	−83	29	61
SMEs	122	34	49	50	7	64	372
Total	**131**	**−25**	**71**	**43**	**−17**	**40**	**318**

Notes: [a]For abbreviations, see table 4.1.
[b]ARC had zero values of employment in Tiny firms in 1991, hence the growth rate cannot be calculated.
Source: *Annual Business Enquiry*, ONS.

Activities, tiny firms are now the most important employers in this sector. In particular, Artistic and Literary Creation has 69 percent of the entire industry employment in tiny firms. This may even be an underestimate of participation in this industry, as this data-set does not include self-employed individuals.

The total employment from the seven creative industries as a set (all firm sizes) has been growing over this sample period. Looking at employment growth in each firm size from table 4.3, tiny firms seem to be most impressive in their performance, which has been well above the average for all firms. Large firms also seem to be performing above average in Software Consultancy and Advertising. Artistic and Literary Creation has been particularly strong, with an average employment growth rate of 318 percent over all firms and 968 percent growth in employment in tiny firms. Architecture and Engineering Activities and Motion Picture and Video Production have, however, both suffered from overall decline in employment levels over this period. This may be a reflection of how improvements in technology in design and production have impacted particular creative industries. Computer-aided design (CAD) software could arguably be replacing draftsmen in architecture firms, film editing now relies more on software, and special effects are computer-simulated.

By summing the data for the seven industries and all firm sizes to form a creative industries set, we can examine the overall significance of these industries in terms of employment growth for each region. The national average employment share of these seven industries as a group stayed the same in both 1991 and 2000, at 3 percent, even though there has been

Table 4.4 *Top 20 UALAD SME employment growth performance, 1991–2000*

Rank	UALAD	Absolute growth
1	Westminster, City of	12,658
2	Camden	7,608
3	Islington	6,192
4	Edinburgh, City of	5,044
5	London, City of	4,007
6	Wandsworth	3,966
7	Richmond-upon-Thames	3,865
8	Kensington and Chelsea	3,832
9	Aberdeen, City of	3,486
10	Hounslow	3,230
11	Southwark	3,210
12	Leeds	3,052
13	Manchester	2,889
14	Hammersmith and Fulham	2,778
15	Hackney	2,764
16	Aberdeenshire	2,764
17	Milton Keynes	2,706
18	Tower Hamlets	2,649
19	Wycombe	2,642
20	Elmbridge	2,553

Source: Annual Business Enquiry, ONS.

a divergence in performance between them. Districts in London and the South of England produced significantly larger shares and the highest was found in Hammersmith and Fulham, which in 2000 had a fifth of its total employment in the seven creative industries. Table 4.4 shows that in terms of numbers of jobs created, it is the districts in London and in other urbanized areas that are significant.

4.4   Measuring clusters

Employment distribution data for creative industries' SMEs provide evidence of high geographical concentration. However, the employment distribution *per se* indicates the geographical concentration of the industry without controlling for the overall population and the size of each area's economy. The main hypothesis to be tested in this chapter is that there is a positive correlation between employment growth in creative industries' SMEs and geographical concentration or clustering. However, measuring cluster intensity is not a simple task.

One way to do this is by calculating the Location Quotient (LQ) for each industry. This is a measure of relative concentration and is defined (Department of Trade and Industry 2001) as:

$$LQ = \frac{\left(\frac{E_{ij}}{E_j}\right)}{\left(\frac{E_{in}}{E_n}\right)} \quad \text{or} \quad LQ = \frac{\left(\frac{E_{ij}}{E_{in}}\right)}{\left(\frac{E_j}{E_n}\right)}$$

Where E_{ij} is employment in industry i in area (region, county or UALAD) j, E_j is total employment in area j, E_{in} is national employment in industry i, and E_n is total national employment. Thus, an LQ greater than one indicates that there is an above-average proportion of employment in a given industry in a given area. Although the LQ has been used in different studies, it has an important shortcoming in serving as a cluster measure. It measures only the local importance of an industry given the overall economic importance of the area. In other words, it captures whether an area has a higher or lower share of a particular industry than the national share, but does not include any information related to the absolute size of the industry in that area. As a result, it is possible to obtain high LQs in absolute terms for very small local industries. If one assumes that scale matters for clustering results, the LQ omits "mass effects" that could exist when the area's industry is large, regardless of its relative concentration.

One way of dealing with this problem is to cross-check, looking, at the same time, at LQ values and at a measure of size, such as the local share of the national industry or simply number of jobs in the local industry (Department of Trade and Industry 2001). An alternative adopted by Fingleton, Igliori, and Moore (2003, 2004) takes into account the relative local importance of an industry and the size of the agglomeration in terms of number of jobs. Cluster intensity is defined as the number of jobs in the local industry that exceeds its expected number. The expected number is then defined by the number of jobs in the industry that would correspond to the area having the national share of the industry and therefore produce a LQ equal to one. The HC* measure is thus calculated by first computing

$$LQ = \frac{\left(\frac{E_{ij}}{E_{in}}\right)}{\left(\frac{E_j}{E_n}\right)}.$$

Then E_{ij} is replaced by $\hat{E}_{ij}$ to produce

$$LQ = \frac{\left(\frac{\hat{E}_{ij}}{E_{in}}\right)}{\left(\frac{E_j}{E_n}\right)} = 1,$$

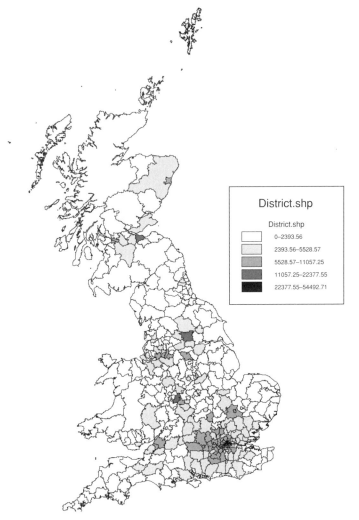

Figure 4.1 Hierarchical clusters distribution, 2000
Source: The authors.

where $\hat{E}_{ij}$ is the number of jobs that makes LQ = one given the other quantities. Finally, the measure of horizontal clustering is obtained as the difference between the actual and expected number of jobs, hence $HC^* = E_{ij} - \hat{E}_{ij}$. This variable produced interesting results in previous research[2] but does not seem to fit very well for the models estimated in this chapter. Its main limitation refers to the absence of any geographical information, in particular the area of each of the administrative areas (UALAD) considered. This is very important for the current analysis given our interests in examining congestion effects associated with high cluster intensity.

To take into account the size of each of the UALAD and include information about geographical proximity of firms, we use as a measure for cluster intensity simply employment per unit area in this chapter. Our independent variable for cluster intensity is then calculated as:

$$HC = \frac{E_{ij}}{A}$$

where A is the area of the UALADi.

This measure represents the employment density in each of the UALAD. It does not take into account the relative employment concentration with regards to the national average but captures the mass effects, which could be responsible for the generation of positive externalities advocated in the cluster literature. Its main advantage relates to the information regarding the geographical proximity of employment that seems to be important when trying to analyze the impact of agglomeration effects and also congestion costs over employment growth (Fingleton, Igliori, and Moore, 2005, have used a similar measure for analyzing computer services). Figure 4.1 shows the distribution of the HC variable across Great Britain in 2000 (figures increase from white to black, excluding Ireland).

4.5   Model specification

In this section we set out a model that endeavors to explain the change in employment in the creative industries over the period 1991–2000. The difference between the employment level by UALAD (*sieg*) at these points in time is the dependent variable of our analysis. We related these employment changes by UALAD to what we refer to as "horizontal clustering,"

---

[2] Using similar modeling, Fingleton, Igliori, and Moore (2003) show that HC^* positively impacted employment growth in Computing Services SMEs over the period 1991–2000; however, they did not consider congestion costs.

as previously defined. In doing this, we anticipate that as cluster intensity increases, the close juxtaposition of firms in a confined area will have some beneficial effects for growth because of the net effects of positive externalities. However, we also envision negative externalities becoming increasingly relevant to the growth of employment as the cluster intensity becomes greater. Notice that the negative externalities are sector-specific, they concern the intensity of creative industries' SME employment.

We envisage a nonlinear relationship between horizontal clustering and employment growth due to the effects of (sector-specific) congestion. Hence, in the initial stages of increasing cluster intensity, it is likely that employment growth will increase as the externalities associated with clustering become more powerful. However, it is likely that at some point negative externalities associated with congestion will also start to have an effect that will increasingly counteract the positive externalities as cluster intensity increases, to the point that employment growth will fall to zero and then become negative. In order to test this hypothesis, we assume that employment change is a quadratic function of cluster intensity and is linear in a set of control variables, X, that are also assumed to determine employment change, hence:

$$sieg = aHC^2 + bHC + cX + d.$$

This model should have significant regression coefficients for both horizontal clustering (HC) and the square of horizontal clustering (HC^2), with a positive coefficient on the former and a negative coefficient on the latter. The hypothesis of increasing congestion effects is rejected if the coefficient on HC^2 is either insignificantly different from zero or is positive.

To structure our econometric model, we have selected a set of control and environmental variables, X, that could have direct or indirect impacts on the SME employment performance of an industry in a particular location. The basic idea is to test the relationship between employment growth and a set of initial conditions present in the region, including the level of horizontal clustering. In selecting the control variables, we have been guided by the literature reviewed above, suitably adapted to the characteristics of creative industries' SMEs.

The first set of control variables aims to reflect demand-side conditions and also the supply of factors that are inputs to SME production. We selected three variables. The first one is the total SME employment growth in the UALAD, including all industries (*steg*). Here, the variable captures the demand producing SME growth regardless of industrial sector. It also reflects the provision of inputs from SMEs in other sectors. The second variable is the large-firm employment growth in the industry that occurred in the area (*lieg*). This captures the role of large firms in creating opportunities for SMEs in the same industry. It also reflects inputs from large firms in the sector. The third variable is the total large firms' employment growth that occurred in the area (*lteg*). This variable is a proxy for the demand coming from large firms in other industries. It also represents the provision of inputs from large firms in other sectors. Notice that because these variables measure change in levels rather than percentage growth, they capture the effects of the size of the local economy.

Given that creative industries are knowledge-based, the second set of controls focus on human capital as the key factor market variable. We include two variables in this group. The first one is a simple indicator of the level of education in the area measured by the percentage of the UK population in 1991 with A level or above (*Educ*). The second variable aims to catch the impact of the presence of a science base in the area as a source of technology transfer but also as a source of highly qualified labor. We used a variable derived from the Research Assessment Exercise 1996, which measures the scale and quality local universities present in the area (*univimp*).[3]

The quality of infrastructure provision also contributes to the competitiveness and growth of firms in the area. It is thus possible to say that firms that benefit from better infrastructure have better conditions in which to compete and generate jobs. We represent this by the variable (*NT_pop*), which represents the so-called New Towns in which production conditions have been enhanced by government policy. In areas with New Towns, the variable takes a value equal to the area's population in 1991, otherwise its value is zero.

The fourth type of control variable focuses on market structure and firm rivalry. Arguably, a region with higher degree of competition may offer better incentives for innovation and productivity, contributing to the industry's performance and therefore its employment growth. The variable we used is the number of establishments per employee in 1991 (*Mktstr*).

4.6   The spatial-weight matrix

The spatial-weight matrix (called henceforth the *W* matrix) is used for modeling spatial effects, where we hypothesize that spatial interaction between areas will produce interarea dependency that is a function of the distance separating each pair of areas. There are very many optional definitions of interarea distance, ranging from an indicator of the existence or absence of contiguity, depending on whether areas share a common

---

[3] See the appendix (p. 82) for a detailed description of this variable.

Table 4.5 *Commuting distances in Great Britain, km.*

Distance	<2	2–4	5–9	10–19	20–29	30–39	>40 km
%	26.8	25.2	20.8	15.8	5.0	2.1	4.3	**100.0**

Source: Special Workplace Statistics, 1991 UK Census of Population.

boundary, to complex distance functions combining geographic and economic distance. In this chapter, we attempt to create an economic distance measure using commuting flows to calibrate a distance function, hence:

$$W_{ij} = \exp(-\delta_i d_{ij}) \qquad i \neq j$$
$$W_{ij} = 0 \qquad\qquad\quad i = j$$
$$W_{ij} = 0 \qquad\qquad d_{ij} > 100\text{km}.$$

This shows that the value allotted to cell (i, j) of the W matrix is a function of the (straight-line) distance (d_{ij}) between areas and an exponent δ_i that reflects the area-specific distance decay. We base our choice of the exponent δ_i on empirical comparisons with observed census data (Census of Population 2001)[4] on travel to work patterns. Table 4.5 shows the overall proportion of workers[5] living in Great Britain traveling various distances to work. Given observed travel percentages for each area, the exponent δ_i for each area was chosen by iterating the function $\exp(-\delta_i d_{ij})$ through a range of values to obtain the value giving the closest fit[6] to each area's commuting data. The idea behind this approach is that, for any given area, the relative weights of neighboring areas should approximate to the ratio of the number of commuters traveling in from each.

This specification has implications for the estimation of an additional explanatory variable created as a result of the matrix product of the dependent variable *sieg* and W, which is used to capture spatial effects due to spillovers and spatial externalities (see Fingleton 2003a, 2003b).

4.7   Econometric analysis

As a preliminary analysis, we fit the "full" model by Two-Stage Least Squares (2SLS) to take account of the potential lack of consistency caused

---

[4] Special Workplace Statistics, available from NOMIS (Official Labor Market Statistics).
[5] Total employees and self-employed with a workplace coded.
[6] Minimum of the sum of the squared deviations of the observed proportions in each distance band up to 40 km and the proportions of the sum of the function $\exp(-\delta_i d_{ij})$ calculated using the upper limit of each distance band.

Table 4.6 *2SLS estimates*

	Estimate	Standard error	$t(398)$
Constant	−524	88.034531	−5.955679
Isteg	0.08267	0.006758	12.232278
Ilieg	0.0166	0.049147	0.336839
Ilteg	0.02963	0.007975	3.715294
HC	8.422413	1.063229	7.921543
Univimp	−0.1567	0.033749	−4.643065
Educ	3799.908991	613.144919	6.197408
Mktstr	−31.976087	121.320401	−0.263567
NT_pop	−0.627111	0.598420	−1.047945
HCsq	−0.004973	0.000855	−5.815340

Source: The authors' calculations.

by the presence of endogenous variables.[7] In order to carry out the 2SLS estimation, it is essential to obtain instruments. We use the *three-group* method (described in Johnson 1984 and Kennedy 1992), which is commonly used to overcome measurement error problems. The instruments comprise the three levels of *steg*, *lieg*, and *lteg* with levels −1, 0, and 1 according to whether the values of the variables were low, high, or in between. In addition we use the exogenous variables (*HC*, *univimp*, etc.) plus the lags of the exogenous variables (*W* multiplied by *HC*, etc.) to provide additional instruments.[8] The assumption is that the instruments thus defined are both independent of the errors and are correlated with the endogenous regressors. Leser (1966) shows that in general the three-group method gives consistent estimates on the assumption that the errors are not so large that they correlate with the groups.

The results of fitting the model using 2SLS are given in table 4.6. The letter *I* prefixing the variable name indicates the instrumental variables. On the one hand, the initial model estimate suggests that *steg*, *lteg*, *HC* and HC^2, *univimp*, and *Educ* are probably significant variables that should be retained in the final model, while *lieg*, *Mktstr*, and *NT_pop* can probably be eliminated. Therefore the initial indication is that the demand and supply conditions in the local economy are significant, although the

---

[7] The variables potentially subject to endogeneity problems are *steg*, *lieg*, and *lteg*. These are also growth variables and not initial conditions. Therefore, the causality directions are not clearly established, and the standard exogeneity assumption is not guaranteed. We have run variable-specific tests due to Hausman (see Maddala 2001), which confirmed the endogeneity problem.

[8] However the higher spatial lags are not used (see Kelejian and Robinson 1993; Kelejian and Prucha 1998) because of the possibility of linear dependence in the matrix of instruments.

lack of significance of *lieg* suggests that the growth of the creative industries *per se* is not important, and there is evidence that high levels of human capital (in the form of educational attainment) also stimulate growth.

On the other hand, the significant negative coefficient for *univimp* suggests that the presence of an important science base has a negative association with the growth of creative industries employment. The signs on HC and HC^2 also indicate a significant quadratic relationship suggesting increasing negative externalities with increasing cluster intensity due to congestion.

In order to obtain an insight as to the significance and sources of misspecification, we first calculate Moran's I, which has power against both residual autocorrelation and other forms of misspecification, such as heteroskedasticity (see Anselin and Rey 1991; Anselin and Florax 1995; Fingleton 1999).[9] We also calculate the more appropriate test suggested by Anselin and Kelejian (1997) for residuals from Instrumental Variables (IV) estimation (referred to as the Anselin–Kelejian test below). In the special case with endogenous variables, but no spatially lagged dependent variable, the test statistic is 3.644 standard deviations above expectation, reaffirming the presence of significant residual spatial autocorrelation. One reason for this could be the omission of a significant spatially autocorrelated variable in the form of the endogenous lag *Wsieg*.

Table 4.7 shows the effect of including an endogenous lag (*Wsieg*). This is a significant variable, and its omission appears to have been responsible for some bias in the coefficient estimated of the preceding models, although the interpretations are very much the same as before. The most notable changes are to the coefficients of the quadratic relationship between HC and *sieg*, which are somewhat smaller than previously, although they remain significant. The coefficient for *univimp* is also smaller, although the significant negative relationship is maintained. The coefficient for *Educ* is larger, reaffirming the significance of this dimension of human capital. Employment change in small firms regardless of sector (*steg*) is highly significant, but large-firm employment growth (*lteg*) is either marginally significant or insignificant (*lieg*). There is no evidence that market structure or investment in New Town infrastructure have any explanatory power. The introduction of the endogenous lag completely

---

[9] Moran's I takes a value equal to 0.05196, which exceeds the 99th value of the randomization distribution (0.024653). The mean of the empirical randomization distribution is −0.005542 and the variance is 0.00007850, so that the observed value is 6.49 standard deviations above the mean. The asymptotic moments are equal to -0.003831 and 0.00009392, so that the observed value in this case exceeds the mean by 5.757 standard deviations.

Table 4.7 *2SLS with endogenous spatial lag*

	Estimate	Standard error	$t(397)$
Constant	−438.926837	86.883927	−5.051876
Wsieg	0.01021	0.001993	5.123579
Isteg	0.07693	0.006641	11.584804
Ilieg	0.0380	0.047788	0.795519
Ilteg	0.01412	0.008297	1.701891
HC	5.405215	1.186331	4.556247
Univimp	−0.0873	0.035383	−2.467751
Educ	3079.988508	610.292583	5.046741
Mktstr	−38.041991	117.517857	−0.323712
NT_pop	−0.240328	0.584529	−0.411148
HCsq	−0.002750	0.000935	−2.941406
$R^2 = 0.7798$	Sq. corrn. = 0.8080	$\sigma^2 = 227859$	

Source: The authors' calculations.

eliminates the residual autocorrelation that was evident on the previous specification.[10]

Elimination of the insignificant variables does not introduce significant residual spatial autocorrelation. Using the Anselin–Kelejian test, we see that the distance between Moran's *I* and its expectation is −0.6190 standard deviations, which would be considered insignificant using conventional rules of inference. Table 4.8 gives the reduced model estimates, where each of the retained variables is highly significant.[11]

There is evidently a strong spillover effect (*Wsieg*) with SME creative industries' employment growth greater in areas that are "near" to other areas with large positive changes, and vice versa. We also see significant effects due to overall employment growth in each area (*steg*, *lteg*), and a very significant positive relationship between educational attainment and *sieg*. The other dimension of human capital (*univimp*), relating to the science base in local universities, remains a significant negative factor. It appears that the arts and sciences do not mix! As a simplification, it appears that in areas where the science base is strong, creative industry

[10] The Anselin–Kelejian test (as above, but also with an endogenous lag) gives a test statistic equal to −0.7556 which is very typical of the $N(0,1)$ null distribution. The observed value of Moran's *I* is −0.01157 and this is only −0.5691 standard deviations from expectation using the asymptotic moments of the randomization distribution, and when referred to its empirical randomization distribution, it falls between the 31st and 32nd value and is −0.4636 standard deviations from the mean of the empirical randomization distribution.

[11] While we have focussed on eliminating spatial autocorrelation, the possibility of residual heterogeneity remains. We therefore also obtained bootstrap estimates with ninety-nine replications, which are robust to nonnormality and error heterogeneity. The results are similar to the 2SLS estimates, though not reported.

Table 4.8 *2SLS estimates of the reduced model*

	Estimate	Standard error	$t(400)$
Constant	−473.366547	78.446756	−6.034240
Wsieg	0.00983	0.001953	5.035286
Isteg	0.07684	0.006500	11.820831
Ilteg	0.01773	0.007416	2.390847
HC	5.453871	1.175031	4.641470
univimp	−0.0962	0.033959	−2.832895
Educ	3222.887615	587.088246	5.489614
HCsq	−0.00277	0.000918	−3.019518
$R^2 = 0.7777$	Sq. corrn. = 0.8087	$\sigma^2 = 225420$	

Source: The authors' calculations.

employment growth is weak. On reflection, we can attribute this to the positive benefits we have highlighted elsewhere (Fingleton, Igliori, and Moore 2003) of a strong science base for other sectors (Computing services) and what we may have identified by this result is a spatial differentiating effect in which local economies become specialized and exclusive as the local factors become focused on the core activity and relatively unattractive to other activities.[12] Finally, the significant quadratic relationship between cluster intensity (*HC*) and *sieg* remains evident. This implies that employment increases with cluster intensity and then falls as the cluster becomes very intense and the negative externalities associated with congestion begin to take effect. We explore the implications of this relationship in the next section.

4.8   Dynamic implications of the model

The quadratic function linking employment change to cluster intensity has important implications for the dynamics of both the level of cluster intensity and employment change. In order to clarify the implications of our estimates, we isolate the quadratic function linking *sieg* and *HC* by calculating adjusted employment changes for each area. This is done by deducting the contribution due to the variables other than *HC* and HC^2 from the fitted values ($si\hat{e}g$) given by the table 4.8 model. These other variables (*lteg, steg, Educ, univimp*) are denoted by X_1, X_2 below.

---

[12] This result does not rule out the contribution of universities to employment growth in creative industries. As we do not have the nonscience knowledge base in our variable we cannot provide evidence on the contribution that large and strong departments of Arts and Humanities would make to the sector. This is a subject for further research.

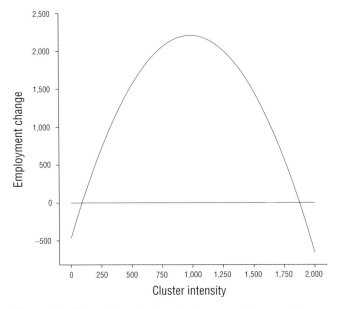

Figure 4.2 Cluster intensity in relation to employment change

Hence if

$$si\hat{e}g = \hat{Y} = \hat{b}_0 + \hat{\rho} Wsieg + \hat{b}_1 X_1 + \hat{b}_2 X_2 + \hat{b}_3 HC + \hat{b}_4 HC^2$$

then the adjusted employment changes are given by

$$adj.si\hat{e}g = si\hat{e}g - (\rho Wsieg + \hat{b}_1 X_1 + \hat{b}_2 X_2) = \hat{b}_0 + \hat{b}_3 HC + \hat{b}_4 HC^2.$$

In other words, the adjusted employment changes are simply those that would occur having nullified the effects of variables other than cluster intensity. Plotting $adj.si\hat{e}g$ against HC identifies the dynamics implied by the model. Since $\hat{b}_4 \neq 0$ and $0 \leq \hat{b}_3^2 - 4\hat{b}_0\hat{b}_4$ then there is a solution to the quadratic with two roots (which would be coincident if $\hat{b}_3^2 = 4\hat{b}_0\hat{b}_4$). Solving for the roots using

$$x = \frac{-\hat{b}_3 \pm \hat{b}_3^2 - 4\hat{b}_4\hat{b}_0}{2\hat{b}_4}$$

gives the points (91,0) and (1878,0). Figure 4.2 is the outcome using the 2SLS estimates given in table 4.6. This shows that, assuming all areas are identical apart from cluster intensity, areas with more than 1,878 employees per km^2 experience falling employment until they reach the stable equilibrium point at zero employment change. In these cases, the negative congestion externalities more than offset the positive externalities deriving from the concentration of activity. Areas with fewer than 91 employees per km^2 see employment falling to zero. Areas between the two roots experience positive employment change up to the stable equilibrium. Therefore, we have both a declustering process involving falling employment density and a clustering process with increasing employment per km^2.

In reality, each area will have different roots due to the effect of the other variables (*lteg, steg, Educ, univimp*). The precise dynamics for any given area depend on its initial cluster intensity and on the initial cluster intensity of its neighbors in relation to the roots. Let us consider first only the dynamics implied by each of the areas as if their respective neighbors did not impact them. If an area's initial cluster intensity lies below its unstable lower root, then employment change is negative, which further diminishes cluster intensity and induces even more negative employment change, so that the cluster intensity tends to zero (since a negative cluster intensity is impossible). If the area's cluster intensity is above the lower root, then the area converges to the upper root, either from below or above. If its initial position is above the stable upper root, then employment change is negative, and the area's cluster intensity converges on the equilibrium from above, at which point employment change is zero. If the area's initial cluster intensity lies between the roots, then employment change is positive, so that cluster intensity increases until the upper root is reached. Therefore, in this set-up, history matters, with the final outcome depending on the initial conditions. The resulting dynamics for the whole set of areas are complex; an area with lower cluster intensity can end up at a higher equilibrium than an area with an initially higher cluster intensity, because the relevant factor is the initial position in relation to the roots.

Considering the more realistic assumption where their neighbors impact each of the areas, the dynamics are a little more complicated. Although we can find the roots at which employment change in an area is zero using the above method, it relies on all other areas simultaneously having zero employment change. Assume that an area is below the lower root as calculated above, but surrounding areas have positive employment change. On the one hand, spillovers across areas may have the effect that, given that ρ is positive and sufficiently large, a positive contribution from ρWY produces positive net employment change, thus moving the area towards the upper root when it would otherwise have moved in the opposite direction. On the other hand, while congestion may contribute a negative component to an area's employment change when it lies above the upper root, this may be counteracted by positive employment change due to spillover from neighbors, causing movement further away from the upper root, although this results in an even stronger congestion effect. Therefore, in this set-up, both history and geography matter, since the initial position of an area with respect to its roots governs its path, but its location *vis-à-vis* other areas also plays a part.

While it is interesting to note that, in theory, equilibria exist, it is also important to recognise that, in practice, their existence relies on the stability of variables and coefficients – and, in reality, particularly over the longer term, we would expect these to shift, in which case the equilibria to which areas converge will also change, or may no longer exist if the quadratic relationship breaks down. For the shorter term, we can assume that the coefficients and variables will be more or less stable and the model estimated from data could provide a reasonably realistic forecast.

4.9   Conclusion

The presence of agglomerations and clustering has been advocated as important factors for local economic performance. In this chapter, we contribute to the cluster literature by empirically testing the hypothesis that the level of horizontal clustering positively impacts the subsequent employment growth of SMEs in creative industries in Great Britain. We also test if, after a certain point, the level of horizontal clustering starts to impact employment growth negatively due to congestion effects.

The estimated spatial econometric model provides evidence supporting the presence of positive and negative externalities associated with different levels of cluster intensity, with respect to employment growth in the creative industries. Some of the control variables are also significant, and the model suggests that local demand and supply conditions are important factors explaining the change in creative industries' employment, and supports the role attributed to human capital as proxied by educational attainment. It is also apparent that external effects spill over across area boundaries. This finding points to the importance of local spin-offs and knowledge flows creating technological externalities that transgress area boundaries.

The dynamics implied by the model allow us to identify the relative sizes of positive and negative externalities associated with different levels of cluster intensity. The quadratic specification suggests that there are cluster-intensity lower and upper thresholds. These thresholds show whether the levels of cluster intensity are likely to generate larger positive externalities than negative ones creating employment. As the analysis suggests, we can have the opposite situation where negative externalities predominate, and employment is destroyed.

These findings reinforce the claim that agglomerations and clustering play an important role in economic performance, as suggested by the literature. However, they also indicate that the positive effects of cluster intensity have upper thresholds, and clustering can negatively impact employment growth due to congestion effects. The model also suggests that each locality has its own thresholds and is therefore subject to individual dynamics. Moreover, neighboring effects can either reinforce or counteract the individual trajectories. These results have important policy implications, as it is clear that the promotion of clustering can be only justified on the basis of a case-by-case analysis. Understanding the peculiarities of individual cases goes beyond the scope of this chapter and provides material for further investigation.

APPENDIX   THE UNIVERSITY IMPACT VARIABLE (UNIVIMP)

In order to build a variable that could serve as a proxy for the impact of universities over SMEs' employment growth in creative industries, we considered two key aspects: research quality and staff size. The data source was the 1996 Research Assessment Exercise and the departments considered were the following: Agriculture; Anatomy; Applied Mathematics; Biochemistry; Biological Sciences; Chemical Engineering; Chemistry; Civil Engineering; Clinical Dentistry; Clinical Laboratory Sciences; Community Based Clinical Subjects; Computer Science; Earth Sciences; Electrical and Electronic Engineering; Environmental Sciences; Food Science and Technology; General Engineering; Hospital Based Clinical Subjects; Mechanical, Aeronautical and Manufacturing Engineering; Metallurgy and Materials; Mineral and Mining Engineering; Nursing; Other Studies and Professions Allied to Medicine; Pharmacology; Pharmacy; Physics; Physiology; Pre-Clinical Studies; Psychology; Pure Mathematics; Statistics and Operational Research; Veterinary Science.

The first step consists in deriving a number for each university. In order to do that we initially multiply the rate of each department by its Category A Research Active Staff. We then sum the department numbers, obtaining the university impact measure. In the second step, we construct the variable for the area considered (UALAD or county), only adding up the numbers of the universities located in each area.

REFERENCES

Anselin, L. and R. Florax, 1995 "Small Sample Properties of Tests for Spatial Dependence in Regression Models: Some Further Results," in L. Anselin and R. Florax (eds.), *New Directions in Spatial Econometrics*, Berlin: Springer-Verlag: 21–74

Anselin L. and H. H. Kelejian, 1997. "Testing for Spatial Error Autocorrelation in the Presence of Endogenous Regressors," *International Regional Science Review*, 20: 153–182

Anselin, L. and S. Rey, 1991. "Properties of Tests for Spatial Dependence in Linear Regression Models," *Geographical Analysis*, 23: 112–131

Antonelli, C., 1999. "The Evolution of the Industrial Organisation of the Production of Knowledge," *Cambridge Journal of Economics*, 23: 243–260

Begg, I. G. and D. Hodson, 2001. "The Location of Jobs in High-Technology Industries in Great Britain in the 1990s," London: South Bank University, Mimeo

Camagni, R., 1991. *Innovation Networks: Spatial Perspectives*, London: Belhaven Press

Census of Population, 2001. London: ONS

Department for Culture, Media and Sport (DCMS), 2001. *Creative Industries Mapping Document*, http://193.128.182.36/creative/index.html

Department of Trade and Industry (DTI), 2001. *Business Clusters in the UK – A First Assessment*, London: DTI

Fingleton, B., 1999. "Spurious Spatial Regression: Some Monte-Carlo Results with a Spatial Unit Root and Spatial Cointegration," *Journal of Regional Science*, 39: 1–19

2003a. "Increasing Returns: Evidence from Local Wage Rates in Great Britain," *Oxford Economic Papers*, 55(4): 716–739

2003b. "Externalities, Economic Geography and Spatial Econometrics: Conceptual and Modeling Developments," *International Regional Science Review*, 26(2): 197–207

Fingleton, B., D. Igliori, and B. Moore, 2003. "Employment Growth of Small Computing Services Firms and the Role of Horizontal Clusters: Evidence from Great Britain 1991–2000," in B. Fingleton (ed.), *Regional Growth in Europe*, Berlin: Springer Verlag: 267–291

2004. "Employment Growth of Small Computing Services Firms and the Role of Horizontal Clusters: Evidence from Computing Services and R&D in Great Britain, 1991–2000," *Urban Studies*, 41(4): 773–779

2005. "Cluster Dynamics: New Evidence and Projections for Computing Services in Great Britain," *Journal of Regional Science*, 45(2): 283–311

Freeman, A., 2002. *Creativity: London's Core Business*, A Report for the Greater London Authority, at http://www.london.gov.uk

Freeman, C., 1995. "The 'National System of Innovation' in Historical Perspective," *Cambridge Journal of Economics*, 19: 5–24

Fujita, M. and J. F. Thisse, 1996. "Economics of Agglomeration," *Journal of the Japanese and International Economies*, 10: 339–378

Johnston, J., 1984. *Econometric Methods*, 3rd edn., New York: McGraw-Hill

Keeble, D., 2000. "Collective Learning Processes in European High-Technology Milieux," in D. Keeble and F. Wilkinson (eds.), *High-Technology Clusters, Networking and Collective Learning in Europe*, Aldershot: Ashgate: 182–198

Keeble, D., C. Lawson, B. Moore, and F. Wilkinson, 1999. "Collective Learning Processes, Networking and Institutional Thickness in the Cambridge Region," *Regional Studies*, 33: 319–332

Keeble, D. and F. Wilkinson (eds.), 2000. *High-Technology Clusters, Networking and Collective Learning in Europe*, Aldershot: Ashgate

Kelejian, H. H. and I. R. Prucha, 1998. "A Generalized Spatial Two-Stage Least Squares Procedure for Estimating a Spatial Autoregressive Model with Autoregressive Disturbances," *Journal of Real Estate Finance and Economics*, 17: 99–121

Kelejian, H. H. and D. P. Robinson, 1993. "A Suggested Method of Estimation for Spatial Interdependent Models with Autocorrelated Errors, and an Application to a County Expenditure Model," *Papers in Regional Science*, 72: 297–312

Kennedy, P., 1992. *A Guide to Econometrics*, 3rd edn., Oxford: Blackwell

Krugman, P., 1991a. *Geography and Trade*, Cambridge, MA: MIT Press
    1991b. "Increasing Returns and Economic Geography," *Journal of Political Economy*, 99(31): 483–499
    1995. *Development, Geography*, and *Economic Theory*, Cambridge, MA: MIT

Leser, C., 1966. *Econometric Techniques and Problems*, London: Griffin

Maddala, G. S., 2001. *An Introduction to Econometrics*, New York: Wiley

Marshall, A., 1920. *Principles of Economics*, London: Macmillan

Porter, M. E., 1990. *The Competitive Advantage of Nations*, London: Macmillan
    1998. *On Competition*, Boston: Harvard Business Review Press

Storper, M., 1997. *The Regional World: Territorial Development in a Global Economy*, New York: Guilford Press

Part II

Institutional and spatial aspects of information and knowledge flows

5   Tacit knowledge in production systems: how important is geography?

Meric S. Gertler

5.1   Introduction

Within the field of innovation studies and technological change, the distinction between tacit and codified knowledge has recently been accorded great significance. Much of this interest was stimulated by Nelson and Winter (1982), whose classic work *An Evolutionary Theory of Economic Change* made extensive use of the concept of tacit knowledge in their analysis of how organizational routines shape technological change. In so doing, these authors have helped revive widespread interest in the earlier work of Michael Polanyi (1958, 1966), to the point where tacit knowledge has come to be recognized as a central component of the learning economy (Lundvall and Johnson 1994) and a key to innovation and value creation.

Moreover, tacit knowledge has come to be acknowledged as a prime determinant of the geography of innovative activity, since its central role in the process of learning-through-interacting tends to reinforce the local over the global. Those interested in the geographical structure of production and innovation systems have argued that the strong tacit component of leading-edge technical knowledge induces (indeed, requires) spatial clustering for the purposes of knowledge sharing that leads to innovation (Cooke and Morgan 1998; Maskell and Malmberg 1999). For a growing number of scholars, this explains the perpetuation and deepening of geographical concentration in a world of expanding markets, weakening borders, and ever-cheaper and more pervasive communication technologies.

Recently, the concept of tacit knowledge has received more critical attention within the fields of industrial economics and economic geography, where a process of re-examination and debate has begun. Some skeptics question the presumed distinction between tacit and explicit knowledge (see, for example, Cowan, David, and Foray 2000; Johnson, Lorenz, and Lundvall 2002). Others accept the distinction as valid, but question the argument that geographical proximity *per se* is a precondition for the effective transmission of tacit knowledge between economic actors (Allen 2000; Amin and Cohendet 2004). Considering the somewhat loose and indiscriminate way in which the term has come to be applied, and in the light of the generally superficial understanding of the origins of tacit knowledge prevalent in the literature, this recent debate is a welcome development.

The ongoing debate over the importance of geographical proximity for the sharing of tacit knowledge has, to this point, rested on very slim conceptual and empirical foundations. In this chapter, I seek to bring greater clarity to this debate by exploring an important, but hitherto neglected, aspect of tacit knowledge in the firm – namely, its institutional underpinnings. I argue that the geography of tacit knowledge cannot be properly understood without considering a prior question: How is tacit knowledge produced, and what role do institutional frameworks play in this process?

This chapter proceeds in four sections. In section 5.2, I review the standard definitions of tacit knowledge and discuss the reasons for its heightened importance in recent scholarship on economic change. In section 5.3, I further probe the concept of tacit knowledge by examining the question of how readily it can be transferred from one location to another (section 5.4). In section 5.5, I explore these arguments through the use of a case study, examining attempts to transfer tacit production knowledge between geographically distant partners. Finally, I conclude the chapter in section 5.6 with a reassessment of the nature and origins of tacit knowledge, in which I examine the role and importance of institutional context more fully. Here my aims are twofold: first, to recenter the analysis of tacitness away from its predominantly cognitive foundations and, second, to reconsider systematically the institutional origins of much that we recognize as tacit knowledge.

5.2   The essence of tacit knowledge: tacit and explicit definitions

In his classic work *The Tacit Dimension*, Michael Polanyi's distinction between tacit and explicit or codified knowledge is captured most vividly in his felicitous phrase "we can know more than we can tell" (1966: 4). Polanyi's underlying motivation was to argue that "scientific" knowledge is produced by individuals who imbue their search for new knowledge with deeply personal content. In other words, the knowledge of scientists is not fully reducible to a clearly articulated set of axioms, rules, algorithms, and statements (Sveiby 1997). However, there is an all-too-rarely-acknowledged degree of ambiguity in Polanyi's much-repeated aphorism, which is perhaps the source of continuing confusion about the meaning of tacitness. When it comes to specifying *why* we can know more than we can tell, there are at least two distinct ideas bound up in this statement.

First is the issue of awareness or consciousness. The tacit dimension of knowledge exists in the background of our consciousness, enabling us to focus our conscious attention on specific tasks and problems. Analysts, in their paradigmatic examples, used to illustrate this idea, whether in Polanyi's own work or elsewhere (Nelson and Winter 1982; Nonaka and Takeuchi 1995; von Krogh, Ichijo, and Nonaka 2000), tend to focus on the performance of psychomotor skills, such as swimming, identifying a person's face, riding a bicycle, or landing an airplane. In each case, the successful performance of a skill depends on "the observance of a set of rules which are not known as such to the person following them" (Polanyi 1958: 49) – i.e. knowledge that is "imperfectly accessible to conscious thought" (Nelson and Winter 1982: 79), leading to "levels of action that are not open to full, conscious deliberation" (Hodgson 1988: 126). In Polanyi's own famous example, skilled swimmers often remain unaware of the fact that one of the ingredients of a successful performance of this skill is keeping one's lungs filled with a sufficient quantity of air to enhance one's buoyancy – a practice that most of us implement unconsciously, without reflection. When skilled performers attempt to describe or explain their performance to an unskilled pupil, they must first try to develop their own awareness of all of the key components of success before they can attempt to communicate these to their student. Frequently, teachers will fail to achieve complete self-awareness, despite their best efforts.

The second idea pertains to communication difficulties and the inadequacies of language in expressing certain forms of knowledge and explanation, even when a person has achieved full self-awareness. This is the idea that symbolic forms of communication, such as spoken or written words, cannot convey all of the knowledge necessary for successful execution. Even pictures, though helpful, will not fully suffice. In the face of such challenges, one common response is to communicate the correct practice through an actual performance ("since I cannot explain this very well, let me show you instead").

In other words, the tacit component of the knowledge required for successful performance of a skill is that which defies codification or articulation – *either* because the performer herself is not fully conscious of all the "secrets" of successful performance *or* because the codes of language are not well enough developed to permit clear explication. The best way to convey such knowledge is through demonstration and practice, such as in the classic master–apprentice relationship in which observation, imitation, correction, and repetition are employed in the learning process (Polanyi 1966; Nonaka 1991).

This leads us to a closely related idea: that tacit knowledge can be acquired only through experience. Hence, Howells (2000: 53) refers to tacit knowledge as "know-how that is acquired via the informal take-up of learned behavior and procedures." Maskell and Malmberg (1999: 172) go a bit further in asserting that tacit knowledge "can only be produced in practice." This is so either because such knowledge must be shared between teacher and pupil (or master and apprentice) for the reasons described above, *or* because it was produced in the first place as a practical solution to a specific problem. Notice that such practical, problem-based knowledge may be produced either privately – for example, by a single worker figuring out how to extract greater productivity from a piece of machinery, akin to Arrow's (1962) classic idea of "learning-by-doing" – or collectively through a group-based problem-solving exercise. The collective nature of this process enables us to make the final link: between tacit knowledge and social context.

In this literature, the relationship between tacit knowledge and context is a reflexive one, since tacit knowledge both defines, and is defined by, social context. On the one hand, tacit knowledge is an essential complement to explicit knowledge, in the sense that it supports the acquisition and transmission of explicit knowledge through tacitly held constructs such as the rules enabling speech, reading, and writing. Furthermore, as we shall see below, the routines, customs, and conventions that govern much economic behavior contain a strong tacit component (Nelson and Winter 1982; Hodgson 1988). At the same time, a key idea is that tacit knowledge can be shared effectively between two or more people only when they also share a common social context: shared values, language, and culture. For example, Lundvall and Johnson (1994: 30) contend that "tacit knowledge is often specific to its original context. One might say that important elements of tacit knowledge are collective rather than individual." I shall return to this theme below.

Having reviewed the definition of tacit knowledge, two obvious questions are: Why has this concept received so much attention in recent times? Why does it matter to scholars of innovation and regional economic change? One compelling answer arises from the competence-based view of the firm and the nature of modern competition (Penrose 1959; Kay 1993). The idea is that, in a competitive era in which success depends increasingly upon the ability to produce new or improved products and processes, tacit knowledge constitutes the most important basis for innovation-based value creation. As Maskell and Malmberg (1999: 172) have famously put it, when everyone has relatively easy access to explicit/codified knowledge, the creation of unique capabilities and products depends on the production and use of tacit knowledge.

Maskell and Malmberg go further to suggest a fundamentally spatial argument: that tacit knowledge is a key determinant of the *geography* of innovative activity. There are three closely related elements to this argument. The first is alluded to above: that tacit knowledge, because it defies easy articulation and is best acquired experientially, is difficult to exchange over long distances. Second, its context-specific nature makes it spatially sticky, since two parties can exchange such knowledge effectively only if they share a common social context, and the most important elements of this social context are defined locally. The third element relates to the changing nature of the innovation process itself and, in particular, the growing importance of *socially organized* learning processes. The argument here is that innovation has come to be based increasingly on the interactions and knowledge flows *between* economic entities, such as firms (customers, suppliers, competitors), research organizations (universities, other public and private research institutions), and public agencies (technology transfer centers, development agencies). This is fundamental to Lundvall and Johnson's (1994) learning economy thesis, and is especially well reflected in their concept of "learning through interacting." When one combines these three features of tacit knowledge and the innovation process, it becomes apparent why geography now "matters" so much. As we shall see below, however, this argument has recently become contested.

5.3   How portable is tacit knowledge?

Since the mid-1990s, the centrality of knowledge, learning, and innovativeness to firms' competitive success has come to be more widely appreciated. Over this time, a new interest in "knowledge management" (KM) began to emerge (see, for example, Leonard 1995; Prusak 1997; Sveiby 1997; Davenport and Prusak 1998). The goal of KM, at least as seen from the business perspective, is to create value by accumulating and "leveraging" intangible (especially knowledge) assets. In order to do this, firms must overcome a number of central obstacles or problems that arise at several different sites or scales: inside the firm (between individual workers or groups of workers), between divisions and branches (local and non-local) within the individual firm, between firms (locally), and between firms separated by substantial distance (as well as regional and national boundaries).

Much of this literature (as well as the corresponding interest within economic geography, industrial economics, and innovation studies) focuses on a single problem – can tacit knowledge be transferred from place to place or firm to firm and, if so, how and under what circumstances? However, as I shall argue below, one cannot understand this issue of transferability without first developing a better appreciation for the manner in which tacit knowledge is generated in the first place.

As I noted at the outset of this chapter, the problem of how to spread tacit knowledge around more widely, once it has been produced, identified, and appropriated has received more attention than the question of how it is generated. Although this is an issue of central importance to economic geographers, for obvious reasons, it has recently become a concern of overriding importance within the management literature as well as within industrial economics and the innovation systems literature. It can be thought of as a problem of how to promote social-learning processes.

This issue presents a special problem for "distributed organizations" in which different units are situated in different locations separated by long distances. Particularly for large, multi-divisional, and multi-branch firms, a key challenge that has been recognized within the KM literature is how to find – and, once located, appropriate – tacit knowledge. This arises as a management challenge precisely because of the localized, nonubiquitous, context-specific nature of tacit knowledge discussed earlier. Within the KM literature, the processes of search and appropriation are frequently described as acts of "capture," "harvest," or "unlocking." The effective manager's challenge – indeed, responsibility – is to track down tacit knowledge wherever it may reside in the far reaches of the organization, then to appropriate it for productive re-use to benefit the firm. A recurring theme here is the problem of transferring tacit knowledge from the individuals who comprise the firm (and jointly produce tacit knowledge), to the larger organization so that it may be more widely exploited (Kogut and Zander 1992).

If there is one assertion on which there is widespread agreement, it is that the transmission or diffusion of tacit knowledge is not straightforward. This is principally because successful sharing depends on close and deep interaction between the parties involved (Lundvall 1988). However, as we shall see below, there is considerable disagreement concerning how "close" should be defined, as well as multiple rationales as to *why* it is important. Some contend that the process, if it works at all, may depend on the conversion of knowledge from its tacit to its explicit form ("externalization," according to Nonaka and Takeuchi 1995). Others remain more skeptical about the possibility of this actually being achieved successfully.

Looking more carefully at this issue, it becomes clear that there are really two different problems in one. The first problem is concerned with the "moment" of innovation (whether of the "big bang" variety or a more incremental form): if innovation has become an increasingly social process resting on the production and exchange of tacit knowledge, then how "close" must those participating in the process be to one another for it to work? And what kinds of proximity matter? Is simple physical proximity sufficient? How important is cultural commonality? Or is organizational or relational proximity the crucial factor?

The second problem is concerned with difficulties in the *diffusion* of innovations (including what are commonly referred to as "best practices") throughout a large organization, especially when the innovations must be transmitted across regional and national boundaries as well as cultural and other divides. Not surprisingly, a large proportion of the recent KM literature has focused on this problem. According to Prusak (1997: xii), the problem can be stated in the following terms: "Geography brings additional challenges: if knowledge is only transferred through proximity and exposure, how long does it take for something that is known in Munich to make it to Michigan?" Here, Prusak seems to support the argument made by Maskell and Malmberg (1999) that in a world in which access to codified knowledge is becoming ever easier, a firm's ability to produce, access, and control tacit knowledge is most important to its competitive success.

However, it is also evident that Prusak sees the problem of how to reproduce or share tacit knowledge as being closely bound up with the issue of finding and appropriating it. This dual nature is evident in a quote he reproduces, which he attributes to Lew Platt, former chairman of Hewlett-Packard (HP): "If only HP knew what HP knows, we could be three times more productive!" (Prusak 1997: xii). I shall explore the deeper significance of this quote below, but it is already clear that this problem is considerably more complex than simply taking an inventory of a firm's knowledge base, because knowledge is more like a dynamic process than a static product.

Given the attention that has recently been focused on tacit knowledge, it should come as no surprise that there is now a lively debate over the prospects for overcoming the problems outlined above. Most of the discussion has been centered explicitly on the issue of how easily tacit knowledge can be shared and transferred across longer distances. At least three distinct positions are evident within the literature, each of which produces its own distinctive vision of the geography of tacit knowledge.

The learning-regions thesis is now well established in economic geography, regional economic planning, and the (regional) innovation systems literature (see Florida 1995; Asheim 1996; Morgan 1997; Cooke and Morgan 1998; Maskell and Malmberg 1999). In a nutshell, its proponents argue that tacit knowledge does not "travel" easily. This is because its transmission is best shared through face-to-face interaction between partners who already share some basic similarities: the same language; common "codes" of communication; shared conventions and norms; personal knowledge of each other based on a past history of successful collaboration or informal interaction. In addition to enabling mutual understanding, these commonalities are said to serve the vital purpose of building trust between partners – which, in turn, facilitates the local flow of tacit knowledge between partners.

Because this approach has adopted the learning-by-interacting model as the cornerstone of its conceptual framework, it argues that the production of tacit knowledge occurs *simultaneously* with the act of transmission – primarily through the mechanism of user–producer interaction (Lundvall 1988). According to this perspective, knowledge does not flow unidirectionally from technology producers to users. Instead, users provide tacit knowledge to producers in order to enable the latter to devise innovative solutions to users' practical problems. But at the same time, by supplying users with innovative technologies, producers are also sharing their tacit knowledge with their customers. The end product arising from this close interaction benefits both users and producers, and embodies within it new tacit knowledge that could not have been produced by either party working in isolation. This, in effect, describes a social process of joint innovation and tacit knowledge production.

On the related issue of finding and appropriating tacit knowledge, proponents of the learning-regions approach at least imply that firms will search locally first, for reasons well justified in economic terms. Their intimate knowledge of other local firms and their capabilities is built up through past interaction and/or word-of-mouth referrals and local reputation (i.e. network) effects. This "local knowledge" greatly improves their odds of finding the right "match." Moreover, as is clear from the above discussion, appropriation (access to and successful absorption) of another firm's tacit knowledge is greatly facilitated by the bonds of trust that have developed between such local partners over time, or which are supported by strong locally grounded deterrents to opportunistic behavior by potential innovation partners with respect to the use of one another's intellectual property.

The economic geography associated with this perspective is clear and unequivocal: since spatial proximity is key to the effective production and transmission/sharing of tacit knowledge, this reinforces the importance of innovative clusters, districts, and regions. Moreover, as Maskell and Malmberg (1999) point out, these regions also benefit from the presence of localized capabilities and intangible assets that further strengthen their centripetal pull. Many of these are social assets, but produced one level above the scale of the individual organization – i.e. they exist *between* rather than within firms (Leonard and Swap 2000). Although they are therefore not fully appropriable by individual firms, only local firms can enjoy their benefits. These assets also include the region's unique institutional endowment, which can act to support and reinforce local advantage. As Maskell and Malmberg argue (1999: 181), because such assets exhibit strong tendencies of path-dependent development, they may prove to be very difficult to emulate by would-be imitators in other regions, thereby preserving the initial advantage of "first-mover" regions.

Allen (2000) has raised some important questions about the "self-evident truths" at the heart of the learning-regions thesis. In particular, he doubts the validity of the underlying assumption that tacit knowledge can be connected only to the local scale, while codified knowledge is necessarily global in reach or availability. He sees this dualism as unhelpful to our understanding of the geography of knowledge flows, considering it "a flawed, if not spurious, exercise" (Allen 2000: 30). He suggests that "distanciated contacts and 'thick' relationships may span organizational and industry boundaries, as can the puzzles and performances which constitute them" (Allen 2000: 28). In asserting that "the translation of ideas and practices . . . [is] likely to involve people moving to and through "local" contexts, to which they bring their own blend of tacit and codified knowledges, ways of doing things and ways of judging things" (Allen 2000: 28), Allen's arguments anticipate a second position evident in the literature.

More recently, another group of scholars has emphasized the central role of "communities of practice" as key entities driving the firm's knowledge-processing activities. These analysts argue that routines and established practices *shaped by organizations* (or subset communities within organizations) promote the production and sharing of tacit knowledge (Brown and Duguid 1996, 2000; Wenger 1998). They define communities of practice as groups of workers informally bound together by shared experience, expertise, and commitment to a joint enterprise. These communities normally self-organize for the purpose of solving practical problems facing the larger organization, and in the process they produce innovations (both product and process). The commonalities shared by members of the community facilitate the identification, joint production, and sharing of tacit knowledge through collaborative problem-solving assisted by story-telling and other narrative devices for circulating tacit knowledge (Denning 2001).

Thus, according to these analysts, organizational or relational proximity and occupational similarity are more important than geographical proximity in supporting the production, identification, appropriation, and flow of tacit knowledge (Amin and Cohendet 1999, 2004). The resulting tacit knowledge geography is distinctly different from that which is envisioned by adherents to the learning-regions approach. In this view, the joint production and diffusion/transmission of tacit knowledge across intra-organizational boundaries is possible, so long as it is mediated within these communities. Moreover, because communities of practice may extend outside the single firm to include customers or suppliers, tacit knowledge can also flow across the boundaries of individual organizations.

To this point, the argument does not appear to differ substantially from the user–producer interaction perspective inherent in the learning-regions approach. However, proponents of the communities-of-practice approach argue strongly that tacit knowledge will also flow across regional and national boundaries if organizational or "virtual community" proximity is strong enough – a phenomenon that Bunnell and Coe (2001) refer to as the "de-territorialization of closeness." In other words, as Amin (2000: 14) argues, the sharing of codified and tacit knowledge need *not* be subject to the frictional effects of distance if relational proximity ("ongoing organizational routines and the social practices of collectives implicated in a common venture") is present, supported by advanced communications and transportation infrastructure. Rather than seeing "the local as a unique source of tacit knowledge for competitive advantage," Amin (2000: 14) argues that "it is within organizational spaces, with their complex geographies blending action at a distance and local practices, that codified and tacit knowledge are mobilised for competitive advantage."

In other words, in place of *local context*, advocates of this perspective substitute *organizational context* as the crucial social environment shaping tacit knowledge production, identification, appropriation, absorption, and circulation. These arguments are useful reminders of the importance of relationships and the strength of underlying similarities rather than geographical proximity *per se* in determining the effectiveness of knowledge-sharing between economic actors. However, they do beg one very important question: What forces shape or define this "relational proximity," enabling it to transcend physical, cultural, and institutional divides? How are "shared understandings" produced? What role does social context play in embedding narratives to enable effective transfer of tacit knowledge between community members? Most proponents of the communities-of-practice approach are largely silent on this question, although Brown and Duguid (1996, 2000) stand out as a clear exception.

Brown and Duguid openly acknowledge a potential problem when they argue that tacit knowledge cannot be assumed to circulate freely just because the technology to support its circulation is available. In sharp contrast to the arguments reviewed above, Brown and Duguid (2000) stake out a very different position on the spatial reach of communities of practice, by arguing that the latter "are usually face-to-face communities" whose members "continually negotiate with, communicate with, and co-ordinate with each other directly in the course of work" (Brown and Duguid 2000: 143). On the use of information technologies *per se*, they are equally unequivocal in arguing (Brown and Duguid 2000: 146) that, "for the sort of implicit communication, negotiation, and collective improvisation that we have described as part of practice, learning, and knowledge sharing, it's clear that there are advantages to working together." In their view, the narratives and social ties so crucial to the flow of knowledge within communities of practice are deeply embedded within the social systems in which they arise. This view provides a convenient bridge to the third perspective on tacit knowledge problems.

In contrast to the optimistic view expressed in the communities-of-practice literature (Brown and Duguid excepted), another recent group of analysts begins from a rather different premise. They argue that although organizations may be able to *produce* tacit knowledge effectively (implicitly, using spatially concentrated resources to achieve this), it is devilishly difficult to disseminate or *share* it more widely ("harness" it) within the organization. This problem has become the focus of a huge effort by firms (especially large ones) and has come to be recognized – even by those who originally promoted the idea of a "knowledge-creating company" – as a very significant obstacle to greater innovativeness (Ichijo, von Krogh, and Nonaka 1998; von Krogh, Ichijo, and Nonaka 2000). These analysts set out to document some of the creative ways in which some firms have responded to this situation, emphasizing the key role of knowledge enablers – that is, "knowledge activists" who aim to span boundaries within the large organization, acting as agents for the diffusion of tacit knowledge – normally with at least partial codification in the process of transmission.

The boundary-spanning strategies of these knowledge activists make heavy use of story-telling as a key mode of tacit knowledge transfer. But even this can work only when supported by direct, face-to-face interaction and communication between people. For this reason, another key element of a knowledge-enabling strategy is the circulation of key personnel between head office and branch locations (or between different branches) around the globe.

The geography of tacit knowledge implicit in this approach is subtly, but importantly, different from either of the first two positions reviewed above. Although the *production* of tacit knowledge remains strongly localized, the possibilities for its dissemination – once produced – create large spread effects within multi-divisional and multi-locational organizations. There is also at least the potential for wider diffusion of this knowledge outside the organization, if the appropriate enablers are in place.

von Krogh, Ichijo, and Nonaka (2000) argue that "microcommunities of knowledge" play a key role in ensuring the success of this tacit knowledge circulation within large organizations. These are small groups (typically no more than five–seven people) whose members are strongly bound together through common work histories and who employ face-to-face interaction as their most important *modus operandi*. Of course, von Krogh, Ichijo, and Nonaka recognize that "geography" makes all of this more difficult and challenging. It is clear from their discussion that, for them, "geography" signifies both physical separation and local cultural differences. Although they emphasize the importance of a common or shared "social context" in facilitating the flow of tacit knowledge, they view the creation and shaping of this context as *primarily within the purview of the firm*. Furthermore, although they offer detailed renderings of case studies involving the attempted transmission of tacit technological knowledge between culturally (as well as physically) distant sites (e.g. advanced intercity rail technology being transposed from Switzerland to India), they provide no real insights into how "local culture" is produced.

5.4   "Local culture" and the transfer of tacit production knowledge: a case study

In order to approach a resolution of the central question above – how easily does tacit knowledge flow across physical distance, especially when there are also cultural differences at work? – I offer a brief case study of one attempt to bridge such distances. The story told here revolves around the experiences of a large German engineering firm and, in particular, its in-house division producing special machinery and industrial automation systems. At the time of my first visit, this division employed over 300 people. While a substantial proportion of its revenue was earned through sales to customers outside the firm, largely in the automotive, computer, and electronics sectors, the majority of its yearly turnover came from the sale of specialized production equipment to other divisions of the parent firm. Virtually all of the division's work involved the design and production of advanced, highly customized products, in which each system was designed and built to order, according to customers' own production requirements.

On this first visit, quite by chance, I found the division to be work-ing on the final production stages of two identical flexible manufacturing systems (FMS) for the assembly and testing of a small automotive part. These two FMS lines had already been fully constructed and were being fine-tuned, tested, and debugged prior to being disassembled and shipped to the customer plants for reassembly. In fact, both lines were being pro-duced for plants within another division of the firm. One of the lines was intended for a plant in another region of Germany where the automotive part was to be produced. The other was destined for another of the par-ent firm's plants, located in the southern United States, manufacturing a number of different products for the North American market.

The FMS lines were complex and technologically sophisticated, dic-tated in part by the characteristics of the finished product. The auto part being assembled was fairly small, with narrow tolerances permitted in order to ensure high performance. Moreover, the quality of this part was crucial to the performance of the vehicle into which it would ultimately be installed. Hence, each of the two FMS systems featured sophisticated robotics, advanced sensor devices, and programmable controls. Although the two lines were identical, the contrasts between the two ends of the plant in which each was being tested were striking. At the "German" end, all was peaceful. A few engineers wearing white coats could be seen qui-etly running tests, recording data, and making adjustments. But the "US" end was a hive of activity. Here, a dozen workers from the US plant were following around the division's German engineers and technical staff, watching them debug and break in the new line.

The senior manager in charge of this project indicated that the objective of this exercise was to provide US workers the opportunity to acquire vital tacit knowledge, learning how to solve problems occurring on the FMS line by observing the process of problem identification and correction as practiced by the firm's German engineers. It was management's hope that when problems arose during normal operation of the FMS lines in the US plant, the tacit knowledge and problem-solving skills learned through observation in Germany would be applied at home in order to correct difficulties more quickly and easily. Additionally, the firm hoped that its US workers might learn how to avoid many such problems in the first place. In either case, the intent was to reduce down-time or unacceptable variations in product quality due to operational difficulties. Moreover, in order to support this learning process, the parent firm had attempted to reduce the cultural distance between their American and German workers by immersing the American workers in three months of German-language training in the United States before sending them overseas. The length of their stay in Germany was a generous eight weeks, in order to allow sufficient time for the requisite skills and tacit knowledge to be transferred.

Asked to account for the striking difference between the two ends of the plant, senior management indicated that they were aware of the radically different levels and type of worker training in the US south compared to Germany. Their prior experience had taught them that American workers would typically be far less well trained, especially with respect to advanced skills such as the use of electronic controls and the ability to solve production problems on the job. Anticipating future problems at the US plant, the parent firm's management had directed its special machinery division and its US management to do all they could to avoid or minimize their occurrence. Management was confident that they could overcome any difficulties by pursuing this strategy.

Moreover, this approach was supplemented by other measures. In particular, the special machinery division enlisted the support of its North American subsidiary in the United States, which was asked to serve as an intermediary during the line's initial set-up and subsequent operation in the US plant. The firm was also taking the further precaution of providing an electronic link-up between the US plant and German headquarters in order to enable engineers at the head office to monitor production data in real time and assist with troubleshooting if necessary.

By contrast, the relative calm at the German end of the plant was explained by the firm's confidence in the ability of their domestic workers to solve problems or avoid them altogether, thanks to their lengthier and more extensive training. This training was acquired through both a rigorous technical college program as well as a three-and-a-half year apprenticeship period required of all workers as part of the "dual" training system typical of German manufacturing industries.

A second visit to the division's headquarters in Germany one year later provided an opportunity to monitor the success of the technology implementation process. This second round of discussions with the division's management revealed that they had planned for a six-month period to transfer the lines to the two plants, set them up and break them in. During this time, there were frequent exchanges of engineers and operators across the Atlantic between the two user plants, with the special machinery division and its US subsidiary also heavily involved. The idea was to allow the exchange and sharing of information and experiences in the FMS implementation: in other words, to create an interplant and international community of practice engaging in social learning through joint problem-solving.

However, the subsequent process did not unfold as expected. The break-in process and time required to reach "normal" operation were significantly longer and more difficult in the case of the US plant. There were several reasons for these difficulties. Among the more mundane of these, the US line had to operate under conditions of higher average temperature and humidity, producing problems of part recognition, handling, and alignment. Furthermore, this was compounded by more variable or poorer-quality components from outside suppliers based in the United States. These problems in quality control and materials, while relatively minor, were still significant and – given the parent firm's lengthy experience in the operation of a US plant – it is surprising that they were not anticipated during the design process in Germany.

Other sources of difficulty were more fundamental in nature. It transpired that the training provided for the worker-operatives from the US plant was not sufficient, even with the lengthy eight-week visit to division headquarters. A few months' training was simply not enough to overcome the absence of a basic foundation of background knowledge and skills in the US workforce. To restate this in somewhat different terms, their deficiencies in the codified forms of knowledge that they had previously acquired undermined their ability to absorb the new knowledge (both tacit and codified) required to operate and troubleshoot the machinery properly. Furthermore, the firm found that its US maintenance and support personnel were also poorly prepared for the task, either through formal education or experience. Finally, and perhaps most importantly, employee turnover proved to be a very serious source of difficulty for the US plant. Management had indeed anticipated that this might be a problem, but had thought that by investing in the training of their workers, and by trying to build a stronger relation between them, they might instill a sense of commitment and loyalty to the firm among their American workers. However, such was not to be the case. Indeed, once their workers had received what (in the local context) amounted to such relatively extensive training, they became much-sought-after commodities in the regional labor market. In a fashion typical of US-style labor markets, these workers were poached by other manufacturers in the same region and, as a result, the firm's investment in their training yielded very little return for the US plant.

To complete the case study, I visited the US plant some eighteen months later. Discussions with managers at the plant emphasized the fact that many adjustments to the original design had been implemented to adapt the FMS line to US conditions and respond to the difficulties encountered. Operation of the line had eventually reached the point where disruptions were relatively infrequent and tolerable, although this state had been achieved in a matter of years rather than months. Moreover, another interesting difference was revealed. The line in the US plant was now producing parts more cheaply than its German counterpart, largely due to US management's freedom to work the machinery more intensively – for longer hours each week, and with fewer shutdowns for weekends or holidays. In contrast, the German line was producing parts of significantly better quality. Indeed, German managers confirmed that the quality differences were substantial enough to be perceptible to their customers in the automotive industry. This had become the source of some concern, since their customers had expected the US-made parts to be cheaper but of equal quality.

5.5   Tacit knowledge revisited: from Michael to Karl Polanyi

The discussion in section 5.3 of this chapter provides ample evidence of the considerable disagreement and confusion that persists concerning the nature of tacit knowledge and its relationship to the geography of innovation. I will argue in this section that the principal reason for this confusion stems from the relatively limited and superficial interpretation of the concept adopted by most scholars up until now. Furthermore, these limitations arise from a too literal reliance on Michael Polanyi's own particular conception of tacit knowledge. In reflecting on the case study just presented, my goal here is to reconstruct our understanding of tacit knowledge based on more robust foundations that allow us to develop a deeper understanding of the true meaning and significance of local context or culture.

Recalling our earlier discussion, Polanyi's original conception of tacit knowledge is primarily experiential and cognitive, though only weakly contextual. It is experiential in the sense that he conceives of tacit knowledge as an understanding of "know-how," acquired through experience. It is cognitive in the sense that it defies conscious articulation – meaning that (1) we may not even be aware of it, or of the way it influences our behavior, and (2) even if we are, when we try to articulate or explain it to someone else, communicating this knowledge in verbal, written, or diagrammatic form will never be fully equal to the task. For these reasons, tacit knowledge must be learned by demonstration, imitation, performance, and shared experience. Polanyi does assert that tacit knowledge is context-dependent in the sense that common rules shared between one person and another are important for the successful transmission of tacit knowledge. However, perhaps the reason so many have gone astray in applying Polanyi's concept is that he never fully specified how "rules" and context are produced. Instead, their origins remain idiosyncratic, pre-modern and "cultural" in the superorganic sense (McDowell 1994), in line with his larger project to legitimize the personal, passionate pursuit of knowledge by individual scholars as the driving force behind scientific advance (Polanyi 1958: 266).

Unfortunately, although those who have followed in Polanyi's footsteps almost always acknowledge the importance of social context, this rarely goes beyond lip-service. We have already reviewed those contributions from proponents of the communities-of-practice and knowledge-enablers approaches, for whom the analysis of context and the origins of shared rules, routines, norms, customs, and habits rests primarily on occupational similarity, common histories of project-based interaction (both past and recent), and organizational cultures *shaped by the firm*. On the other hand, the economic-geography literature evinces a considerably stronger recognition that larger institutional forces may play a part in shaping social context and rules, although the analysis remains underdeveloped. Hence, Storper (1999: 37–38) acknowledges "labor markets, public institutions, and locally or nationally derived rules of action, customs, understandings, and values" as part and parcel of the region-specific untraded interdependencies that support and sustain localized, innovative growth. He also invokes the idea of "conventions," which he defines as "common languages and rules for developing, communicating, and interpreting knowledge" (Storper 1999: 40) and "taken-for-granted rules and routines" (Storper 1999: 42).

In more recent work, Storper and Leamer (2001: 650) emphasize the continuing "importance of face-to-face interactions in the production and distribution of new or complex ideas," but only hint as to the institutional foundations of social context. Hence, they recognize the importance of "mutual trust and mutual understanding. The parties therefore need to 'know' each other, or have a broad common background which goes well beyond their direct contact" (Storper and Leamer 2001: 651), but their analysis of "common background" stresses other processes. In their view, the shared context so necessary for achieving true mutual understanding emerges from common membership in "communities defined by cultural affiliation, language, ideology, desire, mutual identification, and other powerful forms of bonding" (Storper and Leamer 2001: 653).

In comparison, Cooke and Morgan (1998) outline in considerably greater length the institutional foundations of tacit knowledge creation and transmission. Because the phenomenon they are trying to explain is spatially concentrated innovative growth based on localized learning dynamics, there is a natural tendency here to emphasize local and regional institutional forces more heavily than others. Nevertheless, they give due recognition to national institutions, including national systems of innovation, which they define (following Lundvall) as "a nationally structured system of interactive learning" (Cooke and Morgan 1998: 25). In fleshing out this definition, they emphasize nationally distinctive ensembles of education and training institutions, financial systems, and inter-firm relations. However, when it comes to tacit knowledge *per se*, the institutional dimensions seem to fade into the background. Although they do assert (Cooke and Morgan 1998: 25) that "national boundaries are proxies for physical, cultural, political, and linguistic nearness and sameness, which continue to affect the transfer of tacit knowledge from person to person and from organization to organization," elsewhere they treat tacit knowledge exchange as a strongly localized phenomenon. In doing so, their approach echoes Maskell and Malmberg's (1999: 181) important argument reviewed earlier, that "the region's distinct institutional endowment . . . embeds knowledge and allows for knowledge creation."

These latter ideas point us productively in the direction of an institutional analysis of the origins of tacit knowledge, while stressing the local and regional scale. More generally, they suggest that we cannot sort out the geography of tacit knowledge without inquiring more systematically into the fundamental nature of "culture" and the institutional underpinnings of economic activity. Ironically, the source for a more helpful perspective on this issue is another well-known Polanyi – Michael's older brother, Karl Polanyi (1944) – whose classic work yields the central insight that markets and the behavior of economic actors are *socially constructed, embedded, and governed*. According to Zysman (1994: 244), this means that "markets do not exist or operate apart from the rules and institutions that establish them and that structure how buying, selling and the very organization of production take place." This insight has important implications for my analysis. It suggests that the ability of individual workers or firms to produce and share tacit knowledge depends on much more than spatial proximity, cultural affinity, or corporate culture. In particular, it depends on institutional proximity – that is, the shared norms, conventions, values, expectations, and routines arising from commonly experienced frameworks of institutions. This form of proximity or affinity may rival or override organizational proximity (common corporate ownership and culture) or relational proximity (occupational similarity, or bonds arising from past interaction) if the organization in question extends geographically across institutional divides.

Karl Polanyi's work also suggests that the ability of firms to find and appropriate the tacit knowledge produced by individual workers on the shop (or office, or laboratory) floor, or by teams (communities), will be highly sensitive to the institutions governing the employment relation which, themselves, vary geographically by nation and region (Kochan and Osterman 1994; Wever 1995; O'Sullivan 2000).

These insights suggest that we need to devise an alternative conception of tacit knowledge, since (Michael) Polanyi's famous aphorism "we can know more than we can tell" has deflected our attention away from the broader (geographically defined) context within which tacit knowledge is produced and shared. Following Karl Polanyi's inspiration, then, we can more productively interpret the origins of routines, characteristic practices, "settled habits of thought," and "second nature" as arising from concrete institutional origins: although corporate agency and the distinctive "culture" of the firm undoubtedly play a major role, they do not exist within a vacuum (Schoenberger 1997; Glasmeier 2001) and, contrary to the underlying premise of much of the KM literature, managers do not fully (or even largely) shape their own destiny. They operate within a possibility set that is constrained by larger forces – particularly the institutional and regulatory frameworks at the national and regional scales (Whitley 1999; Lam 2000).

These frameworks influence firms' practices, values, and expectations in fundamental ways. For example, Lam (2000: 489) has demonstrated convincingly how nationally distinctive education and training systems and labor-market features "shape the social constitution of knowledge." Her goal is to show how "micro-level learning activities" are shaped by "macro-level societal institutions" (Lam 2000: 487). She documents how nationally characteristic organizational forms (themselves shaped by national constellations of education and labor market institutions) create or inhibit possibilities for tacit knowledge production and transmission to varying degrees. Hence, the "J-form" organization typical of large Japanese firms, based on stable employment, nonhierarchical teams, and strong corporate cultures, "is marked by a tremendous capacity to generate, diffuse and continuously accumulate tacit knowledge through 'learning-by-doing' and interaction" (Lam 2000: 498). She contrasts this with other organizational forms such as the "machine bureaucracy," characterized by "the standardization of work process, a sharp division of labor and close supervision." This latter organizational form (far more typical of Anglo-American systems) "operates on the basis of 'encoded knowledge.' A large part of tacit knowledge is naturally lost in the translation and aggregation process" (Lam 2000: 495–496).

Extending this analysis considerably further, Christopherson (2002) has argued that the kinds of organizational features and labor market characteristics of interest to Lam are strongly shaped by the structure of capital markets and "investment regimes" determined at the national level. Moreover, these different investment regimes produce the societal conditions for divergent forms of competitive advantage in global markets. For example, Christopherson lays out what she considers to be the central features of a US-style "market governance model" dominated by the drive to maximize short-term investment returns. This model has promoted the emergence of US strengths in a set of "project oriented" industries including electronic media and entertainment, advertising, management consulting, public relations, engineering and industrial design, computer services, and R&D related to computing and telecommunications.

5.6   Conclusion

There are two general points arising from this analysis. The first is that "context" is, to a very large degree, defined by institutional features. Of course, as Maskell and Malmberg (1999: 173) point out, the institutional endowment of a region or nation accumulates over time, and "thus represents the intricate contemporary interaction between elements of different ages . . . from the very old (religion, beliefs, values) to the recent/current (contemporary industry standards, current regulations, etc.)." The second point – and the explicit link to tacit knowledge – is that such institutional influences are subtle, but pervasive: indeed, often so subtle that firms and individuals are not even conscious of the impact they exert over their own choices, practices, attitudes, values, and expectations. The reasons for this stem from the taken-for-granted quality which managers' attitudes acquire after years of training and experience in a particular societal/economic system. Particular practices and attitudes become naturalized through repetition and reinforced through repeated and frequent interaction with other like-minded economic actors. In this sense, we can accept one of the alleged hallmarks of tacit knowledge – that it is "imperfectly accessible to conscious thought." However, we now have a firmer understanding of why managers and workers remain unaware of such attitudes and their influence over practice, as well as whence such "knowledge" arises in the first place. Based on this, one might be tempted to recast Michael Polanyi's famous aphorism as "we do not understand what we know, or *how* it shapes what we do."

That firms remain almost completely oblivious to the influence of these institutional forces – or greatly underestimate their impact – becomes readily apparent whenever they attempt to engage in learning that spans institutionally defined contextual divides, whether this is between different firms or between different divisions/branches of the *same* firm situated in different institutional settings.

The discussion of such circumstances in the brief case study described above shows how national institutions governing labor markets and corporate governance shape the norms, taken-for-granted knowledge, and

unconsciously held assumptions of managers concerning production processes and technology use. After all, the firm in question was attempting to transfer a blend of codified and tacit knowledge concerning the
proper operation of a complex production system from one plant to
another. Because both production systems were identical, and because
both implementing plants were under the same corporate umbrella, relational proximity of the sort described by Allen (2000) and Amin and
Cohendet (2004) was assured. The firm also engineered the formation
of an international community of practice to enable this knowledge flow.
Nevertheless, the gulf it was attempting to bridge was not only physical
and cultural, but also institutional in nature. It is clear from the case
study that, despite the presence of organizational or relational proximity
(not to mention the considerable financial and human capital resources
of the large parent firm), institutional distance appears to have trumped
all other forms.

Examining the differences between the two plants more carefully, I
found that a crucial source of variation was in the way that labor markets are socially constructed and regulated in the two countries. The high
rates of employee turnover among both shop floor workers and managers
at the US plant, which proved to be the source of so many implementation problems, are encouraged by the characteristic features of US labor
market regulation described above. Hence, the high rate of employee
turnover and instability in the workforce frustrated the firm in its efforts
to retain the US workers who had undergone extensive training. This
instability was itself heightened by the unwillingness of other employers
in the region to invest in training their own workers, given the likelihood
that these workers, once trained, might be poached by other firms seeking similar skills. As a consequence, they were aggressive in their pursuit
of the case-study firm's skilled employees. Such behavior can be understood to have been induced by the systemic influence of flexible employment rules, which enhance the ability of firms to deploy labor with few
encumbrances, and which fuel the mobility of workers. Moreover, the
firm's continuing quality problems were likely to have been exacerbated
by a reluctance to spend more funds on training newly hired workers so
extensively. Thus, despite the firm's best efforts, their objective of implementing a skill-intensive production process to produce a high-quality
product was seriously compromised by the contours of an "unfriendly"
institutional environment in which their US plant was located.

Furthermore, it is clear that those who designed the advanced production system in Germany were themselves operating on the basis
of a set of taken-for-granted, tacitly held beliefs about the workplace
setting in which their technology would be implemented, based on

experience designing production systems for use in Germany. Foremost among these was the tacit assumption that the workers operating the machinery would have received a high level of both theoretical education and practical training prior to joining the firm. They also apparently assumed that the employment relation in the implementing workplace was stable, with minimal employee turnover; meaning that workers would have ample time to learn how to exploit the full capabilities of the new machinery on the job *and* that this knowledge would remain inside the firm over time. As a result of high levels of education and training, and stable on-the-job experience sustained over an extended period, the operators would demonstrate well-developed problem-solving (and problem-avoidance) skills, and would require minimal technical information to be supplied in codified form in operational manuals (see Gertler 2004 for a more extended discussion of these issues).

The engineers who designed the advanced manufacturing technology clearly (and mistakenly) assumed that the above features accurately described the operations and practices in both the German and US plants. Furthermore, their ability to engage their new overseas "customers" in a process of close learning-through-interacting, mediated by a community of practice, was frustrated and undermined by the widely divergent sets of tacitly held norms, expectations, and beliefs that shaped their respective attitudes and practices. Indeed, it was possibly only at this point – when they failed to transcend institutionally defined spatial divides – that the German technology producers even became aware of the mindset and settled habits of thought that had guided their approach to the design of production systems for use in the German workplace.

On the basis of this case study, it appears that institutional systems of industrial regulation continue to exert a very strong influence over firms' day-to-day practices in the workplace. They also act to limit the extent to which tacitly held and acquired work practices and technologies can "travel" successfully across international borders.

This case study demonstrates that learning involving tacit knowledge transfer, when attempted across major institutional–contextual boundaries, will be subject to formidable obstacles, even in the presence of substantial corporate wealth and resources. It also throws into sharper relief the quote cited earlier from the former chairman of HP: "knowing" what HP knows is more than a matter of simply identifying, cataloguing, and providing ready access to all knowledge in the firm (itself a daunting prospect). The inevitable geographical variations in institutionally defined local context are endemic to organizations as large as HP, meaning that fully "knowing" what some key employee, situated in a far-flung corner of the corporation, knows will be all but impossible. And even if one *could* know this, the ability or inclination of central management to act on this knowledge will also surely be limited.

The conclusion is that transcending the bonds of spatial proximity may be possible, but it will also be difficult and expensive, because of the fundamentally different institutional environments involved – what we might understand as the distinctive and uneven, though systematic, economic geography of context. Technological fixes and corporate hubris may not be sufficient to overcome these obstacles. Nor will occupational similarity or even mobile "knowledge enablers." The barriers that matter most in these situations are less cognitive and more institutional in origin. Although they may scan as "cultural" differences, the divergent attitudes, practices, and norms underlying them can be linked to very concrete differences in the macro-institutional architectures. For these reasons, it may well be true that "the death of geography has been greatly exaggerated," to paraphrase Morgan (2004).

In conclusion, the line of argument I pursue in this chapter suggests that students of innovation need to consider more carefully how tacit knowledge and context are *produced* before we can say anything intelligent about how easily tacit knowledge can be shared – that is, when "proximity" is important: what types and why. When we examine the process of tacit knowledge production more carefully, we learn that the social context that Michael Polanyi (and everyone since) acknowledged as being so important rests on concrete institutional foundations.

REFERENCES

Allen, J., 2000. "Power/Economic Knowledge: Symbolic and Spatial Formations," in J. R. Bryson, P. W. Daniels, N. Henry, and J. Pollard (eds.), *Knowledge, Space, Economy*, London: Routledge: 15–33

Amin, A., 2000. "Organisational Learning Through Communities of Practice," Paper presented at the Workshop on The Firm in Economic Geography, University of Portsmouth, March 9–11

Amin, A. and P. Cohendet, 1999. "Learning and Adaptation in Decentralised Business Networks," *Environment and Planning D: Society and Space*, 17: 87–104

2004. *Architectures of Knowledge*, Oxford: Oxford University Press

Arrow, K. J., 1962. "The Economic Implications of Learning by Doing," *Review of Economic Studies*, 29: 155–173

Asheim, B., 1996. "Industrial Districts As "Learning Regions": A Condition for Prosperity?," *European Planning Studies*, 4: 379–400

Brown, J. S. and P. Duguid, 1996. "Organizational Learning and Communities-of-Practice," in M. Cohen and L. Sproull (eds.), *Organizational Learning*, London: Sage

2000. *The Social Life of Information*, Boston: Harvard Business School Press

Bunnell, T. and N. Coe, 2001. "Spaces and Scales of Innovation," *Progress in Human Geography*, 25: 569–589

Christopherson, S., 2002. "Why Do National Labor Market Practices Continue to Diverge in the Global Economy? The "Missing Link" of Investment Rules," *Economic Geography*, 78: 1–20

Cooke, P. and K. Morgan, 1998. *The Associational Economy*, Oxford: Oxford University Press

Cowan, R., P. A. David, and D. Foray, 2000. "The Explicit Economics of Knowledge Codification and Tacitness," *Industrial and Corporate Change*, 9: 211–253

Davenport, T. H. and L. Prusak, 1998. *Working Knowledge: How Organizations Manage What They Know*, Boston: Harvard Business School Press

Denning, S., 2001. *The Springboard: How Storytelling Ignites Action in Knowledge-Era Organizations*, Boston: Butterworth-Heinemann

Florida, R., 1995. "Toward the Learning Region," *Futures*, 27: 527–536

Gertler, M. S., 2004. *Manufacturing Culture: The Institutional Geography of Industrial Practice*, Oxford: Oxford University Press

Glasmeier, A., 2001. *Manufacturing Time: Global Competition in the Watch Industry, 1795–2000*, New York: Guilford Press

Hodgson, G. M., 1988. *Economics and Institutions*, Cambridge: Polity Press

Howells, J., 2000. "Knowledge, Innovation and Location," in J. R. Bryson *et al.* (eds.): 50–62

Ichijo, K., G. von Krogh, and I. Nonaka, 1998. "Knowledge Enablers," in G. von Krogh, J. Roos, and D. Kleine (eds.), *Knowing in Firms*, London: Sage: 173–203

Johnson, B., E. Lorenz, and B.-Å. Lundvall, 2002. "Why All This Fuss About Codified and Tacit Knowledge?," *Industrial and Corporate Change*, 11: 245–262

Kay, J., 1993. *Foundations of Corporate Success*, Oxford: Oxford University Press

Kochan, T. A. and P. Osterman, 1994. *The Mutual Gains Enterprise*, Boston: Harvard Business School Press

Kogut, B. and U. Zander, 1992. "Knowledge of the Firm: Combinative Capabilities, and the Replication of Technology," *Organizational Science*, 3: 383–397

Lam, A., 2000. "Tacit Knowledge, Organizational Learning and Societal Institutions: An Integrated Framework," *Organization Studies*, 21: 487–513

Leonard, D., 1995. *Wellsprings of Knowledge: Building and Sustaining the Sources of Innovation*, Boston: Harvard Business School Press

Leonard, D. and W. Swap, 2000. "Gurus in the Garage," *Harvard Business Review*, 78: 71–82

Lundvall, B.-Å., 1988. "Innovation as an Interactive Process: From User–Producer Interaction to the National System of Innovation," in G. Dosi, C. Freeman, G. Silverberg, and L. Soete (eds.), *Technical Change and Economic Theory*, London: Frances Pinter: 349–369

Lundvall, B.-Å., and B. Johnson, 1994. "The Learning Economy," *Journal of Industry Studies*, 1: 23–42

Maskell, P. and A. Malmberg, 1999. "Localised Learning and Industrial Competitiveness," *Cambridge Journal of Economics*, 23: 167–186

McDowell, L., 1994. "The Transformation of Cultural Geography," in D. Gregory, R. Martin, and G. Smith (eds.), *Human Geography*, Minneapolis: University of Minnesota Press: 146–173

Morgan, K., 1997. "The Learning Region: Institutions, Innovation and Regional Renewal," *Regional Studies*, 31: 491–504

2004. "The Exaggerated Death of Geography: Learning, Proximity and Territorial Innovation Systems," *Journal of Economic Geography*, 4: 3–21

Nelson, R. R. and S. G. Winter, 1982. *An Evolutionary Theory of Economic Change*, Cambridge, MA: Harvard University Press

Nonaka, I., 1991. "The Knowledge Creating Company," *Harvard Business Review*, 69: 96–104

Nonaka, I. and H. Takeuchi, 1995. *The Knowledge-Creating Company*, Oxford: Oxford University Press

O'Sullivan, M., 2000. *Contests for Corporate Control*, Oxford: Oxford University Press

Penrose, E., 1959. *The Theory of the Growth of the Firm*, Oxford: Basil Blackwell

Polanyi, K., 1944. *The Great Transformation*, New York: Rinehart

Polanyi, M., 1958. *Personal Knowledge*, London: Routledge & Kegan Paul

1966. *The Tacit Dimension*, New York: Doubleday

Prusak, L. (ed.), 1997. *Knowledge in Organizations*, Boston: Butterworth–Heinemann

Schoenberger, E., 1997. *The Cultural Crisis of the Firm*, Oxford: Blackwell

Storper, M., 1999. "The Resurgence of Regional Economics: Ten Years Later," in T. J. Barnes and M. S. Gertler (eds.), *The New Industrial Geography*, London: Routledge: 23–53

Storper, M. and E. E. Leamer, 2001. "The Economic Geography of the Internet Age," *Journal of International Business Studies*, 32: 641–665

Sveiby, K. E., 1997. *The New Organizational Wealth*, San Francisco: Berrett-Koehler

von Krogh, G., K. Ichijo, and I. Nonaka, 2000. *Enabling Knowledge Creation: How to Unlock the Mystery of Tacit Knowledge and Release the Power of Innovation*, Oxford: Oxford University Press

Wenger, E., 1998. *Communities of Practice*, Cambridge: Cambridge University Press

Wever, K. S., 1995. *Negotiating Competitiveness*, Boston: Harvard Business School Press

Whitley, R., 1999. *Divergent Capitalisms*, Oxford: Oxford University Press

Zysman, J., 1994. "How Institutions Create Historically Rooted Trajectories of Growth," *Industrial and Corporate Change*, 3: 243–283

6   The self-aware firm: information needs, acquisition strategies, and utilization prospects

Amy Glasmeier

6.1   Introduction

Debate about the extent to which regions can foster innovation moves in two divergent directions. The first set of analysts takes a normative approach in suggesting what makes regions and firms competitive, innovative, and resilient. Their perspective draws largely on case studies of "successful" regions or firms where learning either occurs or is suboptimal (Lam 1997; Amin and Cohendet 1999; Capello 1999; Keeble and Wilkinson 1999; Lawson and Lorenz 1999; French 2000; Henry and Pinch 2000; Florida 2002; Lambooy, 2002; Storper 2002; and Gertler 2003a, 2003b). The second set of analysts' perspectives takes a positive approach to firm learning and investigates the practice of information acquisition, knowledge creation, and behavioral change in firms (Glasmeier 1991, 1999, 2001; Glasmeier *et al.* 1995; Feller, Glasmeier, and Marks 1996; Harrison and Glasmeier 1997; Glasmeier *et al.* 1998; Meeus, Oerlemans, and Boekema 2000; and Oerlemans, Meeus, and Boekema 2000). While the first set suggests that firms can and do act deliberately and with forethought, the second set suggests that firms are reactive, incremental, and myopic, and are motivated by factors that include life-style considerations rather than profit maximization.

The first type of investigation supports the belief that to be successful in the new economy, firms must have superior abilities to network, acquire new information, turn it into knowledge, learn from its internalization, and act upon it (Cooke 2002; Gertler and Wolfe 2002; Storper 2002).

Gertler and Wolfe (2002: 3) suggest that neither firms nor the public sector "are the source of all wisdom; rather, the process of innovation and institutional adaptation is essentially an interactive one in which the means for establishing supportive social relations and of communicating insights and knowledge in all its various forms are crucial to the outcomes." They argue that:

This insight suggests a higher order of learning by institutions – one based on a capacity for reflexivity and the ability to apply institutional memory and intelligence to monitor the success of institutions in adapting to ongoing changes in the environment. This higher order is learning-by-learning, where the [institutional] self-monitoring of the learning process itself becomes an integral feature of the institutional structure.

From a policy perspective, the key is to discover how to promote – and, if possible, reproduce – these behaviors in other contexts. These authors operate from the perspective of normative economics of "what should be," given today's competitive context. It is from this perspective that we can discern the importance of networks and collaboration as contributors to regional success and as mechanisms to enhance competitiveness and overcome bottlenecks to learning.

Authors from the second group use surveys of public-sector institutions created to encourage learning or studies of firms and their knowledge acquisition and learning processes. Their research highlights the rather mundane, rote, and limited search processes undertaken by most firms in acquiring strategic information. They agree that firms' limited search behaviors diminish the likelihood of using information provided by public-sector organizations to improve their competitiveness. The reason is a lack of trust and a belief that such organizations know little about the problems of modern business, much less understand the experience of individual firms (Meeus, Oerlemans, and Boekema 2000; Cooke 2002).

This second set of authors builds upon positive economics and argues that the more descriptive case-study-based line of research is uncritical, inexact, and overgeneralizes from the (few) experiences of firms engaged in innovative activities and the behavioral and environmental keys that lead to competitiveness. Critical of this body of case-study research, Meeus, Oerlemans, and Boekema (2000: 193) comment that:

[An] alternative explanation of regional economic performance [has] made relationships and networks an important variable on the research agendas of organization theory, institutional economics, and systems of innovation but, at the same time, raise[s] a number of questions. The literature of innovation systems either lacks theoretical rigor or applies a naïve, unidirectional approach in which institutional differences explain differences in innovative behavior and performance. The fad of network research produced an enormous literature, which is very fragmented and also rather uncritical. This partly explains the strong bias toward descriptive accounts of strong linkages and the benefits of local co-operation, whereas the under utilization of local resources, the drawbacks of networks and weak ties are generally neglected.

If one set emphasizes what is needed and the other identifies what is done in practice, how can we reconcile these two perspectives on firm behavior? How might reconciliation shape proposals about public-sector involvement in the firm knowledge creation and innovation process?

In a study of firm information acquisition and utilization behaviors, I explore the extent to which firms identified, acquired, internalized, and then acted on information obtained to solve a range of business problems. My research focused on several questions: How do firms actually make decisions; What kind of information do they use; How do they search for information; How do they answer questions; and How do they solve problems? In other words, do most firms naturally assume a baseline strategic posture when it comes to decisionmaking in the face of uncertainty, or does their action accord with our normative vision of how we think (or would like to think) firms work?

In this chapter, I frame the process of firm learning as a function of two overarching competencies: (a) information acquisition and (b) the ability to take purposeful action based upon that acquired information. This process is fairly complex. The firm must identify signals in the environment such that the information enters the firm; then, the information must circulate and be decoded, stored, and used. The firm's actions on this information result in experiences that further clarify and moderate the future acquisition and use of information. In examining this process, I seek to answer two simple, interrelated questions: (1) How do firms acquire strategic information, and what are their sources and uses of this information, and (2) What actions do they take based on the information acquired?

The chapter is organized into four sections. Section 6.2 provides a short description of literature on firm information acquisition and utilization behavior; section 6.3 describes the research project; section 6.4 reports the results of a multi-firm survey in which I collected information from a target and a control group sample of firms; and section 6.5 explores the results of my thirty in-depth case study interviews with firms across the eastern United States. The chapter concludes with some observations about firm behavior and public policy.

6.2   The relevance of firm learning

Analysts suggest that two interrelated and overarching competencies are necessary for effective organizational learning: (1) an ability to make environmental assessments and acquire information about potential actions in the face of environmental challenges, and (2) the firm's capacity to act on the newly acquired information. Neither of these competencies alone is sufficient for learning to occur. Information without an organizational ability to act renders the information impotent; action without information is likely to be dangerous and risky.

Many analysts of firm behavior suggest the following:

- Firms scan the environment through their networks for the information that they need, but differ greatly in management's emphasis on external scanning, the propensity of the organization to scan systematically and regularly, the intensity of scanning activities, and the range of information sources utilized (see Fuellhart 1998 for a full discussion of this literature).
- Firms scan for information related not only to strategic levels of decisionmaking, but to routine activities as well (Glasmeier *et al.* 1998; Fuellhart and Glasmeier 2003).

Analysts of information acquisition draw significant distinctions between small- and large-firm behavior (Fuellhart and Glasmeier 2003; Jocoy 2004):

- Acquisition strategies depend on the type of information – simple information is acquired from run-of-the-mill sources, whereas strategic information often has to be explicitly acquired from suppliers of information (Lam 1997).
- Large firms are more systematic and have more complex systems of information gathering than do small firms. Large firms usually have R&D departments, planning departments, and differentiated venues for information acquisition (Capello 1999).
- Large firms have search processes that take advantage of information supply regardless of location. Large firms have the resources to buy professional expertise and have the contacts to find the expertise required.
- Information-acquisition behavior is heterogeneous between big and small firms, and homogeneous across small firms (Henry and Pinch 2000). Big firms are known to use a variety of sources from R&D to business management to human resource assistance.

Finally, many analysts suggest that there are constraints on a firm's ability to learn, based on:

- Competitiveness (Porter 1990); many geography analysts consider this point of departure.
- Organization-specific resources, bounded rationality, and absorptive capacity (Cohen and Levinthal 1990).

In summary, firms primarily scan for basic information on a routine basis; search processes vary by size of firm; firms rarely act in the face of information – the more uncertain the situation, the less likely they are to change their behavior dramatically.

Geographers and regional scientists speak more about the external information environment and have less to say about information after it has been absorbed by the organization. Traditionally, geographers have operated under the assumption that firms in proximity have a greater propensity to learn than those dispersed by virtue of the information that naturally circulates within a "community" of such firms (Gertler 2003a, 2003b; Amin and Cohendet 1999). This type of enhanced-learning effect occurs when a number of firms in the same or similar industries share a space (localization economies) or locations with complementary firms and organizations and thereby collectively enhance information flows (Capello 1999; Lawson and Lorenz 1999; French 2000; Malmberg and Maskell 2002; Fuellhart and Glasmeier 2003).

6.3   The research design

The research discussed in this chapter stems from a survey that we conducted of firms in six different settings. We identified firms using a commercially distributed data set of firm-location information. Through a combination of sampling, surveys, and case studies conducted through site-visit interviews, we studied firms in the eastern United States, with a control group of firms drawn from around the rest of the country.

The approach presented here encompasses environmental assessment/ information acquisition and action. This twofold conception of firm learning enabled a review of the problem of firm competitiveness from three standpoints: (a) the channels and sources of information available (and unavailable) to firms in the surrounding area; (b) the organizational capacity of firms to sort through and assess the relevance and value of information; and (c) the ability to incorporate the acquired information into an executable action plan. On the basis of this perspective, the research team surveyed firms to analyze the (1) types of information firms desire or need; (2) the sources through which information is sought or desired and the characteristics of those sources; and (3) the ways in which such information is used.

Sample

The sample of establishments involved thirteen separate 2- and 3-digit SIC sectors, which we reduced to five major industrial groupings: textiles (SIC 22); carpets (SIC 227); plastics/rubber (SIC 30); fabricated metals (SIC 34); and industrial machinery (SIC 35) (tables 6.1 and 6.2.)

We attempted to select a sample that reflected the size and ownership characteristics of the firms in a particular industry on a national basis. We

Table 6.1 *Industries sampled*

SIC code	Description
2821	Plastic materials, synthetic resins, non-vulcanized elastomers
3082	Unsupported plastic profile shapes
3084	Plastic pipes
3085	Plastic bottles
3086	Plastic foam products
3087	Custom compounding of purchased plastic resins
3088	Plastic plumbing fixtures
3089	Plastic products, n.e.c.
3544	Special dies and tools, jigs and fixtures, and industrial molds

Note: n.e.c. = not elsewhere classified.
Source: The author.

Table 6.2 *Sample region and response rate*

Sample regions (counties)			
Ohio	Ohio	Kentucky	West Virginia
Adam	Jefferson	Boyd	Cabell
Athens	Lawrence	Elliot	Lincoln
Belmont	Meigs	Lawrence	Logan
Brown	Monroe	Carter	Mason
Carroll	Morgan	Greenup	Mingo
Cleremont	Muskingum		Wayne
Columbiana	Noble		
Coshocton	Perry		
Gallia	Pike		
Guernsey	Ross		
Harrison	Scioto		
Highland	Tuscarawas		
Hocking	Vinton		
Holmes	Washington		
Jackson			

Source: Author's survey results.

obtained this information through *American Business Disks*, a CD-ROM database that allows the selection of individual business organizations on a variety of criteria, including industrial sector and geography (specific county-level location).

We mailed the surveys[1] to 750 SMEs. In the Appalachian region, we selected all firms in the industries we studied for this project. We also investigated a comparison group. In order to achieve a (rough) regional/industrial sector perspective, we sampled plastics SMEs in the Boston and southern/eastern Ohio regions; metals and machinery SMEs in northern Pennsylvania, Missouri, and the southern tier of New York; and textile and carpet SMEs primarily in North Carolina, South Carolina, and Georgia. (This regional breakdown is not absolute; for example, we found machine-tool plants in the plastics region.)

In all, 235 organizations returned the survey, which corresponds to a response rate of 31.3 percent. In final form, we asked survey respondents to provide information regarding six areas: (1) organizational characteristics; (2) topics for which additional business information was needed; (3) the frequency of use of information sources; (4) the credibility, relevance, and availability of those information sources; (5) a listing of the four most important information sources and the location of those sources; and (6) the degree of organizational change in an affiliate.

We asked sample organizations to rate the frequency with which they used a variety of common business-information sources that are, for the most part, *external* to the organization. We asked them to rate each information source on a 7-point scale, where 1 indicated the lowest level of usage and 7 represented the highest level of usage. Respondents ranked the availability, relevance, and credibility of a range of information sources. We also asked them to indicate the extent to which organizational change had occurred in several business realms as a result of the acquisition of information over the previous eighteen months on a five-point scale (ranging from 1 for no organizational change to 5 for fundamental levels of organizational change).

Participants

The sample included a preponderance of small firms (not unlike the population of firms throughout the study regions). Almost half (49 percent)

---

[1] Before mailing to the selected sample, we tested the instrument, both in person (by visiting establishments local to the State College of Pennsylvania area and discussing the survey) and through a sample mailing to organizations in the Erie, Pennsylvania, area.

Table 6.3 *Descriptive characteristics of responding firms*

Mode of ownership		Organizational affiliation	
Ownership status	% of total	Affiliation	% of total
		No affiliation	63.64
Corporation	72.5	Branch plant	25.0
Sole proprietor	21.6	Subsidiary	6.8
Partnership	5.9	Affiliate	4.5
Overall	100.0[a]	Overall	100.0[a]

Size of firms		Age of production equipment[b] (years old)				
Size class (no. of employees)	% of total		<3 (%)	4–7 (%)	8–12 (%)	>12 (%)
1–25	45.1	Mean	15.1	19.4	22.9	42.00
26–100	39.2	Minimum	0.0	0.0	0.0	0.00
101–250	7.8	Maximum	75.0	75.0	100.0[a]	100.00
251–500	5.9					
501–1,000	2.0					
1,000+	0.0					
Overall	100.0[a]					

Notes: [a] Columns may not total to 100% due to rounding.
[b] Firms were asked to indicate the proportion of production equipment in each of the four age categories. The mean represents the average percentage of production equipment in each category across all responding firms. The minimum and maximum represent the lowest and highest answers for each category.
Source: Author's survey data

of the responding firms had fewer than twenty-five employees; 24 percent had between twenty-six and 100 employees. Thus, nearly 75 percent of responding firms reported fewer than 100 employees.

The largest sectoral representation was in the carpet and rug producer category, with approximately 15 percent of responding firms. When we added cotton products (7.5 percent), fabric dyeing or finishing (3.5 percent) as well as textile manufacturing (3.0 percent) and screen printing/fabric printing (2.9 percent), we covered approximately 32 percent of responding firms.

Participating firms were predominantly organized as corporations. Approximately 76 percent of all the surveyed firms listed their organizational structure as corporate. Partnerships – representing only 8 percent of total firms responding to the survey – comprised the least common form of organization (table 6.3).

Information needs and sources

Firms indicated very similar information needs, acquisition behaviors, and judgments about the relative merits of information sources. Their primary information needs were narrowly focused on marketing, quality control, and production processes. Their primary information sources were conventional and very limited. The most important sources of strategic information were their own business experience with managers, vendors, customers, magazines, trade shows, and firms in the same industry. Seldom-used sources included state and federal assistance programs, online/databases, university-based programs, consultants, new employees, and firms in other industries, respectively.

Firm size: big differences in information-use behavior

Larger firms were more likely to indicate a need for information about production processes, inventory control, quality control, human resource and training, quality assurance, and regulatory procedures than were small firms. Larger firms were more likely to use customers, vendors, firms in other industries, universities, seminars, trade shows, online/databases, consultants, and trade associations than were small firms. Small firms rated only their own practice and experience higher in the use category.

Larger firms were considerably more likely to consider university and state and federal technical assistance programs as credible, relevant, and available than were smaller firms (all scores were substantially above the mean for larger firms). Other important differences in perceptions of credibility, relevancy, and availability attributable to firm size included information from new employees, customers, seminars, trade shows, databases, consultants, and trade associations.

Both large and small firms had a narrow focus for their information needs (table 6.4). They reported their primary areas of information need as being marketing, quality control, and production processes. Similarly, sources of information were conventional in nature and very limited in number. In descending order of identification, firms listed own practice, customers, vendors, and trade magazines as their primary information sources. The perceived importance of such sources paralleled their general usage. Information source location was largely outside the state of residence. Although there were modest, but discernible, differences in firm perceptions of the relevance, reliability, and availability of sources of information, customers, vendors, trade shows, and trade magazines were nonetheless considered credible, relevant, and available sources of

Table 6.4 *Information needs*

Business area	Mean	Standard deviation	Minimum	Maximum
Marketing strategy	4.6	1.7	1	7
Production processes	4.3	1.7	1	7
Quality assurance	4.2	1.6	1	7
Human resources and training	3.9	1.6	1	7
Procurement	3.8	1.6	1	7
Regulatory environment	3.8	1.7	1	7
Inventory control	3.6	1.7	1	7
Finance	3.3	1.8	1	7

Source: Author's survey data.

information. Firms in a particular industry also considered other firms in the same industry as credible and relevant information sources.

Finally, based on information-acquisition behavior, firms indicated their relative immunity to change. Organizational change based on newly acquired information strongly suggests that conventional behavior governs the action of firms. They are more likely to change suppliers, production technologies, and prices over a two-year period than to change marketing, product mix, etc. In both cases, this type of change is usually the result of events exogenous to the firm (i.e. a supplier goes out of business or the price of a critical input increases unexpectedly). These are common events that occur with unpredictable frequency:

Findings from this study appear robust with respect to geographic location and industry. We found no significant statistical variation between the firms in the sample and the control group. Differences in information use and preferences were predicted by variables such as firm size or amount of recently purchased production technology far more than by other factors. We attribute the findings regarding firm size to the ability of larger organizations to dispense funds to acquire information and to the fact that they have more elaborate structures of information acquisition and utilization.

Our baseline estimations of firm-information acquisition and utilization behaviors largely explain the status quo strategic intent of firms. The extent to which conventional practice governs information-acquisition behavior says a good deal about the schism between the normative view of firm behavior and actual practice. Firms did not appear to venture far from well-worn paths governing information acquisition. Thus, public- and private-sector efforts to alter the path or pattern of information acquisition that deviate substantially from prior experiences may be missing important targets of opportunity. Certainly, one area ripe for further research is the vendor–supplier relationship and its intersection with customers.

There are very clear patterns of information acquisition: firms use particular sources of information and generally do not deviate very far from these preferred sources. The data presented above show that the firms generally did not make significant changes due to the acquisition of strategic information. The results of the mail survey and firm interviews covered these issues in several important ways.

In many cases, the reason for the frequent use of particular sources seemed to be self-evident: individual experience is the most available and probably the most trusted – and, of course, the easiest and cheapest to draw upon. Information from customers and vendors is required constantly within the course of daily business activities, as an organization needs a stable supply of inputs, the proper equipment and processes with which to manufacture the product, and a market in which to sell the goods. However, we did not find an obvious way in which information flows into and is assessed within the firm. Similarly, we could not determine the degree of firms' self-aware acquisition and use of information. Finally, we did not find clear reasons for firms' decision not to use particular sources of information.

6.4   Case study interviews

In this section, I draw heavily on our experiences within "enlightened" organizations in the Appalachian region, in addition to the quantitative analysis, to clarify these points. In particular, I cover two areas:
1. Information flows into and within the firm, and their subsequent use.
2. The ability of firms to act in a self-aware manner.
I conclude with brief comments on the policy significance of these findings.

Information flows

Our survey and the subsequent case-study interviews lend some insight into these questions. We discovered at least three factors in our case-study interviews that were particularly indicative that firms effectively managed information flows into and within their organizations: (1) strong leadership dedicated to an enhanced flow of information into and within a firm; (2) multiple assessments of the information within the firm; and (3) the use of multiple information sources.

We found that one of the most critical variables in distinguishing firms with advanced capabilities to acquire and then use information was strong leadership. Many small firms have only one or two owners/managers. The ability of such firms to learn is tied closely to the priority given to learning by these managers.

Another important factor that influenced the ability of firms to acquire and then use information was the number of multiple assessments of information within the firm. Such assessments allowed the various constituencies within a firm to discuss and analyze the possible impacts of action based upon new information.

Multiple sources of information also were critical to maximizing information flows, to ensuring that this flow was continuous, and to facilitating internal analysis. A philosophy of constant learning and information utilization from a wide variety of sources, including employees, consultants, and trade shows, improved firms' overall competitive position while opening the possibility of acquiring information from many sources. In the long run, this strategy may assist firms in successfully identifying future opportunities and threats.

In summary, the firms that were successful in managing information flows had multiple sources of information, multiple persons who assessed the information, and the leadership to implement identified areas in need of change. In addition, successful firms saw the facilitation of information flows and analysis as continuous; they were organized to learn all of the time, not just when particular problems arose. Unsuccessful firms, by contrast, had limited information flows and assessments and were sometimes plagued by information flows that they did not fully understand.

The ability of firms to be self-aware

An important aspect of firm learning is the degree to which a firm is self-aware of the constant need to acquire information, to translate it into meaningful knowledge, and to then take action. This perspective accords with that of Gertler and Wolfe (2002) in their representation of successful learning behavior. Gertler and Wolfe believe that such behavior reflects reflexivity and the ability of firms to "learn to learn." Self-awareness is a condition experienced by and reflected in the personalities and identities of individuals associated with a firm. It is a purposeful state of awareness that is distinctive and deliberate. The measurement of self-awareness is not captured conveniently through the enunciation of questions about actions. Rather, self-awareness is demonstrated in reactions to, steps toward, and anticipation of, changes in the internal and external environment of the firm – all of which constitute states of awareness, purposeful action, and controlled guidance. Unlike Gertler and Wolfe (2002), we found reflexivity to be a condition with multiple states of being, ranging from reactive to directive in nature.

Reactive self-awareness

Empirical examples of firms' self-aware behavior help us to understand the importance of this attribute. A readily identifiable symbol of self-awareness is the ability to recall the process of deliberation leading up to a major strategic decision. Several potential states of being reflect such awareness. Perhaps the most common mode of self-awareness arises in response to some type of external stimulus. One large textile firm we visited self-consciously displayed its prior efforts to increase its awareness of the importance of external events. The walls in the waiting room sported plaques demonstrating the various management makeovers the firm had undergone, including training in Continuous Quality Improvement (CQI) and the principles of W. Edward Deming. Conversations with the Vice-President for Development revealed elements of the latest fad in management philosophy. Although gestures to become and remain self-aware were evident, more detailed discussions revealed that the firm undertook such actions "because it was what everyone else was doing." Thus the impetus to act came in reaction to others' behaviors, not from within the organization.

Reflective self-awareness

Another mode of self-awareness reflects a firm's ability to evaluate itself based on past experience and the ability to change in reaction to past modes of behavior. In this instance, a firm might still lack an ability to act completely self-awarely by anticipating how a change could and would alter the future trajectory of the firm. The manager of a machine shop that manufactured turbine blade replacements used the metaphor of an emergency room to describe the firm's mode of operation. The firm is called into service by desperate customers willing to pay almost any price to make their capital equipment operational. (A power plant disabled by a broken turbine blade can lose as much as $50,000 a week in revenues.) The manager was able to diagnose how such a metaphor came to shape the behavior of the firm and how it influenced its organization. The ability to react did not translate into self-awareness of the impact of present and future gestures that would unalterably shape the trajectory and therefore the organization of the firm. In an effort to get off the "emergency room tread mill," the firm was presented with the possibility of a long-term contract for the production of a standardized product. The rapidity with which the decision was made to move into mass manufacturing precluded the time needed to contemplate how such a decision would affect a firm's operations. Given the firm's past history with handling everything on an "emergency" basis regardless of cost, the general manager only vaguely understood the transformation associated with moving towards a standardized product market. As he noted, "we will respond to changes as they occur."

Directed self-awareness

A more complex understanding of cause and effect in the acquisition and application of information is the firm's self-aware decision to move in a new direction and to have the will and ability to make the necessary adjustments to achieve that goal. The acquisition of a simple accounting program to manage payroll and inventory presented a carpet firm with the opportunity to automate virtually all the phases of its business. The owner and his administrative assistant jointly developed the firm's future vision and its subsequent direction. The President assessed the trajectory of the market and saw it evolving towards higher standards achieved only through the application of significantly more sophisticated technology and managerial practice. The administrative assistant recognized that this vision would have to encompass a very different type of internal organization. Over the course of ten years, the firm made major investments in software and organizational training, substantially in excess of the industry average. The firm persistently recognized that the firm's growth was firmly tied to new information acquisition and application, a recognition that influenced hiring decisions and was reinforced by a decentralized system of information acquisition and adaptation. The firm is in an intermediate stage of internalizing this new information acquisition and adaptation ability. In addition, it is constantly revisiting "staying the course," while feeding back into the planning process lessons learned during this period of change that will determine its future direction.

Firms, like people, demonstrate varying degrees of self-awareness. Some firms simply copy others, thus relying on someone else's assessment of the significance of environmental change. Other firms understand the world by reflecting on past experiences and a historical view rather than one informed by future trends. A small number of firms combines the experience of their histories with an acute awareness of what is possible – and, therefore, what is likely to occur in the future – and then acts. These organizations, to the greatest extent possible, control aspects of their destiny.

6.5   Conclusions

By juxtaposing and integrating a broad-based survey of firm needs, uses, and perceptions of strategic business information with case-study findings, I provide a broader, more representative assessment of the capabilities of SMEs in acquiring and utilizing strategic business and technical information than is provided through the use of a methodological approach alone.

My analyses of the information sources used by firms reveal significant differences across firms based on size. It should be noted, however, that while there are significant differences between the use of particular sources and firm size, some rankings are low in absolute terms for both large and small firms. For example, large firms use university resources more often, but both large and small firms place little emphasis on this source of information.

Analyses of the relationship between firm size and perceived credibility, relevance, and availability of information sources support relevant distinctions between the groups. Differences associated with the size of the firm also are evident in comparisons of the likelihood of organizational change based on externally acquired information. Larger firms were more likely to change as a result of the acquisition of external information than were small firms in all significant cases. However, again, all areas of organizational change are relatively close to the midpoint of the 5-point scale used in this question. In general, firms in this study either see little need to change or are highly change-averse. To the extent that policies are considered a means to enhance information, particularly in the case of small firms, new information will most likely be accepted if it is conveyed within the context of existing small-firm search strategies. Similarly, new information has to be in a form that small firms can absorb and that is delivered by trusted intermediaries. This would include sales, distribution links, and technically-based business organizations.

Perhaps the final conclusion loops back to the introduction. There, I contended that academic notions of how firms work are crude approximations of actual occurrence. If this is indeed the case, then analysts need to rethink many of our notions of what underlies firm practices and outcomes. This leads us to a behavioral theory of the firm and away from the more normative tendencies evident in aspects of current research on learning regions. Certainly policy and public programming would have a greater chance of getting closer to the target of improving firm competitiveness if they were based on a realistic appraisal of how firms actually operated on a day-to-day basis.

REFERENCES

Amin, A. and P. Cohendet, 1999. "Learning and Adaptation in Decentralised Business Networks," *Environment and Planning D: Society and Space*, 17(1): 87–104

Capello, R., 1999. "Spatial Transfer of Knowledge in High Technology Milieux: Learning Versus Collective Learning Processes," *Regional Studies*, 33(4): 353–365

Cohen, W. and D. Levinthal, 1990. "Absorptive Capacity: A New Perspective on Learning and Innovation," *Administrative Science Quarterly*, 35(1): 128–152

Cooke, P., 2002. "Regional Innovation Systems and Regional Competitiveness," in M. Gertler and D. Wolfe (eds.), *Innovation and Social Learning: Institutional Adaptation in an Era of Technological Change*, London: Palgrave: 177–203

Feller, I., A. Glasmeier, and M. Marks, 1996. "Issues and Perspectives on Evaluating Manufacturing Modernization Programs," *Research Policy*, 25(2): 309–319

Florida, R., 2002. "The Learning Region," in M. Gertler and D. Wolfe (eds.), *Innovation and Social Learning: Institutional Adaptation in an Era of Technological Change*, London: Palgrave: 117–138

French, S., 2000. "Re-Scaling the Economic Geography of Knowledge and Information: Constructing Life Assurance Markets," *Geoforum*, 31: 101–119

Fuellhart, K., 1998. *Networks, Location and Information Acquisition: An Analysis of Small Manufacturing Establishments*, Department of Geography, Pennsylvania State University, unpublished dissertation

Fuellhart, K. and A. Glasmeier, 2003. "Acquisition, Assessment and Use of Business Information by Small- and Medium-sized Businesses: A Demand Perspective," *Entrepreneurship and Regional Development*, 15(3): 229–252

Gertler, M., 2003a. "A Cultural Economic Geography of Production: Are We Learning by Doing?," in K. Anderson, M. Domosh, S. Pike, and N. Thrift (eds.), *Handbook of Cultural Geography*, London: Sage: 131–146

    2003b. "Tacit Knowledge and the Economic Geography of Context, or the Undefinable Tacitness of Being (There)," *Journal of Economic Geography*, 3(1): 75–99

Gertler, M. and D. Wolfe, 2002. *Innovation and Social Learning: Institutional Adaptation in an Era of Technological Change*, London: Palgrave

Glasmeier, A., 1991. "Technological Discontinuities and Flexible Production Networks: The Case of Switzerland and the World Watch Industry," *Research Policy*, 21: 469–485

    1999. "Territory-Based Regional Development Policy and Planning in a Learning Economy: The Case of 'Real Service Centers' in Industrial Districts," *European Urban and Regional Studies*, 6(1): 73–84

    2001. *Manufacturing Time: Global Competition in the Watch Industry, 1795–2000*, New York: Guilford Press

Glasmeier, A., I. Feller, M. Marks, and K. Fuellhart, 1998. "The Relevance of Firm Learning to the Design of Manufacturing Modernization Programs," *Economic Development Quarterly*, 12(2): 107–123

Glasmeier, A., A. Kays, J. Thompson, and R. Gurwitt, 1995. "Branch Plants and Rural Development in the Age of Globalization," State Overview Series, Rural Economic Policy Program, The Aspen Institute, monograph

Harrison, B. and A. Glasmeier, 1997. "Why Business Alone Won't Redevelop the Inner City: A Friendly Critique of Michael Porter's Approach to Urban Revitalization," *Economic Development Quarterly*, 11(1): 29–38

128 *Amy Glasmeier*

Henry, N. and S. Pinch, 2000. "Spatializing Knowledge: Placing the Knowledge Community of Motor Sport Valley," *Geoforum*, 31: 191–208

Jocoy, C., 2004. *Contrasts in Learning: The Social and Spatial Context of Learning in Innovative Firms*, Department of Geography, Pennsylvania State University, PhD dissertation

Keeble, D. and F. Wilkinson, 1999. "Collective Learning and Knowledge Development in the Evolution of Regional Clusters of High Technology SMEs in Europe," *Regional Studies*, 33(4): 295–303

Lam, A., 1997, "Embedded Firms, Embedded Knowledge: Problems of Collaboration and Knowledge Transfer in Global Collaborative Ventures," *Organization Studies*, 18(6): 973–996

Lambooy, J., 2002. "Knowledge and Urban Economic Development: An Evolutionary Perspective," *Urban Studies*, 39(5–6): 1019–1035

Lawson, C. and E. Lorenz, 1999. "Collective Learning: Tacit Knowledge and Regional Innovative Capacity," *Regional Studies*, 33(4): 305–317

Malmberg, A. and P. Maskell, 2002. "The Elusive Conception of Localization Economies: Towards a Knowledge-Based Theory of Spatial Clustering," *Environment and Planning A*, 34(3): 429–449

Meeus, M. T., L. A. Oerlemans, and F. W. Boekema, 2000. "Innovation and Proximity: Theoretical Perspectives," in M. Green and R. McNoughton (eds.), *Industrial Networks and Proximity*, London: Ashgate: 17–46

Oerlemans, L., M. Meeus, and F. Boekema, 2000. "Learning, Innovation, and Proximity: An Empirical Exploration of Patterns of Learning: A Case Study," in F. Boekema, K. Morgan, S. Bakkers, and R. Rutten, (eds.), *Knowledge, Innovation, and Economic Growth: The Theory and Practice of Learning Regions*, London: Edward Elgar: 137–165

Porter, M., 1990. *Competitive Strategy*, Cambridge, MA: Harvard University Press

Storper, M., 2002. "Institutions and the Learning Economy," in M. Gertler and D. Wolfe (eds.), *Innovation and Social Learning: Institutional Adaptation in an Era of Technological Change*, London: Palgrave: 177–203

7   Theorizing the gendered institutional bases of innovative regional economies

Mia Gray and Al James

7.1   Introduction

During the past two decades, scholars and policymakers have debated how best to promote and harness innovation in regional economies. Much of the resulting regional literature focuses on creating conditions conducive to knowledge creation, information dissemination, entrepreneurship, and learning. However, although this literature extensively documents the formal interactions that underpin innovative regional economies, it is less satisfying in its treatment of the informal socioinstitutional bases. Critically, we still do not fully understand how distinctive patterns of social relations reinforce more formal interactions within these regions, and hence how they contribute to economic performance. Although many analysts typically suggest something intangible that permits innovation to proceed in some places but not in others, they often fail to specify the exact nature of the processes through which key sociorelational structures promote innovative activity more successfully in some regions than in others.

One major component of this problem is a dominant tendency within the regional learning and innovation literature to treat elite workers as an homogeneous group with little differentiation across gender, race, or cultural background. Although scholars argue that collective learning and innovation processes are enhanced by a shared social environment that supports interaction (e.g. Lorenz 1992; Keeble and Wilkinson 1999), this shared social environment is too often conceptualized as implicitly masculine, and hence distinctive patterns of female work and social interaction are sidelined. In part, this gap in the literature potentially reflects the limited numbers of women working in the fields of science and technology at the national and international scales. However, while women are

Thanks to Linda McDowell, Amy Glasmeier, Bhaskar Vira, and Irene Hardhill for their helpful comments on earlier drafts of the chapter. Al James would also like to thank his Mom. The research on which this chapter draws was funded as part of the "Regional Impact of the Information Society on Employment and Integration" (RISESI) project.

underrepresented in high-technology (high-tech) firms' total workforces, their proportion in the high-tech workplace has nevertheless increased from the late 1980s when much of the new industrial-district literature was written. There is also considerable national variation: while women make up only 22 percent of the professional ICT workforce in the United Kingdom, this compares with 33 percent in the European Union, and 45 percent in the United States (AMICUS 2002).[1] Further, we argue that the lack of attention to gender in the regional learning and innovation literature is also a function of the social construction of elite workers within high-tech firms. Over time, the attributes needed to fulfill a job successfully within a particular firm become imbued with socially constructed job characteristics and thus are often characterized as predominantly "male" or "female" (see also McDowell 1997). As regional learning and innovation scholars have drawn on these corporate case studies, so their theoretical accounts have inevitably mirrored dominant social constructions of the "typical" high-tech worker as inherently "male."

Encouragingly, however, a growing number of scholars have begun to unpack these dominant social constructions within high-tech firms' workforces, focusing on the social construction of skill, occupational segregation, and the gendered nature of low-end contingent and high-end elite workers in high-tech labor markets (see, e.g. Massey, Quintas, and Wield 1992; Henry and Massey 1995; Massey 1995). Massey, Quintas, and Wield (1992), in particular, explore high-tech industries' spatial organization, social divisions of labor, and social inequality, focusing on the development of science parks in the United Kingdom. They analyze the intersection between social construction of skill and women's exclusion from many elite scientific jobs. However, while we welcome these studies, they still fail to specify the *processes* by which the reworked gender composition of high-tech workforces affects intra-firm and interfirm learning and innovation processes in the region. Crucially, rather than simply describing the gendered sociorelational *properties* of these regions, we need to specify *how* these social relations affect female workers' abilities both to access and use new sources of information and expertise on behalf of their respective firms, relative to their male colleagues. These socioeconomic phenomena form the focus of this chapter. Specifically, we examine gendered patterns of work, employment, and networks of social interaction within the ICT sector in Cambridge, England, one of Europe's foremost high-tech regional economies. For this analysis, we follow Benner (2002), who distinguishes between changes in how we work (work) and changes in the work contract (employment).

---

[1] This figure includes technical and administrative professionals. The estimate comes from AMICUS, the union that organizes the IT industry in the United Kingdom.

We argue that many women's working time is structured in a way that minimises opportunities to exchange tacit knowledge, which undermines their role in diffusing knowledge both within and between firms in the region. As such, we root our gender analysis within a broader focus on the social determinants of competitiveness, productivity, and innovative capacity that span the spatial scales of the individual worker, firm, and region. Crucially, these issues all have central public-policy relevance yet often remain sidelined in sociocultural accounts of firms in the region. This therefore forms the basis for our final discussion, which centers on the wider implications of our analysis and the need for more socially informed regional development policies. We are also keen to move beyond the simple male–female gender binaries that characterize much of the literature to show how gender is a much more nuanced phenomenon, typically premised on parental responsibilities, age, and position in the life-cycle.

7.2   Theorizing innovation and learning in the region

Over the last two decades, processes of knowledge production, learning, and innovation have been widely recognized as fundamental to understanding patterns of regional economic development. In many high-tech subsectors, the very terms of capitalist competition are said to have undergone a fundamental shift in favor of quality, innovativeness, responsiveness to market trends, and timeliness (Best 1990; Leadbeater 1999). As such, competitiveness is sustained only by becoming a moving target, through technological learning and innovation, to anticipate and outrun attempts at imitation by competitors (Porter 1990; Castells 1996; Storper 1996). Innovation may involve new-product development based on R&D, or new-process development based on the application of new technologies for continuous incremental improvements in the production process (Gray and Parker 1998). Either way, those firms that can learn and innovate faster become more competitive because their knowledge is scarce and therefore cannot be immediately imitated or transferred to new market entrants (Lundvall 1992). Firms that innovate more consistently and rapidly thus often demand higher skills, pay higher wages, and offer more stable prospects for their workforce (OECD 1996). As such, the regional sociorelational underpinnings of innovative firms have attracted considerable policy and academic attention.

Specifically, scholars have focused on how formal networks of relationships between firms, the public sector, and financial, educational and research institutions serve as sources of knowledge dissemination and innovation within the region (e.g. Cooke and Morgan 1993, 1998; Morgan 1997; Wolfe 1997; Braczyk, Cooke, and Heidenreich 1998;

Hudson 1999; Maskell and Malmberg 1999). Additionally, they recognize that informal networks of interaction between firms' employees are crucial, premised on interpersonal face-to-face contacts, which aid the circulation of tacit (non-codified) knowledge within the region (Lundvall and Johnson 1994; Malmberg and Maskell 1997). When individuals with diverse and partially overlapping knowledge come together and collectively seek to articulate their ideas about a new product or technology, they are forced to clarify those ideas and to derive more adequate concepts and models about the technology they are trying to develop (Lawson and Lorenz 1999: 312). Innovation is therefore increasingly regarded as a fundamentally interactive process and hence inseparable from the regional sociorelational context in which it occurs (Malecki and Oinas 1999; Gertler, Wolfe, and Garkut 2000; Asheim 2001). However, even with the theoretical developments that have occurred in industrial district and regional learning theories over the last two decades, the exact nature of the links between regional social structures, the workings of innovative regional economies and the firms within them, are still not fully understood.

Problematically, while scholars return again and again to the sociorelational *properties* of these regions, they rarely specify the exact nature of the mechanisms and processes by which regional social structures promote innovative activity more successfully in some regions than in others (Asheim 1996; Storper 1997). There is often circularity in these arguments: innovation occurs because of the presence of certain social institutions, and those social institutions are what exist in regions where there is innovation. Part of the problem, we argue, is that scholars rarely distinguish between different gendered patterns of work and social interaction in the region. This is a glaring omission. Not only do our results suggest that intra-firm learning and innovation processes are fundamentally gendered, but that gender relations also impact on the mechanisms by which information is diffused *between* firms in the region. Our analysis focuses on the high-tech regional economy centered on Cambridge. Although this region has already been the subject of various high-profile studies, scholars have largely sidelined the role of gender in their analyses of the region's technological growth dynamic. However, we argue that we can never hope fully to understand the workings of innovative regional economies outside of these gendered social relations.

7.3   Silicon fen? Exploring the "Cambridge phenomenon"

Few other regions have been so consistently held up as an example of successful high-tech growth in the United Kingdom by politicians, policy analysts, and academics alike than Cambridge. Notably, the European Union, in its annual ranking of member states' innovative capacities, praised the Cambridge region for its high rates of innovation and enterprise. The study ranked the European Union's 148 regions on seventeen indicators, such as human resources, the creation of new knowledge, the transmission and application of knowledge, and innovation finance. It found that the UK Eastern region, where Cambridge is located, is ranked in the top ten in these innovation measures (European Commission 2002). Cambridge has thus come to represent a key European center of scientific and technological innovation (Keeble 2001). The level of success experienced by firms in Cambridge's high-tech cluster (as well as the lack of attention given to various corporate failures) has inevitably led politicians to use the region, in both symbolic and material ways, as a model for other regions in the United Kingdom. Indeed, in April 2002, Lord Sainsbury (2002) highlighted the Cambridge economy as *the* exemplary high-tech growth cluster in the United Kingdom, outlining the efforts of the Department of Trade and Industry (DTI) to sustain growth in the Cambridge economy *and* to replicate the region's success in other areas of the UK economy.

Through a series of studies, scholars have shown that while the Cambridge high-tech economy is clearly smaller than some other so-called "blueprint" industrial districts, it is nevertheless based on the same socioeconomic structure as other regional innovation systems, technopoles, or learning regions (Castells and Hall 1994; Lawton-Smith *et al.* 1998; Keeble *et al.* 1999; Lawson 1999; Heffernan and Garnsey 2002). Scholars have consistently attributed Cambridge's high-tech growth to interfirm networks of social relationships and untraded interdependencies that underpin the region's formal institutional infrastructure. Notably, Lawton-Smith *et al.* (1998) argue that high-tech growth in the Cambridge region is underpinned by a high degree of social and cultural cohesion between both firms and individuals. Other studies have also found high rates of interfirm interaction in Cambridge's high-tech economy. For example, Lawson *et al.* (1997) found that over three-quarters of firms in their sample had close links with other firms in the Cambridge region. Keeble's work on the region also reinforces this interpretation, demonstrating a high level of formal and informal networking among individuals, firms, and other lead educational, government and research institutions within the Cambridge region (Keeble 2001).

However, despite the high rates of innovation and new-firm formation, Cambridge's regional growth rates have disappointed many regional commentators. As early as 1989, Saxenian (1989: 448) argued that "upon closer examination, the promise of Cambridge and its scores of

high-technology businesses disappears like the Cheshire cat's grin."
Studying the Cambridge economy in the late 1980s, Saxenian found
that small firms in Cambridge tended to remain small and focused only
upon a narrow range of activities – rarely going beyond the research
stage into development, prototyping, or manufacturing (Saxenian 1989).
Saxenian's work has subsequently been extended by Athreye (2004),
who argues that although the region excels in creating new start-ups,
widespread poor marketing strategies and managerial skills mean that
few firms are able to grow to even medium size. Of course, small firms
are not necessarily bad for regional growth; indeed they are rightly celebrated as an essential component of growth. However, a regional economy that only has small firms with few large firms anchoring growth has
fewer means to respond to market changes. This point has been made by
Walter Herriot, a local-industry player whom many consider the "grand-
father of the Cambridge phenomenon." He has spoken publicly about
the Cambridge region's lack of world-class companies and the inability
of many firms in the region to move beyond the research stage, concluding
that "Cambridge has failed to fulfill its potential" (Herriot 2004).

However, despite these two sets of authors having highly divergent
views on the validity of Cambridge as an exemplar high-tech regional
economy, they are nevertheless united in their sidelining (indeed, totally
ignoring in many instances) the role of gender relations in shaping the
socioinstitutional bases of the region. Similarly, although Massey and her
colleagues' research does offer a valuable exception as already described
(see Massey, Quintas, and Wield 1992; Henry and Massey 1995; Massey
1995), they have yet to link gendered divisions of labor – and their underlying expectations regarding males' versus females' available work hours
and flexibilities – to firms' innovative capacities. In this chapter, we therefore extend this earlier work to examine explicitly the impact of gender
structures on key patterns of work and social interaction widely theorized to underpin learning and innovation at the levels of the firm and
the region.

To explore these issues, we focus specifically on the ICT sector, which is
particularly well represented in the Cambridge region. Estimates of the
size of the ICT sector in Cambridgeshire vary extensively, as different
bodies use different definitions of sectors comprising the ICT sector.
However, using very conservative methods, we estimate that it currently
comprises almost 1,000 companies that employ over 17,000 workers.

The subsectors most heavily represented within Cambridge's ICT
sector and their associated SIC codes are: Software consultancy and
supply (SIC 72.20), Telecommunications (SIC 64.20), and Scientific
instrumentation (SIC 33.20), and together these subsectors account for

Table 7.1 *Employment and location quotients in the ICT industry in Cambridgeshire, 1999*

SIC	Description	Cambridge employment	Location quotient
	Manufacture of		
30.02	Computers and other info processing machinery	1721	5.6
31.30	Insulated wire and cable	290	2.0
32.10	Electronic valves, tubes and other electronic components	933	2.6
33.20	Instruments for measuring, checking testing or navigation	2824	3.8
64.20	Telecommunications	2896	1.6
72.10	Hardware consultancy	267	2.5
72.20	Software consultancy and supply	5974	2.7
72.40	Database activities	161	1.8
72.60	Other computer-related activities	1376	2.3

Note: SIC = Standard Industrial Classification.
Source: Cambridge County Council (1999).

67.5 percent of ICT employment within the Cambridge region. The relative strength of these subsectors in terms of employment is manifest in their respective location quotients, a measure of concentration and specialization (table 7.1).

The ICT firms in Cambridge are also characteristic of the UK high-tech industry at the national scale (see e.g. Keeble 1989, 2001). First, almost 60 percent of all ICT firms in Cambridgeshire employ ten or fewer workers (indeed, only 10 percent of all ICT firms have over fifty employees). Second, these small ICT firms in Cambridge also display a social structure that parallels the industry nationally, in terms of a persistence of strong gendered occupational segregation (see e.g. Humphries and Rubery 1995; Crompton, Gallie, and Purcell 1996; McDowell 1997). Women represent 6.6 percent of employees working in engineering and technology occupations in the United Kingdom (table 7.2). However, this figure includes engineers in many manufacturing industries where women are particularly poorly represented.

When we examine the ICT sector by itself, women's representation rises slightly. For example, in a study, Millar and Jagger (2001) found that 13 percent of workers employed in the UK ICT industry in 2001 were female. These figures seem to be reflected in the Cambridge region, where women hold between 9 and 15 percent of all ICT jobs (Gray and Damery 2003). More fundamentally, female labor-force participation

Table 7.2 *Employees in UK professional occupations, by gender, Spring 2000 (%)*

Occupation	Men	Women
Engineers and Technologists	93.4	6.6
Architects, Town Planners, Surveyors	84.9	15.1
Business and Financial Professionals	66.6	33.4
Natural Scientists	64.8	35.2
Health Professionals	56.4	43.6
Legal Professionals	56.4	43.6
Teaching Professionals	36.3	63.7
Other Professional Occupations	44.9	55.1
All Professional Occupations	57.7	42.3

Source: Labor Force Survey (2001).

rates in the ICT sector continue to increase from the late 1980s when much of the new industrial literature was written. It is therefore imperative that we factor women into our analyses of high-tech regional economic development.

7.4   Methodology

To explore the impact of gender upon workers' abilities to contribute to intra-firm and interfirm learning and innovation processes, we conducted initial interviews with eighty-eight employees in ten leading firms in Cambridge's software and engineering sectors. This approach was based on the premise that if we are to understand the dynamics of a regional economy then we should focus on its *lead* sectors (following Markusen 1994). Focusing predominantly on elite high-tech workers, our respondents included both female and male human resources managers, chief executive officers (CEOs), and local engineers, scientists, and technologists. In the second phase of the study, we focused on a subset of three of the initial ten firms. We conducted a series of ten group interviews with between three and seven male and female professional and scientists and technologists sitting in on each interview. We segregated group interviews by gender to facilitate freer exploration of issues related to gender.

We used an open-ended interview protocol to facilitate the acquisition of detailed "insider knowledge" not amenable to more structured questionnaire methods (Schoenberger 1991). Our interviews typically lasted between one and one-and-a-half hours and, to ensure consistency, we used a checklist of topics to be covered with all respondents, while simultaneously allowing them freedom to describe their own experiences in their own terms. We questioned respondents across a series of themes, including formal corporate interactions, informal socializing, and their intra-firm and interfirm peer relationships. We also encouraged respondents to reflect upon their implicit and explicit responsibilities at work and their fulfillment of them. We tape-recorded the interviews and pushed respondents for concrete examples wherever possible. We also employed various secondary data sources (annual reports, memos, etc.) as part of a source triangulation strategy to verify interview responses.

We systematically analyzed the interview transcripts through an iterative process of progressive qualitative hypothesis testing. This involved coding the data to break them down, recategorizing them, examining the links between groups, and then developing hypotheses with regard to the mechanisms and patterns that best fit the data and helped explain them. In order to make our analysis more robust, we also employed "member checking" – that is, checking the credibility of our analytic categories, constructs, and hypotheses with members of the group from which we originally obtained the data. Although these respondents do not have privileged access to the truth, they *do* have privileged access to their own opinions and meanings (Baxter and Eyles 1997), and it is upon these experiences that our analysis has been primarily based. Further, we gleaned through highly personal, albeit formalized, exchanges much of the information upon which we base this analysis and have therefore not named names in the write-up itself. Instead we describe the relevant respondent's position as far as possible within the boundaries of anonymity and also refer to firms by pseudonyms to protect the confidentiality of our sources.

7.5   Deconstructing the gendered social bases of innovative regional economies

In the following subsections, we describe ways in which gender relations shape distinctive patterns of work and sociocultural interaction among male and female workers within Cambridge's high-tech regional economy, focusing on how female workers' abilities to contribute to processes widely theorized to positively underpin learning and innovation at the levels of the firm and the region are constrained relative to their male colleagues. There are four key areas: intensity of work hours; nature of job contract; patterns of labor mobility; and patterns of informal afterwork socializing. We now cover all of these.

High intensity of work hours

In her analysis of Silicon Valley and Route 128's divergent performances through the 1980s, Saxenian (1994) highlights how Silicon Valley's engineers, often young men without wives or families, instead developed shared identities around the project of advancing new technologies. She argues that their lack of local family ties allowed them to work long unsociable work hours and enhanced their willingness to be committed to the firm. This, in turn, facilitates the completion of large workloads in short periods of calendar time, particularly when bringing a new product to market, and hence significantly contributes to the region's technological dynamism. In the same vein, Reich (2000: 159) explores lengthening work weeks in high-tech firms: "high-powered jobs in the emerging economy tend to demand total commitment. It's all or nothing – fast track or slow track. If you want to remain on the fast track, you have to work late with customers and clients, be available at all hours, develop your contacts and connections, and stay abreast of new developments." The necessity of long working hours is often regarded as particularly important in information-intensive industries where competition is based on constant new product development, which allows monopoly pricing practices until market rivals emerge.

These intense working patterns are largely self-reinforcing within the New Economy, based on mutual expectations within the firm. Many studies suggest that employees work long hours as a visible display of loyalty and commitment to the firm[2] (Williams 2000; Perrons 2002). However, others argue that there is a clear relationship between increased work hours and productivity. Notably, the National Center on the Education Quality of the Workforce (NCEQW) estimates that, for nonmanufacturing firms, a 10 percent increase in work hours results in a 6.3 percent increase in establishment productivity (US NCEQW 1995). This suggests that employees are not merely marking time or sending a signal of commitment, but using the extra hours to accomplish necessary work. Whether actually correlated with increased productivity or not, long hours have become expected and required in many high-tech firms, certainly among many of those in the ICT sector.

However, while yielding a perceived strategic advantage to the firm, these intensive work patterns have direct implications for employees' abilities to balance the ever-increasing demands of work with an active home

---

[2] For example, Perrons (2002) highlights how employees not only work long hours, but also actively advertise their commitment to the firm, and high levels of work stress, by including deliberate errors in e-mails and making appointments difficult to arrange.

life. As such, we argue that they are fundamentally gendered. Specifically, the expectations parallel Williams' (2000) notion of the "ideal worker" who *can* maintain long work hours, because of a supportive partner and few domestic responsibilities, both of which are premised on traditional *male* patterns of work. Despite the inroads made by women into elite occupations in the high-tech sector, many women still perform the majority of duties at home (Schor 1992; Hochschild 1997; McDowell, 2001). Family and home commitments therefore make it difficult for many women to work the long "unsociable hours"[3] required not only for their own career progression, but also potentially for *firm* productivity in high-tech markets in which time-to-market or a quick response to customer needs is key.

Our results also suggest that many elite female employees working in Cambridge's high-tech economy opt for shorter average work-weeks with fewer total hours relative to their male colleagues. Many of our female respondents consistently outlined how their work-weeks are distinctively structured, driven primarily by family responsibilities and childcare commitments, which actively "gate" their hours at work. Gated hours, in turn, undermine female employees' abilities to take part in everyday events and interactions that are widely theorized to underpin firms' innovative capacities and which assume employees *are* available outside of normal working hours:

Kick[ing] in at the crack of dawn is not attractive to females. I'm not saying women don't have the same amount of energy, but it's very difficult to sustain when they have to get back to their child-care. They can't just jump on a plane off to Japan tomorrow . . . Whereas our single blokes, through their own enjoyment of work *are* able to work whatever hours God sends. (Head of Personnel, BSN, male with children)

Indeed, the pattern is well illustrated by many of our female respondents who once worked very long work-weeks but have since actively reduced them following the birth of their child in order to spend more time with them:

In my last job I was working sixty to eighty hours per week, and travelling a lot. It was quite tough, but not too bad because I didn't have any kids. Once I had my first kid I went back to work full time after about 4 months, but now my full time week is only forty-ish hours. While I typically go into the office four times a week, I tend to do quite a lot of work at home in the evenings when the kids have gone to bed. (Engineer, TUJ, female with children)

---

[3] See Perrons (2000).

Our results are further consistent with McDowell's (2001) analysis in which she seeks to make visible the social reproduction that occurs in the home and which *allows* male employees with children to "work all the hours God sends." Crucially, many of our male respondents can only work these intense hours *because* they are supported by female partners who do *not*:

Fundamentally we expect people to work ludicrously long hours at times. But blokes *can* do that more easily. So my wife could not work [here]. At the end of the day she bears the brunt of the kids, even though the fact we have child-care etc., the fact is that she's the one there now making the kiddies their tea, not me. If I was to take on that more balanced parentage, I couldn't work here. (Head of Personnel, BSN, male with children)

In response, many firms make extensive use of flexible work hours as a means to enable their employees to balance commitments at home and work. However, while women are able to take advantage of flexible time arrangements to fit work hours around childcare or school hours, and so fulfill their work commitments in terms of *absolute* numbers of hours, this type of flexibility nevertheless has several intangible drawbacks for the employee. Significantly, our female respondents consistently highlighted how, relative to their male colleagues, they miss out on crucial informal interactions within the firm in which knowledge, often tacit, is circulated:

There's sort of a prescribed coffee and tea time each afternoon and each morning. Generally I don't go because I feel that I'm already there for such a short period of time that I find it difficult to justify. What you're doing is doing your hours as opposed to being able to contribute fully to what is a very high commitment, very passionate organisation. I don't know how to reconcile that. (Scientist, NSD, female with children)

Indeed, several respondents highlighted how missing out on the informal knowledge and gossip also potentially constrains females' occupational mobility within the firm relative to their male colleagues, demonstrating how issues of gender equity and innovative capacity in the firm are inseparable.

Overall, our results suggest that work patterns within the firm are fundamentally gendered and have significant implications for firms' innovative capacities, primarily through female workers' constrained abilities to contribute to informal information diffusion within the firm. We are not arguing that these issues are solely the preserve of female employees; however, our interviews do suggest that they are experienced to a greater degree among females than males, also confirmed by our male respondents themselves. Nevertheless, this is not to argue for some monolithic "female high-tech worker." Many of the young female respondents do not

find the long-hours' culture problematic, as they have few family commitments at this point in their life-cycle. These younger women often
work the same intense hours as their male colleagues and can therefore
be seen as "honorary males" (Acker 1990):

You can't be seen to go home before ten o'clock, then you have to be back in at
8 in the morning . . . I've done the whole thirty-six hours on the trot routine.
(Female engineer, BSO, single no children)

However, when they do form families, women often find it increasingly
difficult to join in the long-hours' work cultures which predominate in
high-technology firms. However, participation is not solely based on gender, but also on active parental duties. Many of our male respondents,
especially those who are active parents, also find it difficult to take part in
the long-hours culture. Either way, conventional analyses tend to ignore
these key constraints; constraints that are not only fundamentally gendered, but which also shape patterns of information and knowledge transfer within and between firms.

Nature of job contract

The second area in which gender relations shape innovative capacity
within Cambridge's high-tech regional economy concerns the nature of
job contracts and workers' differing professional status. In contrast to
Benner's (2002) research on non-standard work in Silicon Valley, our
results suggest that within ICT firms in the Cambridge region, full-
time jobs are regarded as an icon of validation, consistent with Massey's
broader (1997) analysis of occupational structure in the high-tech sector.
Although most jobs in the sector are full-time, significantly the vast majority of part-time workers that we encountered in our study were women,
even within high-end elite positions. Further, all of the human resource
managers we interviewed stated that very few of their firms' male employees worked part-time. Although the managers and others often framed
the ability to work part-time in a positive discourse of increased flexibility
and employee choice, we argue that it also has negative implications both
for part-time employees and for the firms that employ them. There are
three key areas.

First, our female respondents consistently outlined how these contracts
mean that they often forgo job promotion:

My contract has been for three years, full time in the beginning, then one and a
half years into the contract, I had my second child and took five or six months
completely off work. After that I worked part time for several months. At the end
of the day, I'm judged on my performance, but no-one takes into consideration

that what I've achieved has been done in two years even though it was a three-year contract. So really I am disadvantaged by having had children. (Scientist, NSD, female with children)

Our female respondents were also keen to outline how it is not simply they that lose out personally, but that the firm itself also loses out through its not fully capitalizing on female employees' skill-sets, knowledge, and social contacts.

Second, as with reduced intensity of work hours, the predominance of females in part-time work contracts in our case-study firms was consistently presented to us in terms of female employees' missed opportunities for informal, yet crucial, social interactions through which information and tacit knowledge[4] is circulated in the firm:

Yeah, we are immensely flexible. People work flexitime: some start work at 7.30 in the morning, whereas others start at 10.30 and other times in between. Most people on part time contracts of different types are female. Although we are predominantly a male company, 80% of the company is male, 70% of our part-timers are female – half in their career and half at home. You end up with female employees that are no longer so connected to the social capital at work, which is mainly a bunch of blokes nattering around the cooler about whatever big is going on right now. (HR Manager, BSN, male with children)

This highlights how it is more difficult for an engineer on a part-time schedule to participate in informal social interactions within the firm. For example, female part-time respondents often commented that they needed to "make every minute at work count" and thus felt guilty about taking any tea breaks or chatting with colleagues in the halls. This time-pressure on part-time employees closes a major route through which tacit knowledge is disseminated within the firm.

Third, the predominance of females in part-time work contracts also means that they often tend to be assigned piecemeal non-essential work, in which they are able only to contribute to a wider project rather than see their own project through from start to finish themselves. This work is regarded as non-stimulating:

The commercial demand for us to roll out projects at a high rate means that generally part timers are given less project-critical work, which normally means less exciting technical work. So we've had female part-timers taking redundancy

---

[4] Notions of tacit knowledge draw on the work of Michael Polanyi, and refer to the knowledge or insights that individuals acquire which is ill-defined or uncodified and which they themselves cannot fully articulate. Polanyi argues that explicit (or codified) knowledge is knowledge that is transmittable in formal, systematic language. Tacit knowledge is personal, context-specific, and difficult to formalize and communicate – "we know more than we can tell" (Polanyi 1967: 4). However, the distinction between "tacit" and "explicit" knowledge is not fixed.

because they weren't feeling technically stimulated enough in the work that they did. (HR Manager, BSO, female no children)

The wider impact of this type of work is that women on part-time con-tracts often end up leaving the firm, or indeed the labor market altogether, meaning a loss of knowledge, skills, and competencies to the firm and the region.

Job-hopping and employees as embodied competencies

The third area in which gender shapes firms' innovative capacities con-cerns processes of interfirm labor mobility and hence information dif-fusion within the region, which our results suggest significantly differ between male and female employees in Cambridge's high-tech economy. The regional learning and innovation literature has consistently high-lighted the benefits of wider networks of association and interaction (e.g. Scott 1988; Saxenian 1990, 1994; Capello 1999; Lawson and Lorenz 1999; Leadbeater 1999; OECD 1999; Hotz-Hart 2000) – and, in par-ticular, of mobile employees acting as important channels of informa-tion exchange between firms. When employees move between firms in the region and meet individuals with partially overlapping knowledge, comparisons of evolving ideas are made with other practices that are not internally generated. Thus, there is an increased potential for new unexpected ideas, interpretations, and synergies to develop; that is, for increased learning and innovation (Grabher 1993; Malecki and Oinas 1999). Employees may also maintain advantageous *ongoing* links between their new firm and their previous firm via personal relationships.

However, our results show that female employees in Cambridge's high-tech economy change jobs much less frequently than their male col-leagues, and that when female employees *do* change jobs, it is often not for their own personal career advancement but to accommodate their part-ner's move (see also Dex 1987). Many of our female respondents outlined how they have often sought "compromise jobs"; that is, jobs not pursued for career advancement but which allow for accommodation of their exist-ing home responsibilities and childcare needs. These latter commitments are largely dictated by their partner's job taking precedence, because of its generating a higher income or being a more socially prestigious position:

So when you find a situation that will accommodate you and you fit in, you stay with it, even if you start to dislike the job. This is a shame, because if you're at work six, seven or eight hours a day it's boring, and it's a shame that you have to stick that out. (Scientist, TUJ, female with children)

Significantly, this dynamic occurs in the elite professional workforce within our case study; that is, it is not (as often portrayed) solely an attribute of women working in the secondary labor market. This has implications for female workers' abilities to access external sources of information on behalf of their respective firms, relative to their male colleagues. Beneficial information transfer between firms through labor mobility typically functions only when employees remain in the *same* sector or move into similar sectors where those same types of information, skill, and competencies are also valued. Significantly our female respondents highlighted how frequent transfers *between* occupations and sectors not only serve to devalue these embodied skills, but also the social networks of relationships between individuals *within* firms which take time to develop; a form of corporate social capital which nonself-motivated labor mobility devalues and undermines.

Overall, this lower level of occupational mobility, as evidenced by women in our Cambridge case study, maintains segregation *within* the female worker group itself, based on a generational divide, itself heavily correlated with childcare responsibilities. The key difference exists between females who are predominantly young with minor or no home and childcare responsibilities, compared with their older female colleagues who often have children (see also Dumelow, Littlejohns, and Griffiths 2000). Crucially it is more difficult for this latter group of older female high-end workers to move between firms, thus limiting their abilities to act as agents of information and knowledge diffusion within the region. At the same time, these women are also less likely to move up through occupational hierarchies within firms, reinforcing the mechanisms outlined in the previous section in which female employees' skill-sets, knowledge, and competencies are not fully utilized within the firm. These mechanisms function to short-circuit one of the major routes through which knowledge is diffused from the firm to other firms in the region, yet nevertheless remains invisible in the regional learning and innovation literature.

Informal afterwork socializing and tacit knowledge transfer

The fourth area in which gender shapes workers' abilities to access wider sources of information on behalf of their respective firms concerns processes of informal afterwork socializing, which our results suggest significantly differ between male and female high-tech workers. The regional learning and innovation literature has consistently demonstrated how personal contacts between firms act as conduits of information and reinforce more formal types of corporate interaction. As employees swap knowledge and ideas about how things are done in other firms interaction helps to raise knowledge throughout the industry (Henry and Pinch 2000). Indeed, Powell (1990) argues that social networks are *the* most efficient organizational arrangement for sourcing information given that information is difficult to price in a market and difficult to communicate through a hierarchy. Ideas are thus recombined in different firms in new ways with existing skills, technology, know-how, and experience, and in this way, information diffusion through informal social networks helps stimulate innovation (Saxenian 1990; Capello 1999; Lawson and Lorenz 1999).

Significantly, these social interactions are found in both formal and informal settings within the region. For example, Saxenian (1994) highlights specifically how Silicon Valley's engineers, migrating to California from the East Coast, lacked any roots or family ties, and instead developed shared identities around the project of advancing a new technology, premised on a porous division between work, social life, and leisure activities (Saxenian 1994: 60–64). While employees frequently meet at trade shows, industry conferences, seminars, talks, and other social activities organized by local business organizations, crucial interactions also occur in more informal venues, such as bars, clubs, pubs, cafes, and coffee shops. In these social contexts, relationships are easily formed and maintained (Saxenian 1990), technical and market information exchanged, contacts established, and new ideas conceived.

Consistent with the above patterns, many of our male respondents embrace (sometimes quite self-consciously) this social networking model in order to ensure participation in formal and informal exchanges with business colleagues. In contrast, however, patterns of social interaction among many female employees within the Cambridge high-tech regional economy are instead characterized by a sharper division between work and social life, premised on childcare and other domestic responsibilities, of which many women bear the brunt within the home. Many of our female respondents either felt they could not attend social functions outside of work because of commitments at home, or else chose not to attend because of worries about work dominating their home-lives.

Not only are corporate social events often difficult to attend, but our results also suggest that many are structured in inherently masculine ways, therefore impacting on female employees' willingness to engage in these types of social event where they might otherwise act as agents of informal information exchange between firms in the region:

The main thing I find about the corporate social events that take place in Cambridge is that most of them tend to start at 6.30 [p.m.], and if you have kids, that's just the worst time, it's just impossible to get to them. These events rule out people with kids practically, well the women at least. So while there's a mixture [of socialising events], they all tend to be dominated by men, 85% men probably. (Vice President, TUJ, female with children)

Our female respondents consistently outlined how their male colleagues often develop a strong sense of identity that they do not share. Importantly, their absence from social events also leads to widespread feelings of exclusion from industry news among our female respondents:

You can't suddenly drop everything and go out to an event, so I do feel out-of-the-loop sometimes. I've lost that spontaneous socialising thing, and I find it hard sometimes. So I rely on the people who can go to these things to do the networking on behalf of the company, but you lose some of the networking there. (Entrepreneur, ALC, female with children)

Also, in similar ways as outlined in relation to female employees taking "compromise jobs" to accommodate their partners, females that have been able to maintain "noncompromise jobs" are nevertheless often forced to adopt compromise levels of informal social networking relative to their partners at both the intra-firm and inter-firm levels:

I used to work a lot more hours before I had kids and spend a couple of hours every day wandering around doing who knows what but not having the extra time means you have less socialising with colleagues, less time standing around chatting, spontaneous coffee. I suppose the other bit is in the evenings, where people go to the pub a lot. I do always feel a bit of an outsider as a result because I don't go to social things. So I do miss out. (Scientist, NSD, female with children)

While we share responsibility for the kids, typically [my partner] does the mornings and I tend to pick the kids up between 4.30 and 5. But he travels more. The company I'm with now, I don't travel, other people in the company have to do it. It's a big problem because now I don't attend conferences at all. Partially because it's a huge networking opportunity on an international scale. Because of my personal life I had to take the decision, and I can't do it. It puts a lot of pressure on families when the parents travel. (Entrepreneur, SUJ, female with children)

Overall, our results therefore suggest that female elite high-tech employees are often unable to attend business-oriented social events with the same frequency as their male colleagues. This is especially true for females with children, who consistently highlighted how they consciously reduced the amount they travel outside the local area; often do not attend trade shows and industry conferences; and minimize their attendance at local seminars and talks. Many also minimize their informal interactions in restaurants and pubs after work. Simultaneously, many of our female respondents without children often also avoided industry social events due to the predominant male culture at these events. With regard to alternative social events, while the majority of respondents unable to travel or attend social events outside the firm did attend *internal* firm events (e.g. firms' Christmas parties or summer barbeques) and occasionally entertained work-friends at home, very few felt able to do any more than that. Further, while some of our female respondents participate in online women's work forums, none felt this to be an adequate substitute for face-to-face industry-oriented social events.

These gendered patterns of socialization shape the processes of information diffusion between firms in the region in three key ways. First, the unequal distribution of home and childcare commitments make social activities out-of-work hours difficult to attend, which in turn affects female employees' abilities to act as conduits for interfirm information diffusion. Second, limits on the hours women are able to work make the work-experience more intense, and as a result they have less time to socialise *at* work, again affecting their ability to access and exchange (often tacit) knowledge within the firm. Third, the masculine nature of many social events often make them unappealing to women, thus encouraging them to limit their attendance, in turn constraining their ability to access and exchange information on behalf of their respective firms. We therefore need to recognise that employee attendance at informal afterwork social events, and hence employees' abilities to act as agents of information diffusion in the region, are fundamentally gendered phenomena.

7.6   Hard at work: women in high-tech industry

Our results therefore suggest that gender affects firms' abilities to access and use new sources of information in four key ways, as summarized in table 7.3, contrasted with the dominant assumptions within the regional learning and innovation literature regarding the ways in which elite high-tech engineers and programers "ideally" work and socialise. To sideline gender analyses in the regional learning and innovation literature is therefore a glaring omission.

Relative to their male colleagues, many of our female respondents typically experience shorter working hours, more part-time and "flexible" work, labor mobility not suited to the strategic pursuit of their own career progression, and fewer opportunities for intra-firm and interfirm socializing. These traits contrast with those consistently highlighted in the literature as positively underpinning firms' innovative capacities. These

Table 7.3 *Unpacking the "contents" of firms' embedding in gendered patterns of work, employment, and social interaction*

Patterns identified in the regional literature (positively underpinning innovative capacity)	Self-identified patterns among female respondents
High intensity of working hours – Blurred work and social identities Completion of large workloads over short periods of calendar time – Reduced time-to-market for products	**Gated working hours** – Around home and childcare commitments – Conscious decision to reject long hours – No longer "part of the team"
Full-time job contract – Icon of validation – team player – Increased chances of promotion – Increased job satisfaction	**"Flexible" job contract** – Part-time work more prevalent – Less time at work for informal interactions – Reduced work satisfaction – Reduced chance of promotion – Premature exit from firm/industry – loss of skills to the region
Job hopping self-motivated – Firms rarely innovate in isolation – Diffusion of embodied (tacit) knowledge – Multiple evaluations of own knowledge – Exploit partially overlapping technical knowledges – Firms gain new competencies – Shared resources/expertise/costs/risks	**Nonself-motivated job hopping** – Remain in less satisfying job to facilitate work–life balance – Moving to accommodate male partner – Tacit knowledge, most valuable when occupationally or sectorally specific
Informal socializing away from work – Increased channels of information exchange – Reinforce more formal interactions between firms – Blurring of work and social identities – Informal information networks – Diffusion of embodied (tacit) knowledge	**Minimal afterwork informal socializing** – Rigid separation of work and social life – Social events dominated by men – Women treated differently at events – Socializing takes other forms

Source: The authors.

patterns are particularly acute for the parents of younger children in our respondent sample, who recognise that they need to function at work in a different way than they did before they had children. For many of our female respondents, the heavy demands at home result in their needing to keep their efforts at work within boundaries that often did not exist when they were younger and which still do not exist for many of their male colleagues. Elite high-tech female employees, at least once they have family commitments, are typically less able, willing, *or expected*, to commit to work in the same way that their male colleagues are often expected to do. This therefore impacts on the ability of elite, high-tech, female employees to transmit and receive tacit knowledge on behalf of their respective firms in the manner that is consistently highlighted in the regional learning and innovation literature as central to high-tech regional dynamism.

We are not, however, arguing that women are the only ones to reassess their role at work once they become parents. Many men, who are actively involved in child-rearing and home-based responsibilities, share the constraints this places on commitments at work. Evidence from our interviews suggests that many fathers of young children experience similar tensions, as various individual and societal expectations regarding the active involvement fathers in child-rearing change over time. Overall, therefore, we cannot theorise the impacts of gender relations in the region outside of the division of parental and household duties more widely, nor from generational divisions in the workforce. We need to assess how the pressures to perform at work and the inability of all employees to perform in that manner changes through their life-cycles. We also need to examine how gendered constraints on the types of social interaction widely regarded as central to regional innovation system functioning vary over an employee's life-cycle.

Many of our professional female respondents with families are characteristic in making occupational choices that do not further their personal careers, at least in the short term, but instead enable the family unit to function. Nancy Folbre, a feminist economist, refers to this as maximizing the family's utility function, rather than an individual's utility function, something that she argues is characteristic of women's "economic algebra" (Folbre 1994). Our results seem to support this notion. For example, many of our female respondents consciously put boundaries around the number of hours they put in at work (minimizing total hours worked, corporate travel, or attendance at after-work events) to take on additional home and childcare duties. This, in turn, allows their partners to perform at a higher level at work. McDowell (1991, 2001) has also explored this dynamic, outlining how the expectations of female partners ensure social reproduction of the household unit. Another way of viewing this is that females with "compromise" work patterns actually support elite male workers in their work efforts. However, despite extensive research on dual-career couples buying domestic and childcare help to allow both members of the couple to function at work (Gregson and Lowe 1998; McDowell 2001), our results suggest that purchased help is still often insufficient to allow women to devote themselves fully to work – that is, as one of Williams' (2000) "ideal workers," or in a manner consistent with the work patterns identified in the regional literature as central to high-tech dynamism. Many women must also make additional effort to supplement purchased domestic help with their own labor in the home.

For women without children, the issue appears to be more of a cultural one. Many female employees often feel unwelcome or patronised at social events dominated by men. Similarly, although many younger women often feel comfortable in intra-firm socializing, they feel less so with interfirm socializing. This serves to limit their ability to access and exchange information at an interfirm level, with wider implications for firms' innovative capacities, as outlined earlier. We further argue that this diversity of social interaction is made invisible in the literature by the focus on male social interaction that is theorised as gender-neutral. As such, little work specifically examines the different gendered types of corporate social interaction and the impact of that on firms' learning and innovation processes. For example, all of our female respondents socialise, but do so in a different manner than that captured by conventional theories on innovative or learning regions. Instead of socializing around the basis of work, alternative social outlets for female employees often focus on friendships, children, or other interests. Little is known about the extent to which these networks overlap with firm-based networks. Indeed, the only analyses that try to explore women's specific impact on the firm tend to be culturally essentialist accounts of how more "feminine" traits of empathy, compassion, mutual support, and understanding are key in the "New Economy," and that female employees are thus naturally at an advantage relative to their male colleagues (see e.g. Wachs-Book 2000). We remain so far unconvinced by such arguments.

Nevertheless, we argue that firms themselves have a vested interest in understanding how many of their female employees face constraints that minimise their willingness and ability to function at work in the ways widely theorised as central to success in high-tech sectors. Gender impacts on both intra-firm and interfirm dynamics in the region. As such, these are not only issues of individual women paying a price for trying to achieve a work–life balance, but also of firms themselves simultaneously bearing a cost. Women who are not supported in their efforts to balance the demands of work and homelife either withdraw their labor or set limits on their efforts within the workplace – neither of which is good for the firm for whom the employee represents embodied knowledge (Burton-Jones, 1999). Further, if women need to curtail their work involvement by minimizing extra-work activities, or because they feel unwelcome, this suggests that their embodied knowledge is not being fully utilized and, thus, one of the firm's mechanisms to spur innovation is weakened. In this regard, we must ask if Cambridge's disappointing growth rates in the

ICT industry are partly due to underutilization of the industry's human and social capital.

If elite female high-tech workers must, at some points in their career, curtail their expected social functions relative to many of their male colleagues – traveling less, displaying less interfirm mobility, socializing less outside and inside of the firm – does that, in turn, reinforce their weaker position in the high-tech labor market relative to their male colleagues? We must question the extent to which the ability to work late and long hours, travel, and socialise outside of work also function as material markers of a committed "ideal worker." In fact, the human relations managers we interviewed did not see their female employees as any less innovative than their male colleagues, but did think that they made different decisions in the labor market. We must ask to what extent a firm's hiring, retention, and promotion decisions intensify the fundamental problem that many working women, particularly those with young children, face. These are key questions for future research. By expecting such high levels of commitment from employees, the firm itself sets standards that may be hard for employees to meet.[5]

Likewise, Regional Development Agencies (RDAs) also have a vested interest in understanding how many female employees face constraints and inequalities that minimise their willingness and ability to function at work in ways widely theorised as central to regional high-tech economic success. Specifically, as regional development agencies seek to elevate the position of their respective areas to "hold down the global," one way they might capitalise more fully on women's embodied skills and knowledge is through the policy levers of childcare provision and work–life balance programs. Our results show that the lack of flexible and high-quality childcare provision and measures to help workers achieve a better "work–life balance" are major barriers that constrain women's abilities to participate in key corporate and social events that underpin intra-firm and interfirm innovation and learning processes. Problematically, however, childcare and work–life balance policies are too often regarded as pastoral add-ons to keep employees happy, rather than as fundamental enabling mechanisms that allow firms and regions alike to capitalise fully on employees' embodied competencies. As such, we argue that childcare and work–life balance policies should come under the umbrella of more socially inclusive regional economic development policy. This is especially the case in England where recent devolution of economic development funds to the

---

[5] Indeed, the changing division of labor at home and changing norms surrounding active parenting mean that firms are likely to witness an increasing number of *male* employees also adopting these self-imposed limits on the intensity of work and social interaction.

regional level through the RDAs, gives these agencies both the power and the legitimacy to act within this sphere.

7.7   Conclusion

In this chapter, we have critiqued the dominant tendency within the regional learning and innovation literature to divorce learning and innovation processes within innovative regional economies from *people* with very real gendered identities and commitments that unavoidably motivate and shape their daily work activities. Drawing on the case study of the ICT sector in Cambridge – one of Europe's blueprint high-tech regional economies – we have outlined significant differences in the dominant patterns of work and social interaction among female versus male employees. Crucially, we have also outlined how gendered patterns of work and social interaction constrain female workers' abilities to contribute fully to the processes widely theorised in the geographical literature as underpinning innovation and learning processes at the scales of the firm and the region, and have grounded our analysis in terms of the specific manifestations of that gender impact. As such, our results highlight the need for a realignment of conventional thinking with regard to the sociorelational underpinnings of industrial district success, and of the need for a change in policy to encourage women's full participation in regional innovation systems. At the same time, our analysis also highlights how appropriate solutions to these problems must be multiple-scaled, premised on a rethink of how and when firm-based and regional networking events take place, of how to encourage women to participate in those events, and of how to encourage a regional industry approach to childcare provision. Clearly, there exists a very powerful and socially significant research agenda in this vein. Strangely, however, it is one that remains largely absent from the extant regional learning and innovation literature.

REFERENCES

Acker, J., 1990. "Hierarchies, Jobs, Bodies: A Theory of Gendered Organisations," *Gender and Society*, 4: 139–158
AMICUS, 2002. *Internal Figures on UK and European ICT Female Workforces*, London: AMICUS
Asheim, B. T., 1996. "Industrial Districts as 'Learning Regions': A Condition for Prosperity?," *European Planning Studies*, 4: 379–400
    2001. *"The Learning Firm in the Learning Region: Broad Participation as Social Capital Building,"* Presented at the Annual Conference of the Association of American Geographers, New York , February 27–March 3

Athreye, S. S., 2004. "Agglomeration and Growth: A Study of the Cambridge Hi-Tech Cluster" in T. Bresnahan and A. Gambardella (eds.), *Building Hi-Tech Clusters: Silicon Valley and Beyond*, Cambridge: Cambridge University Press: 121–159

Baxter, J. and J. Eyles, 1997. "Evaluating Qualitative Research in Social Geography: Establishing 'Rigour' in Interview Analysis," *Transactions of the Institute of British Geographers*, 22: 505–525

Benner, C., 2002. *Work in the New Economy: Flexible Labour Markets in Silicon Valley*, Oxford: Blackwell

Best, M. H., 1990. *The New Competition: Institutions of Industrial Restructuring*, Cambridge: Polity Press

Braczyk, H.-J., P. Cooke and M. Heidenreich (eds.), 1998. *Regional Innovation Systems: The Role of Governances in a Globalized World*, London: UCL Press

Burton-Jones, A., 1999. *Knowledge Capitalism: Business, Work and Learning in the New Economy*, Oxford: Oxford University Press

Capello, R., 1999. "Spatial Transfers of Knowledge in High Technology Milieux: Learning Versus Collective Learning Processes," *Regional Studies*, 33(4): 353–365

Castells, M., 1996. *The Rise of the Network Society*, Oxford: Blackwell

Castells, M. and P. Hall, 1994. *Technopoles of the World: The Making of the Twenty-First Century Industrial Complexes*, London: Routledge

Cooke, P. and K. Morgan, 1993. "The Network Paradigm: New Departures in Corporate and Regional Development," *Environment and Planning D*, 11: 543–664

     1998. *The Associational Economy: Firms, Regions and Innovation*, Oxford: Oxford University Press

Crompton, R., C. Gallie, and K. Purcell (eds.), 1996. *Changing Forms of Employment: Organizations, Skills and Gender*, London: Routledge

Dex, S., 1987. *Women's Occupational Mobility: A Lifetime Perspective*, London: Macmillan

Dumelow, C., P. Littlejohns, and S. Griffiths, 2000. "The Relation Between Two Careers and a Family for English Hospital Consultants: A Qualitative, Semi-Structured Interview Study," *British Medical Journal*, 320: 1437–1440

European Commission, 2002. *European Innovation Scoreboard, 2000*, at http://www.edis.sk/ekes/kneldok/dokument/innovation_scoreboard_2002_en.pdf

Folbre, N., 1994. *Who Pays for the Kids? Gender and the Structure of Constraint*, London: Routledge

Gertler, M. S., D. A. Wolfe, and D. Garkut, 2000. "No Place Like Home? The Embeddedness of Innovation in a Regional Economy," *Review of International Political Economy*, 30: 688–718

Grabher, G. (ed.) 1993. *The Embedded Firm: On the Socioeconomics of Industrial Networks*, London: Routledge

Gray, M. and S. Damery, 2003. *Regional Development and Differentiated Labor Markets: The Cambridge Case*, Report to the European Commission, IST Program, available from the authors

Gray, M. and E. Parker, 1998. "Industrial Change and Regional Development: The Case of the US Biotechnology and Pharmaceutical Industries," *Environment and Planning A*, 30: 1757–1774

Gregson, N. and M. Lowe, 1998. *Servicing the Middle Classes: Class, Gender and Waged Domestic Work in Contemporary Britain*, London: Routledge

Heffernan, P. and E. Garnsey, 2002. *The Growth of High Technology and Knowledge-Based Business in the Cambridge Sub-Region*, Working Paper, Centre for Technology Management, Department of Engineering, Cambridge: University of Cambridge

Henry, N. and D. Massey, 1995. "Competitive Time–Space in High Technology," *Geoforum*, 26(1): 49–64

Henry, N. and S. Pinch, 2000. "Spatialising Knowledge: Placing the Knowledge Community of Motor Sport Valley," *Geoforum*, 31: 191–208

Herriot, W., 2004. "Speech to the Technology in Action Press Day," St. John's Innovation Centre, March

Hochschild, A. R., 1997. *The Time Bind: When Work Becomes Home and Home Becomes Work*, New York: Metropolitan Books

Hotz-Hart, B., 2000. "Innovation Networks, Regions and Globalization," in G. L. Clark, M. P. Feldman, and M. S. Gertler (eds.), *The Oxford Handbook of Economic Geography*, Oxford: Oxford University Press: 432–450

Hudson, R., 1999. "The Learning Economy, the Learning Firm and the Learning Region: A Sympathetic Critique of the Limits to Learning," *European Urban and Regional Studies*, 6(1): 59–72

Humphries, J. and J. Rubery (eds.), 1995. *The Economics of Equal Opportunity*, London: Equal Opportunities Commission

Keeble, D., 1989. "High-Technology Industry and Regional Development in Britain: The Case of the Cambridge Phenomenon," *Environment and Planning C*, 7: 153–172

2001. *University and Technology: Science and Technology Parks in the Cambridge Region*, Working Paper, 218, ESRC Centre for Business Research, Cambridge University

Keeble, D., C. Lawson, B. Moore, and F. Wilkinson, 1999. "Collective Learning Processes, Networking and Institutional Thickness in the Cambridge Region," *Regional Studies*, 33(4): 319–332

Keeble, D. and F. Wilkinson, 1999. "Collective Learning and Regional Development in the Evolution of Regional Clusters of High Technology SMEs in Europe," *Regional Studies*, 33(4): 295–304

Lawson, C., 1999. "Towards a Competence Theory of the Region," *Cambridge Journal of Economics*, 23(2): 155–166

Lawson, C. and E. Lorenz, 1999. "Collective Learning, Tacit Knowledge and Regional Innovative Capacity," *Regional Studies*, 33(4): 305–317

Lawson, C., B. Moore, D. Keeble, H. Lawton Smith, and F. Wilkinson, 1997. *Inter-Firm Links Between Regionally Clustered High-Technology SMEs: A Comparison of Cambridge and Oxford Innovation Networks*, Working Paper, 65, ESRC Centre for Business Research, University of Cambridge

Lawton-Smith, H., D. Keeble, C. Lawson, B. Moore, and F. Wilkinson, 1998. "Contrasting Regional Innovation Systems in Oxford and Cambridge," in J. de la Moethe and G. Paquet (eds.), *Local and Regional Systems of Innovation*, Dordrecht: Kluwer: 125–148

Leadbeater, C., 1999. *Living on Thin Air: The New Economy*, London: Viking

Lorenz, E. H., 1992. "Trust, Community and Co-operation: Toward a Theory of Industrial Districts," in M. Storper and A. Scott (eds.), *Pathways to Industrialisation and Regional Development*, London: Routledge: 195–204

Lundvall, B.-Å., 1992. *National Systems of Innovation: Toward a Theory of Innovation and Interactive Learning*, London: Frances Pinter

Lundvall, B.-Å. and B. Johnson, 1994. *The Learning Economy*, Presented to the European Association for Evolutionary Political Economy conference, Paris, November 4–6

Malecki, E. J. and P. Oinas (eds.), 1999. *Making Connections: Technological Learning and Regional Economic Change*, Aldershot: Ashgate

Malmberg, A. and P. Maskell, 1997. "Towards an Explanation of Regional Specialization and Industry Agglomeration," *European Planning Studies*, 5: 25–41

Markusen, A., 1994. "Studying Regions by Studying Firms," *Professional Geographer*, 46(4): 477–490

Maskell, P. and A. Malmberg, 1999. "The Competitiveness of Firms and Regions: 'Ubiquitification' and the Importance of Localised Learning," *European Urban and Regional Studies*, 6: 9–26

Massey, D., 1995. "Masculinity, Dualisms and High Technology," *Transactions of the Institute of British Geographers*, 20: 487–499

1997. "Economic/Non-Economic," in R. Lee and J. Wills (eds.), *Geographies of Economies*, London: Arnold: 27–36

Massey, D., P. Quintas, and D. Wield, 1992. *High Tech Fantasies: Science Parks in Society, Science and Space*, London: Routledge

McDowell, L. M., 1991. "Life Without Father and Ford: The New Gender Order of Post-Fordism," *Transactions of the Institute of British Geographers*, 16: 400–419

1997. *Capital Culture: Gender at Work in the City*, Oxford: Blackwell

2001. "Father and Ford Revisited: Gender, Class and Employment Change in the New Millennium," *Transactions of the Institute of British Geographers*, 26: 448–464

Millar, J. and N. Jagger, 2001. *Women in ITEC Courses and Careers*, Report WITI 20, Department for Education and Skills, HM Government

Morgan, K., 1997. "The Learning Region: Institutions, Innovation and Regional Renewal," *Regional Studies*, 31: 491–503

Organization for Economic Co-operation and Development (OECD), 1996. *Technology, Productivity and Job Creation: Best Policy Practices*, Paris: OECD

1999, *Managing National Innovation Systems*, Paris: OECD

Oinas, P. and E. J. Malecki, 1999. "Technological Trajectories in Space: From 'National' and 'Regional' to 'Spatial' Innovation Systems," Presented at the North American Meetings of the Regional Science Association International, Montreal, November

Perrons, D., 2000. "Flexible Working and Equal Opportunities in the United Kingdom: A Case Study from Retail," *Environment and Planning A*, 32: 1719–1734

2002. "Social Divisions in the New Economy," Presented at the Regional Studies Association Conference, Geographies of the New Economy, London, October, 25

Polanyi, M., 1967. *The Tacit Dimension*, London: Routledge & Kegan Paul

Porter, M. E., 1990. *The Competitive Advantage of Nations*, London: Macmillan

Powell, W. W., 1990. "'Neither Market Nor Hierarchy': Network Forms of Organisation," *Research in Organizational Behavior*, 12: 295–336

Reich, R., 2000. *The Future of Success: Work and Life in the New Economy*, London: Random House

Sainsbury, Lord, 2002. "Prospects for Cambridge: What Government is Doing to Make Cambridge More Successful," Speech given to the Cambridge Network and Greater Cambridge Partnership, Cambridge

Saxenian, A. L., 1989. "The Cheshire Cat's Grin: Innovation, Regional Development and the Cambridge Case," *Economy and Society*, 18(4): 448–477

   1990. "Regional Networks and the Resurgence of Silicon Valley," *California Management Review*, 33: 89–112

   1994. *Regional Advantage: Culture and Competition in Silicon Valley and Route 128*, Cambridge, MA: Harvard University Press

Schoenberger, E., 1991. "The Corporate Interview as Research Method in Economic Geography," *Professional Geographer*, 43: 183–189

Schor, J., 1992. *The Overworked American: The Unexpected Decline of Leisure*, New York: Basic Books

Scott, A. J., 1988. *New Industrial Spaces: Flexible Production, Organisation and Regional Development in North America and Western Europe*, London: Pion

Storper, M. J., 1996. "Innovation as Collective Action: Conventions, Products and Technologies," *Industrial and Corporate Change*, 5(3): 761–790

   1997. *The Regional World: Territorial Development in a Global Economy*, New York: Guilford Press

US National Center on the Educational Quality of the Workforce (NCEQW), 1995. *The Other Shoe: Education's Contribution to the Productivity of Establishments*, National Employer Survey, EQW, Catalogue no. RE02

Wachs-Book, E., 2000. *Why the Best Man for the Job is a Woman: The Unique Female Qualities of Leadership*, New York: HarperCollins

Williams, J., 2000. *Unbundling Gender: Why Family and Work Conflict and What to Do About It*, Oxford: Oxford University Press

Wolfe, D. A., 1997. "The Emergence of the Region State," Prepared for the *Bell Canada Papers*, 5, *The Nation State in a Global Information Era: Policy Challenges*, John Deutsch Institute for the Study of Economic Policy, Queen's University, Kingston, Ontario

8 Multinationals and transnational social space for learning: knowledge creation and transfer through global R&D networks

Alice Lam

8.1 Introduction

Multinational enterprises (MNEs) are unique knowledge-creating organisations because of their superior ability to engage in knowledge transfer across national borders within the context of interorganisational networks (Kogut and Zander 1993; Gupta and Govindarajan 2000). The ways in which MNEs develop their transnational social space for learning, however, differ significantly between firms on the basis of the dominant organizational model and patterns of learning derived from the home contexts. In this chapter, I build on the institutional perspective, which stresses the strong influence of home-based institutions on the structure and behavior of MNEs (Pauly and Reich 1997; Doremus *et al.* 1998; Whitley 1999, 2001; Morgan 2001). I examine the ways in which national patterns of organization and innovation affect firms' global R&D networks and transnational learning activities. One notable recent trend in the management of innovation within MNEs has been the extension of R&D activities and competence portfolios on a global scale (Gerybadze and Reger 1999; Pearce 1999) to augment the knowledge base of the firm (Howells 1990; Florida 1997; Kuemmerle 1997, 1999a, 1999b). In the science-based high-technology industries in particular, a growing element of firms' strategies involves collaboration with world-class academic institutions and research centers, and recruitment of the best scientific personnel on a global scale (Kaounides 1999). Accordingly, I examine the organizational and human resource strategies adopted by US and Japanese MNEs in managing their global R&D networks and transnational learning in the pharmaceutical and ICT sectors. My empirical evidence is based on case studies carried out in the R&D laboratories of US and Japanese MNEs in the United Kingdom. In particular, I focus on

The research on which this chapter is based is part of a multi-country study funded by the European Commission, DGXII, TSER Program SOE1-CT97–1054.

how these MNEs tap into the foreign academic knowledge base and scientific labor through collaborative links with universities. The main aim of the study is to understand how national institutions shape the nature and boundary of firms' transnational space for learning, and their ability to tap globally dispersed knowledge networks.

8.2   Global R&D networks: from technology transfer to organizational learning

Firms in most of the industrialized countries have increased the proportion of their R&D investments abroad since the mid-1980s (Patel 1995; Roberts 2001). US firms were pioneer investors in R&D facilities abroad, but Japanese firms established their foreign R&D sites only much later and their foreign subsidiaries have a lower level of R&D intensity compared with US firms (Cantwell 1995; Doremus *et al.* 1998). As a result of their intensive investment activity since the mid-1980s, Japanese pharmaceutical and electronics firms in the mid-1990s operated 32 percent more R&D sites abroad than US firms and more than twice as many sites as European firms, according to Kuemmerle's survey (1999a).

The global dispersion of R&D has been driven by firms' needs to acquire new knowledge and capabilities and to gain access to unique human resources (Howells 1990; Florida 1997; Dunning and Wymbs 1999). Since the mid-1980s, the overseas R&D units of many MNEs no longer confine themselves to the transfer of parent-company technology to host countries, but are developing major innovations for the global market by leveraging the unique knowledge resources of some host-country environments. Gerybadze and Reger (1999) argue that the proliferation of national innovation systems and knowledge centers at various locations throughout the world has strengthened the incentives for MNEs to go for global knowledge sourcing. When deciding to establish or expand R&D abroad, firms are increasingly motivated by the wish to gain access to sophisticated resources that cannot be found anywhere else.

These changes are clearly demonstrated in Pearce and Papanasatassiou's (1999) survey of the evolution of overseas R&D labs in the United Kingdom. The authors distinguish three different roles of laboratories: support, locally integrated, and internationally interdependent categories. Their study shows that the internationally interdependent type, whose main aim is to generate new scientific knowledge that can underpin the technological distinctiveness of the MNE, has emerged as the most prevalent type of laboratory in MNEs' units in the United Kingdom. They suggest that supply-side factors, namely the UK technological capability and research infrastructure, and the availability of local scientific personnel, are most important in affecting the strategic positioning of these labs.

A key element in the global learning strategies of MNEs has been the growth of transnational collaborative relationships with academic institutions. This trend is particularly prominent in the science-based industries where the traditional barriers between scientific and technological disciplines are breaking down, and where there is an increased interchange between basic and applied research. Forging close links with academic institutions helps to speed up innovation and also to broaden the boundary of knowledge exploration. Large MNEs also seek to establish strong links with local higher-education institutions to gain early access to the best students and academic researchers. In the dynamic technological fields, competitive advantage increasingly depends on tacit competence and unique configurations of knowledge resources. Recruitment of scientific personnel is one of the main ways for MNEs to tap effectively into new clusters of knowledge located abroad.

The United States and United Kingdom have been popular locations for MNEs seeking to establish links with higher-education institutions because of the high-quality academic knowledge base, the openness of their academic institutions, and the presence of a large pool of well-trained scientific personnel. For Japanese companies without a strong overseas R&D presence, collaboration with academic institutions in the United States or Europe represents an attractive avenue for gaining access to leading scientific expertise. MNEs internationalize their university collaborations in general; but Japanese firms appear to have internationalized their university collaborations to a larger extent (Granstrand 1999).

8.3   The "social embeddedness" of MNEs: R&D networks and transnational organizational learning

As firms seek to use knowledge and innovation generated on a global scale, the development of international R&D organization becomes a central issue. Zanfei (2000) describes the new organizational mode of transnational innovation as "a double network" comprising the internal and external networks. The internal networks refer to the organizational mechanisms for the co-ordination and integration of distributed R&D units, while external networks are constituted by relations with actors outside of the firm. A number of authors argue that a subsidiary's ability to gain access to local knowledge sources is dependent upon its embeddedness in the host-country context and the social relations of technological innovation (Blanc and Sierra 1999; Frost 2001). What makes

MNEs unique as knowledge-creating organisations is their ability to create "transnational social spaces" for learning. This is achieved by linking their internal networks with their external and locally embedded knowledge networks spanning diverse organizational and institutional contexts.

The ways in which MNEs develop "transnational learning spaces" and their ability to tap into local knowledge sources, however, differ between firms of different national origins, as suggested by the institutional approach to organisations (Pauly and Reich 1997; Doremus *et al.* 1998; Whitley 1999, 2001; Morgan 2001). In a similar vein, the national innovation system authors (e.g. Lundvall 1992; Nelson 1993) emphasise the impact of distinctive national institutions on firms' innovation patterns and technological trajectories. Several authors also note the strong influence of national innovation systems on the technological and innovation activities of MNEs (e.g. Patel and Vega 1999; Pavitt and Patel 1999).

Drawing on this earlier work, I argue that the transnational learning activities of MNEs continue to bear the strong imprint of "home-country effects." This does not imply the replication of home-based organizational forms and learning patterns in the global arena, but refers to the ways in which home-based institutions shape the nature and boundary of firms' "transnational learning spaces" and their ability to tap into local innovation networks. In particular, I suggest that US MNEs will be able to develop a greater organizational capacity, compared with their Japanese counterparts, for co-ordinating globally dispersed learning and embedding themselves in the local innovation networks. This is because the liberal market institutional environment within which US firms have developed allows them considerable flexibility to extend their organizational and human resource systems across institutional and geographical boundaries. By contrast, Japanese MNEs are likely to be more limited in their transnational learning because of the much more tightly integrated organizational and business system within which they are embedded. More specifically, the home-based institutions shape MNEs' transnational learning spaces in three main ways: (a) modes of international R&D organisation; (b) transnational collaboration with academic institutions; and (c) human resource strategies and links with local labor markets.

Modes of international R&D organization

MNEs adopt a variety of global R&D structures and management styles in co-ordinating globally dispersed R&D units. A key managerial problem is the balance between autonomy and control of overseas R&D units

Table 8.1 *Five typical forms of international R&D organization*

Type of R&D organization	Organizational structure	Behavioral orientation
Ethnocentric centralized R&D	Centralized R&D	National inward orientation
Geocentric centralized R&D	Centralized R&D	International co-operation
Polycentric decentralized R&D	Highly dispersed R&D, weak center	Competition among independent R&D units
R&D hub model	Dispersed R&D, strong center	Supportive role of foreign R&D units
Integrated R&D network	Highly dispersed R&D, several competence centers	Synergetic integration of international R&D units

Source: Gassman and von Zedwitz (1999: 235)

and the use of different types of co-ordinating mechanisms for effective knowledge transfer. Gassman and von Zedwitz (1999) identify five ideal forms of structural and behavioral orientation in international R&D organization (table 8.1). The authors argue that there is an evolution towards integrated R&D networks. This is seen as the most advanced form of R&D organization whereby the central R&D department evolves into a competency center among interdependent R&D units that are closely connected by flexible and diverse co-ordination mechanisms. The role of the central R&D unit shifts from a control center to a group with rights and duties equal to those of the dispersed units. Overseas R&D units assume a strategic role affecting the entire company. They enjoy a high degree of autonomy and perform distinctive roles in knowledge creation through their extensive external networks.

The extent to which different types of MNEs are able to adopt the integrated R&D network model, however, will tend to vary. Existing empirical evidence suggests that Japanese firms have not developed this mode of R&D organization as much as leading US and European MNEs (Gassman and von Zedwitz 1999; Gerybadze and Reger 1999). They appear to experience a strong isomorphic pull towards the hybrid modes of "ethnocentric," "hub," model of international R&D organization (Sakakibara and Westney 1992; Gronning 2001). This is characterized by the dominance of the main laboratory at home in all research and advanced development activities, tight control over decentralized activities by means of long-term R&D programs as well as through resource and personnel allocation.

The different modes of international R&D organization reflect the dominant system of managerial co-ordination adopted by firms which, in turn, are rooted in differing national approaches to technological innovation and their internationalization strategies. Japanese MNEs in general tend to be tightly integrated and seek to maintain a high level of internal organizational proximity and coherence (Westney 1999). They develop their internationalization strategies by building on and extending their existing technological expertise to overseas markets. This is achieved by maintaining a close integration between the technological competencies based at home and those transferred to overseas subsidiaries. Their R&D activities have therefore remained highly centralized in the home laboratories, and the level of R&D intensity of their foreign subsidiaries is low compared with that of the US or European MNEs (Meyer-Krahmer and Reger 1999; Belderbos 2001). The Japanese approach to product innovation is characterized by a tight integration between R&D and manufacturing operations and frequent rotation of people across functional boundaries. This particular feature of the Japanese innovation system further inhibits the decentralization of R&D activities to foreign subsidiaries.

The dominance of the home-country R&D organization is also a result of the country's long years' of experience as a "technology follower" (Sakakibara and Westney 1992; Westney 1993, 1994). Japanese firms have spent several decades developing organisations and knowledge-transfer systems to acquire foreign technology. The patterns of R&D organization have been designed to acquire and adapt external technology for product development back at home. This inward-learning pattern has led Japanese firms to treat overseas R&D units primarily as "technology listening posts" or highly specialized units within the corporation. The implication of this tight home-centered structure is that Japanese overseas R&D facilities may be limited in the scope of their innovation activities and their ability to integrate themselves within local innovation networks. Blanc and Sierra (1999) argue that there is a trade-off between internal organizational proximity and the ability of the firm to develop diverse relations of proximity to actors external to the firm. One would expect Japanese firms, then, to experience a higher degree of organizational tension in managing their overseas R&D units (Asakawa 2001), especially in basic research where organizational autonomy is most needed to foster innovation.

US MNEs, by contrast, are less likely to be inhibited by their dominant system of management co-ordination and home-based innovation system from moving towards the integrated R&D network structure. US MNEs in general are more decentralized and their subsidiaries are loosely co-ordinated via financial performance measures. This allows the subsidiaries a greater degree of autonomy in managerial decision-making and local adaptation. One would also expect US firms to have a stronger inclination than Japanese firms to develop globally distributed

R&D networks because of the national innovation system's focus on achieving scientific breakthroughs and radical innovation (Doremus *et al.* 1998; Hollingsworth 2000). This kind of innovation system requires firms to develop highly flexible and permeable organizational structures to acquire knowledge from a wide variety of external sources (Hage and Hollingsworth 2000; Whitley 2000).

Transnational collaboration with academic institutions

In the United States, universities have historically played a prominent role in the national innovation system (Mowery and Rosenberg 1993). This builds on their important role in performing a large proportion of publicly funded basic research and a long history of close collaboration between university researchers and industrial scientists and engineers. Policy developments over the past two decades have strengthened the incentives for academics to engage in industrially relevant research (Hane 1999; Spencer 2001). Another important factor contributing to the innovative role of the US university system is the tight coupling of research and graduate education. This has important effects on students as professional researchers and also as sources of technology transfer (Feller 1999: 83). US firms recruit a large number of PhD scientists into their laboratories, which cements the links between the two sectors and facilitates reciprocal knowledge flow (Westney 1993). As a result, US firms have been able to draw upon a strong academic science base at home to support their radical and entrepreneurial innovation strategies. One can argue that US firms do not have to look abroad for basic research and academic links. However, like firms from elsewhere, they are subject to intense competitive pressures to broaden the scope of innovative search in order to sustain and strengthen their existing innovation strategies. Since the early 1990s, many leading US MNEs have sought to create a global scientific space through their global R&D networks and academic links. The key objectives appear to be the broadening of the firm's external knowledge networks and the search for unique capabilities and human resources.

Japanese firms' motives for developing overseas academic links are very different. They appear to use globalization as a strategy to compensate for the weaknesses of home-based institutions and to "disrupt" their existing patterns of learning. Nakayama and Low (1997: 249) argue that the growing internationalization of R&D and investment in overseas universities are evidence of Japanese industry's lack of confidence in the research function of Japanese universities. The academic science base in Japan is relatively weak in a number of fields and the role of universities in the national research system has been less significant. The post-war economic policy of Japan placed a heavy emphasis on firms creating their own technical capability to "catch-up" with the West in selected areas (Baba Kikuchi, and Mori 1995; Kodama and Branscomb 1999). Public funding in basic research is relatively low compared with that of other advanced economies, and the university sector has been deprived of increases in public funding for the last two decades (Clark 1995; Nakayama and Low 1997). The role of universities in Japan has been primarily that of knowledge "disseminators," providing a steady stream of graduates for industry, rather than knowledge "generators" (Oka 1993; Methé 1995). Formal linkages between university and industry in R&D collaboration have also been severely handicapped by the historic institutional separation between the two sectors (Hane 1999) and, at least until recently, the lack of institutional arrangements and incentives for Japanese universities to perform commercially relevant research. Thus, Japanese firms have not developed strong links with universities at home and have limited experience in conducting basic research. Their innovation strategies have tended to focus on applied R&D projects to promote a cluster of continuous and incremental product innovations.

However, since the mid-1980s Japanese firms have become more concerned with the need to develop more creative research organisations with greater capabilities in basic research and radical innovation. Instead of looking towards their home-based institutions, they go abroad to search for productive university ties and set up basic research facilities. Japanese firms expect their overseas facilities to play two roles. The first is to enable them to learn the organizational routines of basic research, and the second is to help them to acquire basic research findings and academic knowledge in certain specialized areas not available at home (Methé 1995; Turner, Ray, and Hayward 1997). Thus, an analyst would expect Japanese MNEs' relationships with overseas academic institutions to be more focused and specific, evolving around the advancement of new technologies as opposed to the broad objectives of knowledge networking exhibited by the US MNEs.

Human resource strategies and links with local labor markets

US firms have traditionally relied on an external learning strategy that takes advantage of the country's mobile and open professional labor markets. The open recruitment of scientists and engineers has enabled US firms to pursue a radical innovation strategy through continuous renewal of their knowledge base and creation of new technological possibilities.

Moreover, the strong links between industry and university facilitate human resource mobility between the two sectors. This allows firms to gain access to a large supply of professional researchers who are conducting advanced research at universities. The professional-oriented career structures and open employment systems facilitate the development of a decentralized global R&D structure and allow overseas units a greater degree of autonomy in local recruitment than that of Japanese MNEs. US MNEs may, therefore, enjoy an institutional advantage relative to their Japanese counterparts when they seek to extend their learning and human resource systems across geographical boundaries.

Japanese firms, by contrast, have historically built their innovative capabilities on a well-established firm-based internal labor market with a strong emphasis on internal knowledge transfer. The high degree of internal job rotation and career mobility is accompanied by a relative absence of horizontal labor mobility in the large-firm sector. The insular nature of the human resource system in R&D is further reinforced by the institutional separation between industry and academia, and the reluctance of Japanese firms to recruit university-trained PhDs into their organisations (Westney 1993; Nakayama and Low 1997). When Japanese firms set up R&D units in the United Kingdom and the United States, they are likely to come under pressure to alter their human resource systems to accommodate the demands of a more open, externally oriented learning pattern. This may conflict with their home-based labor market institutions and employment systems. One would expect Japanese firms to experience greater tensions in adapting their human resource practices to facilitate the development of globally dispersed knowledge networks.

8.4   Research methods and the interview sample

This study is based on four case studies of two US MNEs, one in the ICT sector (US-ICT) and the other in pharmaceutical (US-Pharma); and two Japanese MNEs also from the same two sectors (J-ICT and J-Pharma). They are all large MNEs operating in the science-based industries. The two ICT firms are comparable in terms of their size, scale of R&D investment, and the duration of their R&D operations in the United Kingdom. US-ICT's Bristol Laboratory was established in 1985, and J-ICT's Cambridge Laboratory in 1989. The two companies in the pharmaceutical sector, however, cannot be claimed to be directly comparable because of the substantial differences in their size and R&D investment (see p. 177). Moreover, US-Pharma's R&D site in the United Kingdom was established in 1955, whereas J-Pharma's London Laboratory was initiated in

Table 8.2 *The interview sample*

Company	Position/background of staff interviewed	No. of interviews in companies	No. of interviews with local academic collaborators
US-ICT	Managing Director of R&D Lab; Human Resource Manager; External Collaboration and Academic Liaison manager; Departmental managers (four areas); R&D Divisional Manager; Senior engineers (engaged in collaborative projects with partner universities)	11	2
US-Pharma	Vice President of Laboratory; Human Resource Director; Learning and Development Manager; Director of Discovery Biology; Recruitment and academic liaison manager (2 areas); Head of external technology acquisition; Licensing and collaborations manager; Director of Project Management; project leaders and other scientific staff engaged in collaborative projects	16	3
J-ICT	Headquarters: General managers, R&D Group (2); General Manager of Global R&D; Managers, human resources and recruitment (3); Cambridge Laboratory: Manager (Japanese)	7	1
J-Pharma	Headquarters: Director of Planning and Co-ordination in Clinical Research Director (formerly co-ordinator and researcher in UK Lab) R&D Planning (formerly laboratory manager in US Lab) London Laboratory: Research Director (Japanese); researcher (Japanese)	4	1

Source: The author.

1990. The "bias" of my sample is inevitable because of the contrasted national patterns of sectoral development in pharmaceuticals between the two countries.

The case studies focus on the MNEs' R&D laboratories in the United Kingdom. All four units studied are research labs with the objectives of exploring new technologies or researching new scientific fields. The two US laboratories are part of the globally distributed R&D centres, whereas the Japanese ones are campus-based laboratories, reflecting the distinctive pattern of Japanese overseas R&D investments. I collected data using semi-structured interviews with senior managerial and technical staff in R&D, human resource, and academic liaison groups, as well as those directly engaged in collaboration with the universities. Also, I conducted a small number of interviews with the key academics in the partner universities to gain a balanced understanding of the collaborative relationships.

In the case of the Japanese firms, I did the interviews with senior management at the headquarters in Japan. This was necessary to collect essential company information not readily available in the United Kingdom. The contacts with the headquarters were also important for gaining access to the UK laboratories. The Japanese interview sample is much smaller, owing to the difficulties in gaining access to key staff in Japan and the small scale of the local laboratories. Access to J-Pharma in Japan was relatively restricted, and only four interviews were carried out. However, this was compensated by the fact that the two interviewees at the headquarters in Japan had previously worked in the overseas laboratories in the United States and United Kingdom, and they were able to provide rich information on the role of these laboratories.

The interviews in Japan were conducted in Japanese and, in the United Kingdom, in English. I conducted the interviews with the two US MNEs between 1999 and 2000 and those with the Japanese MNEs during 2001 (see table 8.2 for the interview sample). I recorded and transcribed all the interviews, supplementing these data with company documents, press releases, and other relevant published materials.

8.5   US MNEs' R&D laboratories in the United Kingdom

The two US MNEs examined here have sought to build an integrated form of network R&D organization on a global basis since the early 1990s. An important policy focus of the R&D organizational restructuring in recent years has been to enhance global co-ordination and integration of the geographically distributed research laboratories into the global knowledge networks. Both the UK laboratories enjoy a clearly defined and controlled autonomy within the MNE groups in terms of their R&D and business strategies, and relationships with local education and research systems. Both companies manifest a strategic aim to build a systematic and all-encompassing approach to the way they interact with local universities. Gaining access to and recruitment of scientific personnel appears to be a key strategic objective of their university links. Moreover, the companies also increasingly seek to enlarge their space for the search of scientific expertise by tapping into the wider European labor markets. This is particularly notable in the case of US-Pharma.

US-ICT: The Bristol Corporate Laboratory

Global R&D networks and knowledge sourcing   US-ICT is a company dedicated to the design, manufacture, and provision of services and systems for measurement, computation, imaging, and communications. In 2000, it had 88,500 employees and over 540 sales and support offices and distributors worldwide in more than 120 countries. Since 1998, US-ICT has undergone radical transformation, attempting to reinvent itself from a hardware manufacturer to an enterprise service producer and systems integrator. The R&D conducted by US-ICT is distributed between the corporate laboratories and R&D groups at the divisional level. Its central research organization is globally distributed, employing 800 employees at laboratories in six sites around the world. Its headquarters are in California and Bristol. The Bristol site employs approximately 240 people and is the second largest research site.

An important consequence of the restructuring has been an increase in the global co-ordination of the corporate laboratories, now having become a single distributed center. There is thus only one central laboratory, with sites in California and Bristol. Projects are conducted on a global basis, involving expertise and resources located in the geographically dispersed R&D units. Co-ordination is achieved via global project teams and the promotion of systematic human resource strategies. Another significant shift in US-ICT's R&D strategy has been the closer alignment of the research programs with business activities. This has resulted in a change in the focus of the research towards application oriented and short-term objectives. To counterbalance this, US-ICT is seeking to maintain its basic research capability by widening its technological base through external collaboration and networking. This has also been prompted by the need to speed up the learning process and to create new competencies in an environment where the rate of change is dramatic. Another issue facing the company has been the growing intensity of competition for scientific personnel. The critical issues facing the company's corporate laboratories are thus twofold: (a) the need to sustain the vitality and originality of the fundamental core of scientific knowledge available to the group; and (b) to ensure that they have a stable supply of core R&D staff.

Building strategic partnerships with universities A key aspect of the company's policy response has been to develop closer links with major research universities in order to gain early access to the best scientific expertise. Since the mid-1990s, there has been a conscious policy effort to develop more systematic and stronger links with universities. A new position responsible for external academic links was created in 1995 at Bristol. The mandate of this new role is the development of a "Strategic University Relations Program" on a global scale together with their counterparts at the US headquarters. The mission of this program has been to concentrate resources on a small number of key institutions from which the company is most likely to resource its human and intellectual capital. The term "strategic partnership" is used to denote the intention to forge long-term and trusting relationships with key institutions. These are sustained by a range of linking mechanisms including an industrial input to curriculum development, student placements, exchange of staff, and collaboration in research.

The intention behind all these measures, according to the academic relations manager, is to have "early access to the most talented people" and "trusted access to the best ideas." By becoming a trusted partner in the academic community, US-ICT would be in a better position to catch the best students early, but also have opportunities to influence the education and training of future researchers. Student placement is an especially important linking mechanism and recruitment channel. US-ICT favors recruiting students who have spent a period of internship with them, the purpose of this being that students will have gained the business understanding and organizational knowledge, and hence will have become more qualified and suitable than those with purely specialist academic training.

The competition for scientific expertise and the need to gain access to wider knowledge networks are key factors driving US-ICT to establish strategic partnerships with universities. The company recognises that "there is no better way to access knowledge than through people." US-ICT is developing these links on a global scale, but the main focus is on the UK and US institutions.

Linking global and local innovation networks: a strategic partner-ship with the University of Bristol   Although US-ICT's university links are co-ordinated on a global scale, the regional factor plays an important role. The close relationship between Bristol Laboratories and the University of Bristol illustrates this. The company has historically developed various links with the university and has recently identified it as one of its global strategic partners. The relationship has intensified in recent years, and become more focused on the Computer Science Department and more recently, also the Mathematics Department. The links have developed around two types of activities: (a) the funding of specific research projects; and (b) personnel-based exchanges including student placements, exchange of staff, and participation of the company's staff in curriculum development and project supervision. These links are guided by a broad policy framework agreed between the university and the company. It includes a mission statement defining a long-term initiative to facilitate the exchange of knowledge through the exchange and sharing of people. The company is currently funding two research projects, both of which are basic in nature. The research objectives are very broadly defined, leaving the academics with a great deal of discretion in defining their own agenda. It appears that the main objective is to use the research projects as vehicles for gaining access to the expertise and knowledge networks of an eminent professor in computer science, rather than the generation of specific technology or intellectual properties. The recruitment of students is seen as a very important part of the partnership:

> Transfer through people is the most effective way of working in partnership over a long period of time with a key university, and as a result their students come to work with us. These mechanisms are very effective. (Managing Director, HP Lab Bristol)

> The recruitment side is very important. They [US-ICT] want to be able to get access to students and to try and target and persuade the best ones, the ones that fit their profile. They want those as early as possible because the experience is they can often be put to use almost immediately. And even if they couldn't, it would be worth investing in further development of them until they can. So that's what a lot of it's about. (Head of Computer Science Department)

Another focal point of interaction is the Basic Research Institute in Mathematical Science (BRIMS). This is a hybrid research organization located at the interface between the company and the university. It seeks to create a permeable boundary between the company and university to facilitate the interchange of people and flow of knowledge. BRIMS was set up in 1994 as part of the company's "Basic Research Initiative" to widen its research base. It is dedicated to pure basic research without any immediate obligation to transfer technology. It has developed close relationships with the Department of Mathematics at Bristol University. The relationships are maintained primarily through joint appointments of key research staff and various informal exchange activities. The research staff are funded by the company, but are formally employed by the university. They represent "joint human capital" shared between the company and the university. For the company, BRIMS helps to enhance its visibility and reputation in the academic world and acts as a vehicle for attracting top researchers. The director of BRIMS described the organization as a "recruitment porthole" for the company.

The relationship between US-ICT and Bristol University represents a model of industry–university partnership structured around the interchange of people and the reciprocal flow of knowledge. The recruitment of students and gaining access to top academic researchers appear to be the priority goals. Forging strong institutional links with key universities amounts to the formation of an "extended human resource system" for the company. It ensures that the company has a stable supply of core R&D personnel and enables the company to broaden the scope of human resources and knowledge networks into the wider academic community. By embedding itself in the local higher education and research system, US-ICT seeks to integrate the local knowledge resources with its global R&D networks.

US-Pharma: central research in the United Kingdom

Global R&D networks and knowledge sourcing US-Pharma is a global pharmaceutical company, which has been experiencing rapid growth and expansion in recent years. The company boasts the industry's largest pharmaceutical R&D organisation: its Global Research and Development division, with approximately 12,000 employees, six discovery sites, and a planned investment in total R&D of about $5 billion in 2001. The company has formed alliances with more than 250 partners in academia and industry that strengthen its position in science and biotechnology. The case study presented here is based on interviews I carried out at US-Pharma's Central Research in the United Kingdom. It is the company's largest research facility outside the United States with over 1,500 employees at the site. It is also the company's European headquarters for the discovery and development of new drugs.

Central research at US-Pharma is organized on a global basis, with a central research committee overseeing the whole portfolio, covering the different sites worldwide. Project-based management has become a key managerial tool for the co-ordination of global R&D. Research teams and project managers located at the different sites increasingly work in co-ordination with each other. US-Pharma has increasingly recognized the need for external collaboration, and has significantly increased its external technology investments over the last five years. Although external collaborative projects at US-Pharma are co-ordinated on a global basis, most of the company's academic links in the United Kingdom have developed on a personalized basis through the contacts of individual scientists. There is a strong emphasis on encouraging a "bottom-up" approach and "getting the science right." About 30 percent of the company's external collaboration budget is spent on academic links. The bulk of the linkage activities takes the form of a "quasi-subsidy" whereby the company does not demand a precise contribution or service. This includes the following categories: (a) *"goodwill grants"* – that is, money that is given to universities to fund a course or student project; and (b) *CASE studentships* that are partly funded by the company and partly by government. The main aim is to use these as mechanisms for building relationships with individual academics or departments, although there have been examples where student projects led to important findings that were valuable for the company.

Higher on the collaborative scale are (c) projects that have a *"semi-commercial"* component, whereby the company's requests are clearly defined, even though the expected return is usually quite flexibly defined. *Post-doctoral collaborations* belong to this category in which "the science" is an important consideration. It is seen as the most important form of collaboration and "good value for money." A large proportion of the money for academic collaboration goes to this form of scheme, and the company currently funds about thirty post-docs. It also funds (d) larger-scale projects, referred to as *"strategic collaboration,"* but this seems to be rather rare. The main project that has been identified is the collaboration with the Biosciences Department at the University of Dundee that involves a consortium of five pharmaceutical companies and the Medical Research Council. The collaboration enables the company to gain quick and cost-effective access to an extremely complex area in which it has previously had little experience. It facilitates rapid development of new expertise and provides networks of academic contacts to support in-house innovation. The company also recognises that recruitment of students is another important beneficial aspect of the collaboration.

Employee resourcing: building strategic partnerships with universities and increased "Europeanization"   In the face of growing competition for qualified scientific personnel, US-Pharma has sought to develop a more focused and targeted approach to the ways it relates to higher-education institutions. The Director of Human Resources in Central Discovery described recruitment as a very "tough" area. Forging closer academic links has become so important that the company has recently created "strategic recruitment specialists" in chemistry and biology, staffed by scientists with PhD qualifications, to liaise and develop strategic relationships with their "preferred institutions." As part of its employee-resourcing strategies, US-Pharma provides teaching funds for a number of UK universities to develop courses in key areas that have skills shortages. However, more significant efforts to boost skills supply take place at the industry level, with US-Pharma engaged in initiatives through working groups within the Association of the British Pharmaceutical Industry (ABPI) to attract graduates to Combinatorial Chemistry. The company is also involved in similar initiatives in Bioinformatics and is a leading member of the UK Life Sciences Committee Working Party on postgraduate and postdoctoral training.

Another significant development in the company's recruitment strategy is the trend towards "Europeanisation." This was initially driven by shortages of people, but the company has increasingly recognized the qualitative benefits of casting its recruitment net wider. At the PhD level, it is notable that the company's European strategy has been prompted mainly by the need to compete for the best scientific talent, especially in biology and biotechnology. There is a growing awareness of the importance of tapping into the European science base in order to gain early access to "new and "emergent" ideas.

8.6   Japanese MNEs' R&D laboratories in UK universities

The two cases I examine here are both university-based laboratories and can be considered as typical of Japanese firms' approach to tapping into the foreign academic knowledge base. They were established some ten years ago and the companies have made a substantial investment in them. They represent the European nodes in the companies' tripolar global research network. The global R&D organization of the two companies, in contrast to the two US cases, approximates the "hub model" rather than an "integrated network." The central research laboratories at home maintain tight control over the research programs in the overseas units through allocation of resources and close monitoring. Both laboratories are managed by Japanese research scientists dispatched from the central laboratories at home. The pharmaceutical company's initial attempt to appoint a foreign research director and grant its London laboratory autonomy proved to be "unsuccessful" from the viewpoint of the parent company. This subsequently led the company to take strong measures to reintegrate the overseas unit within its domestic research facilities. Moreover, in both cases, the relationships with the universities revolve around the advancement of specific technologies core to the companies' product development strategies.

J-ICT: the Cambridge Laboratory

Global R&D networks and knowledge sourcing J-ICT is one of the world's leading global electronics and ICT companies, with 1,069 subsidiaries, including 335 overseas corporations. It has seven corporate research laboratories in Japan, employing a total of 2,700 research staff. The Central Research Laboratory is the largest, employing 930 research staff. J-ICT's tripolar research networks include four research and design centres in the United States and five sites in Europe. The scale of these laboratories is relatively small. The US facilities employ a total of sixty people and the European ones around thirty. In the United States, J-ICT focuses mainly on medium-term applied research in the semiconductor area, whereas in the United Kingdom a key objective has been to strengthen fundamental research. The relationship with Cambridge University, on which this case study is based, appears to be the most important and visible one. The European sites are co-ordinated by a parent organisation, the Corporate Technology Group, based in the United Kingdom. The management team of the Group is solely Japanese, comprizing a general manager and four local laboratory managers, all of whom are Japanese expatriates.

The Cambridge Laboratory: an "embedded laboratory" for collaborative research and knowledge transfer The J-ICT Cambridge Laboratory (JCL) was established in 1989 in close collaboration with the Microelectronics Research Centre (MRC) of Cambridge University. It aims to create new concepts of advanced electronic/opto-electronic devices. J-ICT made an initial donation towards the building of the laboratory and its subsequent extension, and rents laboratory space in MRC. It also pays an annual collaboration grant decided in a written agreement drawn up with the university on a five-year basis. Subjects of research are agreed with the university, J-ICT owns all of the IPRs generated from collaborative research with the university, receiving royalties on all commercial benefits from patents and research exploitation.

JCL is relatively small, employing seven permanent research staff and two fixed-term contract staff. It collaborates with twenty-four researchers from the university, led by the Director of the MRC. The total team size of about thirty is considered appropriate for fundamental research. J-ICT refers to the Cambridge Laboratory as an "embedded" laboratory. This involves the research group of JCL being physically located within the same building as MRC, the frequent sharing of research staff and information, and intimate co-operation in research. J-ICT considers the main advantage of an embedded laboratory to be its ability to share and influence the purpose and targets of research identified within MRC. Indeed, one of the main roles of JCL is to integrate the fundamental research conducted at the university with the strategic objectives of the company.

JCL is funded by the Central Research Laboratory in Japan. The subject areas and future direction of JCL are regularly discussed at an annual advisory committee meeting at Cambridge, involving people from J-ICT and the collaborating academics. The laboratory manager of JCL is a Japanese researcher from the Central R&D who acts as the key liaison person between J-ICT and JCL. He visits Japan at least twice a year to report on progress and decide the future objectives of JCL. J-ICT also makes intensive use of progress reviews and frequent written reports for monitoring the progress and research direction of JCL.

There are currently three collaborative projects, one of which has reached a stage whereby it is currently in development in collaboration with the Central Research Laboratory in Japan. This project, one of the most publicised, has been heralded as a breakthrough in semiconductor memory technology. The project started ten years ago at the initiation of JCL, with research on single-electron devices lasting for seven years, representing a cumulative learning period necessary to gain the expertise that formed the foundation of this invention. JCL regards its role in interfacing "the scientific" with the "development" world as being critical for the innovation. The laboratory manager interviewed stressed the importance of having Japanese staff based in JCL to fulfill this important knowledge-transfer function.

The role of the Cambridge Laboratory in J-ICT's global knowledge networks JCL plays two roles in J-ICT's global knowledge networks. The first is the making of scientific breakthroughs through collaboration with MRC, and the second is managing the transition from scientific to development work in conjunction with the Central Research Laboratory in Japan. It appears that JCL is simultaneously fulfilling the role of an "innovator" as well as that of a "contributor." The organizational learning capability of JCL is augmented by its ability to leverage the scientific expertise within MRC. The collaboration with MRC enables the company to collaborate with some of the most highly qualified researchers in the United Kingdom and to gain access to a vital source of human resources. JCL itself employs only seven permanent researchers but is able to collaborate with twenty-plus research staff of MRC. JCL also funds postdocs and doctoral students, who work on projects jointly devised and supervized by the academics and JCL. This further strengthens the links with the University and helps to promote knowledge exchange.

The evidence thus far suggests that the JCL–MRC collaboration has been a success, in terms of both tangible outputs and its apparent strategic importance for J-ICT. Both the J-ICT management and researchers at Cambridge described the partnership as "stable and successful." A number of factors may have contributed to this. First, JCL has been able to embed itself within the university, both physically and socially. It has established strong personal and social networks within the university and has engaged in reciprocal knowledge sharing. A senior Cambridge researcher interviewed emphasized the importance of the "two-way process" and how JCL "brings in a lot of extra scientific expertise and knowledge to the university group." Secondly, J-ICT has made large investments in its domestic R&D and established a strong scientific culture at its Central Laboratory at home. This facilitates scientific communication with the overseas researchers and the appropriation of scientific breakthroughs. Finally, the tight personnel linkages have also contributed to the integration of research at JCL with product innovation at home.

It is, however, worthy of note that JCL is relatively small. Its collaborative objectives and research focus have remained highly specific and tightly connected with the product innovation strategy at home. This indicates that the innovative capabilities may be limited or circumscribed, in that if they were more extensive, they would be able to conduct a more varied spectrum of research and broaden their scope of knowledge search. It could be argued that JCL remains primarily a "strategic listening post" rather than being developed into a distributed center of excellence with its own distinctive capabilities and autonomy. The JCL–MRC collaboration is itself just one node within J-ICT's global knowledge networks. J-ICT also participates in several other university collaborations within Europe, Japan, and the United States. At the time of the study, these have not yet been fully integrated at the global level, with the Central Laboratory in Japan acting as the co-ordinating center.

J-Pharma: the London Laboratory

Global R&D networks   J-Pharma is the fourth largest pharmaceutical company in Japan. Nevertheless, its annual turnover and R&D investment are quite small compared with those of the global giants.

US-Pharma, for example, with a turnover of £8.8 billion ($15 billion) was able to invest £1.7 billion ($2.9 billion) in R&D in 1999 compared with J-Pharma's R&D investment of £265 million ($450 million). Originally founded in 1936, J-Pharma's overseas operations were initiated in 1979 with the establishment of East Asia Regional Services in Singapore, and J-Pharma USA in 1981. In 1982, J-Pharma's basic research facilities became operational with the construction of the Tsukuba Research Laboratory. It functions as the nucleus of drug development activities and employs around 400 research staff. Overseas R&D facilities were commenced through the establishment of the J-Pharma Research Institute in Boston in 1989 and the initiation of J-Pharma's London Research Laboratories in 1990. Together, these form the company's tripolar research network, with the Tsukuba Laboratory acting as the focal link.

The London Research Laboratory: an experiment in dual-channel organizational learning   J-Pharma's initial investment of £12 million ($20 million) to build and equip the London Research Laboratory (hereafter referred to as the Japan London Laboratory, JLL) at University College London (UCL) was heralded as "the largest and the longest-term funding arrangement that any company has ever made with a university in the UK" by the Committee of Vice Chancellors and Principals (Financial Times 1990). An eminent American cellular neuro-biologist was appointed research director in 1992. Several academics at UCL were closely involved in the setting up of the laboratory and sat on its Advisory Board. JLL had a multinational research staff of forty, including some scientists seconded from the main research laboratories in Tsukuba. JLL's initial focus was basic research in cell and molecular biology, aiming to discover novel ways of treating certain disorders of the central nervous system. For the first five years, JLL developed close links with the academics through consultancy, student projects, and other informal exchange activities. There was a strong expectation on the part of the academic community that JLL would be integrated into the university and engaged in reciprocal scientific exchanges.

The establishment of JLL represented an experiment in what Methé and Penner-Hahn (1999) describe as "dual-channel" organizational learning, in that J-Pharma perceived its weakness to lie in pharmaceutical discovery research, especially in biotechnology. Therefore, it was not only engaged in "single-loop" learning in acquiring the scientific expertise in molecular biology, it also was engaged in "double-loop" learning in attempting to acquire the organizational routines necessary for independent basic research. JLL thus placed emphasis both on the transfer of knowledge and also on gaining an understanding of the research process conducted at JLL. However, in 1997 there was a dramatic change in the JLL's research orientation. Its research focus was shifted from basic research to applied (drug discovery) research, and the American research director was replaced by a Japanese, an experienced drug development researcher from Tsukuba Laboratory. The shift in research focus and tightening of organizational control have had significant adverse effects on JLL's links with the university and its capacity for learning.

The shift from basic to applied research: a failure in organizational learning? JLL was initially conceived so as to focus on basic, curiosity-driven research that might provide new drug candidates that would then be developed at the Tsukuba research laboratories in Japan. Initially the lab was given sufficient independence to carry out this mandate. However, after a few years without producing what was felt to be significant drug candidates, it was reintegrated within the research activities of the Tsukuba lab. JLL currently collaborates on projects with the Tsukuba laboratory, whereby project team members concurrently conduct research on the same project. Tight control is maintained through project management with intensive two-way communication between the two labs via the internet and visits of researchers. The role of JLL appears to have shifted from being that of an "innovator" in the global R&D network to a "contributor" within the product development system at home.

The reason given for this dramatic change of research orientation and management, according to the interviews with J-Pharma, was that following three or four years of investment, no new drug candidates had been discovered. It was stated in the interviews that the president of J-Pharma became impatient for some return on the investment made. However, this expectation and the subsequent change of direction seem remarkable given the fact that J-Pharma's president had stated that the aim of JLL "is to produce good medicines for the central nervous system. It will take at least five to six years – and in many cases more than 10 years – to reach that stage" (Financial Times 1990). It can be argued that the change in research orientation partly reflects the "failure" of J-Pharma to gain an understanding of the research process conducted at JLL and hence to evaluate its research progress appropriately. The tangible output of drug candidates used to evaluate the achievements of JLL may not be a sufficient measure of the success of the collaboration. The academic at UCL responsible for the initial setting up of JLL repeatedly pointed out in the interview that "there were some very serious misunderstandings" about the nature of doing basic research and the role expected of JLL:

The real problem was this misunderstanding about direction from the beginning. Their claim was they had always had the same thing in mind, they wanted to see drugs on line in three to five years and that was not on the table in the early years.

The dramatic shift in the research direction of JLL also reflects the wider change in the strategic focus of the company. After the mid-1990s, J-Pharma concentrated its resources on a number of strategic therapeutic areas, with the research in neurology conducted at JLL being the most important one. The Tsukuba laboratory has taken the lead in the development of new drugs in this field. Indeed, the change of research director at JLL, from an American academic scientist to a Japanese researcher with drug development experience, can be considered as an attempt to harness and exploit the research conducted at JLL. A related factor arose from the need to achieve tighter organizational control. Head office managers considered that the foreign research director sought too much independence and could not be held accountable for the direction of research. Following the appointment of a Japanese research director, JLL became more integrated within J-Pharma.

The dramatic change in research direction resulted in very high staff turnover, with half of the research staff leaving, and the subsequent alienation of numerous academics and cessation of substantial links with the university. There is now little formal collaboration between JLL and the university. Informal contacts and personnel exchanges also appear to be minimal. One of the key academics initially active in the links claimed that JLL is now "a non-entity to the university." He described the change in research direction as "an enormous disappointment," and reckoned that "none of the really good basic research at the university will ever find its way through the doors of J-Pharma." This is because the community of academic scientists on campus no longer felt that they were connected. This raises questions about its long-term ability to build academic links and tap into the wider knowledge networks. J-Pharma itself has also expressed doubts about the value on return for the investment in JLL and its long-term viability.

The collaboration between J-Pharma and UCL has not been considered a success by either of the parties concerned. J-Pharma has not been able to sustain its initial effort in dual-channel organizational learning and has failed to establish close ties with the local academic community. The company was unable initially to co-ordinate the research conducted at JLL owing to its independence, and hence took strong measures to integrate JLL within its domestic research facilities. This alienated the local researchers and academics and weakened JLL's ability to tap into the local knowledge networks. The experience of JLL demonstrates the tension of adaptation and integration of this dispersed center of learning within J-Pharma's global knowledge network. JLL's apparent lack of success also reflects a deeper problem in organizational learning facing the company.

Although J-Pharma is one of the most research-intensive Japanese pharmaceutical companies, its R&D investment remains very small. The company's traditional weakness in basic research and its strong reliance on a cohesive product-development system means that it might not have developed the necessary organizational routines to recognise the value and harness the outputs of basic research conducted abroad. The "misunderstandings" between the company and the university highlighted in the case study are symptomatic of the "communication distance" between them. Evidence elsewhere suggests that the organizational learning difficulties experienced by J-Pharma are common problems for firms in the Japanese pharmaceutical industry (Roehl, Mitchell, and Slattery 1995; Chikudate 1999).

8.7   A comparative analysis of the cases

The case studies reveal some fundamental differences between the US and Japanese MNEs in the ways they manage their global R&D networks and seek to tap geographically dispersed scientific knowledge and expertise. To start with, the mode of co-ordination and integration of overseas R&D units differs significantly between firms from the two countries. The US MNEs have sought to develop globally integrated networks of R&D co-ordinated by project management. The local R&D facilities were granted a considerable degree of autonomy to generate links with the local academic institutions and research communities, while both the Japanese MNEs were characterized by a more centralized R&D structure in which intensive use was made of communication and Japanese nationals to integrate the overseas facilities into the product-development systems at home. Their international R&D organization displays the characteristic features of a "hub model" in which the central R&D at home maintains strong technological leadership and exerts tight control over the decentralized R&D units overseas. Empirical evidence based on other studies also supports these observations (Chiesa 1999; Gassman and von Zedwitz 1999; Asakawa and Lehrer 2003).

The case studies also show a significant contrast between the US and Japanese firms in their patterns of interaction with local universities. In the case of the US MNEs, it appears that the main motives behind the establishment of overseas basic research and academic links are the desire to tap globally dispersed scientific labor pools and to augment the basic research capability that previously existed within corporate R&D. Both companies studied have sought to extend their knowledge networks to academic institutions in a fluid and expanded way through research collaboration, personnel exchanges, participation in education and training programs, and recruitment of students. Indeed, the sourcing of scientific human capital and recruitment of students are the primary objectives in their development of "strategic partnerships" with universities.

In contrast, the Japanese MNEs have not developed this type of broad-based university relationships and human resource strategies. The Japanese R&D facilities established at the universities are relatively small and engaged in rather focused research activities. They are established primarily for the acquisition of specialized expertise and to help the Japanese firms develop new organizational routines in basic research. This is especially important for J-Pharma. This reflects a distinctive mode of R&D globalization among Japanese firms generally whereby overseas academic collaboration is used to compensate for the weakness of basic research at home. Both of the facilities are located on-campus, and they enable the Japanese firms to gain access to local academic expertise through research collaboration. However, the recruitment of local scientific personnel does not appear to be a key motive behind the collaboration.

Using Santoro and Chakrabati's (2001) typology of industry–university relationships, I argue that the US MNEs are acting more as "collegial players" in that they seek to establish long-term "strategic partnerships" with key academic institutions forging multi-dimensional and trusting relationships through personnel exchanges and recruitment. This has enabled them to build strong social networks and personnel linkages with the local academic community, enhancing their ability to tap into the local knowledge sources. Conversely, the Japanese MNEs appear to act more as "aggressive" or "targeted players" in that they seek more tangible research outcomes and are more restricted in their attempts to access local knowledge networks.

Another striking contrast between the MNEs from the two countries concerns the role of human resource strategy in global co-ordination and local knowledge sourcing. The US firms have placed a strong emphasis on developing a global human resource system and international project teams to co-ordinate the decentralized R&D networks. There are exchanges of scientific staff among the different R&D units, and recruitment is also carried out on a global basis. Another important aim of their human resource strategy is to support integration within the local external

Table 8.3 *Global R&D networks and transnational learning: summary of key differences between the US and Japanese approaches*

	US MNEs	Japanese MNEs
Home-based model of learning and innovation	Professional community model	Organizational community model
International R&D organization	Integrated R&D networks	Hub model
Nature of relationships with local universities	Collegial players	Aggressive or targeted players
Human resource strategy	Recruitment of local scientific personnel important	Recruitment not important
Degree of embeddedness in local innovation systems	High	Limited

Source: The author.

networks through recruitment and personnel exchanges with their academic partners. It could be argued that the US MNEs have sought to develop a human resource system at the global level and also to extend this to the local academic institutions in order to create a global scientific network for knowledge sourcing.

The human resource strategy of the Japanese MNEs, by contrast, focuses predominantly on internal integration and knowledge transfer between the R&D center at home and the overseas units. The key actors are the Japanese expatriate managers and researchers whose main role is to monitor local progress and to appropriate knowledge acquired from the local units. The human resource systems of the Japanese firms remain ethnocentric, with limited extension of the home-based internal labor market to the global arena. The price they pay for this strong internal focus is that they lose an important aspect of knowledge sourcing through linkages with local labor markets and personnel exchanges.

The implication of these differences is that the US MNEs have been able to embed themselves to a greater extent within the local innovation networks. The Japanese MNEs, by contrast, appear to be more limited in the scope of their knowledge sourcing and their ability to tap into the wider knowledge networks. The main results of the case studies are summarized in table 8.3.

The differences between the US and Japanese MNEs observed in the study reflect the contrasting logics of the "professional community" and the "organizational community" models of learning and innovation playing out in the global arena (Lam 2000, 2002). In the case of the

US firms, the professional model allows firms considerable flexibility to extend their human resources and learning systems across organizational and geographical boundaries. Moreover, US firms have historically established strong links with academia, leading to a greater degree of human resource mobility between the two sectors, and the formation of research networks within a global scientific space (Mahroum 2000). In contrast, the Japanese organizational community model, characterized by a strong firm-based human resource system and internal organizational proximity, appears to have inhibited the ability of firms to create a transnational learning space through extended professional networks.

It could be argued that US firms, compared with Japanese firms, enjoy an institutional advantage in developing transnational learning spaces to broaden the scope of their knowledge exploration. This advantage may be reinforced when they locate their R&D units in an environment where labor market institutions and systems of higher education are congruent with those at home. Both the US and UK employment systems are organized around liberal market institutions conducive to horizontal labor mobility and external learning. The two countries also share a similar background of having a strong higher education sector and research base. This institutional proximity may have facilitated the transfer of home-based learning and human resource practices, and led to a higher degree of local embeddedness of the US firms. The Japanese firms, on the other hand, appear to be more limited in the scope of their transnational learning because of the constraints imposed by their home-based institutions. The divergence between the UK institutions and the Japanese MNEs' domestic ones may also have created a bigger barrier to learning.

Another factor to be taken into account is the relative strength of different sectors in national innovation systems and how this affects firms' globalization strategies and learning patterns. This is especially significant in the case of Japan where there are substantial differences between the ICT and pharmaceutical industries in terms of their domestic R&D capabilities and global competitiveness (Kitschelt 1991; Odagiri and Goto 1996). The Japanese ICT and electronics industry has been able to maintain a large domestic R&D capability and sustain its global competitiveness over the last three decades. Firms in this industry developed their overseas capabilities only reluctantly in recent years, indeed, their overseas basic research laboratories were established primarily to act as strategic "listening posts."

Conversely, the Japanese pharmaceutical industry is younger, firms are much smaller in size, and firms have less-well-developed domestic R&D capacity. Until recently, Japanese pharmaceutical companies did not receive the level of government backing enjoyed by the ICT sector.

There had been a significant historical underinvestment in R&D in the pharmaceutical sector. Because a firm's absorptive capacity is a function of its level of prior related knowledge, and because those with greater capacity in internal R&D are also able to contribute more to a collaboration as well as learn more extensively from it (Cohen and Levinthal, 1990), I argue that J-ICT's relative domestic strength in R&D has enabled it to have the absorptive capacity to appropriate the scientific discoveries made in its overseas units and also to engage in more effective learning. By contrast, J-Pharma may not possess the necessary "absorptive capacity" to benefit from the knowledge gained from its overseas research facilities without significant augmentation of domestic research capabilities. Such sector differences appear to be less evident in the case of the US firms.

8.8   Conclusions

Relative to many Japanese MNEs, US firms have developed a greater organizational capacity for co-ordinating globally dispersed learning and embedding themselves in local innovation networks. This is because the liberal institutional environment within which US MNEs have developed enables them to extend their organizational and human resource systems across institutional and geographical boundaries. By contrast, Japanese MNEs appear to be more limited in their transnational learning because of the much more tightly integrated organizational and business system within which they are embedded. The evidence I present here generally supports the "social embeddedness thesis" of the institutional perspective, namely that home-based institutions provide the basis for the development of MNEs' transnational social spaces, and thus their strategic behavior and organizational forms will continue to diverge.

Three further related points are worthy of attention. The first is that the concept of "transnational social space" needs to be broadened to incorporate the external, local networks of firms. Morgan's (2001) and Whitley's (1999, 2001) analysis of the "transnational social space" of MNEs focuses narrowly on the internal governance structures and application of firms' existing competencies. It neglects the external dimension of firms' transnational social space and puts too little emphasis on the dynamics of organizational learning within MNEs. My analysis suggests that external networks and the local embeddedness of the subsidiary R&D units are critical to organizational learning and innovation within MNEs. The innovative behavior of MNEs cannot be fully understood without taking into account how national institutions shape their transnational learning spaces, encompassing the internal as well as external networks.

The second point concerns the need to revise the notion of "social embeddedness." While the nature and boundaries of firms' "transnational learning spaces" are heavily influenced by their home-based institutions, the dynamics of the interaction between home-based and local institutions may also be relevant. A growing body of work attests that learning is essentially a social and interactive process rooted in spatial and relational proximity (Lundvall 1992; Saxenian 1994; Gertler, Wolfe, and Garkut 2000). MNEs are attracted to places rich in knowledge sources and technological capabilities in order to exploit the innovative richness arising from the social dynamics of local learning (Gertler 2001). Institutional proximity between the home- and host-country environment may lead to a greater ease in local learning and knowledge transfer. Future research should consider the role of the host-country context in influencing the dynamics of learning and innovation within MNEs. A revised "social embeddedness" thesis should be flexible enough to accommodate a role for the host-country context in the explanatory framework.

A final point to note is that the emphasis on national institutional logic underlying the innovative behavior of MNEs does not imply national uniformity and the absence of sectoral variation. Countries with different institutional arrangements develop and reproduce varied systems of economic organization with different social and innovative capabilities – in particular, industries and sectors. Globalization of innovation may indeed reinforce, and not dismantle, nationally distinctive patterns of innovation (Cantwell 1995). In this chapter, I illustrate with case studies the social dynamics underpinning this process. Future research should examine in greater detail whether the differences in the global R&D organization and learning activities of MNEs support their differing innovation trajectories.

REFERENCES

Asakawa, K., 2001. "Organisational Tension in International R&D Management: The Case of Japanese Firms," *Research Policy*, 30: 735–757
Asakawa, K. and M. Lehrer, 2003. "Managing Local Knowledge Assets Globally: The Role of Regional Innovation Relays," *Journal of World Business*, 38: 31–42
Baba, Y., J. Kikuchi, and S. Mori, 1995. "Japan's R&D Strategy Reconsidered: Departure from the Manageable Risks," *Technovation*, 15(2): 65–78
Belderbos, R., 2001. "Overseas Innovations by Japanese Firms: An Analysis of Patent and Subsidiary Data," *Research Policy*, 30: 313–332
Blanc, H. and C. Sierra, 1999. "The Internationalisation of R&D by Multinationals: A Trade-Off Between External and Internal Proximity," *Cambridge Journal of Economics*, 23: 187–206

Cantwell, J. A., 1995. "The Globalisation of Technology: What Remains of the Product Cycle Model?," *Cambridge Journal of Economics*, 19: 155–174

Chiesa, V., 1999. "Technology Development Control Styles in Multinational Corporations: A Case Study," *Journal of Engineering and Technology Management*, 16: 191–206

Chikudate, N., 1999. "Generating Reflexivity from Partnership Formation: A Phenomenological Reasoning on the Partnership Between a Japanese Pharmaceutical Corporation and Western Laboratories," *Journal of Applied Behavioural Science*, 35(3): 287–305

Clark, B. R., 1995. *Places of Inquiry: Research and Advanced Education in Modern Universities*, Berkeley, CA: University of California Press

Cohen, W. M. and D. A. Levinthal, 1990. "Absorptive Capacity: A New Perspective of Learning and Innovation," *Administrative Science Quarterly*, 35: 128–152

Doremus, P. N., W. Keller, L. Pauley, and S. Reich, 1998. *The Myth of the Global Corporation*, Princeton, NJ: Princeton University Press

Dunning, J. H. and C. Wymbs, 1999. "The Geographical Sourcing of Technology-Based Assets by Multinational Enterprises," in D. Archibugi, J. Howells, and J. Michie (eds.), *Innovation Policy in a Global Economy*, Cambridge: Cambridge University Press: 184–224

Feller, I., 1999. "The American University System as a Performer of Basic and Applied Research," in L. M. Branscomb, F. Kodama, and R. Florida (eds.), *University–Industry Linkages in Japan and the United States*, Cambridge, MA and London: MIT Press: 65–101

Financial Times (FT), 1990. "Japanese Put Pounds 50M into University Research," *Financial Times*, September 12: 10

Florida, R., 1997. "The Globalization of R&D: Results of a Survey of Foreign-Affiliated R&D Laboratories in the USA," *Research Policy*, 26: 85–103

Frost, T. S., 2001. "The Geographic Sources of Foreign Subsidiaries' Innovations," *Strategic Management Journal*, 22: 101–123

Gassman, O. and M. von Zedwitz, 1999. "New Concepts and Trends in International R&D Organisation," *Research Policy*, 28: 231–250

Gertler, M. S., 2001. "Best Practice? Geography, Learning and the Institutional Limits to Convergence," *Journal of Economic Geography*, 1: 5–26

Gertler, M. S., D. A. Wolfe, and D. Garkut, 2000. "No Place Like Home? The Embeddedness of Innovation in a Regional Economy," *Review of International Political Economy*, 7(4): 688–718

Gerybadze, A. and G. Reger, 1999. "Globalization of R&D: Recent Changes in the Management of Innovation in Transnational Corporations," *Research Policy*, 28: 251–274

Granstrand, O., 1999. "Internationalization of Corporate R&D: A Study of Japanese and Swedish Corporations," *Research Policy*, 28: 275–302

Gronning, T., 2001. "Towards the 'Integrated Network' as an Organisational Mode for Global Innovative Activities? A Comparative Study of Two Japanese Pharmaceutical Corporations Eisai and Chugai," Paper presented at ESRC Conference on Multinationals, University of Warwick, September

Gupta, A. K. and V. Govindarajan, 2000. "Knowledge Flows Within Multinational Corporations," *Strategic Management Journal*, 21: 473–496
Hage, J. and J. R. Hollingsworth, 2000. "A Strategy for the Analysis of Idea Innovation Networks and Institutions," *Organization Studies*, 21(5): 971–1004
Hane, G., 1999. "Comparing University–Industry Linkages in the United States and Japan," in L. M. Branscomb, F. Kodama, and R. Florida (eds.), *University–Industry Linkages in Japan and the United States*, Cambridge, MA and London: MIT Press: 20–61
Hollingsworth, J. R., 2000. "Doing Institutional Analysis: Implications for the Study of Innovations," *Review of International Political Economy*, 7(4): 595–644
Howells, J., 1990. "The Internationalization of R&D and the Development of Global Research Networks," *Regional Studies*, 24(6): 495–512
Kaounides, L. C., 1999. "Science, Technology, and Global Competitive Advantage: The Strategic Implications of Emerging Technologies for Corporations and Nations," *International Studies of Management and Organisation*, 29(1): 53–79
Kitschelt, H., 1991. "Industrial Governance Structures, Innovation Strategies, and the Case of Japan: Sectoral or Cross-National Comparative Analysis," *International Organisation*, 45(4): 454–493
Kodama, F. and L. M. Branscomb, 1999. "University Research as an Engine for Growth: How Realistic is the Vision?," in L. M. Branscomb, F. Kodama, and R. Florida (eds.), *University–Industry Linkages in Japan and the United States*, Cambridge, MA and London: MIT Press: 3–19
Kogut, B. and U. Zander, 1993. "Knowledge of the Firm and the Evolutionary Theory of the Multinational Corporation," *Journal of International Business Studies*, 24(4): 625–646
Kuemmerle, W., 1997. "Building Effective R&D Capabilities Abroad," *Harvard Business Review*, March–April: 61–70
  1999a. "Foreign Direct Investment in Industrial Research in the Pharmaceutical and Electronics Industries: Results from a Survey of Multinational Firms," *Research Policy*, 28: 179–193
  1999b. "The Drivers of Foreign Direct Investment Into Research and Development: An Empirical Investigation," *Journal of International Business Studies*, 30(1): 1–25
Lam, A., 2000. "Tacit Knowledge, Organisational Learning and Societal Institutions: An Integrated Framework," *Organisational Studies*, 21(3): 487–513
  2002. "Alternative Societal Models of Learning and Innovation in the Knowledge Economy," *International Social Science Journal*, 171: 67–82
Lundvall, B.-Å., 1992. *National Systems of Innovation: Towards a Theory of Innovation and Interactive Learning*, London: Pinter
Mahroum, S., 2000. "Scientists and Global Spaces," *Technology in Society*, 22: 513–523
Methé, D. T., 1995. "Basic Research in Japanese Electronic Companies: An Attempt at Establishing New Organisational Routines," in J. K. Liker,

J. E. Ettlie, and J. C. Campbell (eds.), *Engineered in Japan: Japanese Technology-Management Practices*, New York: Oxford University Press: 17–39

Methé, D. T. and J. D. Penner-Hahn, 1999. "Globalization of Pharmaceutical Research and Development in Japanese Companies: Organisational Learning and the Parent–Subsidiary Relationship," in S. L. Beechler and A. Bird (eds.), *Japanese Multinationals Abroad: Individual and Organisational Learning*, New York: Oxford University Press: 191–210

Meyer-Krahmer, F. and G. Reger, 1999. "New Perspectives on the Innovation Strategies of Multinational Enterprises: Lessons for Technology Policy in Europe," *Research Policy*, 28: 751–776

Morgan, G., 2001. "The Multinational Firm: Organizing Across Institutional and National Divides," in G. Morgan, P. H. Kristensen, and R. Whitley (eds.), *The Multinational Firm: Organizing Across Institutional and National Divides*, Oxford: Oxford University Press: 1–24

Mowery, D. C. and N. Rosenberg, 1993. "The US National Innovation System," in R. R. Nelson (ed.), *National Innovation Systems: A Comparative Analysis*. Oxford: Oxford University Press: 29–75

Nakayama, S. and M. F. Low, 1997. "The Research Function of Universities in Japan," *Higher Education*, 34: 245–258

Nelson, R. R., 1993. *National Innovation Systems: A Comparative Analysis*, Oxford: Oxford University Press

Odagiri, H. and A. Goto, 1996. *Technology and Industrial Development in Japan*, Oxford: Clarendon Press

Oka, H., 1993. "The Industrial Sector's Expectations of Engineering Education," *Economic Eye*, 14: 12–15

Patel, P., 1995. "The Localised Production of Global Technology," *Cambridge Journal of Economics*, 19: 141–153

Patel, P. and M. Vega, 1999. "Patterns of Internationalisation of Corporate Technology: Location vs. Home Country Advantages," *Research Policy*, 28: 145–155

Pauly, L. W. and S. Reich, 1997. "National Structures and Multinational Corporate Behaviour: Enduring Differences in the Age of Globalization," *International Organisation*, 51(1): 1–30

Pavitt, P. and P. Patel, 1999. "Global Corporations and National Systems of Innovation," in D. Archibugi, J. Howells, and J. Michie (eds.), *Innovation Policy in a Global Economy*, Cambridge: Cambridge University Press: 94–119

Pearce, R. D., 1999. "Decentralised R&D and Strategic Competitiveness: Globalised Approaches to Generation and Use of Technology in Multinational Enterprises (MNEs)," *Research Policy*, 28 (2–3): 157–178

Pearce, R. D. and M. Papanastassiou, 1999, "Overseas R&D and the Strategic Evolution of MNEs: Evidence from Laboratories in the UK," *Research Policy*, 28(1): 23–41

Roberts, E. B., 2001. "Benchmarking Global Strategic Management of Technology," *Research Technology Management*, 44(2): 25–36

Roehl, T., W. Mitchell, and R. J. Slattery, 1995. "The Growth of R&D Investment and Organisational Changes by Japanese Pharmaceutical Firms,

1975–1993," in J. K. Liker, J. E. Ettie, and J. C. Campbell (eds.), *Engineered in Japan*, New York: Oxford University Press: 40–69

Sakakibara, K. and D. E. Westney, 1992. "Japan's Management of Global Innovation: Technology Management Crossing Borders," in N. Rosenberg, R. Landau, and D. Mowery (eds.), *Technology and the Wealth of Nations*, Stanford, CA: Stanford University Press: 327–343

Santoro, M. D. and A. K. Chakrabarti, 2001. "Corporate Strategic Objectives for Establishing Relationships with University Research Centres," *IEEE Transactions on Engineering Management*, 48(2): 157–163

Saxenian, A., 1994. *Regional Advantage: Competition and Cooperation in Silicon Valley and Route 128*, Cambridge, MA: Harvard University Press

Spencer, J. W., 2001. "How Relevant is University-Based Scientific Knowledge to Private High-Technology Firms? A United States–Japan Comparison," *Academy of Management Journal*, 44(2): 432–440

Turner, L., D. Ray, and T. Hayward, 1997. *The British Research of Japanese Companies*, London: Insight Japan/Anglo-Japanese Economic Institute

Westney, D. E., 1993. "Country Patterns in R&D Organisation: The United States and Japan," in B. Kogut (ed.), *Country Competitiveness and the Organizing of Work*, New York: Oxford University Press: 36–53

  1994. "The Evolution of Japan's Industrial Research and Development," in M. Aoki and R. Dore (eds.), *The Japanese Firm: The Sources of Competitive Strength*, Oxford: Oxford University Press: 154–177

  1999. "Changing Perspectives on the Organisation of Japanese Multinational Companies," in S. L. Beechler and A. Bird (eds.), *Japanese Multinationals Abroad: Individual and Organisational Learning*, New York: Oxford University Press: 11–29

Whitley, R., 1999. *Divergent Capitalism*, Oxford: Oxford University Press

  2000. "The Institutional Structuring of Innovation Strategies: Business Systems, Firm Types and Patterns of Technical Change in Different Market Economies," *Organisation Studies*, 21(5): 855–886

  2001. "How and Why are International Firms Different? The Consequences of Cross-Border Managerial Coordination for Firm Characteristics and Behaviour," in G. Morgan, P. H. Kristensen, and R. Whitley (eds.), *The Multinational Firm: Organizing Across Institutional and National Divides*, Oxford: Oxford University Press: 27–65

Zanfei, A., 2000. "Transnational Firms and the Changing Organisation of Innovation Activities," *Cambridge Journal of Economics*, 24: 515–542

9 Brain circulation and regional innovation: the Silicon Valley–Hsinchu–Shanghai triangle

AnnaLee Saxenian

9.1 Introduction

After earning a master's degree in electrical engineering at Texas Tech University, Jimmy Lee, like thousands of other immigrant engineers, was drawn to Silicon Valley in the late 1970s. Lee worked for nearly a decade at established companies such as Signetics and National Semiconductor as well as at a start-up, International CMOS Technology, before joining a classmate from National Taiwan University, K. Y. Han, to start their own semiconductor firm, Integrated Silicon Solutions, Inc. (ISSI). After bootstrapping the start-up with their own funds and those of Taiwan-born colleagues, they raised over $9 million, mainly from Asian venture capital funds managed by overseas Chinese engineers.

Lee and Han exploited their connections in both Silicon Valley and Taiwan to grow ISSI. They recruited former colleagues and classmates in the United States to the R&D center in Santa Clara, and they lined up a manufacturing partnership with the recently established foundry, Taiwan Semiconductor Manufacturing Corp (TSMC). They also incorporated a subsidiary in Taiwan's Hsinchu Science Park to oversee assembly, packaging, and testing. In the firm's early years, Han traveled to Taiwan monthly to monitor its manufacturing operations. He soon decided to join thousands of other "returnees" and moved his family home to run ISSI-Taiwan. Lee remained in the Silicon Valley as CEO and Chairman.

ISSI grew rapidly in the early 1990s by selling high-speed SRAMs to motherboard firms that were supplying Taiwan's fast-growing personal computer (PC) industry. Not only did Lee and Han have the linguistic and cultural know-how to sell in this market but many of their classmates from National Taiwan University had moved into leadership positions in local industry. In February 1995, ISSI was listed on Nasdaq, making it one of the first Silicon Valley companies started by Chinese immigrants to go public in the United States. Several years later they spun off ISSI-Taiwan as an independent venture, Integrated Circuit Solution, Inc.

190

(ICSI), so that it could go public on the Taiwan Stock Exchange, which it did in 2001. ISSI still owns 29 percent of ICSI and the firms do not compete directly: ICSI specializes in designing semiconductors for the PC and peripherals markets, while ISSI's focus is on very high-performance integrated circuits (ICs) for networking, Internet, wireless, and handheld applications that demand portability, connectivity, and increased bandwidth.

ISSI grew in the 1990s by exploiting the Silicon Valley–Taiwan connection. In 2001 the firm expanded its connection to China by investing $40 million in Semiconductor Manufacturing International Corp (SMIC), a Shanghai-based semiconductor foundry. This investment was designed to insure that ISSI had advanced process wafer capacity at low cost, while also providing access to the fast-growing China market. The firm also established ISSI-Shanghai nearby, with facilities for design, backend logistics, and sales and marketing. By 2003, ISSI had 260 employees worldwide, including sixty in China and 170 in the United States. It built on the respective strengths of all three regional economies: Silicon Valley, Hsinchu, and Shanghai.

The economic impact of increased international trade and capital flows dominates most contemporary discussions of globalization. However, the growing mobility of labor, particularly that of highly skilled workers, promises to be at least as significant a force in transforming the world economy in coming decades. As the costs of international travel and communications continue to fall, skilled immigrants such as Jimmy Lee and K. Y. Han are transforming the one-way flows of talent from developing to advanced economies into more complex two-way flows of skill, capital, and know-how – a process that can be characterized as "brain circulation" rather than simply "brain drain." ISSI is one of hundreds of such firms that contributed to Taiwan's emergence as a global PC and semiconductor design and manufacturing center, and it is now contributing to a similar process in China.

In this chapter, I argue that a highly mobile community of Chinese engineers and entrepreneurs with work experience and connections in Silicon Valley is transferring know-how and skill between distant regional economies faster and more flexibly than most multinational corporations (MNCs) – and as a result transforming the geography of information technology (IT) production. The focus is the case of the semiconductor industry, although the process is similar in other IT-related sectors. In 1985, the semiconductor industry was dominated by a small group of very large, integrated producers from the United States and Japan. When Taiwan TSMC pioneered the stand-alone foundry that specialized only in manufacturing, it triggered a process of vertical fragmentation in the industry. By the end of the 1990s, Taiwan had become an important center of semiconductor manufacturing and was also home to over 100 independent IC design firms. Mainland China is now rapidly emerging as a center of chip design and manufacturing.

Domestic policymakers have aggressively promoted the development of the semiconductor industry in both Taiwan and China. However, the crucial transfers of technology and skill in the industry have been co-ordinated by a transnational community of overseas Chinese engineers, entrepreneurs, managers, and venture capitalists – most with graduate degrees from the United States and work experience in Silicon Valley. A tightly knit, transnational community of Taiwan- and US-based engi-neers helped transform Taiwan into an IT manufacturing center – and a leader in semiconductor manufacturing – in the 1980s and 1990s. More recently, immigrants from the Chinese Mainland are becoming part of this community and building bridges to coastal urban centers in China at the same time as Taiwan's IT producers are relocating manufacturing across the Taiwan Straits to take advantage of lower-cost engineering and production skills.

This community of highly skilled engineers and entrepreneurs is distin-guished from the broader Chinese Diaspora or "overseas Chinese busi-ness networks" by shared professional as well as ethnic identities and by their deep integration into the technical community of Silicon Valley. Indeed Taiwanese and Mainland-born engineers have different native languages and grew up in very different political and economic systems. They develop collective identities based on common educational and work experiences: many have attended the same elite universities in their home countries and have worked for the same, or related, companies in Silicon Valley. Many also participate in activities of the region's numerous Chinese professional and technical organizations.

I begin this chapter by arguing that the vertical fragmentation of pro-duction in the IT industry has created new entrepreneurial opportunities for highly skilled immigrants. Communities of foreign-born engineers and entrepreneurs are ideally positioned to seed new centers of techni-cal specialization in formerly peripheral regions of the world. I briefly summarize how a community of US-educated Chinese engineers in Silicon Valley created the cross-Pacific collaborations that fueled Tai-wan's emergence as a global center of technology production in the 1990s. The reversal of the "brain drain" – the return of thousands of US-educated Chinese engineers from Silicon Valley to Taiwan's Hsinchu region – in particular, provided the know-how and business connections that facilitated the development of world-class semiconductor and PC manufacturing capabilities.

In the rest of the chapter, I suggest that China is now poised to repeat Taiwan's experience a decade later, although under different conditions. Taiwanese IT investments in the Mainland are exploding (in spite of political tensions across the Taiwan Straits) at the same time as returning entrepreneurs are using their experience and connections in the United States to accelerate the upgrading of China's technology industries. The Shanghai region, in particular, is emerging as an important center of semiconductor production. This is not to suggest that China will soon surpass industry leaders such as the United States and Japan. China remains two or three generations behind in its adoption of leading-edge IC process technologies, and lacks the technology and managerial know-how to operate such facilities efficiently. However, the circulation of world-class engineering and entrepreneurial talent among China, Taiwan, and the United States is altering the economic trajectories of all three countries.

9.2   Technical communities and industrial decentralization

The emergence of new centers of technology, such as Taiwan, in locations outside of the advanced economies, has been possible because of transformations in the structure of the IT sector. The dominant competitors in the computer industry in the 1960s and 1970s were vertically integrated corporations that controlled all aspects of hardware and software production. Countries sought to build a domestic IBM or "national champion" from the "bottom up." The rise of the Silicon Valley industrial model spurred the introduction of the PC and initiated a radical shift to a more fragmented industrial structure organized around networks of increasingly specialized producers (Bresnahan, 1998).

Today, independent enterprises produce all of the components that were once internalized within a single large corporation – from application software, operating systems, and computers, to microprocessors and other components. The final systems are, in turn, marketed and distributed by still other enterprises. Within each of these horizontal segments, there is, in turn, increasing specialization of production and a deepening social division of labor. In the semiconductor industry today, independent producers specialize in chip design, fabrication, packaging, testing, marketing, and distribution as well as in the multiple segments of the semiconductor equipment manufacturing and materials sectors. A new generation of firms emerged in the late 1990s that specialized in providing intellectual property in the form of design modules rather than the design of the entire chip: for example, there are over 200 independent specialist companies in Taiwan's IC industry.

This change in industry structure appears as a shift in market relations. The number of actors in the industry has increased dramatically, and competition within many (but not all) horizontal layers has increased as well. Yet, this is far from the classic "auction market" mediated by price signals alone; the decentralized system depends heavily on the co-ordination provided by cross-cutting social structures and institutions. While Silicon Valley's entrepreneurs innovate in increasingly specialized niche markets, intense communications, in turn, insure the speedy, often unanticipated, recombination of these specialized components into changing end products. This decentralized system provides significant advantages over a more integrated model in a volatile environment because of the speed and flexibility as well as the conceptual advances associated with the process of specialization and recombination.[1]

The deepening social division of labor in the industry creates opportunities for innovation in formerly peripheral regions – opportunities that did not exist in an era of highly integrated producers. The vertical specialization associated with the new system continually generates entrepreneurial opportunities. By exploiting these opportunities in their home countries, transnational entrepreneurs can build independent centers of specialization and innovation, while simultaneously maintaining ties to Silicon Valley to monitor and respond to fast-changing and uncertain markets and technologies. They are also well positioned to establish cross-regional partnerships that facilitate the integration of their specialized components into end products.

The social structure of a technical community thus appears essential to the organization of production at the global as well as the local level. In the old industrial model, the technical community was primarily inside of the corporation. The firm was seen as the privileged organizational form for the creation and internal transfer of knowledge, particularly technological know-how that is difficult to codify.

In regions such as Silicon Valley, where the technical community transcends firm boundaries, however, such tacit knowledge is often transferred through informal communications or the interfirm movement of individuals (Saxenian, 1994). This suggests that the MNC may no longer be the advantaged or preferred organizational vehicle for transferring

---

[1] Firms may specialize without innovating, and they may innovate without changing the division of labor. However, it seems that the deepening social division of labor enhances the innovative capacity of a community: expanding opportunities for experimentation generate ideas. These ideas are, in turn, combined to make new ideas, and so forth, in a dynamic and self-generating process. This suggests that specialization increases innovation and ultimately economic growth.

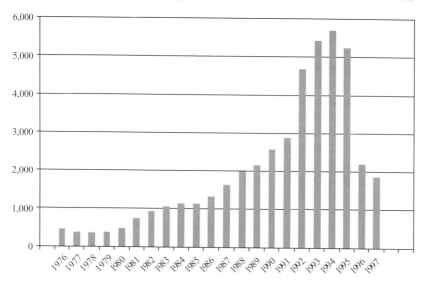

Figure 9.1 Returnees from the United States to Taiwan, 1976–1997
Source: National Youth Council, Taiwan Ministry of Education, 1999.

knowledge or personnel across national borders. An international technological community provides an alternative and potentially more flexible
and responsive mechanism for long-distance transfers of skill and know-
how – particularly between very different business cultures or environments.

9.3   The Silicon Valley–Hsinchu connection

Thousands of US-educated Chinese engineers returned from Silicon
Valley to Taiwan annually in the early 1990s. Some went to start technology companies, others to set up branches of US-based companies,
and still others to work for local companies or to provide professional
services to Taiwan's growing technology community. Most were lured
by the promise of greater economic opportunities, particularly after the
lifting of martial law; and the US recession of the early 1990s served
as a significant push factor. This "reversal" of the brain drain provided
the skill, know-how, and business connections that facilitated the accelerated development of Taiwan's semiconductor and PC manufacturing
capabilities in the 1980s and 1990s (figure 9.1).

The development of a transnational community – a community that
spans borders and boasts as its key assets shared information, trust, and

contacts (Portes, 1996) – has been largely overlooked in accounts of Taiwan's accelerated development. However, the contributions of this technical community have been key to the successes of more commonly recognized actors: government policymakers and global corporations. Both rely heavily on the dense professional and social networks that keep them close to state-of-the-art technical knowledge and leading-edge markets in the United States. The close connections to Silicon Valley, in particular, help to explain how Taiwan's producers innovated technologically in the 1980s and 1990s independent of their Original Equipment Manufacturer (OEM) customers.

The development of an international technical community also transformed the relationship between the Silicon Valley and Taiwan economies. In the 1960s and 1970s, capital and technology resided mainly in the United States and Japan and were transferred to Taiwan by MNCs seeking cheap labor. This one-way flow gave way in the 1990s to more decentralized two-way flows of skill, technology, and capital. The Silicon Valley–Hsinchu relationship today consists of formal and informal collaborations between individual investors and entrepreneurs and SMEs, as well as the division of larger companies located on both sides of the Pacific. A new generation of venture capital providers and professional associations serves as intermediaries, linking the decentralized infrastructures of the two regions. As a result, Taiwan is no longer a low-cost location, yet local producers continue to gain growing shares in global technology markets (Saxenian, 2001; Saxenian and Hsu, 2001).

Taiwan is now home to the world's most sophisticated PC manufacturers and their networks of SME suppliers of components ranging from scanners and keyboards to motherboards and video cards – along with a world-class semiconductor design and manufacturing infrastructure. As one observer notes:

Taiwan claims an advantage as a one-stop shop for every link in the technology production chain, headed by executives with leading edge US tech firms on their CVs and client lists. Chip designer VIA Technologies can have its blueprints etched into silicon by Taiwan Semiconductor Manufacturing and then have the naked wafers packaged by Advanced Semiconductor Engineering (ASE), placed on a motherboard by Asustek Computer, then sold to PC maker Acer – all without ever leaving Taiwan. (*South China Morning Post*, May 23, 2001)

Taiwan's advantage over the United States and Japan lies in its achievements in technology logistics and management as well as process technologies: "no one beats TSMC with logistics of managing 8 fabs [fabricators] with ten billion dollars of investment and 140,000 SKUs [Stock Keeping Units] moving through on a given day to 500 customers globally all ordering different kinds of chips; and no one beats ASE in bringing package and test costs down" (John Paul Ho, speech, 2001).

Taiwan's total IT revenues exceeded $20 billion in 2000, with those of the semiconductor industry reaching $16 billion, from less than $500,000 a decade earlier. And instead of competing directly with Silicon Valley, Taiwan's IT sector has defined and excelled in a distinctive niche. As a result, the Silicon Valley and Taiwan economies remain closely linked, with Taiwan's PC and chip manufacturing expertise complementing Silicon Valley's leading-edge product development, design, and marketing capabilities.

9.4   Cross-straits technology transfers

The transfer of technology and skill from Silicon Valley to Taiwan that occurred in the 1980s and 1990s is now being replicated across the Taiwan straits as well as between Silicon Valley and the Chinese Mainland. In the early 1990s, Taiwan's PC firms, driven by intensifying competition, began locating their most labor-intensive activities, such as the assembly of power supplies, keyboards and scanners, in China to exploit the lower-cost labor and land. Following an earlier generation of Taiwanese footwear, toy, and light consumer-goods manufacturers, they relocated in the south of China, particularly Fujian and Guangdong provinces, where the cost of labor and land were 30 and 40 percent that of Taiwan, respectively (*Nikkei Business Times*, 2001).

By 1999 over one-third of Taiwanese PC manufacturing was located in China, and a majority of these investments were clustered in the city of Dongguan, located between Shenzhen and Guangzhou in the Pearl River Delta, and one of the five Special Economic Zones (SEZs) in China. Although manufacturers moved to exploit lower costs in China, the superiority of Taiwanese managerial and technological capabilities meant that they continued to maintain control over the production process.

This geography shifted significantly after 2000. Faced with intensifying cost competition, the leading Taiwanese PC firms, such as Compal, Mitac, Twinhead, and Acer, began to move their highest value-added activities such as motherboards, video cards, scanners, and even laptop PC manufacturing, to China. However, rather than continuing to invest in South China, they are locating further north, in Shanghai and Zhejiang province, and the nearby cities of Suzhou and Kunshan in Jiangsu province. For example, Quanta, the world's largest laptop manufacturer plans to build a "manufacturing city" in Shanghai that has the capacity to produce 5 million laptops a year.

Most of these investments are not officially permitted under Taiwanese regulations, which until very recently prohibited investments of over $US 50 million per project and in strategic sectors like advanced chip manufacturing.[2] However, the channels for doing so through foreign subsidiaries are well established. This means that the official figures substantially understate total cross-straits investments. A 2001 poll by the Taipei Computer Association found that 90 percent of Taiwan-based high-tech companies have invested or plan to invest in the Mainland. And China has replaced Taiwan as the third largest IT manufacturing center in the world, following only the United States and Japan.

In another break from the past, teams of managers have moved from Taiwan to oversee these sophisticated operations and have encouraged their networks of suppliers to move as well. A manager from component-maker Logitech reports that the firm has encouraged its entire production chain, from ICs to cable wire and plastic mouse cases, to move to Suzhou with it because of the cost advantages of having an integrated local supply base from which to serve international customers. (A typical Taiwanese PC manufacturer relies on approximately 100 different component and part suppliers.) By 2001 there were an estimated 8,000 Taiwanese companies located in the Shanghai area and between 250,000 and 400,000 Taiwanese people, including the family members of plant managers and engineers, living in the region. However, these are far from self-contained operations: the expatriate managers and engineers typically travel back across the straits quarterly, suggesting that these firms continue to rely on their Taiwanese headquarters for strategic decisionmaking and direction.

9.5   Shanghai's Zhangjiang science park

The Chinese government designated Shanghai as the capital of the country's semiconductor industry in 2001, which should deepen as well as diversify the technology base in the region. As in Taiwan a decade earlier, this creates opportunities for mutually beneficial collaborations between local PC and systems producers and IC designers and manufacturers. The Zhangjiang High Tech Park in Shanghai's Pudong New Area is emerging as the locus of new investments in the semiconductor industry. The Park was established in 1992 by the Ministry of Science and Technology as a national center for development of new and high technology. By 2001, with 4.4 km^2 developed area (approximately three times the size of Taiwan's Hsinchu Science Park), the Park was home to 267

---

[2] This ban was ended in late 2001 and replaced by case-by-case evaluation in a policy called "active opening, effective management."

establishments, mostly IT-related, and reported output of close to $US 1 billion.

Both the Shanghai government and the Park Administration have aggressively pursued investment by offering subsidized loans, generous tax exemptions, and a 50 percent discount on land rent in the Park. Zhangjiang's developers have also carefully planned the area's development. The Master Plan includes not only areas for high-tech research, incubation, and manufacturing, but also residential, commercial, and education facilities, green space (40 percent), and mass-transit links. Foreign investment in Zhangjiang Park reached US$ 3.4 billion in 2000, compared with US$ 659,000 investment by Joint Ventures (JVs) and only US$ 451,000 by domestic investors. US firms Motorola, Lam Research, and Sun Microsystems have operations in the Park, but 80 percent of the foreign investments come from Hong Kong and Taiwan.

The semiconductor industry in Shanghai took off following the Chinese government's announcement in July 2000 of substantial tax reductions for the industry, including major cuts in the value-added tax (VAT) charged to domestic semiconductor production and chip design.[3] Later that year, three major manufacturers announced plans to build chip fabrication facilities in Zhangjiang Park–Shanghai Beilin Microelectronics Co., the leading Chinese semiconductor company, and two new JVs: Shanghai Grace Semiconductor Manufacturing Corp (GSMC) and Semiconductor Manufacturing International Corp (SMIC). Even Taiwan's leading foundry, TSMC, recently announced plans to invest in China in the future. According to CEO Morris Chang:

when the Mainland authorities provide such incentives like tax breaks as well as sufficient supplies of high tech personnel and water and electricity, and our competitors have started to use these advantages, we would lose our competitive edge if we did not follow suit. (*South China Morning Post*, August 29, 2001)

These investments have in turn attracted downstream and upstream producers, making Zhangjiang Park home to over 100 IC-related firms, representing all stages of the IC production chain, from wafer manufacturing, IC design, and fabrication to packaging and assembly-and-test. Taiwanese design house VIA Technologies and assembly firms ASE and Siliconware Precision Industries have also located facilities near the park.

The JVs GSMC and SMIC represent a mix of resources and talent from Silicon Valley, Taiwan, and China. GSMC is a high-profile venture

---

[3] Domestic chip manufacturers and designers were subject to 3 and 6 percent VAT, compared to 14 percent for foreign firms. These preferential taxes were eliminated in 2004 under pressure from the US semiconductor industry concerning violation of World Trade Organization (WTO) rules.

founded by Mianheng Jiang, the son of China's former President, Jiang Zemin, and Winston Wong, son of the Chairman of Formosa Plastics and head of Taiwan's most powerful business family. Wong is Chairman and Jiang is Vice Chairman of the Board and principal shareholder of GSMC, which raised US$ 1.6 billion for its first foundry.

The senior executives and managers in both firms have extensive experience in the semiconductor industry in both the United States and/or Taiwan. SMIC, for example, recruited 300 engineers away from Taiwan's leading IC manufacturing firm, TSMC, and another fifty directly from leading Silicon Valley companies. According to one of these recruits, "the salaries here [in China] are lower than they are in the US – but there is a greater upside. Things are moving very fast here. SMIC built its fab in one year, which may be record time. There is tremendous room for growth in China" (interview, January 2001).

The financing for these deals typically comes from US and foreign investors with experience in either Taiwan or China, as well as from local partners. Both are financed from abroad to avoid Taiwan's investment limits and the complex regulatory system in China. SMIC, for example, is incorporated in the Cayman Islands, and is structured as a US Delaware-style corporation so that it can follow US corporate and securities law and governance, which preserves the option of raising capital in the US or Asia public markets. Following Silicon Valley practice, employees of SMIC receive stock options as part of their compensation.

SMIC had also relied almost exclusively on legal and financial advice from Silicon Valley-based professionals. Carmen Chang, a partner from Silicon Valley's leading law firm, Wilson Sonsini, managed the legal details of the SMIC financing and incorporation and oversaw the firm's initial public offering on Nasdaq in 2002. She has also played an active role in related business details, from lobbying for the US government to open its markets to imports of leading-edge chip-making equipment to advising the Chinese policymakers on opening a second board in Shenzhen. Her main clientele in the 1990s was Taiwanese entrepreneurs starting firms in either the United States or Taiwan. Today, she says that business is overwhelmingly from Mainland Chinese – both returnees and Chinese firms setting up operations in the United States – and there are far more requests than she can accept.

Experienced industry observers report that the clustering of the IC industry in Shanghai and the market, technology, talent pool, government support, and capital supply in China today resembles that of Taiwan's Hsinchu region ten or fifteen years ago. Some predict the industry will grow faster than it did in Taiwan because it has a large base of US and Taiwan experience to tap and an existing model to follow. The Chinese market is also a key factor in these predictions: China's accounted for 6 percent (US$ 13 billion) of worldwide demand for semiconductors in 2000, following only the United States, Japan, and Taiwan. This market is predicted to grow at a compound annual rate of 17 percent in the next five years as domestic output of electronics goods grows, yet domestic companies currently supply only 5 percent of the total Chinese demand.

Although there is tremendous room for growth of the domestic semiconductor industry, it is likely that China will continue producing relatively low-end chips (the type used in watches, radios, cell phones, and other consumer electronics products) for the next five–ten years. The IC manufacturing technology in China remains two or three generations behind Taiwan's, and US regulations on export of the most advanced manufacturing equipment to China will slow the adoption of leading-edge process technologies.

McKinsey & Co. consultants in Shanghai predict that the large supply of low-cost engineering talent will allow China to grow more quickly as a center for semiconductor design than for advanced manufacturing, which requires sophisticated technology and management skills. Salaries for chip designers in China are about 20 percent of those in the United States, and the domestic market for IC design in China will reach an estimated US$ 10 billion in 2010 (Chen and Woetzel, 2002). This suggests the possibility that the relationship between China and Taiwan, like that between the United States and Taiwan, will be complementary, rather than competitive, with Taiwan moving up the value chain to provide leading-edge manufacturing services and high-value-added design while China becomes a center of low-end, labor-intensive design and assembly-and-testing as well as nonleading-edge manufacturing.

9.6   China and Silicon Valley: from "brain drain" to "brain circulation"

At the same time that networks of Taiwanese PC and semiconductor makers were moving their low-end manufacturing to the Chinese Mainland, the "best and brightest" of China's youth were leaving to pursue their education abroad. The brain drain, which increased significantly after the 1989 Tiananmen Square events, has been so great that Mainland Chinese are now the largest and fastest growing group of foreign-born students in US universities, with 54,466 students (or 10.5 percent of the total foreign-born students enrolled in 1999–2000). Moreover they have not returned to China in large numbers.

The loss of talent is especially acute in technical fields. Chinese students in the United States are concentrated at the graduate level and

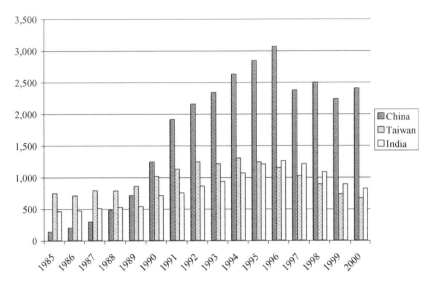

Figure 9.2 US doctorates in science and engineering to foreign-born
students, 1985–2000
Source: National Science Foundation, 2001.

in science and engineering (S&E) fields: about 2,500 Chinese students
per year received doctoral degrees in science and engineering from the
United States in the 1990s – for a total of 28,000 S&E doctorates between
1985 and 2000 (NSB, 2001). This is more than double the total from the
next largest countries of origin of foreign students in the United States –
those from Taiwan, and India (figure 9.2.) Mainlanders have also historically had the highest stay rates of all of these groups. A National Science
Foundation (NSF) study (NSB, 2001) found that 88 percent of Chinese
who earned doctorates in science and engineering in 1990–1 were still
working in the United States in 1995. This is consistent with the data
on visas issued by the United States for workers with exceptional skills:
Mainland Chinese received 20,885 H-1B visas between 1990 and 1999,
second only to immigrants from India.

   Chinese policymakers have recognized the opportunity to tap this
pool of foreign-educated technology professionals for domestic development purposes. Over the past decade, governments at both the local
and central levels in China have pursued two strategies in their efforts
to counteract the brain drain. Following Taiwan, Chinese agencies have
sought to increase professional connections and communications with
the overseas community by sponsoring study tours, conferences, joint

research projects, and short-term work and teaching opportunities. The Ministry of Education, for example, established the Chun Hui Program to finance trips to China by technologists trained abroad to participate in conferences and academic research. Other programs provide opportunities for short-term lecturing, teaching, and postdoctoral appointments in China (Dahlman and Aubert 2002: 9.3). Participants from the United States report that these programs have succeeded in increasing technical exchange between Chinese scholars based in China and the United States. Representatives of cabinet-level ministries, as well as municipal governments from cities such as Shanghai and Beijing, also visit the United States frequently to recruit Chinese professionals by holding dinners or meetings to publicize the favorable incentives and business environment in China.

Competition between municipal and provincial governments for returnees has increased significantly in recent years. There is now an almost continuous flow of delegations of company and government representatives recruiting in Silicon Valley, and they come from all over China – not just coastal urban areas, but central and western provinces as well. Many municipal governments have also established "Returning Students Venture Parks" (or "Overseas Student Parks") within the new and high-tech development zones. These parks are reserved exclusively for companies started by returnees. They offer not only low rent, tax relief, shared infrastructure, and financial benefits like other science parks in China, but they also handle the special needs of returnees, such as accelerating the bureaucratic process involved in establishing residency and ensuring access to housing and prestigious, often bilingual, schools for their children. By 2000 there were twenty-three Returning Students Science Parks across China and many other municipalities had a policy to attract returning students but no park.

Silicon Valley's Mainland Chinese immigrants, like their Taiwanese predecessors, have built extensive professional and social networks both in Silicon Valley as well as back in China. These ties are often co-ordinated through the alumni associations of the elite technical universities such as Beijing University, Tsinghua University, and Shanghai Jiaotong University. In addition, there are close to a dozen specialized Chinese professional and technical associations in Silicon Valley, ranging in size from 200 to over 2,000 members. These organizations breed shared understandings and world-views among their members while providing forums for mentoring and the exchange of contacts, capital, know-how, and information within the community.

The Hua Yuan Science & Technology Association was formed in Silicon Valley in 2000 to "promote the technological, professional, and scientific development of the Chinese business community." Its membership has grown very fast: over 1,000 Chinese engineers attended the 2002 Hua Yuan Annual Conference entitled "Opportunities and Challenges: Riding the China Wave." Their website describes the association's mission: "Hua Yuan assists and encourages professional development and entrepreneurship of our members, facilitates exchange between Chinese and other business communities in the United States, and strengthens cross-border business relationships between Silicon Valley and China" (http://www.huayuan.org/). Hua Yuan maintains a Chinese office in Beijing and describes its role as a "bridge between Chinese and US high tech industries":

Hua Yuan has established strong associations with [the] Chinese business community, and has built up a close working relationship with the Chinese regulatory authorities. Members of Hua Yuan exploring business opportunities in China are backed by our strong networks in China. Such supports include concrete administrative helps [sic] from Hua Yuan's Chinese office located in the center of high-tech development in Beijing. Hua Yuan continues to engage in high-level exchanges between business executives from Silicon Valley and China.

A Hua Yuan meeting in 2004 featured a keynote address by Dr. Char-pin Yeh, President of Macronix Electronics' IC design operation in Suzhou, China. Macronix was started by a Taiwanese engineer who studied and worked in Silicon Valley for fifteen years before returning to start one of the first companies in the Hsinchu Science Park. Dr. Yeh, also Taiwan-born, earned a PhD in electrical engineering from Georgia Institute of Technology, holds twenty-six US patents in microelectronics-related fields, and has worked in the US semiconductor industry for almost fifteen years. His speech was a technical analysis of the "Strengths and Weakness Analysis of Cross-Straits IC Design Industries." He also participated in a forum on the trade-offs between a corporate career and entrepreneurship, the business environment in China, and steps to "start the wheel of business in China."

Hua Yuan and other Chinese professional associations also sponsor regular business tours to China, receive government delegations, and serve as conduits for Chinese firms recruiting in the United States. The delegation from the 2001 Back to China trip sponsored by the Chinese Internet and Networking Association (CINA) gave a series of public presentations on the topic of "The China Wave – A Reality Check" soon after their return. The speakers provided detailed information on the challenges as well as opportunities facing those considering returning to the Mainland, with individuals discussing issues relevant to the telecommunications, wireless, software, and IC sectors.

These associations also provide multiple foras for information exchange and technology transfer between Chinese engineers in the United States, Taiwan, and China. The Chinese Institute of Engineers (CIE), which has branches in all three locations, has sponsored technical conferences that have attracted practicing engineers as well as scholars for decades. Business oriented organizations are also starting to play this role. In 1998 the Chinese American Semiconductor Association (CASPA) sponsored a delegation of local technologists for a two-week study tour of the Shanghai semiconductor industry. After returning, the group produced a technical report assessing the status of the Chinese microelectronics industry that was widely circulated in Silicon Valley.

Equally important, according to one of the group's leaders, Peter Yin of ICT, Inc is the fact that: "we were instrumental in helping our Shanghai counterparts solve current technical problems, [but] we also served as vehicles of knowledge transfer and new modes of thinking." He described an exchange with sessions organized according to detailed technical specializations of the semiconductor engineers and commented:

They benefited a great deal from exposure to advanced technologies and novel analytical methodologies during the sessions, as much as their Silicon Valley colleagues gained first-hand knowledge of China's determination to develop its indigenous IC base and challenges that lie ahead. (CASPA press release, 1998)

These exchanges also help pave the way for returnees. Four former heads of CASPA returned to Shanghai in 2002 alone.

The first wave of high-technology returnees from the United States to China began in the late 1990s, triggered by a combination of Internet enthusiasm, the lure of the large China market, and various government incentives. This group located their businesses primarily in Beijing to be part of the fast-growing Internet and dot.com industries. These returnees came from all over the United States, many were young (recent graduates) with little or no US work experience, and many had business rather than technology backgrounds. Two of the most high-profile firms of this era are AsiaInfo, started by returnees from Texas and now China's largest systems integrator for the telecommunications and Internet industries, and Sina.com, the leading Internet portal in China. Both firms are now publicly listed on Nasdaq. Most Internet start-ups in China failed within a couple of years and the flow of returnees ended abruptly with the collapse of the dot.com bubble.

A larger wave of returnees began in 2001 with the acceleration of foreign investment in China's semiconductor industry. The recruits to these ventures were often older engineers with substantial experience in the semiconductor industry in Silicon Valley and/or Taiwan. Many returned to work in Shanghai, lured by stock options and the promise of professional opportunities not available to Chinese in the United States. The recession in the US economy served as a "push" factor as well, with layoffs growing and new jobs hard to find. When the Shanghai Pudong District High Tech Delegation visited the United States in late 2001, for example, they attracted some 4,000 Chinese students to recruitment sessions in New York, Chicago, and San Francisco (including over 1,000 in Silicon Valley). The delegation included executives from thirty-five Shanghai businesses along with political officials and reported receiving over 2,500 applications for the 238 positions available.

The return rate among US-educated Mainland Chinese has historically been low, below 30 percent according to most estimates and as low as 10 percent among engineers and scientists. However, the Taiwanese case suggests that such trends can reverse quickly and then accelerate because of the networked nature of these communities; news of successes and opportunities travels quickly. In Taiwan the recession of the early 1990s triggered a tripling of returnees within three or four years. The terrorist attacks of September 11, 2001 appear to have had a similar impact on Mainlanders. One career search web site in China reports a dramatic increase in résumés in early 2002: "in the past couple of months we have about 10,000 to 15,000 interested in returning to China to work. Six months ago we would get only 10 to 100 résumés in the same period" (*San Francisco Chronicle*, January 2, 02).

As professional opportunities in Shanghai and elsewhere grow, strengthened by the cross-straits transfers of manufacturing operations and skill, it is likely that more Mainland engineers and managers will return from the United States. According to Lu Chunwei, a software developer who recently returned from a job at Microsoft to start his own business-to-business (B2B) company: "it's a big trend now, people just want to return to China. It's like the Gold Rush. They're successful in the US, but in their hearts they still feel like immigrants. They feel welcome here in China . . . There are not many new opportunities in the US." He added that cheaper labor, lower rents, and better business opportunities in the Mainland were important factors in his decision (*South China Morning Post*, 12 January, 2002).

Chris Xie returned from Silicon Valley to China to start a peer-to-peer computing company after failing to find funding in the Bay Area. He built a partnership with a Shanghai-based biotech company that has provided seed funding and is allowing the start-up to share its office space. Xie reports that the environment for his start-ups was more attractive in China: he tapped into government incentives for $36,000 in cash grants and 390 ft^2 of free office space and hired a staff of ten in Shanghai for what it would have cost to hire a single comparable employee in Silicon Valley (*San Francisco Chronicle*, January 2, 2004).

Of course this does not amount to a reversal of the brain drain. It is likely that the net loss of talent from China will continue for a long time. However the acceleration of the brain circulation and the growing interest in returning to China among US-educated engineers and scientists will have a lasting impact on the economy of the centers of IT production along China's coast.

The emergence of successful role models – either successful start-ups or large firms that provide sizable economic returns for employees with stock options – is likely to be an important turning point in this process. UTStarCom is one such model. The firm, which provides telecommunications network products for the Chinese market, was founded in 1991 by a group of US-educated Chinese engineers. Most of the original founders are classmates from a Ministry of Posts and Telecommunications-run university, and almost all of the senior management team worked at Bell Labs in the United States.

UTStarcom is headquartered in Silicon Valley but 99 percent of its 1,800 employees are at manufacturing and R&D facilities in China as well, and China is also its primary market focus. According to founder Hong Lu, UTStarcom has leveraged its "many connections in China" including its access to Chinese officials, intimate knowledge of the China market, and the ability to combine modern business structures from the United States with this ethnic and cultural know-how. The firm went public on Nasdaq in 2000, and is currently valued at $1.4 billion.

Successes such as UTStarcom remain limited so far. The growing interest of US venture capitalists in funding returning Chinese entrepreneurs from Silicon Valley suggests, however, that the opportunities are there. The Walden International Investment Group (WIIG), for example, was one of the original investors in NeWave Semiconductor. The firm was sold in 2002 to a Silicon Valley semiconductor company for $80 million – making money both for WIIG and also the Chinese government-owned Hua Hong Microelectronics, an entity that had invested $1.5 million. According to WIIG chairman, Lip-Bu Tan, the NeWave experience has taught him that the best strategy in China is to invest in US-educated students who want to return home to start firms. He tried in the early 1990s to invest in Chinese state-owned enterprises (SOEs), but learned that there was no way to get his money out. He then tried to create JVs between US-based and local Chinese companies, but the challenge of bridging the two management cultures proved insurmountable. The key, says Tan, is to find graduates of US universities who have stayed and worked in companies in a place like Silicon Valley for many years: "You have to be reasonably brain-washed in the US." As the Mainland Chinese community in the United States matures, such seasoned start-ups seem increasingly plausible.

9.7   The Silicon Valley–Taiwan–China connection

The growth of a transnational community linking Silicon Valley and China parallels that established a decade earlier between Taiwan and Silicon Valley, and it is creating the third leg in a triangle of professional and business ties linking the economies of Hsinchu, Shanghai, and Silicon Valley. As Chinese technologists extend their technical networks to the Mainland, they are contributing to the growth of an important new center of global IT production and deepening the division of labor between these increasingly specialized – and mutually interdependent – regional economies. The main actors are decentralized networks of transnational entrepreneurs and communities, rather than either individual actors or MNCs. The state and MNCs are involved in the process, to be sure, but it is the Chinese technical community with ties to Silicon Valley that has transferred the technology and know-how as well as the business connections that are the key to economic success in the current era.

The Acorn Campus was established by a team of a half dozen of Silicon Valley's most experienced (and successful) overseas Chinese engineers – Taiwan as well as Mainland-born. The Campus is an incubator in which they serve as "angel investors" and provide mentoring and connections, as well as space, for promising new ventures with Chinese founders. One of their recent investees, Newtone Communications, a telecom software firm, realized that their seed money of $500,000 would go much further in China than in the Bay Area. After moving to Shanghai these returnees doubled their employment without increasing their budget.

This experience spurred the creation of a new Acorn Campus in Shanghai. In raising money for the Acorn Campus Asia Fund, the founders' mission is to "leverage the highest level of Silicon Valley entrepreneurial experiences to create, invest, and incubate high technology startups in China . . . and promote global leadership through Silicon Valley–Asia value chain partnerships." Like WIIG, their target is returning Silicon Valley Chinese entrepreneurs with substantial experience, and their focus is on semiconductor design, wireless infrastructure, and system and software development. They talk about accessing the best resources from different locations: R&D, new product development and marketing in the United States, high-end logistics, design and manufacturing in Taiwan, low-cost engineering in the United States, and manufacturing talent in China.

The power of the transnational community is most evident in the case of the semiconductor industry, which originated in Silicon Valley and has been transferred by Chinese entrepreneurs first to Taiwan and then from Taiwan as well as from Silicon Valley to China. However a similar process is occurring in linked sectors as well. Of course these are not one-way flows. While the Taiwanese IC industry initially grew out of talent and technology from the United States, producers such as TSMC contributed indigenous innovations that, in turn, benefited the entire industry. Likewise, while China remains at a lower technological level than both Taiwan and the United States, it has all of the resources (skill, capital, know-how, connections) to innovate, and there is already evidence that the large Chinese telecommunications market will provide local producers with the opportunity to experiment with, and ultimately innovate in, the field of wireless communication.

REFERENCES

Bresnahan, T., 1998. "New Modes of Competition: Implications for the Future Structure of the Computer Industry," Conference Paper, March
Chen, A. C. and J. Woetzel, 2002. "Chinese Chips," *The McKinsey Quarterly*, 2
Dahlman, C. and J. Aubert, 2001. *China and the Knowledge Economy: Seizing the 21st Century*. Washington, DC: World Bank
National Science Board (NSB), 2001. "Higher Education in Science and Engineering," *Science and Engineering Indicators* NSB-00-1, at http://www.nsf.gov/sbe/srs/
Portes, A., 1996. "Global Villagers: The Rise of Transnational Communities," *The American Prospect*, March-April: 74–77
Saxenian, A., 1994. *Regional Advantage: Culture and Competition in Silicon Valley and Route 128*, Cambridge, MA: Harvard University Press
    2001. "Taiwan's Hsinchu Region: Imitator and Partner for Silicon Valley," Stanford Institute for Economic Policy Research, Policy Paper
Saxenian, A. and J. Hsu, 2001. "The Silicon Valley–Hsinchu Connection: Technical Communities and Industrial Upgrading," *Industrial and Corporate Change*, 10(4): 893–920

Part III

Institutions and innovation systems

10   National systems of production, innovation, and competence-building

Bengt-Åke Lundvall, Björn Johnson, Esben S. Andersen, and Bent Dalum

10.1   Introduction

What follows is a shortened, and slightly revised, version of a paper published in *Research Policy* (Lundvall *et al.*, 2002).[1] In this introduction, We provide a few brief reflections on the innovation system concept in the light of economic geography. We make no attempt to give full justice to the literature on economic geography that predates the literature on innovation systems, however.

While the idea of a national system of innovation (NSI) attempts to explain and understand innovation in economic terms, the concept may also be seen as a combination of different elements – some of which emanate from economic geography and from the development literature. Perroux (1969) and Brookfield (1975), for instance, are among the common references. The overlap of ideas also has to do with timing. The NSI idea was shaped in the first half of the 1980s, and this was also a period of renewal of Marshallian economic geography related to regional studies that referred to industrial districts and clusters (Scott 2000: 29).

It is therefore not so surprising that currently the most advanced and frequent "users" of the concept of NSIs are to be found among economic geographers rather than among economists. This can be documented, for instance, by using the search machine, Google Scholar. Another factor is that economic geographers, for historical and epistemological reasons, are much less inhibited in their use of heterodox ideas emanating from bordering disciplines. They are not "prisoners of their own tool-shed" but willing to bring in new tools if they see them as potentially useful.

Lundvall is the sole author of section 10.1, the Introduction, while the remainder of the chapter was written by all four authors.

[1] We removed sections that did not make explicit reference to the spatial dimension – i.e. sections on "the deepening" of the concept and on "economic development." The only important change is the addition of the reference to the 1982 unpublished OECD paper (OECD 1982) mentioning national systems of innovation.

Defining the analytical core of the NSI concept

An innovation system may be seen as a pragmatic tool for systematic description and mapping of innovation activities and agencies at the level of regions and nations. The basic idea is that innovation comes neither out of the blue nor out of the mind of the individual entrepreneur. Innovation reflects cumulative processes of interaction where different organizations and individuals combine efforts in creating, diffusing, and using knowledge. The division of labor as well as the pattern of collaboration will reflect the distribution of specific competences among agents and organizations as well as the institutions that shape competition, communication, and co-operation. Analysts can therefore understand the rate and direction of innovation by mapping competences and institutional set-ups under the heading of "innovation system."

But innovation systems may also be seen as the outcome of a process of abstraction quite different from the one made by neo-classical economics. The most basic difference is *a double shift of focus from allocation to innovation* and from *rational choice to learning*. In the modern economy, innovation is fundamental for economic performance at the level of both firms and regions. Units that allocate efficiently but keep producing the same product with the same process technology year after year do not survive. It is therefore as legitimate to focus on innovation as it is to focus on allocation.

We have defined "the learning economy" as a context where an increasing share of all agents is exposed to rapid and frequent change (Lundvall and Johnson 1994). In the learning economy, the capability of individuals, organizations, and local systems to learn to cope with new problems becomes a prerequisite for economic success. Production, development, marketing, and trading are processes where agents may learn to become more competent or proficient both in making choices and in doing things.

The major reason that neo-classical economists give attention to allocation rather than innovation is not that the first is more important than the second, but rather that allocation is the phenomenon to which their tools (including mathematical models) can be applied with some efficacy.[2] When they disregard differences in competence and assume that the analysis can be built upon equally competent, well-informed "representative agents," it is not because learning is not relevant – it is because introducing learning overextends the tools whose use they regard

---

[2] Georgescu Roegen's (1971) analysis of how standard economics' view of what is "scientific" gets mixed up with what can be put into numbers (accepting "arithmomorphic" concepts as scientific but rejecting "dialectic" ones, in Georgescu Roegen's terminology) is most enlightening.

Table 10.1 *Four different perspectives in economic analysis*

Perspective	Allocation	Innovation
Choice making	Standard neo-classical	Management of innovation
Learning	Austrian economics	Innovation systems

Source: The authors.

as the most fundamental criterion for remaining scientific. But neither can we argue that allocation and decisionmaking are unimportant. Our reason for bringing *innovation and learning* into focus is that it gives us an alternative "focusing device" – the innovation system – that helps us to see what tends to remain hidden when we use the neo-classical focusing device.

Table 10.1 illustrates how the analytical framework connected to innovation systems as a focusing device relates to, respectively, neo-classical economic theory, Austrian economic theory, and "rationalist innovation management" theory. Austrian economists, such as Hayek and Kirzner, are as preoccupied with allocation as neo-classical economists, but they recognize the importance of learning as being at the core of economic processes. Rationalist versions of innovation management models aim at explaining innovation as an outcome of rational choice. What is proposed here is a double shift of focus.

The micro-foundations of innovation systems

It would not be meaningful to reflect upon "innovation systems" in the abstract world of neo-classical economics. With rational agents making choices on the basis of perfect information, including free and equal access to technological knowledge, it would be legitimate to disregard the role of institutions and organizations. And in the absence of scale economies and IPRs, geographical space would not matter for innovation in this kind of model world.

But, in such a context there would be little innovation. I have argued elsewhere that product innovation – innovation for others, including professional users and other customers – would be infrequent and difficult to explain in a world of isolated producers producing for anonymous markets. Neither the standard neo-classical models nor the transaction-cost models can explain the frequency of product innovation as it is reflected in surveys and in R&D statistics (Lundvall 1985, 1988; Christensen and Lundvall 2004).

As we shall see, this elementary insight forms the micro-foundation for innovation systems, and it leads to a series of necessary modifications of neo-classical economic theory. It implies that most markets – all of those where product innovations play an important role – are not "pure markets." It also implies that the rationality of agents involved cannot be reduced to instrumental, strategic, or opportunistic behavior. To understand innovation, we need to understand both the protection and the sharing of knowledge. And, most importantly, we need to understand interactive learning.

Interactive learning and innovation

One basic assumption emerging from the analysis of how new products are developed that lies behind the NSI concept is that innovation and learning are strongly interconnected and that most relevant knowledge cannot be reduced to time- and space-less "information." Learning is an *interactive, socially embedded, and localized process*. This may be presented as a basic assumption, but it is also borne out by social psychology and empirical evidence.

Some learning may take place by agents engaged in repeated action and operating in isolation. But most meaningful learning takes place when people interact. Teaching is, of course, one example, but apprenticeship relationships are at least as important. Apprenticeship is sometimes associated with how artisans and skilled workers learn, but it is a concept with much wider relevance. It is interesting to note that Nobel Prize winners tend to refer to periods of direct interaction with outstanding senior scholars in their field of research as the most important for developing their ideas (Nielsen and Kvale 1999).

This implies the need for an analytical framework broader than can be offered by "economics." "Social capital" and "social cohesion" need to be taken into account when explaining how and to what degree innovation takes place. Trust and hierarchy are dimensions that affect to what degree and how learning takes place. At a more concrete level, the organization of the education system and the labor-market institutions will reflect and reproduce important regional/national differences in this respect. To emphasize this, we have introduced "competence-building" as an integral part of the title of the chapter.

Geographical distance and the innovation process

From what has been said, it follows that innovation systems have a geographical dimension. But it is also true that in this dimension they are always "open systems." Some stages of the innovation process are truly localized and involve face-to-face interaction and hands-on-experimenting. The engineer may tinker with a prototype machine together with a skilled worker to find a solution to a malfunction problem, or a senior and a junior researcher may work side-by-side in the laboratory trying to explain some unforeseen feature of a new drug.

Other stages may be much less dependent on geographical distance between the interacting partners. Scientists may be able to define a problem in a "global" scientific language and communicate solutions with very low costs across the world. Engineers working in separate, but similar, organizations may exchange information of crucial importance for the innovation process electronically.

A fundamental issue for developing the understanding of the geography of innovation systems is to understand better what types of knowledge and learning are "local" and what types are "global." Another crucial question is how local knowledge may be transformed into a more globally accessible form (and vice versa – how global knowledge may be absorbed and become an element in local systemic knowledge).

I have worked with this issue from two different angles. One has to do with the innovation taxonomy developed by Christopher Freeman and Carlota Perez in the 1980s. The second relates to the distinction between tacit and explicit knowledge and with the distinction between two different modes of innovation – a science-based (STI) and a learning-by-doing (experience)-based mode, which we call Doing, Using, and Interacting (DUI).

Freeman and Perez (1988) make a distinction between incremental innovation, radical innovation, new technological systems, and "technological revolutions." In an earlier paper, I combined these four different types of innovation with four different dimensions of space: economic space, organizational space, geographical space, and cultural space (Lundvall 1999a, 1999b). My first conclusion was that learning processes combined with stationary technology might, in the long run, suppress the importance of space, while radical innovation makes face-to-face interaction necessary. My second conclusion had to do with the trade-off between organizational and geographical distance, especially when it comes to incremental innovation.

One major conclusion was that the technological revolution based on ICTs has had a contradictory impact on the location of the core industries. On the one hand, it makes it less difficult to operate activities long distance; on the other hand, the radical change taking place within the technology itself gives a privilege to agents interacting face-to-face and with opportunities for hands-on experience.

Codification of local knowledge

Technological development and scientific development are characterized by bursts and upheavals followed by more "normal" periods. This is reflected in what engineers and scientists do. Some of them contribute to radical innovation and work out completely new ideas. But most of them develop and refine existing knowledge, or standardize knowledge by codifying it and then diffusing this standardized information to students or other users.

In other words, many knowledge workers make efforts to transform knowledge from a local to a more rootless form both by codifying knowledge and by learning new codes, so that they can receive knowledge from far away. One important reason for making the distinction between tacit and codified knowledge relates to the role of geographical and cultural space in defining innovation systems.

Learning-by-doing, using, and interacting

Kenneth Arrow (1962) made the concept of "learning-by-doing" widely known among economists. He used empirical observations of learning curves and productivity growth patterns from the production of airplane bodies as inspiration for the idea. Later, Rosenberg (1982) developed the idea of "learning-by-using" to explain the rapid reduction in the cost of using complex systems as users become more familiar with them. These kinds of learning take place in all parts of the economy to different degrees. The more frequently innovations occur in terms of new products and systems, the more learning will be imposed upon developers, producers, and users. But still, one might argue that *the impact on the whole economy is limited* since the learning is "local" and "specific" to one specific user or producer – or perhaps it remains embodied in individuals (this is argued in Foray 2000 – in this case, mobility of people becomes crucial for making local knowledge more root-less).[3] This brings us to the core argument that *"learning-by-interacting" is fundamental for the generalization of local learning* (with the side argument that "generalization of local knowledge" does not always take the form of codification!).

---

[3] There are different managerial ways to try to compensate for the limited learning capability of hierarchies. The establishment of a "learning organization," where horizontal communication and interdivisional groups is combined with external networking, may be seen as such an attempt. But learning organizations are as important for innovative capability in firms that have focused their attention on a few steps in the production chain and that operate in technologically dynamic sectors (Christensen and Lundvall 2004).

Learning-by-interacting as an alternative to codification

The major argument against Williamson's (1975) assumption that calculating transaction costs would be sufficient to analyze and explain vertical integration, was that the separation of users from producers into two different organizations actually would enhance interactive learning.[4] The idea is simple. If a producer integrates with a user, or the other way around, the integrated couple tends to become less attractive as partners for interaction, information exchange, and learning *seen from the viewpoint of the remaining independent users or producers*. The independent units have very good reasons to be wary about the self-interest of the integrated units and be reluctant to share information about what they have learned from doing and using. We do not need to introduce "opportunism" – it is simply a question of clear and legitimate self-interest.[5]

The reduction in transaction costs for the integrated couple might be substantial, but the long-term *loss from being locked into learning with only one user (producer) may be much bigger*, especially if we are in a sector with turbulent technology and rapid change in user needs. In the learning economy, users (producers) benefit from being able to draw upon a *diversity of experiences* among users (producers).

And, what is more important for our argument in this chapter: from the viewpoint of the whole economy the learning by interacting has the effect of *transforming local learning into general knowledge embodied in, for instance, new machinery, new components, new software-systems, or even new business solutions*.

Adam Smith and two modes of innovation: DUI and STI

Adam Smith links the development of the division of labor to innovation in two different ways – and, by doing so, he indicates two different modes of innovation. One is *experience-based* and corresponds to what we have called *DUI learning*, referring to learning by Doing, Using, and Interacting. The other is *science-based* and corresponds to what we have called *STI learning*, referring to Science, Technology, and Innovation (see Jensen *et al.* 2004). In the beginning of volume I of *The Wealth of Nations*, Adam

---

[4] The idea of benefits from interactive learning was inspired by a case where a Swedish dairy technology producer (Alfa Laval) kept an affiliate in Denmark in spite of making losses year after year. When we asked the management of Alfa Laval why they did not close it down, they responded that they were willing to pay a price for being close to and learning from the most advanced dairy technology-users in the world.

[5] It corresponds to situations in civil and public life where individuals could not be expected to be impartial and therefore – in spite of being regarded as trustworthy and good citizens – would be declared disqualified.

Smith gives the example of innovation based upon learning-by-doing: the boy who develops an easier way to handle a process in order to get more time to play with his friends. But immediately after that, he refers to "men of speculation" – the scientists – who are "often capable of combining together the powers of the most distant and dissimilar objects" (Smith 1776/1957: 9–10).

Both of these examples (modes of innovation) are relevant for our reasoning about vertical disintegration, diversity, and interactive learning. For instance, the producer of process equipment may be involved in an interaction with users where he draws upon the experiences made by operators in user firms when developing new models and systems (DUI mode). But he might also be involved in an interaction with knowledge institutions – for example, suppliers – in order to get updated on technological opportunities or even to buy R&D results (STI mode).

In both cases, the separation line (some kind of market) between the producer and user may benefit interactive learning at the level of the parties involved as well as knowledge diffusion at the level of the economy as a whole. In the case of STI learning, a certain amount of in-house R&D may be needed to absorb knowledge from the outside sources, and outsourcing R&D has been hampered by different factors. But the diversity argument remains relevant. The research laboratory or the software firm that helps many users with different needs and experiences will learn more by doing so than the in-house-lab or software department getting feedback only from in-house users.

But even if similar mechanisms are at work, it might still be useful to make a distinction between the two modes because the prerequisites for interactive learning to take place are different. In the DUI mode, the generalization of local learning will typically be embodied in new machinery and components, while in the STI mode innovations may reach the user in the form of disembodied codified knowledge. The first type of interaction may be based on social interaction and trust in a broad sense, while the second may be more demanding in terms of overlapping scientific competences, and it might therefore thrive only on the basis of a common professional background. For instance, firms that are users of knowledge produced by academia may need to have, in-house, employees with an academic background.

Summary

The innovation system concept may be seen as a pragmatic tool, taking into account the most updated insights within theoretical and empirical innovation research, and it overlaps with ideas within economic geography. But it might also be seen as a theoretical focusing device derived through a process of abstraction where the focus is moved from allocation and rational choice to innovation and learning.

Innovation systems always have a geographical dimension: in the geographical dimension, they are all open systems. To get a better understanding of the geography of innovation systems, analysts need to work out a theory about what makes some knowledge local rather than global – taking into account that most knowledge is neither absolutely local (individual) nor absolutely generic (global).

Knowledge may be lifted out of its local context through a process of codification. But it may also be done by embodying it into new products and systems helping distant users. I believe that it is useful to introduce the distinction between two modes of innovation – one experience-based (DUI) and one science-based (STI) – that co-exist and complement each other. Both of them will operate in geographical space, but the mechanisms for diffusing knowledge across systems and the absorptive capacity necessary to get real access to the knowledge will be quite different.

10.2   The emergence and spread of the concept of national systems of innovation

In this section we give some background on how the concept of NSI has developed and spread. When using an artifact such as a computer, the user does not need to know how and by whom it was invented, developed, and introduced in the market. Neither is it always necessary for socioeconomic researchers to know how specific analytical tools were shaped. But from time to time, analysts may find it useful to reflect on how a concept such as "NSI" came about, and to see in what direction it tends to be developed. The concept of NSI – as its name clearly indicates – combines ideas taken from rather distinct areas of analysis: economic policy, economic interdependence, and more or less radical economic change. The new combination of such elements, of course, is much shakier than the integration of the elements of a technological innovation such as the modern computer.

The unexpected diffusion

When the idea about the innovation system approach was first discussed in the middle of the 1980s, nobody expected it to become as widely diffused as it is today. Today the OECD, the European Commission, and the United Nations Commission for Trade and Development (UNCTAD) have absorbed the concept as an integral part of their analytical perspective. The World Bank and International Monetary Fund (IMF) have been more reluctant, but even here change seems to be taking place. The US Academy of Science has recently brought the NSI into its vocabulary and now uses it as a framework for analyzing US science and technology policy. Sweden, has given the concept legitimate status in its own particular way by naming a new central government institution (an "ämbetsverk") VINNOVA, which stands for "the Systems of Innovation Authority."

It is interesting to speculate why the concept has diffused so rapidly among scholars and policymakers. One reason may be that mainstream macroeconomic theory and policy have failed to deliver an understanding and control of the factors behind international competitiveness and economic development. Another reason may be that an analytical concept that helped to overcome the extreme specialization among policy institutions and policy analysts was welcomed not least among those responsible for innovation and science policy. It is our impression that the concept to begin with diffused to this more limited community, but that it has now tended to enter into broader circles of scholars and policymakers who are focused on economic growth and development.

A concept with roots far back in history

Although the concept of NSI is of recent origin, it is helpful to see it as a development of much older intellectual endeavors. The most obvious starting point is Adam Smith's (1776/1957) analysis of the division of labor, which not only included knowledge creation in relation to directly productive activities but also the specialized services of scientists. But Adam Smith did not consider innovation and competence building as interdependent and systemic. Rather, the systems perspective goes back to Friedrich List (1841). His concept of a "national system of production" took into account a wide set of national institutions, including those engaged in education and training as well as infrastructure, such as networks for the transport of people and commodities (Freeman 1995a). It was focused on the development of productive forces rather than on allocation of given scarce resources. Thus, List pointed to the need to build *national* infrastructure and institutions, which he argued challenged the "cosmopolitan" approach of Adam Smith. But List obviously lacked the analytical tools for developing his ideas beyond the stage of fairly loose suggestions.

The very first use of the "NSI" concept is to be found in an unpublished paper written by Christopher Freeman in 1982 for an OECD expert group (for the newly published version, see Lundvall 2004). This paper illustrates the key role played by Christopher Freeman in building innovation research, and it refers directly to the work of Friedrich List. In the development of the Aalborg version of the concept, the role of the *home market* for innovations has some connection to the infant-industry argument of List. But here the direct inspiration came from Burenstam Linder, who is a liberal economist and a former conservative minister in the Swedish government (Linder 1961).

Parallel activities around the world

Instead of looking for clear-cut intellectual origins of the innovation system concept, its main background should rather be found in the needs of policymakers and students of innovation. The activities of national governments and international organizations such as the OECD had, during the 1960s and 1970s, led to an immense interest in finding reasons why national growth rates differed. One of the explanations was differences in the research systems of different countries. For researchers who tried to combine general economics with innovation studies, such explanations seemed just to scratch the surface of the issue.

It seemed obvious that most of the new knowledge needed for innovation did not come directly from universities and technical research – and, in many industries, not even from research and experimental development, but rather from other sources, such as production engineers, customers, marketing, etc. The problem was to integrate these broader contributions into a concept of the innovation process. The emphasis on this problem meant that the idea of an NSI was already dominant in the work of the Innovation, Knowledge, and Economic (IKE) dynamics group in Aalborg in the first half of the 1980s. A standard phrase found in several publications from this period was "the innovative capability of the national system of production."

But the concept was dominant also in the international comparisons between national styles of management of innovation pursued at the SPRU, and again it was Christopher Freeman who brought the concept into the literature in 1987 in his book on innovation in Japan (Freeman 1987). And it was certainly dominant in the work of Richard Nelson and other US scholars engaged in comparing the US system of science and technology with other national systems. When Freeman, Nelson, and Lundvall got together in the big project on technical change and economic theory (Dosi *et al.* 1988), they ended up with a book with a four-chapter part on "national systems of innovation."[6]

New models

Over the last decade, there have been several new concepts emphasizing the systemic characteristics of innovation, but with a focus on other levels of the economy than the nation state. The literature on "regional systems of innovation" has grown rapidly since the middle of the 1990s (Cooke 1992; Maskell and Malmberg 1997). Bo Carlsson, with colleagues from Sweden, developed the concept of "technological systems" (Carlsson and Jacobsson 1997), while Franco Malerba developed the concept of "sectoral systems of innovation" (Breschi and Malerba 1997).

Sometimes these concepts have been presented or interpreted as alternatives to the *national* system approach, and it has been argued that many, if not most, interesting interactions in the context of modern innovation tend to cross national borders and that there is no a *priori* reason why the national level should be taken as a given for the analysis. Our view on the issue has always been pragmatic and reflects the fact that we see the policy dimension of the concept as important. As long as nation states exist as political entities with their own agendas related to innovation, it is useful to work with *national* systems as analytical objects.

But the different analytical levels are certainly not only legitimate in their own right – they are complementary. To understand the working of national systems, analysts should see how they are constituted by sectoral and regional systems, including how they are integrated in global networks' relationships. And vice versa, in order to understand the evolution of sectoral and regional systems and industrial clusters, analysts need to determine the way that they are integrated in national systems. Not least, when it comes to designing industrial policy aiming at creating and promoting industrial clusters, policy designers should take the "helicopter view" of the national system approach.

10.3   The evolution of the Aalborg version of the NSI concept

One of Schumpeter's major contributions to the understanding of innovation processes is the interpretation of innovation as *a new*

---

[6] Others who worked along similar lines of thought but with less emphasis on innovation were Michael Porter (1990) and Richard Whitley (1994). Whitley's concept of a national business system is complementary to the innovation system approach in its emphasis on culturally embedded business practices. (For a comparison, see Lundvall 1999a, 1999b).

combination (Schumpeter and Opie 1934). The Aalborg version of the NSI concept may be seen as a combination of four elements: (1) the neo-Schumpeterian reinterpretation of national production systems, (2) empirical work based on the home-market theory of international trade, (3) the microeconomic approach to innovation as an interactive process, and, finally, (4) insights into the role of institutions in shaping innovative activities. This combination reflects the fact that Aalborg analysts developed their version of the NSI concept to get a better understanding of economic growth and trade specialization in a small open economy characterized by high income per *capita* but with a weak representation of science-based firms. It also reflects an emphasis on the economic and technological history of countries with a gradual change in the intra-national and international division of productive and innovative labor. The analysts initially focused on macroeconomic issues, but they also moved gradually toward issues related to microeconomic dynamics.

From systems of production toward systems of innovation

An important starting point for the IKE group's work in innovation systems was a reinterpretation of what appeared to be the "structuralist economics" of Hirschman (1958), Perroux (1969), Dahmén (1970), and their followers. Such theorists seemed to have successfully combined Leontief's input-output analysis with Schumpeter's theory of innovation and entrepreneurship. But, in practice, the input-output perspective easily comes to dominate and "the missing innovation perspective has led to a misjudgement of some of the important mechanisms of the national and regional development process" (Andersen, Dalum, and Villumsen 1981b: 55). It is not easy to recombine Leontief and Schumpeter in a systematic manner (cf. DeBresson 1996; Drejer 1999), but the basic idea gave a new and critical interpretation of many analyses of development and growth and the related policies.

Perroux (1969) and his French followers had developed an analysis of the importance of the structure of national systems of production for economic dynamics, some of it rooted in the Marxian schemes of extended and intensive reproduction. They assumed that different sectors affected growth differently and that the most dynamic elements in the system (the growth poles) were located upstream. This led them into ordering national systems in a hierarchy. They assumed that countries such as the United States and Germany had a stronger economy than France, because their production systems were specialized in the production of machine tools. It also led to somewhat naive recommendations for developing countries to establish, at an early stage, activities belonging to the sector producing machinery. The historical experience of the Nordic countries gave an alternative, more evolutionary, perspective, where well-functioning machinery sectors were the outgrowth of strong user sectors and presupposed a long-term innovative interaction with them.

These problems in integrating a Leontief-style analysis of production systems with innovation and entrepreneurship were found in many types of study, so that in Aalborg there was much discussion of how to avoid the crowding-out of real neo-Schumpeterian perspectives from the theory of growth and development. The immediate solution was to concentrate on a more dynamic approach to vertical linkages in the production system (Hirschman 1958; Dahmén 1970; Stewart 1977). In particular, Dahmén and Hirschman pointed to the opening up of disequilibria as important and sometimes positive drivers in the development process. A related strategy was to apply a life-cycle perspective on national systems (Andersen, Johnson, and Lundvall 1978; Andersen *et al.* 1979). Some of the ideas were later presented for an international audience in Andersen and Lundvall (1988) and Andersen (1992).

With these revisions, the focus was now explicitly on the development of new technology in an interaction between user sectors and producer sectors. The *quality* of demand became an important element in the process. And, while structuralist ideas of the importance of tight national coherence left small countries very limited prospects in terms of growth and wealth, as does the new growth theory today, the Aalborg discussions pointed to a less gloomy future for these countries by emphasizing the *qualitative* characteristics of the home market.

The second element in the combination: the role of the home market for economic specialization

Some of the early empirical work in Aalborg focused on the division of productive and innovative labor in relation to agriculture, and one interesting result was the strong Danish export specialization in machinery to be used in agriculture and related industries (Andersen, Dalum, and Villumsen 1981a: 11). This observation could not be explained without recourse to the role of the home market.

With reference to nonclassical and nonneo-classical contributions to international trade theory by Posner (1961), Vernon (1966), and especially Linder (1961), a series of empirical studies was pursued showing the importance of the home market when it comes to explaining export specialization in process equipment (Dalum *et al.* 1981; Andersen, Dalum, and Villumsen 1981a). The practical test was to analyze the correlation between specialization indexes for the user- and the producer-sector commodity, respectively. The outcome of the test was that the home market did play an important role for many process equipment commodities.

In this context, analysts established that trade statistics offered good opportunities to characterize and compare the production structure and export specialization of national systems at a rather detailed level. If aggregated in new categories of special relevance for economic growth, specialization data could be used to analyze the competitiveness of national systems. The change over time in the specialization pattern in terms of "low-technology" versus "high-technology" products was later followed up by similar studies of high-growth and low-growth products. Further, analyzing the relative uniqueness and stability over time of specialization patterns proved to be a way to underpin the idea of national systems having a certain degree of autonomy (Dalum, Laursen, and Villumsen 1998). Still, analysts who use more or less aggregate statistics cannot reveal the complex process of innovation. For this purpose, they need not only other types of data but also micro-founded theoretical analysis.

From innovation as an interactive process to NSI

The micro-assumptions behind the NSI approach got theoretical inspiration from Nelson and Winter's (1982) evolutionary theory of firms and markets. Another important inspiration came from empirical findings through the 1970s and 1980s made by scholars connected to SPRU and Christopher Freeman. The Sappho study pursued by Freeman and his colleagues at SPRU in the beginning of the 1970s (Rothwell 1977) gave strong support to the idea that success in innovation has to do with long-term relationships and close interaction with agents external to the firm. The presentation of "the chain-linked model," by Kline and Rosenberg (1986), was important, because it gave specific form to an alternative to the cherished linear model, where new technology is assumed to develop directly on the basis of scientific efforts, and, thereafter, to be materialized in new marketed products. All this constituted one important step toward the idea of an NSI, and it indicated a possible micro-foundation for this concept.

The second step was to realize explicitly that the relationships and interactions between agents had to involve *nonprice relationships*. These relationships were presented as *organized markets* with elements of power, trust, and loyalty (Lundvall 1985, 1988). These relationships of coordination and co-operation were identified as the only possible solution to the conundrum of product innovations: on the one hand, pure market interactions (prices and quantities only) were found incapable of transmitting the qualitative information between users and producers. On the other hand, the transformation of markets into hierarchies proposed by transaction-cost theory did not materialize. In order to understand the dynamics, we proposed that the most fruitful perspective was to focus on *interactive learning* rather than only on transactions.

The third step was to realize that different national contexts offer disparate possibilities for establishing organized markets and processes of interactive learning. A series of studies pointed, for instance, to the long-term character of interfirm relationships in Japan and contrasted them with the arm's-length relationships predominating in the Anglo-Saxon countries (Dore 1986; Sako 1990). Furthermore, the literature on the importance of trust and the difficulties in transmitting tacit knowledge pointed to a theory of why the national framework matters for the boundaries of innovation systems: long-term interactive learning is most easily organized in a setting where there are few linguistic and cultural constraints for the transfer of tacit knowledge and where a multilateral system of trust relationships can most easily be organized.

The fourth element in the combination: institutions and institutional economics

The focus on *interactive learning* and national boundaries evokes the important role of nationally organized institutions in determining the rate and direction of innovative activities. Early on, Johnson (1988) insisted on the importance of institutions for innovation and learning processes. *Institutions* understood as norms, habits, and rules, are deeply ingrained in society and play a major role in determining how people relate to each other and how they learn and use their knowledge (Johnson 1992). In an economy characterized by ongoing innovation and fundamental uncertainty, the institutional setting will have a major impact upon how economic agents behave, as well as upon the conduct and performance of the system as a whole.

Which are the most important institutions in the context of innovation and the part of the innovation process that is influenced by the national setting? We emphasize three institutional dimensions that have a major impact and which may differ across nations: the *time horizon* of agents, the role of *trust*, and the *actual mix of rationality*. The distinction between "short-term" as characterizing corporate governance in Anglo-Saxon countries and "long-term" in, for instance, Japanese investment decisions, is one important example of how institutional differences have a decisive influence on the conduct and performance at the national level. This distinction is important not only for the allocation of finance, but also for other aspects of technical innovation. Certain technologies will be developed by agents who only operate with a long-term perspective, while others may be easier to exploit with a short-term horizon.

Trust is a multi-dimensional and complex concept. It may refer to expectations about consistency in behavior, full revelation of what agents regard as relevant information for the other party, and restraint in exploiting the temporary weakness of partners. The institutions that constitute trust are crucial for interactive learning and innovation capabilities. The strength and the kind of trust embedding markets will determine to what degree interactive learning can take place in organized markets. Formal and legal arrangements around the market will reflect, and have an impact upon, this tacit social dimension.

A third category is the predominant rationality. Neo-classical economists assume that instrumental and strategic rationality always dominates human behavior, at least in the private economic sphere. It is correct that market transactions between anonymous agents and a capitalist environment tend to support instrumental rationality. In a context where learning new skills through interaction with other agents is important for success, it is, however, no longer the only kind of behavior that might be selected in the evolving economy. For instance, very little learning would take place if instrumental rationality completely dominated the interaction between professors and students, masters and apprenticeships, or between engineers from R&D labs belonging to different firms. Innovation systems where communicative rationality (Habermas 1984) played a major role in these types of activities might therefore be better off in the long run than the standard exchange economy. The actual mix of rationality in an innovation system may affect its conduct and performance.

In addition to these informal institutions, a number of formal institutional arrangements, such as well-defined and implemented property rights of different kinds – including IPRs, contract laws, corporate law, arbitration institutions and collective bargaining, and other labor-market institutions, are, of course, important for the working of the economy.

In general, we find it useful to think about innovation systems in two dimensions. One refers to the *structure* of the system – what is produced in the system and what competences are most developed? The second refers to the *institutional* set-up – how do production, innovation, and learning take place? Historical analysis may be helpful in demonstrating how the two dimensions co-evolve. Is it the evolution of the structure of production that determines the evolution of the institutional set-up, or vice versa, and how are match and mismatch between the two reflected in economic growth patterns (Freeman 1995b)?

The unfinished synthesis

This outline of the four elements gives a rough impression of how the Aalborg concept of NSI was developed. The basic understanding of the innovation process is that it is neither fully automatic, as in the theory of induced innovation, nor fully deliberate, as in theories of R&D management. The innovation process reflects human initiative and creativity, but it is also deeply influenced by the production structure and the institutional setting. The perspective is one where several partners have roles to play in each innovation process. The focus on innovation systems reflects less a theoretical abstraction and more the practical needs of the participants in the complex division of productive and innovative labor in modern economies. The highly developed institutional, cognitive, and functional specialization and rapid change give rise to a need to establish innovation-related linkages between the component parts of the system. A crucial part of these linkages still tends to be organized on a national basis because of constraints of language and distance in the necessary co-ordination of decisions and in processes of interactive learning of importance for the innovation process.

Compared to other concepts of innovation systems, the Aalborg concept clearly has a complementary role. For instance, the concept implies that NSI are most important in sectors of production where trust and tacit knowledge play a major role in the innovation process, as in the case of product innovations made for professional users by specialized suppliers. As pointed out by Pavitt (1984), these factors are not equally important in all types of innovation. In some sectors a more arm's-length approach to innovation seems appropriate, and here the globalized patterns of sectoral innovation systems are more adequate – although the national system of innovation still has a role to play – for instance, through the national supply of scientific personnel. Similarly, the emphasis on the national level of analysis is not intended to remove attention from innovation systems that have their basis within cities and regions or that come from corporate innovation systems. Still, the national level is a quite handy starting point for the inclusion of many aspects of economic specialization of crucial importance to the innovation process, and it is a level where at least some elements of policy and development strategies are developed and implemented.

10.4   Challenges for the NSI concept

Our on-going research, to some extent, can be seen as a response to challenges to the NSI concept. For brevity, we shall consider only four major challenges. The first concerns the need to base the concept much more strongly on the process of learning and competence-building. The second has to do with the need to broaden the analysis of economic development, and the third is to study how knowledge production is conditioned by, and affects, social and ecological sustainability. The fourth, and final, challenge is to apply the NSI concept to innovation policy and to policy co-ordination.

Innovation systems in the learning economy

In a series of papers, we have argued that the last decades have been characterized by a new context that we call "the learning economy" (Lundvall and Johnson 1994; Archibugi and Lundvall 2001). The new context is more than anything else characterized by a speed-up in the rate of change, giving a stronger importance to learning processes for economic performance. This is why we argue that today the most important elements in innovation systems have to do with the learning capability of individuals, organizations, and regions. The very rapid rate of change gives a premium to those who are rapid learners. This is reflected in the forms of organization inside firms, new mixtures between co-operation and competition, as well as in new forms of governance. It presents all organizations – and especially those specialized in the production, diffusion, and use of knowledge – with new challenges.

So far, analysts studying NSI have given too little emphasis to the sub-system related to human resource development.[7] This includes the formal education and training, the labor-market dynamics, and the organization of knowledge creation and learning within firms and in networks. This subsystem will be confronted with very strong needs for social invention in the near future in all national systems, and quite a lot of the peculiarities of national systems are rooted in it.

Another new focus must be on the part of business services that specialize in producing, gathering, and selling knowledge. This sector is growing more rapidly than any other sector and new empirical studies indicate that it is becoming a key sector in the French structural school sense (Tomlinson 2001). More and more producers of tangible products and traditional services are moving into this field. To understand how such businesses operate within and across national borders is another key to understanding future economic dynamics.

---

[7] An exception is Amable, Barré, and Boyer (1997), where the labor-market and training systems are integrated in the analysis of what they call "social systems of innovation."

The production and diffusion of knowledge is itself changing character. Some elements of knowledge are becoming codified and much more mobile globally, while other key elements remain tacit and deeply embedded in individuals and organizations and localities. To understand these processes may, actually, be a key to establishing a new kind of economy (OECD 2000). This understanding requires an ambitious theoretical research agenda aiming at understanding processes of learning in the context of production and innovation systems.

At the more applied level, innovation analysts need to understand the process of transformation of national innovation systems exposed to "globalization." It is obvious that different national systems respond differently to global trends and challenges – consider the experience of Latin American and Asian countries. Some national systems, for historical reasons, may be better prepared to cope with the new context than others. Some systems may be more innovative than others when it comes to developing policy strategies and institutional reforms that respond to the new challenges.

Contradictions in the era of the globalizing learning economy

In the present era of the globalizing learning economy (Lundvall and Borras 1998; Lundvall 2001), there are contradictions inherent in the economic process that threaten learning and competence-building by undermining social capital. Financial speculation seems to become more and more unhampered, and, increasingly, it is finance capital that judges what is "good practice" among firms as well as among governments. This power of finance capital is one of the major factors that speed up the rate of change, and thereby the need for accelerating learning. At the same time, the uninhibited rule of finance capital gets into serious conflict with some of the fundamental prerequisites for the sustainability of the learning economy.

On the one hand, short-term economic calculations and speedy processes of decisionmaking (especially in financial flows) are becoming more and more important (Jessop 1999). On the other hand, competition depends more and more on dynamic efficiency rooted in knowledge or knowledge-related resources with long-term characteristics. These resources often take a long time and sustained efforts to build, but they may also be quickly destroyed. This is because learning and innovation are interactive processes, which depend on trust and other elements of social cohesion.

One problem is that the speed-up of change puts a pressure on all kinds of established social relationships in local, regional, and national communities. It contributes to the weakening of traditional family relationships, local communities, and stable workplaces. This is important since the production of intellectual capital (learning) is strongly dependent on social capital. To find ways of re-establishing the social capital undermined by the globalization process is a major challenge.

Another problem is that the short-term perspectives promoted by finance capital give little weight to long-term ecological imbalances. The discount rates are very high, not only when it comes to assessing future benefits but also when it comes to assessing ecological costs. Natural capital including unpolluted air in the big cities and clean drinking water is not sufficiently valued in a regime dominated by a governance form where finance capital is directly or indirectly in charge.

These contradictions in the learning economy increase the need for policy co-ordination. Below we shall argue that there is a need for policy learning in terms of building new kinds of institutions for policy co-ordination. Such institutions would have strategic responsibilities to develop a common vision of how to cope with the challenges and contradictions of the globalizing learning economy. At the national level, such a vision has to be based on a deep understanding of the distinct national system of competence-building and innovation on the one hand, and of major trends in the global context, on the other.

Innovation policy

When it comes to supporting innovation processes through different kinds of policy, there is a growing consensus on the need to focus on long-term competence-building in firms and in society as a whole. At the same time, the prevailing institutional set-up and global competition also tends to give predominance to short-term financial objectives in policymaking. At the institutional level, this is reflected in the fact that in most countries ministries of finance have become the only agencies taking on a responsibility for co-ordinating the many specialized area policies. Area-specific ministries tend to identify with their own "customers" and take little interest in the wider objectives of society.

A broad concept of innovation system implies a new perspective on a wide set of policies including social policy, labor-market policy, education policy, industrial policy, energy policy, environmental policy, and science and technology policy. Specifically, the concept calls for new national development strategies with co-ordination across all these policy areas.

All these area-specific policies affect learning and competence-building. They need to be designed with this in mind and brought together and honed into a common strategy. It is highly problematic to leave policy co-ordination exclusively to ministries of finance and to central banks because their visions of the world are necessarily biased toward the monetary dimension of the economy and thereby toward the short term. The analytical efforts aiming at increasing our understanding of the regional, national, and transnational innovation systems need to be supported by new policy institutions in the form of high-level councils for innovation and competence-building at these levels. Such councils should be given authority to take into account issues of social and ecological sustainability and the power to counter short-term views of finance capital.

Another important potential for applying the innovation system concept and pursuing comparative studies of different systems is that it helps to foster a critical understanding of the limits of specific national policy strategies. Policies aiming at promoting industrial development through innovation will often tend to follow specific trajectories, and will often be more successful in reinforcing the system where it is already strong. This was our conclusion in Edquist and Lundvall (1993), where we found that Swedish policies were focused on promoting process innovation while Danish policies were more focused on incremental product innovation. In both countries, the focus was on reinforcing the "strong" sides of the system. In order to overcome this kind of lock-in and the impact of vested interests in defining the policy agenda, the system perspective and its use in comparative analysis is especially helpful.

In a broader perspective, national systems of innovation may be regarded as a tool for analyzing economic development and economic growth. Its commonality with growth accounting is that it tries to bring together the major factors that affect technical progress as registered in standard neo-classical growth models. Such a perspective may be too narrow, however. As pointed out by Freeman (1997), the ecological challenge ought to be integrated into any strategy for economic development, and here we shall argue that in the learning economy, intellectual and social capital are important elements in the development process. We introduce this extended perspective in table 10.2.

Table 10.2 illustrates the fact that economic growth is faced with a double challenge in terms of sustainability and that there is an important risk of undermining not only the material but also the intangible basis of production. The creation of tangible capital may be threatened by a neglect of environmental sustainability, and the production and efficient use of intellectual capital are fundamentally dependent upon social capital (Coleman, 1990; Fukuyama 1995; Woolcock 1998; OECD 2001). A development strategy that focuses only on production capital and intellectual capital is not sustainable.

Table 10.2 *Resources fundamental for economic growth: combining the tangible and reproducible dimensions*

Resources	Easily reproducible resources	Less reproducible resources
Tangible	Production capital	Natural capital
Intangible	Intellectual capital	Social capital

Source: The authors.

Innovation may have a positive role in bolstering sustainability (Johnson 1998). Technical innovation – for instance, in terms of developing substitutes for naturally scarce raw materials – may help to overcome the fact that natural capital cannot always be reproduced. In a similar vein, social innovation and institutional redesign may help to overcome a crisis where social capital is foundering. In both cases it is important to note that the workings of unhampered market forces will erode the basis of economic growth.[8]

This perspective indicates a broader and more interdisciplinary approach to economic growth than is done in neo-classical economics. It also differs in being more explicit in terms of the institutional assumptions made and especially in avoiding any assumption about factors being independent. This reflects the systems perspective and the emphasis on virtuous and vicious circles or match and mismatch between elements and subsystems. Some of the most fundamental contradictions in the new context can also be referred to in terms of the problems of reproducing natural and social capital.

10.5   Concluding remarks

The concept of NSI has evolved and diffused quickly during the last decade. This development has emphasized the need of sharpening the concept and the related policies, and we are confident that much progress will be seen in this vein. There is, however, a tendency to concentrate the efforts in the rich North. We shall therefore use our concluding remarks to comment on the possibilities of widening the concept and its applications.

We believe that the broad concept of an NSI may also be useful, as an analytical tool and as a tool for promoting sustainable economic growth and well-being, in countries in the South. At the same time, we recognize

[8] Environmental sustainability was explicitly introduced into a national innovation system approach by Segura-Bonilla (1999).

the need to adapt and further develop the concept, so that it becomes more relevant for the situation in these countries.

On the positive side, it points to a legitimate national mobilization of efforts and to a co-ordinated policy effort to enhance learning capabilities necessary in order to get a new type of dynamics started in these countries. In order to do so, the NSI concept needs to inspire activities that mobilize broadly across sectors and regions.

On the negative side, there is always a risk that the NSI concept will be misinterpreted as a basis for promoting exclusive science-based institutions and activities with a very limited socioeconomic impact. There is a need for broad efforts to promote the learning capability, including that of weak segments of the population and of the country. Another normative conclusion from the innovation system analysis is that the demand for knowledge should be given as much attention as its supply.

Analytical efforts need to be made to improve how policymakers understand how more complete innovation and competence-building systems may be constructed in the current environment of global competition and networking. The power games of exclusion and inclusion in relation to global knowledge-intensive networks has become of key importance for development and underdevelopment.

REFERENCES

Amable, B., R. Barré, and R. Boyer, 1997. *Les systèmes d'innovation a l'ère de la globalization*, Paris: Economica

Andersen, E. S., 1992. "Approaching National Innovation Systems," in B.-Å. Lundvall (ed.), *National Innovation Systems*, London: Pinter: 68–92

Andersen, E. S., A. Brændgaard, B. Johnson, and B.-Å. Lundvall, 1979. *Industriel udvikling og international konkurrenceevne*, Serie om industriel udvikling, 6, Aalborg: Aalborg University Press

Andersen E. S., B. Dalum, and G. Villumsen, 1981a. *International Specialisation and the Home Market: An Empirical Analysis*, Aalborg: Aalborg University Press

1981b. "The Importance of the Home Market for Technological Development and the Export Specialization of Manufacturing Industry," in C. Freeman (ed.), *Technical Innovation and National Economic Performance*, Aalborg: Aalborg University Press: 49–102

Andersen, E. S., B. Johnson, and B.-Å. Lundvall, 1978. *Industriel udvikling og industrikrise*, Serie om industriel udvikling, 4, Aalborg: Aalborg University Press

Andersen, E. S. and B.-Å. Lundvall, 1988. "Small National Innovation Systems Facing Technological Revolutions: An Analytical Framework," in C. Freeman and B.-Å. Lundvall (eds.), *Small Countries Facing the Technological Revolution*, London: Pinter: 9–37

Archibugi, D. and B.-Å. Lundvall (eds.), 2001. *Europe in the Globalising Learning Economy*, Oxford: Oxford University Press

Arrow, K. J., 1962, "The Economic Implications of Learning by Doing," *Review of Economic Studies*, 29(80): 155–173

Breschi, S. and F. Malerba, 1997. "Sectoral Innovation Systems," in C. Edquist (ed.), *Systems of Innovation: Technologies, Institutions, and Organizations*, London: Pinter: 130–152

Brookfield, H., 1975. *Interdependent Development*, London: Methuen

Carlsson, B. and S. Jacobsson, 1997. "Diversity Creation and Technological Systems: A Technology Policy Perspective," in C. Edquist (ed.), *Systems of Innovation: Technologies, Institutions and Organizations*, London: Pinter: 266–290

Christensen, J. L. and B.-Å. Lundvall (eds.), 2004. *Product Innovation, Interactive Learning, and Economic Performance*, Amsterdam: Elsevier

Coleman J., 1990. *Foundations of Social Theory*, London: Harvard University Press

Cooke, P., 1992. "Regional Innovation Systems: Competitive Regulation in Europe," Geoforum, 23: 365–382

Dahmén, E., 1970. *Entrepreneurial Activity and the Development of Swedish Industry 1919–1939*, Homewood, IL: American Economic Association Translation Series

Dalum, B., M. Gregersen, J. Schmidt, and G. Villumsen, 1981. *Økonomiers langsigtede udvikling: en struktur og teknologidiskussion*, Aalborg: Aalborg University

Dalum, B., K. Laursen, and G. Villumsen, 1998. "Structural Change in OECD Specialisation Patterns: Specialisation and 'Stickiness'," *International Review of Applied Economics*, 12(3): 421–443

DeBresson, C. (ed.), 1996. *Economic Interdependence and Innovative Activity: An Input-Output Analysis*, Aldershot: Edward Elgar

Dore, R., 1986. *Flexible Rigidities: Industrial Policy and Structural Adjustment in the Japanese Economy 1970–1980*, London: Athlone Press

Dosi, G., C. Freeman, R. R. Nelson, G. Silverberg, and L. Soete (eds.), 1988. *Technological Change and Economic Theory*, London: Pinter

Drejer, I., 1999. "Technological Change and Interindustrial Linkages: Introducing Knowledge Flows in Input-Output Studies," Aalborg: Aalborg University, PhD thesis

Edquist, C. and B.-Å. Lundvall,1993. "Comparing the Danish and Swedish Systems of Innovation," in R. R. Nelson (ed.), *National Innovation Systems: A Comparative Analysis*, Oxford: Oxford University Press: 265–298

Foray, D., 2000. *The Economics of Knowledge*, Cambridge, MA, MIT Press

Freeman, C., 1987. *Technology Policy and Economic Performance: Lessons from Japan*: London: Pinter

    1995a. "The National Innovation Systems in Historical Perspective," *Cambridge Journal of Economics*, 19(1): 5–24

    1995b. "History, Co-Evolution, and Economic Growth," IIASA Working Paper, Laxenburg: 95–76

    1997. "Innovation Systems: City-State, National, Continental, and Sub-National," Paper presented at the Montevideo conference, University of Sussex, SPRU, Mimeo

Freeman, C. and C. Perez, 1988. "Structural Crises of Adjustment, Business Cycles, and Investment Behaviour," in G. Dosi, C. Freeman, R. Nelson, G. Silverberg, and L. Soete (eds.), *Technical Change and Economic Theory*, London, Pinter: 38–67

Fukuyama, F., 1995. *Trust: The Social Virtues and the Creation of Prosperity*, New York: Simon & Schuster

Georgescu-Roegen, N., 1971. *The Entropy Law and the Economic Process*, Cambridge, MA: Harvard University Press.

Habermas, J., 1984. *The Theory of Communicative Action*, I, Boston: Beacon Press

Hirschman, A. O., 1958. *The Strategy of Economic Development*, Clinton, MA: Yale University Press

Jensen, M. B., B. Johnson, E. Lorenz, and B.-Å. Lundvall, 2004. "Absorptive Capacity, Forms of Knowledge and Economic Development," Paper presented at the the Second Globelics Conference in Beijing, October 16–20

Jessop, B., 1999. "The State and the Contradictions of the Knowledge-Driven Economy," Development Research Working Papers, Department for Development and Planning

Johnson, B., 1988. "An Institutional Approach to the Small Country Problem," in C. Freeman and B.-Å. Lundvall (eds.), *Small Countries Facing the Technological Revolution*, London: Pinter: 279–298

   1992. "Institutional Learning," in B.-Å. Lundvall (ed.), *National Innovation Systems: Towards a Theory of Innovation and Interactive Learning*, London: Pinter: 23–44

   1998. "Institutional Learning and Clean Growth," in A. Tylecote and J. van der Straaten (eds.), *Environment, Technology and Economic Growth*, Cheltenham: Edward Elgar: 93–111

Kline, S. J. and N. Rosenberg, 1986. "An Overview of Innovation," in R. Landau and N. Rosenberg (eds.), *The Positive Sum Game*, Washington, DC: National Academy Press: 275–305

Linder, S. B., 1961. *An Essay on Trade and Transformation*, New York: Wiley

List, F., 1841. *Das Nationale System der Politischen Ökonomie*, Basel: Kyklos; trans. and pub. under the title, *The National System of Political Economy*, London: Longmans, Green & Co. (1841)

Lundvall, B.-Å., 1985. *Product Innovation and User–producer Interaction*, Aalborg: Aalborg University Press

   1988. "Innovation as an Interactive Process: From User–Producer Interaction to the National Innovation Systems," in G. Dosi, C. Freeman, R. R. Nelson, G. Silverberg, and L. Soete (eds.), *Technical Change and Economic Theory*, London: Pinter: 349–370

   1999a. "National Business Systems and National Innovation Systems," *International Studies of Management and Organization*, 29(2): 60–77

   1999b. "Spatial Division of Labour and Interactive Learning," *Revued'Economie Régionale et Urbaine*, 3: 469–488

   2001. *Innovation, Growth and Social Cohesion: The Danish Model*, London: Edward Elgar

2004, "Introduction to 'Technological Infrastructure and International Competitiveness,' by Christopher Freeman," *Industrial and Corporate Change*, 13(3): 531–539

Lundvall, B.-Å. and S. Borras, 1998. *The Globalising Learning Economy: Implications for Innovation Policy*, Brussels: DG XII-TSER, European Commission

Lundvall, B.-Å. and B. Johnson, 1994. "The Learning Economy," *Journal of Industry Studies*, 1(2): 23–42

Lundvall, B.-Å., B. Johnson, E. S. Andersen, and B. Dalum, 2002. "National Systems of Production, Innovation, and Competence Building," *Research Policy*, 31: 213–231

Maskell, P. and A. Malmberg, 1997. "Towards an Explanation of Regional Specialization and Industry Agglomeration," *European Planning Studies*, 5(1): 25–41

Nelson, R. R. and S. G. Winter, 1982. *An Evolutionary Theory of Economic Change*, Cambridge, MA: The Belknap Press of Harvard University Press

Nielsen, K. and S. Kvale, 1999. "Mesterlære som aktuel læringsform," in K. Nielsen and S. Kvale (eds.), *Mesterlære, Læring som Social Praksis*, Copenhagen: Hans Reitzels Forlag: 9–53

Organization for Economic Co-Operation and Development (OECD), 1982. "Technological Infrastructure and International Competitiveness," Paris: OECD, unpublished paper; see Lundvall (2004)

2000. Knowledge Management in the Learning Economy, Paris: OECD

2001. *The Well-Being of Nations: The Role of Human and Social Capital*, Paris: OECD

Pavitt, K., 1984. "Sectoral Patterns of Technical Change: Towards a Taxonomy and a Theory," *Research Policy*, 13: 343–373

Perroux, F., 1969, *L'Economie du XXe siècle*, 3rd edn., Paris: Presses Universitaires de France

Porter, M., 1990. *The Competitive Advantage of Nations*, London: Macmillan

Posner, M. V., 1961. "International Trade and Technical Change," *Oxford Economic Papers*, 13(3): 323–341

Rosenberg, N., 1982. *Inside the Black Box: Technology and Economics*, Cambridge: Cambridge University Press

Rothwell, R., 1977. "The Characteristics of Successful Innovators and Technically Progressive Firms," *R&D Management*, 7(3): 191–206

Sako, M., 1990. "Buyer–Supplier Relationships and Economic Performance: Evidence from Britain and Japan," University of London, PhD thesis

Schumpeter, J. A. and R. Opie, 1934. *The Theory of Economic Development: An Inquiry into Profits, Capital, Credit, Interest, and the Business Cycle*, Cambridge, MA: Harvard University Press

Scott, A. J., 2000. "Economic Geography: The Great Half-Century," in G. L. Clark, M. P. Feldman, and M. S. Gertler (eds.), The *Oxford Handbook of Economic Geography*, Oxford: Oxford University Press: 18–44

Segura-Bonilla, O., 1999. *Sustainable Systems of Innovation: The Forest Sector in Central America*, SUDESCA Research Papers, 24, Department of Business Studies, Aalborg University, PhD dissertation

Smith, A., 1776/1957. *An Inquiry into the Nature and Causes of the Wealth of Nations*, London: J. M. Dent & Sons

Stewart, F., 1977. *Technology and Underdevelopment*, London: Macmillan

Tomlinson, M., 2001. "A New Role for Business Services in Economic Growth," in D. Archibugi, and B.-Å. Lundvall (eds.), *Europe in the Globalising Learning Economy*, Oxford: Oxford University Press: 97–107

Vernon, R., 1966. "International Investment and International Trade in the Product Cycle," *Quarterly Journal of Economics*, 80(1): 190–207 s

Whitley, R., 1994. *Business Systems in East Asia: Firms, Markets and Societies*, London: Sage

Williamson, D. F., 1975. *Markets and Hierarchies: Analysis and Antitrust Implications*, London: Macmillan

Woolcock, M., 1998. "Social Capital and Economic Development: Toward a Theoretical Synthesis and Policy Framework," *Theory and Society*, 27(2): 151–207

11 Perspectives on entrepreneurship and cluster formation: biotechnology in the US Capitol region

Maryann P. Feldman

11.1 Introduction

Two decades ago, Gaithersburg, Frederick, and Rockville, Maryland, were largely commuter communities for US federal government employees. Today, these Washington suburbs host one of the most dynamic and fast-growing biotechnology (biotech) clusters in the United States (Ernst and Young 2001). While analysts have well documented the tendency for an innovative industry to cluster spatially, they have not answered questions about the development of regional industrial clusters, and the role government policy plays in cluster formation and sustainability. In this chapter, I focus on the emergence of a biotech cluster in the Capitol region.

Based on extensive interviews, I posit that three exogenous sets of factors sparked the nascent entrepreneurial talent in the region, creating the sufficient conditions for the emergence of a biotech cluster: (1) pre-existing resources, (2) entrepreneurship and incentives, and (3) infrastructure provided by government. This emergence was hastened by a series of exogenous events that lowered the opportunity cost of entrepreneurship and promoted the formation of new ventures. Although these changes were national policy initiatives, the Capitol region was in a unique position to capture the benefits. State government policies targeted at the biotech industry reinforced rather than led the cluster formation. My hypothesis is that entrepreneurs and new-firm formation are critical elements in the development of innovative clusters, and occur in those places at a time when the preconditions and incentives are supportive.

The author wishes to acknowledge financial support from MdBio for work that preceded this chapter. In addition, MdBio and the Maryland Department of Business and Economic Development (DBED) provided data and assistance. Johanna Francis provided research support. Specifically, I would like to thank Bob Eaton of MdBio and Will Baber of DBED for their assistance. In addition I would like to thank the individuals who have been interviewed during the course of this project.

To support this hypothesis, I document some of the public initiatives that provided resources for the developing Maryland cluster in section 11.2. Section 11.3 considers the genesis of the dedicated biotech companies, and section 11.4 the role of entrepreneurship in the life-cycle of the Maryland cluster. Section 11.5 provides some reflective conclusions on the technology-intensive cluster development.

11.2   Public initiatives providing resources for the Maryland biotech cluster

The Capitol region biotech cluster is contained almost entirely within the state of Maryland, concentrated mainly in the cities of Frederick, Gaithersburg, and Rockville. The industry has expanded along interstate highway 270 that originates near the National Institutes of Health in the suburb of Bethesda, Maryland, and extends toward Frederick, Maryland. The largest concentration of firms is in the adjacent communities of Gaithersburg and Rockville, Maryland.

These human resources attract large amounts of R&D funding. Maryland ranks second among US states with regard to federal R&D obligations, second only to the state of California. The majority of US federal R&D funds are channeled through the Departments of Agriculture, Commerce, Defense, and Health and Human Services, as well as through the National Aeronautics and Space Administration (NASA). Maryland ranks in the top three states in terms of the total amount of funding received from each of these federal agencies, it is also notable that each of these agencies has a facility located in Maryland. In addition, Maryland ranks sixth in terms of federal R&D expenditures to academic institutions. One single university in the state, Johns Hopkins University located in Baltimore, is the largest recipient of federal R&D expenditures.

These resources translate into measurable inventive activity. The state of Maryland ranked fourth in the number of biotech patents issued in 1997. It also ranked fourth in the number of Small Business Innovation Research (SBIR) awards granted between 1995 and 2000. These awards are given by government agencies hoping to encourage innovation in small firms and are a good indicator of innovation (Black 2002). Given that Maryland is a small state in terms of population, these rankings are impressive. The factors highlighted above have coalesced to form a successful and rapidly growing biotech industry in the state of Maryland. As then Maryland Lieutenant Governor, Katherine Kennedy Townsend (2002), points out:

Table 11.1 *Government laboratories*

Laboratory	Location	Scientific staff	Research budget
Agricultural Research Center	Beltsville, MD	1,040	$97,000,000
NIH	Bethesda, MD (main campus)	10,000	$17,800,000,000
NIST	Gaithersburg, MD	2,800[a]	$400,000,000[b]
Naval Medical Research Institute	Bethesda, MD	150	n.a.
AMRICD	Aberdeen, MD	93	$16,689,000
AMRIID	Frederick, MD	138	$27,000,000
WRAIR	Silver Spring, MD	392	$40,200,000
FDA	Rockville, MD (headquarters and some labs) Bethesda, MD (Labs)	80,000[a]	$1,414,000,000[b]

Notes: [a]Not all scientists; some administrative and other staff included.
[b]These figures are for fiscal year (FY) 2002; entire budget, not only research.
Source: Laboratory websites; data for 2002.
n.a.   Numbers not available.

A healthy, well financed, and daring education system is the indispensable foundation for success in biotechnology. But you also need entrepreneurs, capital, partnerships, and a long-term strategy for reaching your goal. Maryland has all that and more. In 1991, Maryland had approximately 100 bioscience companies. Ten years later, that number had grown to over 300 – second highest per capita [in the nation] – with a market capitalization of $28 billion as of last July. Our biotech industry now employs 20,000 people with another 25,000 working in related R&D – earning a total payroll of $2.1 billion.[1]

An important unique factor in the Capitol biotech cluster is the proximity of US government departments and attendant biotech-relevant laboratories and the amount of government funding they receive. There are eight significant government-funded biotech-relevant laboratories in the Capitol cluster. Table 11.1 details these labs, their locations, number of researchers and research budget. Most important for the biotech industry is the National Institutes of Health (NIH). The NIH is a collection of twenty-seven institutes and centers, each focusing on a specific disease or health topic. The NIH budget, which is generally regarded as the largest

---

[1] The discrepancy in these numbers relative to those presented earlier in the chapter depends on the precise definitions used and the time-frame considered. Market capitalization, for example, is a volatile number and can be very different depending on which quarter and year the data are sampled.

scientific research budget in the world, was $23.56 billion in 2002. Most of this funding, 80–85 percent of the total, is allocated to extramural research, granted mostly to researchers at public and private universities. Approximately 11 percent is allocated to intramural research conducted at the NIH headquarters in Bethesda, Maryland (Baldwin 2002). Although the NIH is the largest government medical research institution in the area, two other very large government laboratories also have their main laboratories in Maryland.

The Food and Drug Administration (FDA) and the National Institute of Standards and Technology (NIST) each have budgets well over $250 million and more than 1,000 employees. The FDA regulates all food and drug products and ensures that they are both safe and effective. The FDA is a particularly important regulatory body for biotech firms that wish to bring new drugs and devices to market, and proximity facilitates this interaction. For example, in order for a new drug to be made available to the public, it must undergo extensive clinical trials. In the Capitol region, there is a large network of hospitals and physicians who undertake clinical trials as well as database firms that manage the records and results. These resources existed to serve the pharmaceutical industry but provide an advantage to the developing biotech sector. NIST is not a regulatory body but rather develops and promotes measurements, standards, and technology to enhance productivity, facilitate trade, and improve the quality of life. Its laboratories produce cutting-edge research in technology and infrastructure. A number of biotech firms have used Cooperative Research and Development Agreements (CRADAs) with NIST as a means to become established. Another large laboratory based in Maryland, the Agricultural Research Center, conducts research particularly relevant to agricultural problems and food safety. There are several other important government laboratories that are smaller and that have a military basis, although they have produced important breakthroughs, particularly in the area of vaccines and infectious diseases.

These government labs anchor the biotech industry in the Capitol region through personnel movements, technology licensing, and government-sponsored co-operative research agreements. Feldman (2001) and Schachtel and Heacock (2002) document the importance of government organizations as a source of entrepreneurs. For example, entrepreneurs from the Walter Reed Army Institute for Research (WRAIR) created some of the earliest dedicated biotech start-ups. Also, at least forty-five biotech entrepreneurs who were previously employed at the NIH have started companies in the state of Maryland. In addition to NIH staff who left to start companies, many more entrepreneurs passed through the NIH at some point, as postdoctoral fellows, graduate students, or as visiting researchers. As well as company founders, many of the young scientists recruited for local biotech companies come from postdoctoral or graduate student positions at the NIH. In general, proximity to these government labs provides biotech companies with a large body of scientists. They recruit the scientists, use them as consultants, and use their ideas. A number of these scientists are either postdoctoral researchers or contract scientists who move easily between their government contract and local companies. In this case, location is a key determinant, as it is simpler to recruit scientists who already work in the same geographical area than to recruit from outside it. The government labs also provided contracts for early-stage biotech companies, allowing them to develop slowly with an initial guarantee of steady contract income.

At the heart of any industrial cluster are firms and the entrepreneurs who start them. Maryland hosts 282 dedicated biotech firms, reflecting the efforts of entrepreneurs who left other employment in the area to start their own firms. These companies range from one-person private start-ups like Protiga, Inc., which provides protein purification services and contract research, to large product development companies like GenVec, which employs seventy-five people and is publicly traded. Leading companies in the region include Human Genome Sciences (HGS) and Celera Genomics Corporation, two key actors in the international effort to map the human genome. In addition, another local company, MedImmune, is currently the world's eighth largest dedicated biotech company with five FDA-approved products on the market. Table 11.2 details the focus of the product-producing companies that currently comprise the Capitol cluster.

The region is internationally noted for its concentration in genomics and bioinformatics and vaccines. Genomics and bioinformatics are related to bioscience software applications and therefore have a natural synergy with the highly developed software design expertise in the region.[2] Delivery systems are related to vaccines development, and are complementary in the sense that delivery systems are the mechanism by which a vaccine reaches its target. Today's vaccines are highly sophisticated; typically the development of the vaccine and the design of the delivery vector are produced in different companies.

Companies are also dedicated to product development on specific disease targets such as AIDs or cancer. Table 11.3 depicts the breakdown

---

[2] Northern Virginia is a fast-growing software and Internet start-up region. Some of these companies have been involved in developing software for the bioinformatics industry, reflecting a regional cross-fertilization. There are a small number of dedicated biotech firms in Northern Virginia.

Table 11.2 *Maryland biotechnology companies by type, 2002*

Product type	Number of companies
Therapeutics	62
Diagnostic products	39
Reagents	38
Genomics/Bioinformatics	17
Vaccines	15
Devices/Materials	15
Bioscience software applications	13
Agricultural	13
Delivery systems	10
Culture media	7
Devices/Instruments	6
Environmental	5
Veterinary	4
Generic drugs	4
Transgenic Animals	2

Source: MdBio (2002); categories provided by MdBio.

Table 11.3 *Disease targets of Capitol biotech companies, 2002*

Disease target	Number of companies	(%)
Cancer	26	31.3
Infectious diseases, excluding AIDS	24	28.9
Neurological	10	12.1
Immunological	7	8.4
Cardiovascular	6	7.2
AIDS	5	6.0
Dermatological	2	2.4
Pulmonary	2	2.4
Gastrointestinal	1	1.2

Source: MdBio (2002).

of disease targets for the eighty-three companies that have provided this information. The largest number of Capitol biotech companies focus on developing products related to various types of cancer (31.3 percent) or infectious diseases (28.9 percent). The remaining 39.8 percent of Maryland's biotech companies are service companies: companies that

Table 11.4 *Service company types*

Service type	Number of companies offering	(%)
Laboratory research	34	35.1
Immunology	12	12.4
Nucleic acid services	11	11.3
Protein services	7	7.2
Viral cell culture	5	5.2
Mammalian cell culture	4	4.1
Bacterial cell culture	2	2.1
Clinical trail support	20	20.6
Contract work	20	20.6
Pre-clinical development/toxicology	18	18.6
Manufacturing/process development	18	18.6
Data management	11	11.3
Drug discovery/screening	9	9.3
Repository/cell banking	6	6.2
Generic testing/forensics	3	3.1

Source: MdBio (2002).

are not involved in their own innovations and product development, but rather perform services, such as contract research and the production of reagents and cell cultures for product-development companies, government and university labs, and other entities. In fact, during the early stages of the cluster's development (1973–80), the first companies were service companies that provided contract research services, produced reagents, medical test kits, or other specialized services for the NIH and various US military departments (see Feldman 2000). Table 11.4 breaks down the type of services offered.

From Table 11.4, we see that the largest number of service companies offer laboratory research services, as well as clinical trial support and contract work. These companies support traditional pharmaceuticals interested in establishing a foothold in biotech products as well as young start-ups, by providing facilities and data management for clinical trials and other FDA testing, as well as R&D work that may be beyond the reach of the contracting company's resources, but which complements their activities. Although service companies are not as flashy as product-development companies, they play an important role in maintaining the cluster and promoting growth. Outsourcing is often a cost-efficient means for young as well as established companies to bring their innovations to market faster and with less risk – for example, by contracting with service companies that have a long history in navigating FDA approval procedures.

Table 11.5 *Biotechnology patent applications, Maryland, 1970–1990*

Year	Number of patents	% of US patents	State rank
1970	5	3.5	11
1975	6	3.1	12
1980	9	2.9	11
1985	27	5.6	6
1990	44	6.1	5
1995	212	6.9	3
1997	103	6.2	4

Note: Patent applications here include only patents granted up to 1999. Patent applications are used rather than patents granted because they more accurately reflect the timing of the innovation. The length of time between patent application and granting results from the US TPO evaluation procedures and does not reflect firm behavior or timing of innovations.

Source: Hall, Jaffe, and Tratjenberg (2001); calculated by the authors from the National Bureau of Economic Research (NBER) Patent Database.

11.3   The genesis of the Maryland biotech cluster

Although the precursors to the biotechnology industry were put in place early in the twentieth century with the discovery of DNA and advances in genetics, the modern biotech industry really began with the Cohen–Boyer discovery of ways to cut and paste DNA to reproduce new DNA inside bacteria in 1973, as well as the production of the first monoclonal antibodies in 1975. Through applying for patents and licensing their innovations to companies, this scientific knowledge gained commercial value. These early successful forays into commercial markets encouraged scientists to begin taking their discoveries out of the lab and into their own companies.

Patents are important in the biotech industry as a measure of both commercial activity and success, albeit a noisy indicator of the latter. To describe the development of the biotech industry in Maryland, table 11.5 depicts the state's relative position in biotech patents.

In 1970, prior to the Cohen–Boyer patents, only 258 biotech patent applications were submitted in the entire United States. The relatively lowly placement of Maryland in biotech patenting up to 1980 reflects the genesis of the cluster and the fact that most of Maryland's biotechs were service companies at that time. Notably in 1980 there were no

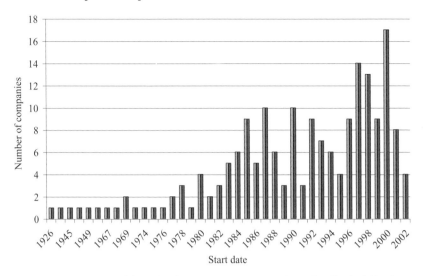

Figure 11.1 Biotechnology company start dates in Capitol Region, 1926–2000

pharmaceutical companies located in the state. Patenting activity among Maryland's biotech firms increased dramatically between 1985 and 1995, with Maryland patents comprising almost 7 percent of total US patents and ranking third overall in biotech patenting.[3] In contrast, the state with the largest biotech activity, California, had almost 30 percent of US biotech patent applications in 1995 (and ranked first in activity).

Correspondingly, figure 11.1 provides the starting dates for the universe of known companies in the Capitol biotech cluster. Vertical bars give an indication of start-up activity over time. Prior to 1973, there were eleven known bioscience companies in the region that were engaged in more traditional technologies and in providing services to government institutions, such as the WRAIR, the US Army and Navy Medical Research Institutes, and the NIH.[4] Some of these early companies were able to adapt to the changing climate and focus on bioscience methods. Companies such as BioReliance, a Rockville, Maryland company

[3] The reason patenting activity appears to have decreased from 1995 to 1997 is likely an artifact of the dataset construction and US TPO patent policy. That is, the decrease reflects only the length of time between applying for a patent and having it granted. Since the database ends at December 1999, patents that were applied for in 1997, 1998, and 1999 but not granted by December 1999, are not included here, thus giving the appearance of a slowdown in patenting activity.

[4] This list cannot be regarded as complete due to the disappearance and lack of evidence on companies that started but did not survive. These data are only an indication of the activity in the region.

established in 1949 to provide development and manufacturing services, and Biomedial Research Institute, established in 1968 to do contract research on vaccines for government agencies, were the precursors to the modern cluster that were able to survive the changes.

From figure 11.1, it appears that biotech companies were created in Maryland in two waves, the first beginning in approximately 1984 and continuing for about eight years. In the next ten years, another 30 percent of the current companies were founded. In 1997 alone, almost 8 percent of the current companies were formed, and in 2000, the largest number of start-ups in a single year – 9 percent – was created. It took a decade to double the number of firms in 1980, and after that less than a decade to triple the number of firms. In 2002, fewer start-ups have been observed than in the previous two years, reflecting the national economic slowdown – and, in particular, the reduction of venture capital funds and initial public offerings.

11.4   Entrepreneurship and the Capitol biotech cluster

The region around the Capitol has recently emerged as a hotbed of entrepreneurial activity in biotechnology and attendant wealth creation and economic growth. This reflects a transformation of the region from an economy dominated by public-sector employment and, in general, not considered innovative or supportive of private-sector activity (Feldman 2001). The emergence of this cluster, rather than the result of direct government intervention, reflects a three-stage process of cluster formation (Feldman and Francis 2002). In this section, I discuss the development of the Capitol biotech cluster and the stages of cluster formation.

Entrepreneurs are a critical element in the formation and the vibrancy of clusters of technology-intensive firms (Feldman 2001). Schumpeter (1942:132) described entrepreneurs not as passive forces in the economy, but as active agents who organize resources and actively refine the environment to be conducive to their pursuits. Through the process of creating new companies, entrepreneurs spark regional industrial transformation, a transformation that exhibits path-dependence, adaptivity, and self-organization. Entrepreneurs, in the process of furthering their individual interests, act collectively to shape their local environments by building institutions that promote their industry needs. The cluster, and the characteristics of the cluster, therefore emerge over time from the individual activities of the entrepreneurs and the organizations and institutions that co-evolve to support them.

Entrepreneurship is an inherently local phenomenon. Individuals start companies based on their previous experience and interests, typically fulfilling some niche that a larger corporation may judge too small, exploiting a new opportunity that may have a risk profile unsuited to an existing company, or using a unique set of skills and knowledge to develop applications from licensed patents. In building their companies, entrepreneurs rely on their local contacts, connections, and knowledge of the business environment. Many individuals have location inertia due to family mobility constraints, locational preferences, familiarity of the environment, the relatively higher costs associated with changing residence, or the high cost of establishing a new company in a thickly populated environment where office and housing costs tend to be higher. As one entrepreneur rhetorically asked: "If you are changing your job, would you also want to complicate your life by changing your residence?"[5] The entrepreneurs involved in the creation of the Capitol biotech cluster came from government institutes, academic institutions, and companies based in Maryland. These "home-grown" entrepreneurs were already in the region working in another local company, at the NIH (located in Bethesda, Maryland) or other government institutions, or they were employed at the Johns Hopkins University or the University of Maryland as postdoctoral students or researchers.

In the case of the Capitol region, prior to 1973, only ten companies related to biotechnology existed, providing services to government labs (Feldman 2000; MdBio 2002). The movement from latent to active entrepreneurship requires some shock, possibly to the demand for entrepreneurs or traditional business, whether private or public sector, as well as a reduction in the opportunity cost of entrepreneurship or an increase in the supply of entrepreneurs; these are all discussed below.

In 1980, as a response to declining American competitiveness, a new era in the transfer of publicly funded intellectual property to industrial firms began with the passage of the Stevenson–Wydler Technology Innovation Act and the Bayh–Dole University and Small Business Patent Act. Large numbers of federal and university labs in the Capitol region were allowed to license their innovations to private firms, and enterprising individuals could license technology out of their own labs in order to create start-up companies. Some had tried earlier, but had faced formidable barriers. These policy changes were designed to facilitate the process of commercializing research findings and provided a stimulus for entrepreneurship. Federal funding was also provided for specific projects in SMEs, with the idea that the federal government could leverage US

---

[5] See Feldman (2001) for interview results.

R&D activity by spurring private enterprise to partner with government institutions. Table 11.6 details these institutional changes. The SBIR program was created in 1982 by federal legislation that required all federal agencies with an R&D budget greater than $100 million to set aside a certain percentage of R&D funds for small business.[6] The Act greatly increased the funding available to technologically oriented small business (Lerner 1996).

In addition, CRADAs, initiated by the Federal Technology Transfer Act in 1986, allow federal agencies to partner with young firms in developing new technologies and drugs. These agreements provide matching resources rather than direct funding. A large number of Maryland companies are described as "CRADA-babies," firms formed around a co-operative agreement with a government lab, although no data exist to quantify this claim. These programs were founded on the basis that small businesses in the United States could provide innovative ideas that meet the R&D needs of the federal government.[7]

Although the policy changes detailed in table 11.6 were national policies, they had a disproportional effect on previously employed scientists and engineers in the Capitol region, in part because there was a highly skilled and trained body of scientists and engineers already working in the government agencies (especially the NIH and the WRAIR). The generally higher level of awareness of the programs in Maryland due to the

---

[6] Eligibility requires the business to have fewer than 500 employees and to be an incorporated for-profit organization. Five federal agencies reserve a portion of their R&D funds to be awarded via the SBIR/STTR program to small business/nonprofit research institution partnerships. These agencies are: Department of Defense, Department of Energy, NASA, Department of Health and Human Services, and the NSF. The SBIR program involves ten federal agencies, including the Department of Agriculture, the Department of Commerce, the Department of Defense, the Department of Education, the Department of Energy, the Department of Health and Human Services, the Department of Transportation, the Environmental Protection Agency, NASA, and the NSF.

[7] For example, BioSpace International (BSI) is a Pharma/Protein products company begun in 1997 with funding from SBIR awards from NASA and the NIH, as well as an investment from the founding members. The company began in a space in the University of Maryland, College Park, incubator and staff were able to conduct their work with collaboration from the Center for Research in Biotechnology in Rockville, Maryland. Subsequently, through the CRADAs program, they began a partnership with NIST where they were able to gain access to sufficient laboratory space to conduct their experiments. In addition, through the CRADA with NIST they were able to gain access to people who, as a small start-up company they "were certainly not in a position financially to hire the caliber of talent that NIST has provided for BSI nor did [they] have a laboratory." Two years later they moved into a new facility in Gaithersburg, Maryland, with an on-site lab as well as several new staff. They developed and patented an electro-mechanical "Dynamically Controlled Crystallization System" known as DCCS. Protein crystallization is a necessary process involved in the discovery of new drugs. Today, BSI has several strategic partnerships, one patent as well as two patents pending, and has been able to create jobs for thirteen people. (Biospace International 2000).

Table 11.6 *Major US policy initiatives favoring science-based entrepreneurship, 1980–1989*

Name and date	Description	Implication for entrepreneurship
Stevenson–Wydler Technology Innovation Act (1980)	Facilitate the transfer of technologies that originated and are owned by Federal laboratories to the private sector	Employees could become entrepreneurs by licensing technology developed at federal laboratories. Other firms could view federal laboratories as a source of technology for transfer
Bayh–Dole University and Small Business Patent Act (1980)	Permitted small business, universities, and not-for-profit institutions to retain title to inventions resulting from federally funded grants and contracts	Encouraged universities to engage in technology transfer to license inventions to industry Allowed federal contracts to engage in commercialization
Small Business Innovation Development Act (1982)	Established the SBIR Program within major federal agencies	Increased funding available for technologically oriented small business
National Co-operative Research Act (1984)	Eased anti-trust penalties on co-operative research	Facilitated joint projects and made it easier for small firms to find niche markets with emerging technologies
Federal Technology Transfer Act (1986)	Amended the Stevenson–Wydler Act to authorize CRADAs between federal agencies and private firms	Allowed small firms to extend R&D capabilities by collaborating with federal labs and agencies on commercialization
National Competitiveness Technology Transfer Act (1989)	Part of a Department of Defense authorization bill, amended the Stevenson–Wydler Act to allow government-owned contractor–operator laboratories to participate	Increased the pool of potential partners and research projects

Note: All federal agencies with an R&D budget greater than $100 million are required to set aside a certain percentage of R&D funds for small business defined as those with fewer than 500 employees and less than $2.5 million in annual sales.
Source: Feldman (2001).

Table 11.7 *Maryland state SBIR funding*

Year	Phase 1 awards	Phase 1 ($)	Phase 2 awards	Phase 2 ($)	Total awards	Total ($)	Rank SBIR/population	Percentage US awards (%)
1997	184	15,537,000	55	34,120,005	239	49,662,000	6	4.4
1998	134	11,491,000	68	41,909,000	202	53,400,000	3	5.1
1999	186	17,396,535	57	32,817,271	243	50,213,806	5	4.9
2000	135	12,921,490	71	43,703,954	206	56,625,444	4	5.3
2001	164	16,334,967	71	37,595,495	235	53,930,462	5	4.7

Source: www.sbirworld.com; calculations by Feldman and Francis (2004).

flow of scientists from the public to the private sector and vice versa, also facilitated agreements between federal agencies and area biotech companies. Weighted by population, Maryland ranked third through sixth in each of the previous five years in SBIR total dollars received. Maryland also received approximately 5 percent of all SBIR funding for the previous five years, although it had approximately 1.9 percent of total US population in each of those years. Table 11.7 shows the SBIR funding and population-weighted rankings.

Although these were national institutional changes, which should have affected all fifty-one US regions (fifty states plus the Capitol region) more or less equally, other exogenous factors promoted biotech development in the Capitol region that did not exist as strongly in other states. Simultaneously with the opportunities provided by federal legislation came changes in federal government employment conditions. Previously, government employment of scientists and engineers was very secure and well compensated. The federal downsizing and switch to outside contracting that began under the Carter Administration, provided an additional push for scientists and engineers to take opportunity of the technology developed in their government labs, and license it for start-ups. It is perhaps both of these factors coming together that promoted cluster formation.

The second phase of cluster development, 1986–95, was dominated by increased entrepreneurial activity as an adaptation to these changes in the external environment. The new start-up firms created soon after the policy changes became particularly fruitful in generating second-, third-, and fourth-generation start-ups. In the earliest period, 1973–80, 20 percent of the start-up entrepreneurs came from the NIH. Between 1981 and 1985, one-third of the entrepreneurs came from the NIH. Notably, however, in the combined time period, 1973–85, the majority of entrepreneurs came from private labs or companies (65 percent). Between 1986 and 1995, approximately half of the biotech entrepreneurs came from government agencies, such as the NIH and the WRAIR, as well as the local universities (predominantly the Johns Hopkins University or the Hopkins Medical School). Having the experience and example of the initial start-ups, the industry becomes self-sustaining: entrepreneurs attracted physical and human capital to the area, public and private networks built up to support and facilitate the ventures, relevant infrastructure was created through public and private initiatives, and services grew up to feed these companies. For some regions, an exogenous shock, such as corporate M&As, may compact the industrial sector into a small number of large MNEs or a more research-oriented cluster, such as the case of the New Jersey electronics industry (Leslie and Kargon 1996).

In the Capitol region, conditions favored new-firm formation, perhaps in part due to the lack of an established large pharmaceutical company that could engineer mergers or acquisitions. It was during this phase that state and local government policies, especially, reinforced entrepreneurship and firm development. Networks of entrepreneurs, policymakers, and secondary industry contractors sprang up; universities, colleges, and technical centers recognized the need for high-tech trained personnel and offered programs to satisfy that demand. The success and experience of the initial activity further generated local recognition of the nascent industry. Local recognition, a reduction in risk, and more opportunities created by the initial companies, contributed to more start-up activities. In this stage, a critical mass of resources was established, some developed within the region and other resources, such as venture capital, locating in the area. It is also at this stage that we see the creation of regional public-sector financing and grant-giving programs. The critical mass of start-up activity has spawned the necessary infrastructure to sustain it, which has in turn attracted more activity to the region. We see that once a minimum efficient level of activity was in place, venture capital was attracted from other parts of the nation. Venture capital lags cluster formation, with firms being attracted to new clusters once there is substantial economic activity with the expectation of future profits.

Over time, as the earliest start-up companies grew and went public, or were bought out by other companies, the dynamics of the region changed. Most notably, local entrepreneurs who had made large fortunes engaged in institution-building to support their activities and to encourage further entrepreneurship. Also important was the emergence of networks of supportive social capital that began as membership organizations to promote networking. These activities were primarily private-sector initiatives, financed with private funds. By collaborating with state and local government programs, these initiatives resulted in cross-fertilization and a common mission to promote the development of industry in the region. There are several cases where early entrepreneurs, who had made personal fortunes, started private incubators to nurture other new companies and made endowments to local universities. These founders were motivated to share their expertise and give something back to the local community. In the process, they contributed to building regional capacity.

Two basic features in this interpretive history stand out: although the Capitol region did not have the generally regarded prerequisites for high-tech development, a confluence of unrelated events created an opportunity for entrepreneurial individuals to create start-ups. Second, the organizations and entrepreneurial ventures co-evolved. The advent of entrepreneurship was reactive and adaptive: locational inertia kept the entrepreneurs in the area and government policies eased the transition

to entrepreneurship. The earliest start-ups were service firms, not originally involved in the types of R&D-intensive activities that generated new
industries. For example, firms such as Bethesda Research Labs were not
launched as flashy product-development firms, although they evolved in
that direction over time. The cluster thus had rather humble beginnings –
service firms do not typically attract attention from venture capital or
local economic development officials. But these firms were relatively less
costly to start and provided a means for entrepreneurs to get started.
Today, product-development firms characterize the cluster, although service companies continue to comprise approximately 35 percent of the
companies.

The third phase of cluster formation is a fully functioning entrepreneurial environment within an innovative and adaptable industrial
cluster. The success of the initial start-ups, and the synergy between
them, has generated new possibilities for further entrepreneurship. Over
time, generations of new firms spun-off from the earliest start-ups and
entrepreneurs who cashed in from one new venture created other companies. It is now possible to construct family trees for various technologies (Eaton *et al.* 1998; Schachtel and Heacock 2002). A region may
be classified as mature, in the biotech industry, once significant spin-off
activity is observed and the region has attracted venture capital, created
state funding programs, and offers steady employment (see Baptista and
Swan 1999). In addition, industrial clusters able to withstand financial
shocks, such as recessions or restructuring of the industry, are typically
considered mature. This appears to be the current observable phase for
this cluster, although only time will tell.

In closing, entrepreneurship in the region was a response to exogenous
factors: underemployed skilled labor brought about by changes in federal
employment policy coupled with new opportunities for the private sector
to contract with the federal government and commercialize new technologies. Most importantly, entrepreneurship picked up momentum in
the cluster and generations of new firms spun-off from the earliest start-
ups. Entrepreneurs who cashed in from one venture created other companies. Entrepreneurs also lobbied for government resources and worked
to change the stance of local universities. As entrepreneurship caught
hold, the cluster emerged and the familiar virtuous, self-sustaining cycles
appeared to be in place.

11.5   Conclusions

Certainly the state of Maryland has a vibrant biotech industry. The emergence of the Capitol biotech cluster can be traced back to institutional
changes that occurred in the early 1980s that favored entrepreneurship.

Maryland was in a particular position to capture this change due to the large number of scientists and engineers employed by federal government laboratories and the large number of bioscience students who were attracted to the region by prominent universities such as the Johns Hopkins University and the University of Maryland. Although it is difficult to determine the exact role that regional government policy plays in cluster formation, our view is that entrepreneurs were the most critical ingredient to cluster formation in a technology-intensive industry. Regional programs, such as the creation of incubator facilities, state funding, and tax initiatives, favor new-firm formation. However, these activities lagged rather than led cluster formation in the Capitol region and reinforced rather than generated the formation of the cluster. Government policy is useful in promoting and furthering the growth of an already existent industry, but it cannot generate a self-sustaining cluster itself. Initiatives undertaken in the United States by individual states to create a high-tech cluster where there was none have largely failed, or the result was different than anticipated. There is a strong evolutionary component to cluster formation.

Other analysts, such as Cortright and Mayer (2001) have also pointed out the idiosyncratic nature of regional development in biotech. This suggests that there are no "one-size-fits all" models for high-tech industrial clusters. Cluster development is better described as a complex, self-organizing process (Feldman and Francis 2002). We emphasize that entrepreneurs are part of this idiosyncratic region-specific component. Every region has a given set of technical workers and entrepreneurs, the interests and expertise of these individuals shape the type of cluster that forms.

The role of government in industrial development, in general, and biotech development, in particular, is not one-dimensional. Various levels of government have unique roles to play, particularly in high-risk, potentially high-return industries such as biotechnology. In the development of the biotech industry, the federal government's role has included setting a national research agenda with broad funding priorities through its labs and grants, and establishing regulations and standards for the industry as a whole. The federal government has historically supported R&D, mostly through its laboratories and grants to research universities, but also to private industry through grants and tax incentives.

Local governments, such as state and county governments, have played, and continue to play, a different role in the development of the biotech industry. Not only is local government involved with more mundane issues than biotechnology, such as issuing building permits for special lab facilities that require current Good Manufacturing Procedures (cGMP), but also it is more focused on attracting firms to its location. States, and counties within states, actively compete with each other to gain promising firms, by providing tax incentives, dedicated funds, and grants to aid in SBIR application preparation, incubators, and other business services and educational opportunities. The reasoning behind the support of private commercial enterprise with public funds is that every dollar invested yields a return many times greater in terms of job creation and contribution to tax revenues.

The cumulative and reinforcing creative environment that anchors an industry depends on a sound infrastructure. The state strategy for long-term growth relied less on firm-specific incentives but instead focused on developing an infrastructure and business climate to support industrial development, especially in building the shared resources that augmented individual company innovative capacity. The state infrastructure includes councils and agencies that work with business; access, quality, and logistics of transportation networks; school systems; and utilities. Subsequently, special tax provisions and financing programs aimed at stimulating the biotech industry have led to a substantial investment, but this appears to have reinforced the development of the cluster. Developing or fine-tuning the role of state government in growing a biotech industry requires an understanding of how firms develop; policy must be technologically specific or industry-specific to provide maximum benefit. Each industry, building on a unique set of technologies and applications, has correspondingly unique challenges in its development and growth stages. Perhaps most importantly in our specific case, state policy may facilitate the conditions that affect the formation and development of entrepreneurial firms that are the building blocks of an industrial cluster.

REFERENCES

Baldwin, W., 2002. "An Introduction to Extramural NIH," National Institutes of Health Report, at <http://grants1.nih.gov/grants/intro2oer.htm>
Baptista, R. and Peter Swann, 1999. "A Comparison of Clustering Dynamics in the US and UK Computer Industries," *Journal of Evolutionary Economics*, 9: 373–399
Biospace International, 2000. "Senior Vice President Speech before the Senate Subcommittee on Technology"
Black, G., 2002. "Innovative Activity in US Cities: Evidence from the Small Business Innovation Research Program," Georgia State University, Andrew Young School of Policy Studies Working Paper
Cortright, J. and H. Mayer, 2001. "High Tech Specialization: A Comparison of High Technology Centers," The Brookings Institution Survey Series, Washington, DC, January

Eaton, B., M. Feldman, L. Gerstley, M. Connolly, and G. Mangels, 1998. "Biosciences in Maryland: A Closer Look," MdBio

Ernst and Young LLP, 2001. "Venture Capital Climate for Bioscience in Maryland," report commissioned by MdBio, Inc.

Feldman, M.P., 2000. "Where Science Comes to Life: University Biosciences, Commercial Spin-offs and Regional Economic Development," *Comparative Journal of Public Policy*, 2: 345–336

  2001. "The Entrepreneurial Event Revisited: An Examination of New Firm Formation in the Regional Context," *Industrial and Corporate Change*, 10: 861–891

Feldman, M. P. and J. L. Francis, 2002. "The Entrepreneurial Spark: Individual Agents and the Formation of Innovative Clusters," in A. Quadrio Curzio and M. Fortis (eds.), *Complexity and Industrial Clusters*, Heidelberg: Physica-Verlag

  2004. "Homegrowth Solutions: Fostering Cluster Formation," *Economic Development Quarterly*, 18(2): 127–137

Hall, B. H., A. B. Jaffe, and M. Tratjenberg, 2001. *The NBER Patent Citation Data File: Lessons, Insights and Methodological Tools*, Working Paper no. 8498, Cambridge, MA: National Bureau of Economic Research, at http://papers.nber.org/papers/w8498

Lerner, J., 1996. "The Government as Venture Capitalist: The Long Run Impact of the SBIR Program," NBER Working Paper, 5753

  1997. "Recreating Silicon Valley," *Business History Review*,

Leslie, S. and R. Kargon, 1996. "Selling Silicon Valley: Frederick Terman's Model for Regional Advantage," *Business History Review*, 70(4): 435–472

MdBio, 2002. "MdBio Company Database," at www.mdbio.org

Schachtel, M. R. and S. R. Heacock, 2002. "Founders of Maryland Bioscience and Medical Instrument Companies," Report for Maryland Technology Development Corporation (TEDCO)

Schumpeter, J. A., 1942/1976. *Capitalism, Socialism, and Democracy*, New York: Harper & Row

Townsend, K. K., 2002. "Biotechnology and Humanity at the Crossroads of a New Era," Speech delivered at the Institute for Emerging Issues Forum, at www.ncsu.edu/iei/forums/2002forum/intro02.htm

12 Facilitating enterprising places: the role of intermediaries in the United States and United Kingdom

Christie Baxter and Peter Tyler

12.1 Introduction

Many communities around the world want the economic benefits associated with high-technology jobs and companies. But creating and nurturing centers of high-technology, what we call "enterprising places," is a complex business. Even when a place has the essential resources: an excellent university or research center, land and facilities for companies, and an educated workforce, it is not clear how to sustain a center from them. The efforts of policymakers to do just that comprise a rich source of experimental evidence. In 2002 and 2003, a research team[1] from MIT and the University of Cambridge set out to examine this evidence in five regions known to be centers of high-technology in the United States and United Kingdom.[2]

To guide the research, we focused on four realms that figured prominently in enterprising places: knowledge, finance, policy, and place (figure 12.1). We were especially interested in actions at the intersections of these realms and how they enhanced a location's competitiveness. We defined the "knowledge realm" to include the people, skills and ideas, and related education and research institutions that were located in a particular place. The finance realm represented the capital, institutions, and people that sustain investment in a place over time. The "policy realm" represented the institutional and regulatory context and the public and private policy agents that influenced the development of a place. The "place realm" represented the competencies of the location in terms of proximity, access, and concentration. The players in each realm came from the traditional

---

[1] Other members of the research team include the following: co-principal investigators: Barry Moore, Nicola Morrison, Bernard Frieden and William Porter; research associates: Rob McGaffin, Jean Poteete; research assistants: Monica Otero-Garcia, Myoung-Gu Kang, and Michael Sable.

[2] San Diego, CA; Eastern Massachusetts; Research Triangle NC; Central Belt, Scotland; and the Eastern region, United Kingdom.

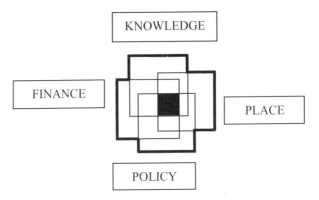

Figure 12.1 The research realms
Source: The authors.

sectors of business, government, academia, and civil society. Knowledge-based companies secured their business objectives at the intersection of these realms.

As analysts such as Castells and Hall (1994) and Quintas, Wield, and Massey (1992) have pointed out, having a few key assets does not necessarily yield a successful enterprising place. The myth of the science park was that a community could become the next major global industrial center by taking "a small dose of venture capital, a university (invariably termed a Technology Institute), fiscal and institutional incentives to attract high-technology firms, and a degree of support for small business . . . Wrap in a glossy brochure illustrated by a sylvan landscape with a futuristic name," (Castells and Hall 1994: 8). Rather, we found that a place's success was determined by the continual development of available assets in the realms of finance, knowledge, place, and policy. This usually resulted from dynamic and effective partnerships between the parties from different sectors within a region. We called the organizations that institutionalized these partnerships "intermediaries." They mediated the differences between sectors and made traditional organizational boundaries sufficiently permeable to generate the innovation necessary to enhance each realm. They also undertook programs that supported the development and vitality of their places. Figure 12.2 identifies, in a schematic way, the different kinds of intermediaries we found in our study regions.

Intermediaries had the following five attributes:

- Missions focused on enhancing realms rather than promoting individual agendas

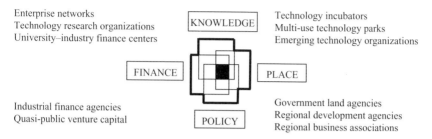

University technology licensing offices
University corporate liaisons
Corporate R&D

Enterprise networks   Technology incubators
Technology research organizations   KNOWLEDGE   Multi-use technology parks
University–industry finance centers   Emerging technology organizations

FINANCE   PLACE

Industrial finance agencies   Government land agencies
Quasi-public venture capital   POLICY   Regional development agencies
                                                             Regional business associations

Regional marketing associations
Industry associations
Technology policy organizations
Benchmarking entities

Figure 12.2 An array of intermediaries
Source: The authors.

- Connections to multiple sectors, this allowed the organizations to attract resources from different sources as the capacity of these sources shifted
- Some separation from government, this permitted organizations to maintain their operations during changes in political leadership and climate
- Structures that enabled entrepreneurship, that is, organizations had both access to resources and the ability to mobilize and deliver them autonomously
- Independent credibility, enabling organizations to influence key decisionmakers in the core sectors of government, business, academia, and civil society.

We chose, for this chapter, to look in depth at intermediaries in two of our study regions: Scotland's Central Belt and Eastern Massachusetts. Both had similar roots in the Industrial Revolution, both had more recent incarnations as electronics industry centers, and both had new and important biotech clusters. We explore the structure and roles played by these intermediaries by asking the following four questions:

- What kinds of organizations were evident at the boundaries of the four realms?
- What happened to these organizations, and to their places, over time?
- How did the organizations advance the development of the places?

- What were the key differences between intermediaries in Massachusetts and Scotland – that is, how did the place influence the organizations?

12.2   Enterprising places and the boundary problem

Enterprising places, as we define them, have concentrations of technology-producing (high-tech) companies; skilled workers and institutions that produce them; centers for basic and applied research, whose work feeds the technology on which resident firms depend; resources such as land, capital, and business support services; and facilitators that enhance the performance of each component, the operation of the place as a whole, and the policy environment. These concentrations, in turn, attract new companies and workers. That is, as the center evolves, the concentration of high-tech workers and companies becomes greater, making the center even more attractive to others.

Our respondents noted that, in their businesses, capital was primarily human, residing in their "knowledge workers." In Massachusetts, for example, students often come to school and then stay in the area, becoming rooted in the community. While some large companies chose to expand their operations into a new community (as, for example, Novartis did in Cambridge, MA), companies generally found it costly and risky to move their existing operations – i.e. key knowledge workers – to a new region. The chief financial officer of a Cambridge, MA biotechnology company reported that the company had paid $1 million to move six people to the Boston area from a mid-western city where a recent company acquisition was located. An executive from a Glasgow-based biotechnology company noted that it was difficult to recruit technology managers to come to Scotland – and, once there, they were reluctant to move elsewhere.

Recognizing the "stickiness" of workers and thus companies, economic development professionals in the two study areas paid great attention to the development and growth of indigenous firms and to workforce development. Even if firms were later acquired by other larger companies – as they often were – their assets, in the form of the workers, were likely to stay put: in that company, another company, or a spin-off. Policies that focused on innovation and entrepreneurship, on nurturing new technologies and new businesses or business units, accompanied such "grow-your-own" strategies.

The influential policy leaders whom we interviewed had paid serious attention to the academic literature and to practical understandings of the processes of innovation and entrepreneurship. Innovation was acknowledged to come from researchers at universities and research centers as well as from "the shop floor" in companies. In designing development strategies, these leaders gave significant attention to breaking down organizational and disciplinary barriers and facilitating the kind of boundary crossing necessary to promote the growth of new companies and, correspondingly, dynamic regional growth.

Academics have long noted that innovation often occurs at the boundaries: of scientific disciplines (Kuhn 1970), of policy (Schön 1971), and of organizations (Peters and Waterman 1982; Saxenian 1994). Such analyses suggest the ways that rigid organizational or industrial boundaries inhibit the processes of innovation and entrepreneurship. More recent attention has been paid to institutions that foster collaboration among businesses and other organizations in industry clusters (Porter 2001).

In our studies, we paid attention to two main forms of boundary issues:
• Projects that facilitated the development of companies from infancy to adulthood. These involved an array of mechanisms to promote the birth of new businesses and to support the growth of companies within the home region.
• Efforts to create systems to facilitate innovation and the corresponding development of new technologies. Efforts focused on promoting the cross-pollination of ideas and fostering connections between universities and research centers and business.

To achieve innovation and entrepreneurship in their communities, the leaders we interviewed sought to break down boundaries between traditional organizations and realms. The goal was to make these boundaries sufficiently permeable to allow ideas and information to flow in new ways, primarily by enabling new connections between people. An important focus was connections between universities and business: moving inventions from university laboratories to commercial markets and moving innovators across the boundaries of different organizations. People we interviewed uniformly identified rigid boundaries, which they often called "silos," as a central constraint to innovation.

For the respondents, connecting universities and industry posed a specific boundary problem: while universities and research centers were seen as important sources of new ideas, respondents on both sides of the Atlantic noted the difficulty of relying on academia to commercialize these ideas. Traditional academic research, while part of a "tree" of new ideas on which new commercial technologies blossomed, was far removed from the demands of the market, and traditional academics were not oriented toward business. Academics were widely regarded as terrible business people. As one of the respondents from Scotland pointed out, "people generally do not become university professors so that they can start companies." And while business might have been very interested in seeing what kinds of innovations universities were generating, it was hard for industry to see what was going on in the university. Academic research and its commercial potential were seen as inaccessible to business. Academics and entrepreneurs speak different languages, and the essential rules of operation in the two sectors differ greatly.

12.3   Overview of the study areas

We focus on two study areas: Massachusetts and Scotland.

Massachusetts

Massachusetts had a population of 6.4 million people and a GDP of $317.7 billion or £173.6 billion in 2004 (US Department of Commerce 2005).

Massachusetts was at the forefront of the Industrial Revolution in the United States, generating income initially from textiles and shoes in the cities of Lowell, Fall River, and Boston, and machine tools and abrasives in Worcester. The region lost most of these manufacturing industries during the 1930s and 1940s.

After the Second World War, and fueled by government spending in the 1950s and early 1960s, new industries emerged that developed and manufactured precision instruments, avionics, missiles, and electrical machinery. Many of the new companies located along Route 128, a circumferential highway built around Boston during the 1940s. Post-Vietnam War reductions in military spending sent the economy into a recession in the early 1970s.

From 1975 through the 1980s, local manufacturers produced minicomputers for the civilian market, then increased specialized production for the military when computer manufacturing moved west during the Reagan era. Many of the big companies, such as Digital Computer Corporation, Wang Laboratories, Prime Computer, and Data General located in the vicinity of another major new interstate highway, 20 miles west of Route 128: Route 495.

During the mid-1980s, local leaders in Worcester, an old manufacturing center west of Route 495, became concerned about the demise of heavy manufacturing and the fact that the computer industry was bypassing the city. They collaborated to initiate a land development project, the Massachusetts Biotechnology Research Park, adjacent to the recently built University of Massachusetts Medical School. The development seeded the biotechnology industry in Worcester.

The end of the 1980s, and the end of the Cold War, brought an economic crisis to the state. The computer industry, the center of the electronics industry in the state, experienced a major downturn, bringing with it a crash in the real estate market and the collapse of a major bank. The state essentially lost its leadership in electronics to Silicon Valley. In work published in the early 1990s, leading analysts of high-tech centers were writing off eastern Massachusetts as a high-tech has-been (Castells and Hall 1994; Saxenian 1994).

The Massachusetts economy rebounded in the 1990s such that, by 2000, the state was widely regarded as one of the most successful centers of the nation's "new economy." Employment, which had declined between 1984 and 1991, increased by 10 percent between 1991 and 2001. Unemployment fell to well below the national average, and real *per capita* income increased by 50 percent, well above the national rate of growth (Massachusetts Office of Economic Development 2002).

The small software and biotechnology companies that replaced the large computer firms chose different locations. By 2003, one real estate observer defined the important high-tech centers in Eastern Massachusetts as Cambridge and Boston's Longwood medical area, for medical technology and biotechnology; and Route 495, for hardware manufacturing and engineering firms. Boston remained the core for business support services: law, accounting, advertising, and shipping, and the most important teaching and research hospitals remained in Boston. Cambridge was the "technical area." Worcester was an emerging center for biotechnology and medical devices.

Scotland's Central Belt

Scotland had a population of approximately 5.1 million (General Register Office for Scotland 2004) and a GDP of £82 billion in 2004 (ONS 2005). The main urban centers are Glasgow and Edinburgh, which lie in the lowlands in the country's "Central Belt." Other significant cities include Aberdeen and Dundee, which lie on the east coast. Although it has a significant history as a separate nation, since 1707 Scotland has been a region of the United Kingdom.

Scotland was at the forefront of the Industrial Revolution in the United Kingdom, with strengths in the textile, shipbuilding and iron, coal and steel industries. However, these industries declined over the course of the twentieth century and, in the late 1950s, the British government offered regional incentives to induce mobile "sunrise" industries to locate in areas such as Scotland. This inward investment strategy prompted a number of large high-tech multinational companies (MNCs) to establish branch, often manufacturing, plants in Scotland. The first major investment came from IBM, which bought land from Scottish Land in the early 1950s. Others followed, including Motorola, National Semiconductor Ltd, Nippon Electronics Corporation, Nikon Precision Europe, and Polaroid Corporation.

By the 1980s, a number of these had relocated to cheaper areas outside of the United Kingdom. The loss of multinational manufacturing triggered a realignment of British economic strategies away from inward investment and towards the development of indigenous businesses.

In 1999, the British parliament granted to Scotland, and the Scottish Executive, authority over matters pertaining to health, education, agriculture, justice, and those economic matters previously under the jurisdiction of the Secretary of State, such as Regional Selective Assistance, infrastructure provision, and Scottish Enterprise (SE). Powers over fiscal and monetary policy, foreign affairs, and defense remained at the national level. At the local level, thirty-two directly elected local authorities now govern Scotland. This political arrangement makes Scotland (as well as Wales and Northern Ireland) more similar (by having three levels of governance) to US states than to regions in England.

The key economic sectors in Scotland in 2003 included biotechnology, ICT, food and drink, forest industries, optoelectronics, microelectronics, creative industries, tourism, oil and gas, textiles, and financial services, mostly located in Scotland's central belt. Dundee has also emerged as a major biotechnology center, following the success in the 1990s of scientists at the University of Dundee in cloning a sheep.

12.4   Three generations of intermediaries

We define "intermediaries" as those organizations that sit on or between the boundaries of different realms. In our conceptual framework, these realms are knowledge, policy, finance, and place (figure 12.1). Some of the organizations we review date back fifty years. Given that the continued operation of these organizations depends on their continuing relevance and productivity, their very longevity is testimony to their effectiveness. Others are much more recent.

We also saw the evolution of new forms of intermediaries over time, as they adapted to new demands. First-generation intermediaries developed on the boundaries of traditional institutions, as entrepreneurs within those institutions sought to adapt their operations to new circumstances. Second-generation intermediaries developed as separate organizations spanning traditional institutions and the realms of policy, place, and finance. Third-generation intermediaries added the knowledge realm. We also found that the characteristics of intermediaries in both the United States and the United Kingdom changed over time. Intermediaries created through the 1970s were largely sector-based, such as government corporations or traditional business trade associations. More recent intermediaries are smaller, mission-driven nonprofit corporations that incorporate participants across the sectors of government, business, academia, and civil society.

A key difference between US and UK intermediaries is that initiative for much intermediary activity in the United States comes from the private sector; in the United Kingdom, the public sector is a more important driver. UK organizations are also more hierarchical relative to each other, often responsible for implementing centrally defined programs. In the United States, board and staff members often have experience in two or more of the sectors. In the United Kingdom, board and staff members are often rooted in the same sector.

First-generation intermediaries

First-generation intermediaries expanded the boundaries of traditional institutions and firms to include players from other sectors. Their mission similarly expanded from an organization-specific agenda to a realm-enhancing agenda. Such intermediaries include:
- Public corporations, which put private, academic, and civic (often labor) representatives on their boards of directors
- Centers embedded in universities and research organizations, often with industry membership, charged with making connections with industry
- Industry organizations representing multiple firms with mandates to influence policy.
Table 12.1 provides examples from Massachusetts and Scotland.

Government-based Beginning in the 1950s, the governments of both Massachusetts and the UK (for Scotland) created organizations and intended to use public resources to encourage the development of private business in the region. For example, the Massachusetts legislature created the Massachusetts Land Bank to convert to civilian use former military facilities being shed by the federal government, and it created the Massachusetts Industrial Finance Authority to issue tax-exempt bonds to support industrial development. Both entities were public corporations modeled on private corporations (Walsh 1978): each had a small board of outside directors – that is, from different sectors – and professional managers who reported directly to the board. The legislature

Table 12.1 *First-generation intermediaries*

Realm connection	Base-sector	Intermediary
Policy–Industry	Government	Massachusetts Land Bank
		Scottish Development Agency
Finance–Industry	Government	Mass Industrial Finance Authority
University–Industry	Academia	MIT Industrial Liaison Office
		MIT Technology Licensing Office
		UK Teaching Company Scheme
		University of Edinburgh Technology
		Transfer Office
Industry–Policy	Industry	Mass High-Tech Council

Source: The authors.

capitalized these organizations with public funds and/or land, but after an initial period of public support, the organizations were expected to pay for ongoing operations with revenues. Each had the power to raise capital by issuing revenue-backed bonds. The state governor made some or all board appointments, but with terms staggered so that it would take several years until a new governor could gain control of a board.

Similar organizations emerged in Scotland. In the 1950s, the Scottish Land agency used the region's land resources to attract industry, and it was successful in bringing IBM to Scotland. The British parliament reorganized Scottish Land, creating the Highlands and Islands Development Board and the Scottish Development Agency to provide a broader range of support to the business community in Scotland and to build international competitiveness. The Scottish Development Agency's focus was on the lowlands, including Edinburgh and Glasgow. The agency held and developed commercial land speculatively, and it used incentives to attract MNCs to Scotland (Firn 2002). Both organizations were accountable to the central UK government.

University-based   In both Massachusetts and Scotland, premier universities often remained quite separate from local industries except where the university could see tangible benefits from corporate connections. For example, while its graduates were busy starting companies in the 1960s and 1970s, the MIT distanced itself from industries in the region, neglecting the region's emerging technology enterprises (Saxenian 1994: 15, 66). William Pounds, Dean of MIT's Sloan School from 1966 through 1980 confirmed that MIT was not seen as a friend to local companies during that era. In his view, companies grew up in and around MIT in spite of, rather than because of, the Institute. An exception is the MIT Industrial Liaison Program begun in 1948 just after the end of the Second World War. The intent was to establish relationships with large corporations that would benefit the Institute through sponsored research and donations.

Similarly, in Scotland as in the rest of the United Kingdom, industry and universities often worked in isolation from each other. As an IBM executive reported, "through the 1960s there were three blocks: skills, industry, and government, and in those days there was no liaison between those three areas." Since UK universities are publicly funded, there has been less of a focus on corporations as a source of donations or research support. One of the earliest efforts to make a university–industry connection, begun in 1975, was the Teaching Company Scheme, through which universities and technical schools received grants to support student and faculty work on projects defined jointly with business. The most active early participants were polytechnics, such as Napier University in Scotland.

In the mid-1980s, universities in both study regions engaged in a new form of industry connection, through technology transfer. MIT's Technology Licensing Office (TLO) was reorganized in 1985 in response to federal legislation regarding patent rights for inventions resulting from federally-funded research. The essential function of the TLO is to license patents on MIT-owned inventions to businesses that will develop the technology commercially. The TLO incorporates a private sector perspective through its staff, which have substantial private-sector experience. The TLO director reports directly to the central MIT administration and ultimately to the MIT Corporation. At about the same time, the University of Edinburgh established the first technology-transfer office in Scotland.

Business-based Trade associations such as chambers of commerce have a long history of serving the collective interests of businesses in a community. More recently, industry-specific organizations have emerged both to provide services to firms and influence policy. For example, in the early 1980s, electronics firms in Massachusetts banded together to change what they saw as an anti-business climate in the state, especially its high taxes. Through the Massachusetts High Tech Council, the industry participated in a successful effort to limit local property taxes in the state.

Second-generation intermediaries

Second-generation intermediaries integrated the realms of policy, place, and finance within their structure. They generally emerged in the 1980s

Table 12.2 *Second-generation intermediaries*

Realm connections	Type	Example
Finance–Place	Multi-strategy public corporation	MassDevelopment
		SE
Policy–Place	Land and sites	MAED
		WBDC
Policy–Finance	Place-based venture funds	Mass Technology Development Corp.
		Scottish Equity Partners

Source: The authors.

and early 1990s in response to various regional development problems – for example, those posed by the demise of the computer industry in Massachusetts or by the relocation off-shore of the Scottish branch plants of MNCs. Accompanying these events was an increasing focus on Small- and Medium-sized Enterprises, especially indigenous firms, and new intermediaries were created to support these enterprises. Other intermediaries sought to exploit the presumed benefits of adjacency to universities: it was the era of the university-related research park. In some cases, existing single-focus agencies merged to create an organization with a more comprehensive mission. Others emerged with more narrow missions: to exploit the advantages the region had in technology, or to provide the necessary venture financing. These second-generation institutions focused on the development or enhancement of a particular kind of asset: land, financial assets, or an expensive commonly needed facility. They increasingly operated as autonomous organizations in that they were not accountable to outside organizations. They ranged from private nonprofits to public corporations (described on p. 263) subject only to indirect state control.

Table 12.2 provides examples of second-generation intermediaries, and identifies their realm connections.

Evolving public corporations In both Massachusetts and Scotland, single-purpose government-based organizations expanded their missions through reorganization. The Massachusetts Land Bank and the Massachusetts Industrial Finance Authority merged in the 1990s to form the Massachusetts Development Finance Corporation, or MassDevelopment, which is empowered to provide a range of fixed-asset financing for business facilities and equipment. MassDevelopment also undertook land development of state and federal properties, such as those previously under the authority of the Land Bank, especially the 4,000 acre former army base, Fort Devens. The legislature capitalized the organization and granted it authority to issue bonds, such as private tax-exempt revenue bonds; it was expected to finance its operations from revenues.

In Scotland, too, an economic crisis prompted a reorganization of the institutional support system for business. The most significant move was the merger of the Scottish Development Agency and the Scottish Training Agency and the creation of Scottish Enterprise (SE) in 1991. SE consists of a central "strategic" body and twelve local enterprise companies (LECs). Each LEC has its own board consisting of local people from the public, private, and civic sectors and with an interest in their local area. Members of the LEC Boards are volunteers, and the staff are employed by SE but seconded to the LECs. Every year, an LEC Board submits a plan along with an application for funding to Scottish Enterprise National. Once SE approves funding, it contracts with the LEC to deliver the economic development activity outlined in the plan. LECs work closely at a local level with organizations in their respective areas, either through projects and programs they devise and implement or through the local delivery of programs mandated by Scottish Enterprise National.

Providing land and sites Other organizations used land development to build a critical mass of enterprise through land development. An example in Massachusetts is Worcester Business Development Corporation (WBDC), a subsidiary of the Worcester Regional Chamber of Commerce with a mission to attract new businesses to the area through the development of industrial parks. In the early 1980s WBDC developed the Massachusetts Biomedical Research Park. The park was initially developed in the mid-1980s, adjacent to the fledgling University of Massachusetts Medical School. The school did not become an active participant in the effort until the 1990s: this development relied on adjacency to the school rather than its active involvement.

In Scotland, the Heriott–Watt Science Park was the first developed in the United Kingdom. Subsequently, the University of Edinburgh began development of the Edinburgh Technopole to provide space for small-to-large technology companies who wanted to locate in proximity to a cluster of research universities and centers in Scotland's Central Belt. A partnership between a private developer and the University of Edinburgh undertook the development.

Company-to-company marketing A Massachusetts intermediary has taken an operational approach to traditional Chamber of Commerce-type regional marketing. To make it easier for companies who want to locate in the state, a consortium of utility, telecommunications, real estate associations, and the state office of business development created the Mass Alliance for Economic Development (MAED) in the early 1990s. MAED serves as a central source for property information for high-technology and other companies interested in locating in the state. The organization also has an "ambassadors" network through which member company executives act as peer resources for visiting executives. Organized as a trade association, MAED's operations are supported by members' fees.

Financing   Place-based financial institutions sought to fill gaps that existed at various places in the local financial system supporting new technology enterprises. New ventures require specialized capital, and our respondents pointed out that venture financing is highly place-related. Policymakers have thus tried to increase the number of new and growing ventures by creating place-based equity investment institutions. For example, in 1978 the Massachusetts Legislature created and capitalized the Massachusetts Technology Development Corporation, a public venture capital fund that invests in technology-based start-up companies, often in partnership with private lenders and state pension boards. SE created Scottish Equity Partners for similar purposes: to invest in new indigenous Scottish companies. It has since been privatized and now provides traditional venture capital funding.

Third-generation intermediaries: building the research infrastructure

Third-generation intermediaries incorporate a greater role for universities, not only as sources of education and technology, but also as partners in regional economic development. The new organizations (and reconstituted existing ones) more fully integrate the realms of place, policy, finance, and knowledge. This was the result of the convergence of a number of streams of analysis in economic development. The first stream is cluster analysis, developed from the work of Michael Porter (1990). The second is the analysis of the role of networks, exemplified by the work of AnnaLee Saxenian (1994). The third is work focusing on the role of technology transfer and the commercialization of university research. The success of Stanford and MIT has contributed greatly to the interest in this area. The fourth is the substantial body of work documenting the importance of the flow of national research funds, in the defense industry, in medicine, and in science. Finally there is the critique of science parks and the underlying premise that spatial adjacency would be sufficient to stimulate university–business connections.

Table 12.3 *Knowledge-related intermediaries*

Strategic focus	Examples
Knowledge–Place	Alba Campus
Organized adjacencies to support	Worcester Gateway Park
technology	Institute for System Level Integration
	Scottish Microelectronics Centre
	Mass Biomedical Initiatives
Finance–Knowledge	Scottish Intermediary Technology Institutes
supporting the research to	MIT Deshpande Center
commercialization gap	Edinburgh Technology Fund
Knowledge–Industry	Edinburgh Research and Innovation Ltd
	SIE
	Technology Ventures, Scotland
Finance–Knowledge–Place	MIT Enterprise Forum
Creating Networks	Scotland CONNECT

Source: The authors.

Examples of knowledge-enhancing intermediaries include entities that incorporate organized connections between research-related functions and business development in land and facility developments, various kinds of technology–business incubators, research organizations with built-in industry partners, and entrepreneurship organizations that make explicit connections to the university and finance realms. While second-generation intermediaries focused on projects, third-generation intermediaries took a more systemic approach, seeking to build a research-to-business system. Leaders we interviewed described the system as the "research infrastructure." It includes institutions engaged in knowledge–business partnerships, and sometimes relies on public funds to support the development of particular kinds of technology.

Table 12.3 identifies some of the third-generation intermediaries we encountered in Massachusetts and Scotland.

Organized adjacencies Universities and research centers are rooted institutions, and during the 1970s and 1980s developers of science parks assumed that if you put enterprises next to universities or research centers, there would be spillovers. However, it is clear from many second-generation efforts that such spillovers effects cannot be taken for granted (Quintas, Wield, and Massey 1992). Such ventures undertaken after the mid-1990s have tended to try to broker interaction more actively. The following are some examples.

The *Alba Campus* is a science park development focused on microelectronics and related technologies. The park promotes interaction among business, students, and researchers through facilitated interactions, such as breakfast networking sessions, and guest lectures. SE facilitated the development of the campus, put in serviced land as its equity contribution, and brought together four universities to develop the Institute for System Level Integration (ISLI), located on the site. The ISLI supports microchip design research and education. A Motorola executive credits SE and the ISLI with prompting the company to establish a systems division in Scotland. A private developer has a 50 percent partnership.

The *Worcester Gateway Project* is a joint development by the Worcester Polytechnic Institute (WPI) and the WBDC on a brownfield site near WPI's main campus. WPI will anchor the development by moving its life-science programs to the parcel in 2007. The site will also house a federally supported bioengineering facility, residences, offices, and retail space. The state is funding brownfields clean-up and infrastructure.

Begun in 2000, the *Scottish Microelectronics Centre* does R&D, and it incubates new companies in the semiconductor industry. It provides wafer fabrication equipment and trains students in fabrication. Research is done through the Institute of Micro and Nano Systems. According to the centre's CEO: "Being involved with the incubator allows companies to get close to the University of Edinburgh's hothouse of ideas." The university covers the capital and operating costs of the building.

Massachusetts Biomedical Initiatives (MBI), Worcester, has several incubator facilities for biotechnology companies, and it supports a network of financing and related services. The organization is a re-formation of the Massachusetts Biotechnology Research Institute, created in the mid-1980s to support biomedical research. MBI spans sectors through its staff and board. For example, the director is a former state legislator, and MBI's board includes some of Worcester's most influential business leaders.

Spanning the research commercialization gap   A number of studies have documented the importance of national funding for research to the development of centers of high technology (Markusen, Lee, and DiGiovanna 1999; Cortright and Mayer 2002). In the Eastern Massachusetts region, a Boston policy leader we interviewed observed that the infrastructure for the resurgence of the area in medical and biotechnology in the late 1990s was also built through capital investment made by MIT and the area's hospitals in the early 1990s. This occurred at a time when little commercial investment was flowing.

In 2003, SE committed £450 million over ten years to institutes intended to extend research in Scotland beyond basic science and into pre-competitive research in designated sectors with particular potential for regional competitive advantage. *Intermediary Technology Institutes* (ITIs) identify emerging market and business opportunities in which Scotland can play a leading role; fund appropriate R&D; and commercialize technology products through member companies, start-up companies, or licensing arrangements. They increase levels of R&D in Scotland by commissioning work from leading researchers in existing research institutions in Scotland and worldwide and by acting as a proxy for corporate R&D. SE has designated the following industry groups for the first three institutes: digital media and communications, life sciences, and energy.

ITIs involve multiple sectors through the research and commercialization steering groups which comprise global industrial players and academics with global reputations in their fields. Each Institute has a core staff of some fifteen people who manage the steering groups and day-to-day operations of the Institutes. ITI directors are leading international entrepreneurs. Private companies participate through institute membership.

MIT's Deshpande Center was launched in 2002 with a private gift of $20 million to MIT. The Center's mission is to address the gap in getting research from the lab at MIT to the marketplace. The Center is guided by a university–industry partnership: a small "steering committee" which includes the founder of a major electronics company and former MIT Corporation chairman, the donor, and a faculty director whose research crosses the boundaries of chemistry, biology, and engineering. The Center's director is an MIT graduate who started and sold several companies.

The Center funds the development of technologies with the potential for commercialization. It offers a proof of concept-funding program, called "Ignition Grants," as well as follow-on funds for product development. These programs support the development of specific technologies and their movement toward commercial markets. However, although funding specific research to market initiatives is a significant part of the Center's program, some see this as less important than its efforts to connect the venture capital community and entrepreneurs to the research community. The Center provides "structured networking" for MIT graduate students; it sponsors fora that showcase MIT technology; and it sponsors other events focused not on technology but on "market opportunities." These activities provide participants with access to the perspectives of players from other realms and fora through which individuals can meet each other to discuss specific mutual interests.

The *Edinburgh Technology Fund* was created in 1999 and jointly funded with £3 million by the European Union and SE. The Fund, which has its own CEO, provides seed funding to close the gap between university output and its commercialization. The Fund serves a consortium of four research institutions plus the University of Edinburgh. Consortium members and spin-outs as well as other companies in designated areas are eligible to apply for grants to start companies, equity contributions, and loans for new firms (EU funds are restricted to certain areas). Funds are intended to complement those from other sources such as SE and the UK Department of Trade and Industry.

Knowledge to industry   Scotland has created several intermediaries that make university–knowledge connections through independent entities rather than through universities themselves. One is Edinburgh Research and Innovation Ltd (ERI), a wholly-owned subsidiary of the University of Edinburgh. Another is the Scottish Institute for Enterprise (SIE), which serves all thirteen Scottish universities.

The University of Edinburgh created ERI in 1999 to centralize the universities' interface with industry. ERI manages technology licensing and outside research; acts as a central consulting service for university staff; manages the Edinburgh Technology Transfer Centre, the university's incubator; and oversees the university's interest in the Edinburgh Technopole. ERI's technology licensing is a formal part of the commercialization process for university patents. Through its consulting arm ERI acts as a "broker" between academics and companies. In its research operations ERI acts as an agent of the university and individual academics when they seek grants.

The SIE provides entrepreneurship education, advice, and guidance to science, engineering, and technology students at all thirteen Scottish universities, including the University of Edinburgh, plus associated institutions who want to start companies. Some programs are patterned after the MIT Entrepreneurship Center. In addition to student support at each school, SIE runs an annual business plan competition plus an annual conference showcasing the finalists' plans and offering networking opportunities to students. SIE also has a patent fund for students. SIE involves private-sector participants through its board and staff, although the board is largely drawn from its university members.

Technology Ventures, Scotland, is an advisory forum that bridges business, academia, and the Scottish Executive, with a focus on education. The forum is staffed by a technology consulting firm that contracts with the public sector to provide technology and business management services to companies and project management services to public clients. For example, electronics suppliers in Scotland were competing globally and Technology Ventures, through its consultant, provided education to help them to do this better. Technology Ventures also seeks to bring different industry sectors together to create new integrated products.

Network oriented connections   Parallel to institutions that directly support R&D are organizations focused on connecting the right players. The idea is to maximize the odds of productive interactions by maximizing the opportunities for informal connections. Multi-service support organizations also support such connections.

The MIT Enterprise Forum links entrepreneurs, new business, and commercializable ideas to the venture capital community. It provides both "windows" on MIT and interactive forums, and is promoted by the MIT Alumni Association.

CONNECT Scotland is a networking and entrepreneurship education program modeled on the successful CONNECT program initiated by the University of California at San Diego. It began at the University of Edinburgh in 1997, but since 2001 it has operated as an independent organization, funded by member fees. Three main programs – a springboard, bootcamp, and annual investment conference – bring researchers, entrepreneurs, and investors together and educate each about the other.

Keeping ahead   Finally, there are intermediaries whose mission is to keep places at the forefront of new research and technology. Massachusetts Technology Collaborative (MTC) is such an entity, It was created by the Massachusetts legislature in the 1980s to improve chip design by giving engineers in the state experience with fabrication through access to a common fabrication facility. The governor appoints MTC's Board of Directors, who represent a broad cross-sector constituency that includes a strong academic component: the deans of all the engineering schools in Massachusetts, including private universities, such as MIT, were represented on the board through the 1980s. When technology support needs changed in the 1990s, MTC sold its chip-fabrication facility, leased the property to a private firm, and transformed itself into a public-interest consulting organization that supports technology-based business. MTC now benchmarks the development of high-tech industries in Massachusetts, supports emerging industry groups, and houses an endowment, the Renewable Energy Trust, which finances the development of alternative energy products.

12.5   Policy through intermediaries

In both Massachusetts and Scotland, the collective activity of inter-mediaries, as well as the direct action of government, influences the development of the enterprising place. Thus policy, defined as intervention, is not restricted to government; it includes public and private policy agents, many acting through intermediaries. Although both Massachusetts and Scotland developed a comparable array of intermediaries over time, policy development and implementation look different in the two regions. In this section, we examine government-linked intermediaries.

Both Massachusetts and Scotland have governmental agencies responsible for the public efforts related to economic development. In Massachusetts in 2003 the executive office was the Office of Economic Development. Its Department of Business and Technology managed enterprise assistance. Massachusetts implemented its public economic development programs through a layered system of intermediaries, each increasingly independent, financially and otherwise, from government. In Scotland, the executive agency in 2003 was the Department of Transport, Enterprise, and Lifelong Learning. Scotland also implemented its programs using intermediaries, but SE, a central entity accountable to the Scottish Executive, designed and monitored the implementation of most programs.

Public enterprise assistance in Massachusetts

The formal governmental level of economic development activity in Massachusetts, in 2003, was rather thin, consisting of five line offices. The operating budget for these five offices, plus funds for public programs undertaken by the Massachusetts Technology Collaborative, was $21 million. Related economic development intermediaries in Massachusetts were far more active than were line departments. For example, in fiscal year 2003 MassDevelopment made investments totaling $860 million in business and nonprofit fixed assets. MassDevelopment was the largest of the economic development oriented intermediaries: most of its 150 employees in 2003 came from the private sector. The Massachusetts Technology Collaborative had fifty-six employees in 2003, Massachusetts Technology Development Corporation had seven employees, and the Mass Alliance for Economic Development had four.

Figure 12.3 illustrates the relationships among government economic development agencies and related intermediaries in Massachusetts in 2003. The first layer, below the level of governor, includes line agencies. The bracket on the right contains the agencies that collectively shared the $21 million budgeted in 2003. The bottom row includes the three primary self-funded government corporations and nonprofits that are part of the primary economic development network.

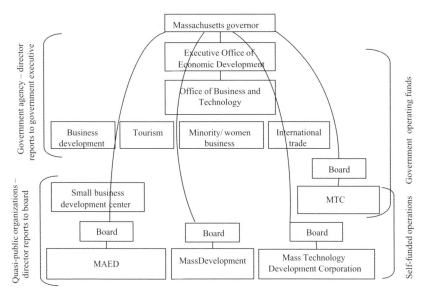

Figure 12.3 Massachusetts enterprise assistance 2003
Source: The authors.

Because the intermediaries responsible for delivering economic development investment and assistance are financially autonomous, the development of a single central policy is difficult, if not impossible. The board of directors of each organization determines the organization's direction. Some directors are accountable to the governor or his or her representative, but others represent other public, private, academic, and civic constituencies. This has a number of implications:

• Policies must be negotiated among different groups
• If the organization ceases to deal with the interests of a particular group, it can withdraw support and resources – this makes the organization highly responsive to some interests
• Creating a policy that affects multiple realms is complicated, in that multiple organizations and groups within the direct policy network must sign on, and many other organizations are outside the system.

For example, Massachusetts policymakers have created a central advertizing campaign, "Massachusetts Means Business," but its implementation remains limited to direct government agencies.

The number of intermediaries in Massachusetts has been subject to some criticism. One respondent noted that the state has a reputation for setting up a new organization every time it wants to solve a new problem: the suggestion was that it was time to consolidate some functions.

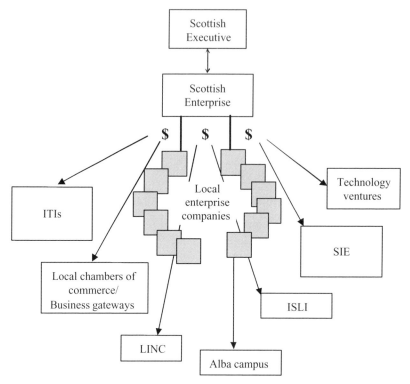

Figure 12.4 Enterprise assistance in Scotland
Source: The authors.

Public enterprise assistance in Scotland

Scotland's line agency in 2003 was the Department of Entrepreneur-ship, Transport, and Lifelong Learning. SE has managed Scotland's enterprise assistance since the early 1990s. In 2003 SE's staff providing enterprise-related assistance totaled 1,490 people (SE 2003b). Almost three-quarters of its enterprise oriented FY 2003 budget of £315.9 million (the equivalent of $547 million) was public (SE 2003a). Over half of the agency's FY 2003 income was paid to its twelve Local Enter-prise Companies the for services they provided. Those receiving the funds are shown in figure 12.4.

Scotland has an "economic development policy" that is centrally deter-mined. Through the 1990s, SE followed a "cluster strategy," directing resources to those industry groups in which Scotland had a competi-tive advantage. During the latter part of the 1990s Scotland shifted its focus to growing indigenous business and the corresponding creation of networking organizations. For example, a commercialization inquiry in 1994–5 led by the Royal Bank of Scotland (RBS) recommended an increase in seed funding, restructuring of universities to facilitate commercialization, and the establishment of networking organizations along the lines of San Diego's CONNECT. The development of the Alba Campus responded to this inquiry.

SE has subsequently pursued strategies to exploit the research and scientific strengths of Scottish universities. It has increased pressure on the universities to commercialize technology, work together, and interact with businesses and investors. It has also created public funding programs to bring new ideas under research closer to the market and to support businesses that want to develop university technologies.

We heard several kinds of criticism of this centralized approach. One was that government did not talk to industry much about its policies, at least in the past. The second was that the cluster strategies were too rigid, failing to account for the development of new industries at the boundaries of traditional industries.

12.6   Conclusions

We conclude by answering the four questions we posed at the start of this chapter.

- What kinds of organizations were evident at the boundaries of the four realms?
- What happened to these organizations, and to their places, over time?
- How did the organizations advance the development of their places?
- What were the key differences between intermediaries in Massachusetts and Scotland – that is, how did the places influence the organizations?

What kinds of organizations were evident at the boundaries of the four realms?

We found a range of organizations, from large government corporations to small independent nonprofits, incorporating players from the private and public sectors. These organizations collectively made connections to multiple realms, and many touched every realm in some part of its organization.

Intermediaries had boards with private-sector members and professional (noncivil service) staff. They used both board membership and staffing choices to bring the viewpoints of the different sectors into the organization. Many allocated board seats for this purpose. Staff and board membership with experience in private for-profit firms figured prominently in most organizations.

What happened to these organizations, and to their places, over time?

In both places, large changes in the regional economy induced by global trends produced periodic crises. These include the search by MNCs for ever-more cost-effective places to locate their manufacturing operations and their exodus from Scotland, as well as the demise of the computer industry in Massachusetts and its shift to Silicon Valley. At the same time, the scientific communities in the two regions participated in technological change that produced the entirely new fields of biotechnology, communications, and nanotechnology, creating opportunities for new enterprises.

The political environment in each place also changed over time. In Massachusetts, the state went from having governors who supported an active role for the public sector in advancing economic development and other programs to having governors who advocated a minimal public role. Economic cycles affected this as well, in that state revenues – income and sales taxes – fluctuated, with the state's economy. In Scotland, national politics were much more influential, with national leadership shifting over time from conservative, minimalist government policies to moderate public intervention. In addition, the devolution of power from the UK government to the Scottish parliament and SE in 1999 was a major event influencing development policy.

In each place, the number, characteristics, and mandates of regional intermediaries changed in response to both crises and opportunities. Existing organizations changed what they did, and changed their organizational formats. Some organizations merged to create larger, more powerful institutions with more comprehensive mandates. New organizations were created over time to solve new problems: traditional organizations opened themselves to players from other sectors, new multi-sector organizations focused on enhancing particular realms – and, increasingly, on the knowledge realm.

These changes affected economic development policy, the availability of resources, and the nature of programs. The emphasis increased on knowledge and technology and the role of universities and research centers in the process. Programs went from being project-based to network oriented.

How did the intermediaries advance the development of their places?

Intermediaries played a number of key roles in the development of place. They provided a vehicle to address the common concerns of business, which were especially important in an era of small endogenous companies. They provided conduits for the development of technology, from the laboratory to commercialization by companies. They enabled the flow of information about technology, finance, facilities, where to get legal advice, and a host of other issues. They made connections between investors, inventors, and entrepreneurs. They provided environments for nurturing new ideas and new companies. In the aggregate, they formed a system to support the operation of the many parts of the place; they looked for "kinks" in this system, and they moved to fix them.

How did the places influence the organizations?

Intermediaries in Massachusetts and Scotland offered a similar array of programs. But there were clear differences between organizations in the two places: in their size, focus, degree of government control, presence of private organizations, and reliance on public funds. We believe this is due largely to the differing institutional structure and history of the two places: Scotland has a history of strong central government, while Massachusetts has both highly autonomous local communities and a history of using mission-specific public corporations to do public work.

First, we found much larger intermediaries in Scotland than in Massachusetts. For example, SE had almost 1,500 employees in development oriented activities in 2003. In the same year, the four most important government-based intermediaries in Massachusetts employed a total of 217 people, while the largest of the Massachusetts development corporations, MassDevelopment, had 150.

Employment differences appear to reflect the premise that government serves business in the United Kingdom. In Massachusetts, government is seen more as a catalyst, as the supplier of the missing piece of the puzzle. Agency measures of performance support this: service oriented indicators such as customer satisfaction are prevalent in SE's annual report. MassDevelopment measures the number of deals closed, agency investment, and private leverage achieved.

Government funding was much greater in Scotland than in Massachusetts. For example, 2003 expenditures by SE for development-related activities were the equivalent of $547 million, of which 82 percent came from the Scottish Executive. State appropriations for the Massachusetts line economic development agency, the Executive Office of Economic Development, were just $21 million in the same year. Mass-Development received no state appropriations, funding its operations from land sales and bond and lending fees. The agency did rely on the bonding authority of the state in its provision of $860 million in investment to economic development projects in FY 2003.

Meanwhile, government control is weaker and more indirect in Massachusetts development organizations. For example, the board of Mass-Development makes policy for the organization. The governor controls the board through appointments. SE also has a board, but the executive director is accountable to the Scottish Executive for all expenditures. The board serves mainly to ensure that the organization hears differing (private-sector) viewpoints.

There was a greater tendency in Scotland for organizations to have comprehensive mandates and for Massachusetts' organizations to have fairly focused mandates. A good example is a comparison between SE, a single entity with multiple development missions, and the array of Massachusetts public corporations, each with a relatively specific mission. And this was true not only for development entities, as a comparison between MIT's Technology Licensing Office, with a dozen professionals who focus on licensing technology, and Edinburgh Innovation and Research Ltd, with a staff of over fifty people who manage consulting, technology licensing, and corporate research, would indicate.

Finally, compared with Scotland, Massachusetts had more private nonprofit organizations mediating between the public and private sectors. In Scotland, there was some evidence that private consulting firms, such as that under contract to Scottish Technology Ventures, performed this public–private mediation.

Implications: sustaining organizations

In addition to the role intermediaries played in sustaining places, their structure enabled them to sustain themselves. Their connections to high-level executives in the diverse realms, usually through board membership, gave the organizations access to a diverse range of resources, both human and financial. Intermediaries were in a good position to learn what their constituents – high-technology companies – needed and act accordingly because these companies often served on the boards of intermediaries and participated in organizational policymaking. Finally, the fact that they were separate from government, combined with their ability to draw from different revenues sources, allowed intermediaries to maintain continuity in their economic development policies during periods of political volatility.

Many interesting questions still remain about how these organizations fit into the new system of regional governance beyond government.

APPENDIX

Our research involved field interviews with 193 leaders of technology-producing companies, universities and their various departments, government, and others responsible for facilitating the development of the

Table 12A.1 *Interview and survey respondents*

	High-tech companies		Universities and research centers interview	Government interview	Other interview	Total interview
Region	Interview	Survey				
Eastern Massachusetts	20	35	14	3	12	49
Research Triangle	3	12	4	2	9	18
San Diego	4	18	3	1	7	15
Total US	27	65	21	6	28	82
Scotland	30	67	20	5	27	82
Cambridge	10	47	2	0	5	17
Eastern except Camb.	2	72	5	1	4	12
Total UK	42	186	26	19	33	111
All regions	69	251	47	16	61	193
Totals by Realm	320		47	16	61	444

Source: The authors.

"enterprising places" in our study. We supplemented these with a survey of 251 technology-producing businesses, the "targets" of economic development policies. Table 12A.1 shows the distribution of the interview and survey respondents across sectors and study areas. Note that the "others" interviewed were predominantly leaders of intermediary organizations plus some investment and real estate firms.

REFERENCES

Castells, M. and P. Hall, 1994. *Technopoles of the World: The Making of 21st Century Industrial Complexes*, London: Routledge

Cortright, J. and H. Mayer, 2002. *Signs of Life: The Growth of Biotechnology Centers in the US*, Washington, DC: The Brookings Institution on Urban and Metropolitan Policy

Firn, J. R., 2002. "Economic Governance and the Scottish Economy," in N. Hood, J. Peat, E. Peters, and S. Young (eds.), *Scotland in a Global Economy: The 2020 Vision*, Basingstoke: Palgrave

General Register Office for Scotland, 2004. *Scotland's Population 2004 – The Registrar General's Annual Review of Demographic Trends*, 150th Edition, July 29, at www.gro-scotland.gov.uk

Kuhn, T. S., 1970. *The Structure of Scientific Revolutions*, Chicago: University of Chicago Press

Markusen, A., S. Lee, and S. DiGiovanna (eds.), 1999. *Second-Tier Cities: Rapid Growth Beyond the Metropolis*, Minneapolis: University of Minnesota Press

Massachusetts Office of Economic Development, 2002. *Massachusetts: Toward a New Prosperity*, Boston: Massachusetts Office of Economic Development, August

Office of National Statistics (ONS), 2005. *First Release: Regional Gross Value Added*, at www.statistics.gov.uk, December

Peters, T. J. and R. H. Waterman, 1982. *In Search of Excellence: Lessons from America's Best-Run Companies*, New York: Harper & Row

Porter, M. E., 1990. *The Competitive Advantage of Nations*, London: Macmillan
    2001. *San Diego: Clusters of Innovative Initiatives*. Washington, DC: Council on Competitiveness

Quintas, P., D. Wield, and D. Massey, 1992. "Academic–Industry Links and Innovation: Questioning the Science Park Model," *Technovation*, 12(3): 161–173

Saxenian, A., 1994. *Regional Advantage: Culture and Computing in Silicon Valley and Route 128*, Cambridge, MA: Harvard University Press

Schön, D. A., 1971. *Beyond the Stable State*, New York: W. W. Norton

Scottish Enterprise (SE), 2003a. *Annual Report 2002/03*
    2003b. *Operating Plan 2003/04*

US Department of Commerce, 2005. Bureau of Economic Analysis website, Press release of June 23, at www.bea.gov/bea/newsrel/2005rd.htm

Walsh, A. H., 1978. *The Public's Business: The Politics and Practice of Government Corporations*, Cambridge, MA: MIT Press

13 Innovation, integration, and technology upgrading in contemporary Chinese industry

Edward S. Steinfeld

13.1 Introduction

China's extraordinary economic transformation over the past two decades has been linked inextricably with the nation's broader process of technological upgrading, industrial restructuring, and integration into the global economy. Beijing's initial policy of "opening up," by permitting inflows of knowledge and information, underscored for domestic observers China's relative economic backwardness (thus raising expectations for reform) while at the same time providing the sorts of overseas contacts needed by nascent industrial firms to link up with international supply chains (thus initiating the sorts of organizational change that alleviate economic backwardness). Domestic institutional and organizational reform, in turn, has enabled Chinese producers over time to deepen their engagement with outside markets, leading to growth outcomes that not only accelerate societal transformation, but also raise popular expectations and imperatives for further reform.

This chapter examines the limits and sustainability of this "virtuous cycle." Chinese firms unquestionably are now major players in global production, but can these firms organizationally develop the sort of innovative capacities that lead to long-term competitiveness? What have the obstacles been to date?

The question is particularly challenging since China's domestic modernization process is hardly the only variable in play. Instead, the international system itself, particularly the manner by which manufacturing activity is structured globally, has changed dramatically in recent years. Technological advances, especially those associated with digitization and modularization, have permitted at least some complex production processes – the kinds of processes that previously took place within single integrated firms – to be split into discrete activities, spread out across multiple firms, and dispersed across great geographical expanses (Baldwin and Clark 2000). Although the end result may be familiar – a branded consumer product associated with a specific company – the research, design, and manufacturing processes behind that product often appear markedly different today from the past.

The emerging pattern of networked production has afforded great opportunities for new entrants – Chinese manufacturers, for example – to capture particular pieces of global manufacturing, pieces that in the past had been inseparable from entrenched incumbent firms (Gereffi and Korzeniewicz 1994). At the same time, as entry barriers to such activities come down, competitive pressures on the new entrants go up. Given the ease with which standardized, nondifferentiated production can be transplanted from firm to firm today – in other words, given the low switching costs faced by downstream buyers – producers face increasing pressures to move into higher-entry barrier activities, precisely those for which the firm can compete on the basis of a unique skill, service, or product. Put simply, opportunities for new entrants have been created, but so too have imperatives for innovation and upgrading.

In some respects, networked production and modularization also create new freedoms to innovate.[1] To the extent that firms participate in multiple supply chains – i.e. by performing a discrete function or producing a particular component that may serve several overlapping production networks – they end up contributing to a variety of downstream final products. Producing the "guts" of myriad final products, the firms enjoy fates that are not exclusively tied to any single one. As such, they are free to innovate in their particular production activity not only in ways that incrementally improve existing downstream products ("sustaining" innovation), but also in ways that utterly destroy existing products by facilitating entirely new replacements ("disruptive" innovation), as defined by Christensen (1997). That such freedom exists may explain the extremely rapid product cycle and almost dizzying pace of innovation characteristic of high-technology (high-tech) industry today, referred to by Fine (1998) as "clockspeed." Moreover, co-ordination and interaction with upstream and downstream firms should afford the producer with learning opportunities that never existed in the past. Innovation, in this sense, may

---

[1] Worth noting is the tension between the terms "modularization" and "networked production." Modularization and codification suggest the ability to standardize activities – and, by extension, spread them geographically and organizationally. The term "network," however, suggests co-ordinated, dense interaction in something deeper than an arm's-length, market transaction sense. Presumably, in networked production there is a spectrum of activities, with those at one pole being completely modularized and codified (essentially "tossed over the wall" through pure outsourcing), those in the middle being codifiable enough to be outsourced but tacit enough to require dense interaction and frequent communication between the producer and the outsourcer, and finally those at the other extreme being so complex and tacit that they must remain within the confines of the original lead firm.

involve not just in-house creativity, but also the creative recombination and reapplication of skills absorbed from external partners.[2]

Given China's status as a prime manufacturing center for global consumer products and components, the fact of the nation's participation in global production networks is beyond dispute. More debatable is the extent to which Chinese firms are coping with pressures to innovate. It is upon this issue, however, that the sustainability of China's current industrial strategy turns. As I shall argue in this chapter, Chinese firms are structured in a fashion that allows them to compete extremely effectively on the basis of low cost in relatively low-value manufacturing activities. The problem is that this structure does not easily allow them to move upward in the production chain into more innovative, higher-return activities: control over brands, provision of unique services, or development of proprietary knowledge. To the extent that Chinese firms remain shut out of these activities and locked in basic manufacturing, they have no choice but to compete on the basis of cost, thus eroding their profit margins and further inhibiting efforts to upgrade.

Had it not been for national economic reforms, Chinese firms could never have entered the global economy. Yet, current bottlenecks in the institutional reform process lead to an enterprise-level corporate architecture that severely limits the manner by which Chinese firms compete globally, the extent to which they can upgrade, and the likelihood that they will challenge either the large MNCs currently integrating and coordinating the global supply chains, or even the more innovative and flexible small firms that have carved out defendable, high-value niches within those chains.

13.2   The phenomenon: price wars and corporate structure

By the 1990s, global manufacturing had migrated extensively to China, thus providing cheaper products for consumers globally, but also inducing worries on the part of various constituencies in Japan, Europe, and North America that Chinese exports were being "dumped" into their markets. A recent example involves efforts by the European Union to restrict television imports from China (Yau 2002). At the same time, while China appeared in global terms to be ascending as a major economic power, many of the nation's individual producers, rather than celebrating, found themselves locked in a downward spiral of cost-based

---

[2] Examples here can be drawn from the silicon chip foundry industry. Foundry producers such as the Taiwan Semiconductor Manufacturing Corporation (TSMC) routinely upgrade through interactions with engineers from upstream design houses.

competition, primarily with one another rather than outsiders. Anecdotes (e.g. Leggett 2001) of cut-throat cost competition across a number of product areas – what in China have been termed the "television wars," the "refrigerator wars," and the "air-conditioner wars," just to name a few – abound. Regardless of product area – whether consumer electronics, electronic components, appliances, apparel, or even steel or fiber-optic cable – much of Chinese manufacturing industry consists of small-scale firms producing nondifferentiated products and competing on the basis of price. In recent years, this has proven as true for the myriad, essentially nameless, subcontractors producing for globally branded MNCs as it has for some of China's better-known companies – Haier in home appliances, Lenovo in personal computers, and Changhong and Konka in home electronics (Leggett and Wonacott 2002).

In theory, this situation could be understood as the prelude to industrywide shakeouts that would eliminate small-scale firms and consolidate activities into a few large-scale producers, presumably the sort of players that might engage in industrial upgrading. In reality, however, evidence of such progression remains sparse. Undoubtedly, thousands of firms – particularly in the state sector – were either liquidated or substantially restructured in the 1990s, often with significant societal ramifications (Hu 1999; Tenev and Zhang 2002). Similarly, the private sector has burgeoned and exhibited considerable churning, with enterprises entering and exiting at high rates (Gregory, Tenev, and Wagle 2000). That said, there has to date been relatively little evidence of rationalization, whether in terms of coherent mergers and consolidation across given sectors, or individual examples of movement into higher-value activities by China's more famous enterprises.

Instead, Chinese firms, particularly in manufacturing sectors, have consistently displayed four attributes that set them apart from many of their global counterparts, as clearly described by Nolan (2001). First, and not surprisingly, given China's relatively recent emergence as a "global shop-floor," Chinese firms tend to be both newer and smaller in scale than their global counterparts. In the World Bank's 2001 survey of 1,500 higher-technology enterprises in China, firms averaged just over 600 employees, and generally had been in existence for only ten to fifteen years.[3] Even China's more famous firms fit the pattern. The nation's

---

[3] The World Bank's survey involved 2,500 "higher-tech" firms (500 firms in each of the following cities: Beijing, Shanghai, Chengdu, Guangzhou, and Tianjin). Included in the survey were firms from the following sectors: vehicles and vehicle parts, electronic equipment, electronic components, apparel and leather goods, IT services, consumer products, communication services, business logistics services, advertising and marketing, and accounting. The survey was relatively skewed toward the manufacturing side, with 995 firms falling into that overall category.

premier computer and information technology firm, the Legend Group (now renamed "Lenovo"), had revenues in 2001 of approximately $3.48 billion.[4] Its nearest MNC analog, IBM, had revenues that year of $85.9 billion.[5] The Chinese state-owned petroleum company, Sinopec, had revenues of $34 billion in 1998, compared with $182.3 for Exxon/Mobil in 1997 (Nolan 2001: 166). Capital Iron and Steel had revenues of $2.16 billion in 1998, compared with Nippon Steel's $21.6 billion. Haier–China's premier home-appliance manufacturer, one of the best known Chinese brands internationally, and the fifth largest producer of white goods worldwide in terms of market share – is dwarfed by its global competitors: Whirlpool, Electrolux, Bosch-Siemens, and General Electric.[6] Even in domestic resource-based sectors such as coal, China's industrial structure is characterized by a proliferation of relatively small firms (in terms of annual output), though consolidation has been underway since the late 1990s (Sinton and Fridley 2000). Relative to leading global firms in their respective industries, Chinese enterprises tend to operate at a significantly smaller production scale, maintain significantly smaller asset bases, and realize significantly smaller annual revenues. The one area in which Chinese firms appear particularly large – whether in steel, petroleum, mining, or manufacturing – is in total employment.[7]

Second, Chinese firms, though international in many respects, tend to be extremely localized in terms of their actual operations. In the World Bank's 2001 survey, 41 percent of the 995 manufacturing firms in the sample reported producing to specifications set by foreign firms, 21 percent reported directly producing parts for foreign firms, and 25 percent reported producing final products for such customers. Indicative of China's liberal policies toward FDI, 25 percent of all firms in the survey reported having foreign equity partners, with the foreign ownership stake on average hovering just over 50 percent. At the same time, the 2001 survey suggested that on average, over 50 percent of upstream suppliers were located in the respondents' own respective cities.[8]

---

[4] 2001 *Annual Report*, at www.legend-holdings.com.

[5] 2001 *Annual Report*, at www.ibm.com.

[6] In the US market, where Haier has recently established a refrigerator manufacturing facility, Whirlpool, General Electric, Maytag, and Electrolux (Frigidaire) account for 98 percent of the refrigerators sold (Sprague 2002).

[7] Industrywide consolidation and shakeouts have been at the top of the Chinese policy agenda across a number of sectors since the late 1990s. Major efforts have been pursued in the coal sector with the creation of the Shenhua Group. At the same time, in a number of sectors, but particularly coal, a large number of small-scale, local government-owned, and often poorly regulated firms persist.

[8] Of the cities surveyed (Beijing, Shanghai, Guangzhou, Chengdu, and Tianjin), Guangzhou proved to be somewhat of an exception to this point, with respondents reporting higher levels of overseas suppliers and lower levels of intra-city supply network concentration.

Approximately 75 percent of the supply network on average was located within China. Downstream, the survey indicated that, for the average Chinese firm, approximately half of the customer base is located within the firm's own municipality.[9]

The localized nature of Chinese commercial networks leads to a third point, the relative shallowness with which Chinese firms integrate into global supply chains. Despite high levels of foreign ownership, only 15 percent of the manufacturing firms surveyed by the World Bank in 2001 reported designing parts for foreign customers. Only 7 percent reported the provision of any R&D or other services.[10] The figures are surprisingly low given that the sample specifically targeted higher-tech sectors such as electronics, vehicle assembly and parts, and consumer products – the very ones in which we might expect a higher degree of innovation, networking, and development of firm-specific proprietary knowledge. Interestingly, firms were failing not only to design for down-stream customers, but also to develop deep relationships of any kind with such customers; 69 percent of the survey respondents reported using trading companies to handle interactions with the broader customer base, thus suggesting essentially arm's-length – rather than deeply enmeshed – relationships with customers.

An interesting exception is the cokemaking sector in Shanxi Province, where the prevailing pattern involves a proliferation of small-scale township and village enterprises (TVEs) (firms producing no more than 600,000 metric tonnes per annum, compared to the 5 million metric tonnes per annum achieved by the largest foreign enterprises), but also extensive direct sales to overseas, namely Japanese, corporate customers (Polenske 2006).[11] Although beyond the scope of this chapter, this issue clearly deserves further exploration. It is an important enough exception to underscore the point that the general phenomena discussed in this chapter should be restricted to manufacturing firms, rather than a broader set of industries that might include those based on natural-resource inputs.

---

[9] Again, Guangzhou was the exception, with respondents reporting 38 percent of the customer base within the city, and 29 percent located overseas.

[10] Conceivably, this is in part driven by concerns on the part of foreign partners regarding the poorly developed state of IPRs protection in China. Executives in foreign firms frequently report concerns on this front. Though leading global technology firms routinely set up R&D centers in China, these centers are occasionally jokingly referred to as "PR&D centers," with the "PR" suggesting "public relations."

[11] This information comes from extensive China-based interviewing and fieldwork conducted by Professor Karen R. Polenske's Alliance for Global Sustainability (AGS) research team, which is detailed in her cokemaking study (Polenske 2006). I am grateful to her for sharing this information with me prior to its publication.

In terms of identifying factors inhibiting greater exports, respondents to the World Bank survey focused on the difficulties of meeting foreign product standards, the high costs of meeting such standards, and especially the intense cost competition faced in all these activities (refer to table 7 in the World Bank report). Managers, all things being equal, apparently preferred to produce for export markets.[12] At the same time, although few managers claimed that targeting the domestic market offered better financial gains, they believed their firms to be severely lacking in the capabilities needed to meet foreign standards in a cost-effective manner. Moreover, they perceived themselves to be in an intensely competitive environment with price pressures bearing down from domestic and foreign competitors alike. Presumably, one reason why managers find the export market (and the domestic market, for that matter) so price competitive is that they neither sell directly to – nor design directly for – customers. If a firm does not sell directly, it cannot develop the sort of service-based, specifically tailored relationships or products that lead to customer loyalty. If the firm – for example, a component producer – does not design directly for the downstream user, it is not likely to have particularly deep interactions with that user, and hence will likely forgo important learning opportunities (whether in terms of product or process technology, or even marketing skills and service provision) from the potentially more sophisticated customer. Nor will the firm likely be able to exert any leverage if the user decides to source elsewhere. Under these combined circumstances, the firm has little choice but to compete on the basis of cost. After all, it is essentially producing a nondifferentiated product that can be "thrown over the wall" to distant, nondifferentiated customers.

That then leads to a fourth and final point, the lack of innovative capacity on the part of Chinese firms. Chinese enterprises today face great pressure to upgrade their technological capabilities, and managers, in turn, frequently report high levels of what they at least perceive to be innovative activity. The pressures are understandable. Modern production, whether for ostensibly low-end goods such as textiles or high-end goods such as semiconductors, virtually by definition entails the management

---

[12] This may be changing over time. In the author's own fieldwork in Zhejiang Province in January 2003, entrepreneurs appeared increasingly interested in serving the domestic market, particularly given the opportunities emerging in Western China. In part, this may reflect regulatory incentives associated with the national government's "Opening to the West" development strategy. It may also reflect the rise of protectionist sentiment – and associated regulation – in key overseas markets in North America and Western Europe. Finally, it also reflects the economic downturn that has affected all of these overseas markets, including Japan.

of complex processes, technology and capital-intensive machinery, highly refined product-specific materials, extremely high-quality requirements by customers, and rapid turn-around times. Simply to be involved in global production networks today, even at the relatively low end, and even just to produce the sort of commodity products that can be "thrown over the wall," new entrants must climb exceedingly steep managerial and technological learning curves, and they must do so with unprecedented rapidity. That Chinese firms are so extensively involved in production for overseas markets represents a major achievement of learning.

There is little evidence, however, that the learning they are engaged in actually constitutes "innovation," at least the kind of innovation that leads to commercially sustainable competitive advantage. In other words, it is not at all clear that these firms are developing intellectual assets, production skills, modes of serving customers, or actual products that can be understood as in any way "proprietary"– things that cannot be duplicated by hundreds or thousands of other firms in their immediate environment. In the 2001 survey, nearly 50 percent of all firms reported innovations in shop floor production processes, and another 46 percent reported innovations in managerial techniques – all measures that allow for the cutting of costs. The type of innovation that few, if any, of the firms reported was one allowing the firm to charge a higher margin rather than a lower one – an innovation, in other words, that would encourage customers to pay a premium for the product.[13] Moreover, given the prevalence of product "wars" and cut-throat competition among the proliferation of small producers in China, it appears that few if any players, even on the production-process front, have achieved the sort of innovations that constitute defendable barriers against new entrants. Instead, one firm's cost-cutting "innovation" simply gets duplicated by the next, and margins continue to erode.

To some extent, this may be driven by the strategic preferences of the entrepreneurs involved. Choosing to operate a portfolio of often unrelated – but often rather basic – manufacturing activities, Chinese business entrepreneurs seem inclined to engage in extensive arbitrage, shifting back and forth between activities as the business cycle shifts. Alternatively, they rarely choose to invest long-term in the building of capabilities in a single sector. Meanwhile, the ineffectiveness of Chinese IPRs protection reinforces incentives to operate in this manner. Even if an entrepreneur did choose to pursue a focused strategy of innovation and

---

[13] Such innovations often include the bundling of value-added services with basic manufacturing. The TSMC, for example, maintains libraries of contacts that allow external chip designers to connect with potential downstream firms that design and produce the final products that use chips.

product differentiation, it is not clear that he or she could defend such intangible assets from piracy or other forms of illegal replication.

Indeed, the response to this dilemma usually entails another activity that survey respondents term "innovation," the introduction of new products or entirely new lines of business.[14] The portfolio of activities expands as commodity producers end up chasing one undifferentiated product market after another. Leading Chinese television manufacturers like Konka – facing declining profits, rising inventories, and overseas import quotas – have moved aggressively, and en masse, into mobile phone manufacturing (Leggett 2001).[15] Similarly, low-end microwave oven producers, facing their own problems of declining profits, have jumped into air-conditioner manufacturing (Lee 2002). The entry strategy almost invariably involves extensive price discounting. Even the most famous, established firms cope with increasing competition by aggressively discounting and expanding sales volume on existing products, entering new product areas in which they can compete again only on the basis of discounting and razor-thin margins, or finally, by trying to export their way out of trouble by pursuing overseas markets.[16]

In essence, firms focus on activities with low barriers to entry. Once the cost pressures become too intense, rather than moving upward into higher-end activities or taking the time to develop proprietary skills, the firms diversify into other low-entry-barrier markets. The products themselves – whether televisions, PCs, refrigerators, or data routers – are standardized. In the local context, therefore, "innovation" becomes associated with flexibility – the ease and rapidity with which a firm can jump from one saturated product market to the next – and cost reduction. In this same local context (let alone globally) neither of these capabilities has proven defendable over an extended period of time.

13.3   Explanations: governmental reform style, state capacity, and industrial policy

The pattern described above in large part results from an interaction between three factors: governmental reform style, state capacity, and

---

[14] In the 2001 survey, 36 percent of the respondents reported the introduction of new products within existing lines, and 21 percent reported new products in entirely new lines of business.

[15] Konka, China's second largest television producer, lost $84.5 million in 2001. TCL International reported a 32 percent drop in profits that same year, and, like Konka, has moved into other appliance manufacturing (see Stevens 2002).

[16] Haier, China's largest refrigerator and air-conditioner manufacturers – and an emerging global brand – suffered a 45 percent year-on-year drop in net profit in the first half of 2002. The company's response involved an increase in exports of low-end air-conditioners, and a further ramping up of refrigerator and air-conditioner production domestically; see Dow Jones (2002).

industrial policy. This interaction has at once permitted the integration of Chinese firms into the global economy and substantially circumscribed the extent of that integration.

Reform style

Since the dawn of reform in the early 1980s, China's policies of market transition have been marked by three features: informality, experimentation, and decentralization. In terms of general policy, central leaders have set the overall aim (economic growth) and the basic constraint (the maintenance, in the vaguest terms, of "socialism"). Local officials, then, have been granted broad leeway to engage in policy experiments, virtually all of which have involved elements of capitalism. "Socialism" is maintained to the extent that the experiments remain informal. When experiments prove successful, the center encourages their implementation – again on informal terms – nationally. If their success continues, the experiments stand to be adopted post hoc as official government policy. Finally, in some – but not all – cases, the center formalizes the outcomes with new institutional rules, many of which directly challenge the initial condition of "maintaining socialism." Through a certain element of semantic gymnastics, that which began as an informal and experimental alternative to socialism (hence its explicitly informal status) ultimately gets legitimized as socialism itself, albeit socialism "with Chinese characteristics."

This progression has proven brilliant in many respects. Without it, China's transition from socialism to what most observers consider capitalism could never have proceeded smoothly.[17] It also explains how private enterprise, which just twenty years ago was anathema in China, now constitutes the predominant ownership form in Chinese industry, and also has official status in the Chinese constitution.[18]

That said, there are far fewer positive organizational ramifications of prolonged informality and extensive decentralization. As the evidence from China suggests, entrepreneurial firms can thrive under such circumstances, and they can engage in international commerce, but their property rights tend to remain either undefined or – to the extent that they

---

[17] For a useful definition of what just such a transformation means, see Kornai (2000) and Steinfeld (2002).

[18] A change in attitude was signaled in 1997, when the Communist Party recognized private firms as an important part of the Chinese economy. That change was followed in 1999 with an amendment to the Chinese Constitution officially recognizing private enterprise. Finally, in 2001, China's President and Communist Party General Secretary, Jiang Zemin, called for the welcoming of private entrepreneurs – capitalists, in effect – into the Communist Party.

tuck themselves under the auspices of a governmental bureau or state-owned firm – inaccurately defined. Deprived of clear property rights, firms have no formal title to assets – and, as such, face constraints in their financing options. In essence, they have little choice but to self-finance, a situation that may be good for guaranteeing a hard budget, but one that also tends to limit enterprise growth.

Similarly, informality results in the firm's facing an extremely tight liquidity constraint. The enterprise response often involves operating on a cash basis, but that then leads to the forgoing of transactions that in more formalized systems allow for greater enterprise expansion. Alternatively, the firm turns to informal channels of financial intermediation, providing credit that tends to be high in price and small in scale (Tsai 2002).

Furthermore, rather than investing in existing business lines and developing specialized skills, cash-starved firms instead jump to alternative – and at times unrelated – businesses simply to maintain cash flow (i.e. "if low-end television production isn't generating revenue today, try low-end mobile phone manufacturing!"). The diversification strategy partly solves liquidity issues, but it does not encourage the development of firm-specific proprietary assets or skills. Firms remain stuck in low-entry-barrier activities.

Informality, because it implies that the firm has no legal standing, also shapes the geographical reach of the firm. Without legal standing, the firm must engage predominantly in trust-based transactions (in terms of both with whom it chooses to deal, and who chooses to deal with it). The surest way to ensure trust is to stay local – essentially, by buying from known local suppliers (or better yet, backward integrating) and selling to reliable local customers. When dealing with international markets, the main option becomes to sell to a local trading company. In essence, the interaction between legal and financial institutions deeply impacts the manner by which firms expand the scale and scope of their production activities. That then impacts the geography of production and innovation more broadly.

From the perspective of a foreign firm interacting with informal organizations, the coping strategy entails either buying from a more formalized state trading company or, alternatively, actually buying the local producer itself. Indeed, FDI, to the extent that it places the recipient into the special regulatory category "foreign owned," constitutes a formalization mechanism, one that benefits provider and recipient alike. As Yasheng Huang (2005) points out, Chinese firms sell their assets to foreign firms at a discount, but in so doing achieve a degree of formality that permits access to credit and insulation from arbitrary governmental policy. The implication as Huang points out, is that China has an inordinately high demand for FDI. In other words, over the past twenty years in China, legal institutionalization has moved forward differentially across owner-ship sectors. Domestic state-owned industry and foreign-invested firms have enjoyed the earliest and most extensive provisioning of legal and regulatory infrastructure – thus permitting these firms to formalize their activities in China – whereas domestic private firms have generally been discriminated against or otherwise shut out of the legal system. Simply to enjoy the preferential access granted foreign firms to public regulatory and legal goods, domestic firms essentially "put on a foreign cap" by selling themselves to an overseas investor.

Like informality, governmental decentralization leaves its own mark on entrepreneurial organizations. Local governments throughout the reform period have been keen to promote economic development, and, as part of that goal, have frequently promoted local entrepreneurship. They have been far less eager, however, to facilitate development that benefits areas beyond the locality. Early in the reform era, this reluctance manifested itself in regional trade wars and overt barriers to inter-provincial trade.[19] More recently in the 1990s, given central crackdowns on such practices, localities have used more subtle methods: "local" content rules ("local" defined as "within the municipality") for local producers, discrimina-tory regulatory enforcement for outsiders trying to enter the local mar-ket, and restrictions on enterprise mergers and acquisitions (Segal and Thun 2001).

To the extent that firms are forced to keep their sourcing networks local, they are in many cases prevented from interacting with the best, most advanced suppliers. In an era of networked production, when innovation is understood as emanating as much from interfirm learning across the supply chain as it is from isolated activities within the individual firm, link-ing up with the best upstream and downstream partners becomes a key component of upgrading. Administratively imposed restrictions on these linkages, particularly ones that limit the linkages to a given municipality, frequently prevent Chinese firms from accessing not only the best global suppliers, but even the best national suppliers. Deprived of high-quality components and important learning opportunities, many Chinese firms are pushed further down the road of low-end manufacturing and cost-based competition. Moreover, when subnational governmental agencies try to keep the firm local, often by inhibiting organic growth beyond municipal and provincial boundaries, or by withholding authorization for

---

[19] For alternative perspectives on the problem, see Naughton (1999) and Young (2000).

mergers and acquisitions beyond such boundaries, the firm's problems of small scale and limited financial resources deepen.[20]

State capacity to co-ordinate and regulate

By the mid-to-late 1990s, the architects of Chinese reform began to recognize and aggressively tackle the problems discussed above. They understood that informality and decentralization, while critical initially for achieving local acceptance of reform (and for easing the ideological problems associated with what ultimately became a wholesale adoption of the market system), had run their useful course and were now inhibiting further growth. Informality has its time and place. Efforts across a variety of areas to formalize China's market system have risen to the top of the policy agenda. The problem, however, is that these imperatives have collided with the reality of extremely limited state capacity in China.

The capacity issue manifests itself in at least two respects: (1) the ability of the center adequately to co-ordinate policy across the government's administrative hierarchy, and (2) the ability of the government as a whole effectively to regulate commercial activity in the civil sphere. The first problem, discussed in section 13.2, has arguably receded in recent years. The second, however – one basically of provision of public regulatory goods – is both more interesting and more vexing. As occurs in any developing market economy, the Chinese system has witnessed a dramatic increase in the complexity and density of interactions between economic actors, most of which are no longer under the direct administrative control of the state. Across the board – whether in terms of financial relationships, contracts, issues of corporate control, or IPRs – demand within the civil sphere has increased for both objective rules and reliable enforcement. Understandably, given the extreme rapidity of Chinese economic growth, the demand for market governance has outpaced the ability of the state to provide such public goods. Courts are overwhelmed with cases, judges are often inadequately trained, and enforcement mechanisms are generally weak at best (Lubman 1999; Alford 2000).

Virtually everyone in China today repeats the mantra that the "rule of law" is essential for sustained growth, though the question remains of how the rule of law can ultimately be achieved. The point is not that the actual causal relationship between economic development and legal

---

[20] Some scholars have argued that Chinese private firms, rather than innovating, spend most of their energy cultivating clientelistic ties with political patrons (see Wank 1999). Others, such as Guthrie (1999) have argued that clientalism has receded in recent years, as institutionalization has increased.

institutionalization is well understood in China, or anywhere else, for that matter.[21] Indeed, China over the past two-and-a-half decades has achieved impressive growth under conditions that can arguably be characterized as lacking in effective legal development. Rather, the point is that since the 1980s, but particularly during the 1990s, the Chinese government was actively promulgating the idea that modernity and development were contingent upon the establishment of rule of the law. By the end of the 1990s, Chinese officials were proudly reporting the issuance of 37,000 new laws, legal measures, and regulations over the preceding two decades (Alford 2000: 5).

Meanwhile, the government and public alike in China seem to accept that the absence of the rule of law encourages rent-seeking behavior that further undermines trust in commercial affairs and in society more broadly. There is certainly some empirical basis for this view. In the area of financial affairs, for example, we have witnessed the emergence of what some Chinese observers describe as a "nonpayment" economy (Zhou 1999: 6). Commercial buyers make purchases, and then refuse to pay. Borrowers take out loans, and then default. Banks accept deposits, and then squander the loan assets. In each case, the victim is left with little recourse. As the current saying in China goes, "you sue, but the court won't accept your case; the court accepts your case, but won't begin the trial; the court begins the trial, but won't issue a judgment; the court issues a judgment, but then doesn't enforce it" (*qi gao bu shou li, shou li bu kai ting, kai ting bu xuan pan, xuan pan bu zhi xing*) (Zhou 1999: 6).

What results is neither utter lawlessness nor an absence of growth. Instead, what emerges is a subtle pattern of tremendous growth in the scope and extent of legal codes, but also of proliferation of unclear rules, low levels of trust, and frequent efforts to skirt the boundaries of legal strictures, conditions that – as indicated earlier – all impact the organizational structure and global competitiveness of Chinese firms. At the very least, they impinge on both the capacity and inclination of firms to innovate.

At the same time, low state capacity, in terms of both administrative co-ordination within the government and provision of public regulatory goods beyond the government, impedes reform of a key chokepoint in the economy, the bank-dominated national financial system. Unable and unaccustomed to operating a modern fiscal apparatus – and unable effectively to co-ordinate the various levels of local government in the fiscal

---

[21] For a skeptical view on this subject, see Alford (2000), at http://credpr.stanford.edu/publications/abstracts.html#58.

system that it has – China, for much of the reform era, has been forced to rely on the state-owned banking system as a quasi-fiscal system. This quasi-fiscal system, in turn, has been employed primarily to channel funds into state-owned firms (Lardy 1998). Over time, that pattern resulted in a build up of nonperforming loans and a situation of technical insolvency in the financial system (Ma and Fung 2002). To its credit, the central government, particularly since the Asian Financial Crisis, has acknowledged the problem and undertaken a series of measures to encourage both the recapitalization and commercialization of the financial system (Steinfeld 2000). The problem, though, is that although it has proven able to freeze credit provision by fiat, the government in the past five years has proven consistently unable to produce modern financial regulations. The banking system remains mired in conditions of moral hazard: bank balance sheets remain awash in red ink, large borrowers have not been shut down, the costs of loan write-offs have either been borne by state agencies or otherwise deferred, and bankers have then been told to loan money on commercial terms. It is no wonder that nonperforming loans continue to build up (Kynge 2002). It is also no wonder that Chinese industrial producers – particularly the newer, more dynamic firms that have no established relationship with state banks – face tight liquidity constraints.

Industrial policy

Lurking behind the aforementioned capacity issues, of course, is the issue of ultimate governmental aims. China throughout the 1990s has pursued institutional reforms that encouraged market deepening and a leveling of the playing field among all participants in the economy. In an overall sense, it is the vast array of smaller state firms that has probably suffered the most from these changes. Nonetheless, it would be incorrect to suggest that the Chinese government has abandoned either the notion of state ownership or the ambition of building key state firms into world-class commercial conglomerates. Indeed, the government still pursues a policy of encouraging development in "pillar industries" – sectors such as autos, steel, machine building, and aerospace.

In this sense, Chinese industrial policy has a rather schizophrenic quality. On the one hand, for all the lessons of the Asian Financial Crisis, China's policymakers remain enamored of Japanese- and South Korean-style industrial policy. The ambition of saving the state sector writ large may have receded, but the goal of building a smaller set of state-owned "national firms" – the "national team" – is alive and well (Nolan 2001: 16). This, after all, is the "grasping the large" side of China's *zhua da fang xiao* ("grasping the large, and releasing the small") enterprise-reform policy.

On the other hand, and at the same time, Chinese policymakers are pursuing what they themselves term a "comparative advantage strategy of development," a strategy embodied by the bold WTO accession effort (Chen 2002). The idea, presumably, is to push domestic reform by binding the nation to external commitments for extensive market liberalization. Although many observers, including this author, applaud the accession effort and believe it represents a genuine effort on the part of the government to further reform, it is hard to understand how that effort is consistent with the goal of building "pillar" industries. After all, it is hard to imagine that a comparative advantage strategy of development will lead to the emergence of vertically integrated industrial giants in China, any more than it did in Japan.

China may for political or social reasons choose to build vertically integrated, self-reliant pillar industries. Yet, the notion that a comparative advantage strategy of development is the way to do so, or that such self-reliant pillar industries can be competitive globally, is problematic at best. In other words, the organizational attributes of old-style Japanese or South Korean-style "national champions" – massive scope, high levels of diversification, extreme vertical integration – are precisely those that globalization trends to discriminate against. Second, the creation of such firms in the past was predicated on a high degree of governmental protection, protection that was tolerated by the world's most advanced economies in previous decades, but is no longer tolerated today. Indeed, China by its own aggressive WTO accession strategy is submitting itself to a degree of market opening that would have been unimaginable to Japanese or Korean industrial planners of yore. Logically, the ambition of building self-reliant pillar industries remains consistent with the government's WTO strategy only to the extent that policymakers believe that the resulting "national champions" will *ipso facto* be globally competitive. Such assumptions require a degree of faith, or perhaps a quality of information, rarely shared by outside observers.

For all those contradictions, however, the goal of building traditional "national industries" has crept into a wide variety of institutional reform measures, including the financial reform measures discussed in brief earlier. Standard moral hazard encourages banks to continue to pour money into large state firms. So too, however, does a governmental industrial policy repeatedly endorsing such firms. The point is that, at least in part because of industrial policy ambitions, the government is impeding the very sort of institutional reforms that would help China's most internationalized firms – those already engaged in networked production – to build competitiveness in an emerging global order.

13.4   Conclusions

The Chinese case is so interesting because it illustrates how institutional evolution interacts with public policy to affect the production decisions of firms at the micro-level, and the overall geography of innovation and production at the macro-level. In terms of actual outcomes, China's particular pattern of institutional change, and its unique approach to post-socialist transition – one characterized by informality, gradualism, and incrementalism on the one hand, and aggressive opening to FDI and foreign commercial partnerships on the other – has led to a rather mixed bag. Entrepreneurship has been unleashed on a grand scale, but a particular kind of entrepreneurship – one that in the face of uncertain and often halting legal development has learned to operate with extraordinary flexibility and learned to adopt coping mechanisms to fill the void left by insufficient governmental provision of public-regulatory goods and property-rights protection. That a vast number of manufacturing firms have emerged to populate China's industrial landscape is testament to the vitality, flexibility, and, frankly, innovativeness of the Chinese entrepreneurial spirit. At the same time, as both a direct and indirect result of public policy, these firms now enjoy extensive interactions and often direct ownership ties with more advanced overseas enterprises. Such partnerships are undoubtedly critical vectors for knowledge transfer, organizational learning, and ultimately industrial upgrading. That Chinese firms today are so extensively involved in global production chains constitutes a major achievement, one that has eluded many other developing countries.

Yet, as I have argued, the full potential of these positive outcomes – the full potential of Chinese entrepreneurship, and the full potential of China's partnerships with overseas commercial actors – has yet to be realized. Chinese entrepreneurs have proven extraordinarily innovative in terms of their ability to promote business development in a highly uncertain political and regulatory environment. Chinese firms, however, in terms of building the sort of innovative capacity that leads to sustainable competitive advantage, have up to this point proven somewhat lacking. Firm-level innovative capacity in China has been impeded by the legacies of Chinese reform style, current bottlenecks in the institutional reform process, and inconsistencies in governmental industrial policy. The problem with drawing long-term implications from this observation, though, is that even in purely analytical terms, so much uncertainty still surrounds the globalization process itself. Three examples are worth noting.

First, the concept of organizational "best practice," at least with regard to innovation and competitiveness, remains highly ambiguous. Chinese industrial policy may be inconsistent, but so too are many of our analytical assertions about the nature of competitiveness. Even given the fact of globalized production networks, the assumptions we make about the nature of those networks can lead to highly divergent implications about policy. To the extent we understand technology as relatively stable, product cycles as fairly long, and production networks as consisting of fully modularized, discrete processes, we could imagine that innovation would primarily fall within the "sustaining technologies" category, and that it would occur within the confines of the incumbent firm. The goal of industrial policy, then, might be to create the kinds of large, self-contained organizations that could dominate a particular piece of the supply chain. Yet, if we understand technology as highly unstable, product cycles as extremely short, and production networks as defined by extensive co-ordination between upstream and downstream producers (in other words, if co-ordination needs undercut full modularization), then innovation would fall primarily in the "disruptive technologies" category, and it might be understood as occurring primarily through interaction between firms. Under such circumstances, the policy goal would be to create not particular kinds of companies, but rather particular kinds of communities (*à la* Silicon Valley). Chinese industrial policy may be creating neither of these, but we can sympathize with the dilemmas that policymakers face. There is no reason to believe that competitiveness in the current global context by definition entails the creation of massive firms operating at massive scale. Niche strategies by smaller players are undoubtedly feasible, and given the sort of firms that have emerged from the Chinese reform process, potentially quite applicable for China. The problem, however, is that, institutionally, the Chinese system is inhibiting the unfolding of either large-scale supply-chain integrators or smaller-scale, specialized niche players.

Second, with regard to the actual enterprise-level picture that emerges from China, there is uncertainty regarding the likelihood of change in the future. I have argued that, for institutional reasons, Chinese firms are upgrading less rapidly than they should, and are in certain respects suffering from a degree of arrested development. Yet, given that the evidence we see today is, in a sense, but one frame in an evolving film, it is conceivable that Chinese firms are simply still at the earliest stages of a more drawn-out upgrading process. As we witness Chinese companies today beginning to make forays into branded product markets in developed countries, how are we to know that this is not analogous to the Japanese auto industry's first steps in similar markets (also initially involving low-end, low-cost products)?[22] The nature of production has changed, as have the ability of home governments – especially in the developing world – to protect their national firms, but the broader point still stands. There is a chance that Chinese firms are following an evolutionary path not entirely unlike that which was taken by their predecessors and other late developers.

Finally, this leads to uncertainty about what the relevant comparison (or "comparator") for China really is. Chinese firms in most sectors are today locked in intense competition, competition for which the dominant strategy still seems to involve deep discounting rather than specialization and innovation. By virtually any measure, Chinese firms are not as innovative as global leaders – namely MNCs producing branded products – in any given supply chain. But are the global leaders really the relevant comparison? China's *per capita* income in 2001 was US$ 890, roughly one-fortieth that of Japan or of the United States (World Bank 2002). It is perhaps not surprising that Chinese firms are failing to unseat incumbents from these far richer countries. Yet, in terms of positioning in global supply chains, can we say that Chinese firms are performing poorly relative to Mexican firms, Malaysian firms, or Thai firms (firms hailing from countries with *per capita* incomes, respectively, six times, four times, and twice China's)? The point is that Chinese firms may not be innovating relative to one another and relative to globally branded leaders. Yet, they are outcompeting rivals from far wealthier developing countries, and they are doing so by rapidly developing competence in increasingly complex manufacturing processes. Simply to remain in the game – simply to compete even on the basis of cost – firms in the contemporary era must upgrade rapidly, and that is precisely what Chinese enterprises have proven able to do. They may not be "innovating" in the traditional sense, but they are keeping pace with a dynamically evolving system of global production, an achievement that appears to elude many of their developing country counterparts. Although that may not fit the Chinese goal of "catching-up," keeping pace represents an achievement worth celebrating – and understanding analytically – in its own right.

---

[22] Chinese motorcycle manufacturers currently dominate Southeast Asian markets, and Haier is trying to carve out the low-end US and European markets for household appliances.

REFERENCES

BOOKS AND ARTICLES

Alford, W., 2000. "The More Law, the More . . .? Measuring Legal Reform in the People's Republic of China," Center for Research on Economic Development and Policy Reform, Working Paper, 59, Stanford University, at http://credpr.stanford.edu/publications/abstracts.html#58, August

Baldwin, C. Y. and K. B. Clark, 2000. *Design Rules: The Power of Modularity*, Cambridge, MA: MIT Press

Chen, Q., 2002. "Promoting Regional Economic Cooperation in Asia Amidst Economic Globalization," Paper presented to the Conference on Asian Economic Integration, Research Institute of Economy, Trade, and Industry, Tokyo, April 22–23

Christensen, C. M., 1997. *The Innovator's Dilemma*, Cambridge, MA: Harvard University Press

Dow Jones, 2002. "China's Haier First Half Profit Down 45% on Low-Priced Exports," *Dow Jones International News*, July 29

Fine, C. H., 1998. *Clockspeed: Winning Industry Control in the Age of Temporary Advantage*, Reading, MA: Perseus

Gereffi, G. and M. Korzeniewicz (eds.), 1994. *Commodity Chains and Global Capitalism*, Westport, CT: Praeger

Gregory, N., S. Tenev, and D. Wagle, 2000. *China's Emerging Private Enterprises: Prospects for the New Century*, Washington, DC: World Bank/International Finance Corporation

Guthrie, D., 1999. *Dragon in a Three-Piece Suit*, Princeton, NJ: Princeton University Press

Hu, A., 1999. "The Greatest Challenge of the New Century: China Enters the Stage of High Unemployement (*Kuaru xinshiji de zui da tiaozhan: wo guo jinru gaoshiye jieduan*)," Chinese Academy of Sciences–Tsinghua University Joint Center for Chinese Studies

Huang, Y., 2005. *Selling China: Foreign Direct Investment During the Reform Era*, New York: Cambridge University Press

Kornai, J., 2000. "What the Change of System from Socialism to Capitalism Does and Does Not Mean," *Journal of Economic Perspectives*, 14(1): 27–42

Kynge, J., 2002. "Creaking Economy Needs Stronger Foundations," *Financial Times*, October 29

Lardy, N., 1998. *China's Unfinished Economic Revolution*, Washington, DC: Brookings

Lee, J. L., 2002. "China's Price Wars Build Pressure on State Companies to Reform," *Dow Jones International News*, April 17

Leggett, K., 2001. "Konka's Loss Shows Effects of Price Wars," *Asian Wall Street Journal*, August 30

Leggett, K. and P. Wonacott, 2002. "China Proving Victorious in the Manufacturing War," *Far Eastern Economic Review*, October 17

Lubman, S. B., 1999. *Bird in a Cage: Legal Reform in China after Mao*, Stanford, CA: Stanford University Press

Ma, G. and B. S. C. Fung, 2002. "China's Asset Management Corporations," Bank for International Settlements Working Papers, 115, August

Naughton, B., 1999. "How Much Can Regional Integration Do to Unify China's Markets?," Paper presented to the Conference on Policy Reform in China, Stanford University, November,

Nolan, P., 2001. *China and the Global Economy*, New York: St. Martin's Press

Polenske, K. R. (ed.), 2006. *The Technology–Energy–Environment–Health (TEEH) Chain in China: A Case Study of Cokemaking*, Heidelberg: Springer

Segal, A. and E. Thun, 2001. "Thinking Globally and Acting Locally: Local Governments, Industrial Sectors, and Development in China," *Politics & Society*, 29(4): 557–588.

Sinton, J. E. and D. G. Fridley, 2000. "What Goes Up: Recent Trends in China's Energy Consumption," Lawrence Berkeley National Laboratory, at http://china.lbl.gov/pubs/up_preprint2.PDF, February 3

Sprague, J., 2002. "China's Manufacturing Beachhead," *Fortune*, October 28

Steinfeld, E. S. 2000. "Free Lunch or Last Supper: China's Debt–Equity Swaps in Context," *China Business Review*, July–August

2002. "Moving Beyond Transition in China: Financial Reform and the Political Economy of Declining Growth," *Comparative Politics*, 34(4): 379–398.

Stevens, C., 2002. "Domestic Chinese Appliance OEMs on the Ropes," *Appliance*, June 1

Tenev S. and C. Zhang, 2002. *Corporate Governance and Enterprise Reform in China*, Washington, DC: World Bank/International Finance Corporation

Tsai, K., 2002. *Back-Alley Banking: Private Entrepreneurs in China*, Ithaca, NY: Cornell University Press

Wank, D. L., 1999. *Commodifying Communism*, New York: Cambridge University Press

World Bank, 2002. World Development Indicators Database, August

Yau, W., 2002. "Mainland TV Makers Tackle European Import Quota," *South China Morning Post*, October 14

Young, A., 2000. "The Razor's Edge: Distortions and Incremental Reform in the People's Republic of China," *Quarterly Journal of Economics*, 115(4): 1091–1135

Zhou, X. (ed.), 1999. *Chongjian yu zaisheng*, Beijing: China Financial Press

WEBSITES

IBM 2001 *Annual Report*, at www.ibm.com
Legend 2001 *Annual Report*, at www.legend-holdings.com

14 Society, community, and development: a tale of two regions

Michael Storper, Lena Lavinas, and
Alejandro Mercado-Célis

14.1 Contrasts in innovation: why should low-tech be so difficult?

Tonalá, near Guadalajara in the state of Jalisco, Mexico, provides the first-time visitor with the impression of a typical Mexican town with narrow, cobbled streets and small adobe houses whose front rooms double as stores. The town center is traditional Mexican plaza style. The streets are clean and well-cared for, with cheerful brightly colored facades; every morning, each family cleans its sidewalks in front of its shop. Overall, there is a jumble of production, residential, and sales spaces. People are all around, with workers moving ceramic products, while trucks almost too large for the narrow streets are crammed full of products, leaving for far-flung destinations, to be sold in American and European chain stores. Hundreds of stores line the streets, one after another, offering a wide array of "typical Mexican" handicrafts. On the two big market days each week when goods are sold not only in shops, but in street markets, people arrive from all over to buy ceramics, furniture, blown glass, and other decorative objects. The work areas are low-tech and work is hard, but the overall feeling is of bustle but not oppression; this is not surprising, since many of the firms are family-owned and operated, and, in many, the owners are former workers in other firms.

On the other side of the Guadalajara metropolitan area, the main street of the town of Tlaquepaque is lined with magnificent colonial houses, the central plaza has a baroque cathedral, and there are fine restaurants, bars, cafes, and high-quality boutiques throughout the town. The products that can be seen in boutiques, showrooms, and tree-shaded courtyards of colonial houses are of high quality, ranging from traditional Mexican-baroque to modern updated hacienda-style design objects. Buyers come from around the world to Tlaquepaque, and a high proportion of its products are exported to the United States, Canada and Europe. Behind many of these courtyards, and interspersed throughout surrounding residential areas, is a multitude of small- and medium-sized workshops.

The vast Northeastern region of Brazil also has well-developed artisanal and handicraft industries – in ceramics, decorative arts, and housewares – as well as industrial production of many low-technology goods, such as wooden and metal furniture, and significant output of clothing and shoes in both large and small firms. Visitors to these firms gain a strikingly different impression from Tonalá and Tlaquepaque (T&T).[1] Some firms are located in the industrial neighborhoods of cities such as Fortaleza or Recife. The feeling is of grueling industrial work, often hazardous and dirty, whether it be in shoes or ceramics. Similar kinds of factories can be found in grimy frontier towns, such as Imperatriz, in the state of Maranhão, on the border between the Northeast and Amazonia, where cheap furniture is made from tropical hardwoods by low-paid workers. The Northeast also boasts its share of industrial estates, where the visitor is stunned to travel down long dusty dirt roads "to the middle of nowhere," and to find modern shoe and textile factories, with the latest Italian and Swiss machinery, staffed by a small number of industrial workers, with managers and engineers there to oversee the machinery and attend to orders from computer rooms linked to the outside world by fiber-optic cables. The workers typically have an air of quiet resignation, and their monthly minimum-wage salaries[2] are supplemented by food baskets containing packages of rice, beans, and other basic necessities. Moreover, the Northeast is not a developmental success in the low-technology industries: its export levels are extremely low, its penetration of national markets in Brazil is fragile and generally limited to low-quality products, and overall developmental indicators, such as the ratio of regional wages to national wages, have not progressed much in forty years of intense policy-led effort to develop the region.

Why has the Northeast failed where these areas of Jalisco have succeeded? Failure and success, we shall argue in this chapter, are closely related to different incentives. Success is based on the incentives that

[1] A word on the scale of the comparison reported in this chapter: we use the term "Northeast" to refer to case studies, which are more precisely about a set of cities and towns in that region, or industrial clusters in cities, including in and around Fortaleza, Recife, Salvador, and Imperatriz. Because, as we argue, failure of the clusters is widespread, we use the term "Northeast" to generalize across these case studies. In Mexico, we use T&T as examples of a different developmental dynamic which is also found, with some variation, across a wider region including parts of the states of Jalisco, Michoacán, and Guanajuato. Thus, the comparison concerns industrial localities set in wider regional contexts in both countries.
[2] Equivalent in May 2003 to US$80, for forty-four hours per week.

flow from generalized confidence in the economic process; appropriate distributional arrangements; and ongoing collective problem-solving and conflict resolution. These differences in incentives are reflected in such areas as entrepreneurship, co-ordination with other firms and actors, and investments in physical capital and skills.

Why are the incentives so different from Jalisco to the Northeast? The three types of incentive are defined by the interaction between what we shall call "societal and communitarian forces" in each region. Think of community as bonding among people with strongly similar backgrounds and interests and society as forms of bridging between those groups; both can be institutionalized in rules, laws, and shared conventions, but societal bridging is more often formal than communitarian bonding.[3] Well-studied low-tech success stories, such as the "Third Italy," are often said to be successful because of the communitarian structures that make collective co-ordination possible. Tight social networks, anchored by mutual trust and reputation effects, facilitate the information flows that underpin an elaborate, highly flexible, and innovative production system. High commitment of individuals to firms and of firms to the region enables skills to be transmitted via socialization in regional networks (Becattini 1987). At the same time, in another part of Italy, economic stagnation is often ascribed to communitarian structures of another sort (Gambetta 1988). The Mezzogiorno is a prisoner of clan-like communities who make normal free markets impossible. Interestingly, this kind of difference is found in debates about sources of success in many other places. Silicon Valley is described by some analysts as a tightly-woven community, whose economic performance depends on informal networks of entrepreneurs and technologists (Saxenian 1994). But by others, it is described as a set of overlapping markets, with research universities, government financing, venture capitalist, law firms, stock options, high labor mobility, and brutal competition (Cohen and Fields 1999). Taiwan's success is sometimes said to stem from family- and community-based systems of co-ordination, and is sometimes criticized for being a form of "crony capitalism"; others claim simply that Taiwan followed the rules of export markets, just as Silicon Valley pushed market logic to its limits in the United States (Wade 1990). Thus, in these stories of economic development, some claim that the right institutions are communitarian, in the sense of strong bonding within social groups that have positive effects on the economic system. Others, however, claim that it is the force of commercial culture, of widely

---

[3] These definitions bear an intentional similarity to those used by Putnam (2000), though in our view the sources of each can be different than those claimed by Putnam. Our position is described in greater detail in Storper (2005).

accepted principles of competition, which are the source of success; it is society, not community, that generates development.

In contrast to both sides in this debate, we argue that *both* society and community are necessary, and it is their interactions that determine whether and to what extent the appropriate incentives to economic development are generated. What matters are the relative strengths of society and community, their institutional forms, and how they interact in shaping incentives, which, in turn, enable the long-term process of economic growth.

The crux of our argument is shown in columns (4) and (5) of table 14.1. Each of the features of successful development depends on both community-based and societal-based relationships between persons, and on the interactions between these two forms of co-ordination. This interaction, when successful, is one of mutual checks and balances; when unsuccessful, the checks and balances are not sufficiently present, allowing the potentially negative effects of society or community alone to make themselves felt.

When the conditions do not exist for society–community interactions of mutual checks and balances then other less-favorable outcomes for economic development are likely to be the result. In the case of North-eastern Brazil, we shall see that relatively strong, but distorted, forms of societal rules, combined with weak communities, generate insufficient public goods; low confidence and high transaction costs; and a distribution of wealth that reduces motivation for entrepreneurship. In Tonalá and Tlaquepaque, by contrast, society and community interact to sustain confidence, shape distributional arrangements, and foster problem-solving such that innovation is ongoing and sustains local development.

14.2 The perverse effects of a "civilizing process": society against community in the Brazilian Northeast

The Brazilian Northeast remains the country's unsolved "regional question," a source of worry for decades.[4] The conventional diagnosis of Brazil's "Northeast problem" is that it stems from the region's imperfect integration into the national society. This is said to be the consequence of a social structure molded by a colonial plantation economy and slavery, leading to a post-colonial society split between a landowning economic

---

[4] We provide some basic indicators of economic development for the two areas in the appendix (tables 14A.1–14A.2, pp. 336, 337). The Northeast is a much bigger region than Jalisco and Michoacán (40 million versus 10 million people, representing, respectively, about 25 percent of Brazil's population and 12 percent of Mexico's). However, both are regions with big cities.

Table 14.1 *The economic effects of society–community interactions*

Incentives necessary to long-term development (1)	Principal microeconomic effects of each incentive (2)	Operational institutions: behavior, routines, regularities (3)	Role of communitarian "bonding" in bringing about each incentive (4)	Role of societal "bridging" in bringing about each incentive (5)
Generalized confidence↓	– Reduces transactions costs – Reduces moral hazards – Raises expectations and efforts →	– Encourages Schumpeterian entrepreneur – Improves co-ordination of firm–firm transactions – Raises investment levels ↓→	– Reputation effects, shared conventions, identities (depends on process of group formation) – Overcome certain information problems in low-cost way (but can encourage rent-seeking) →	– Overarching rules promote transparency and limit rent-seeking, help to complete markets ←
Effective and acceptable distributional arrangements↓↓	– Precedent encourages ongoing "sacrifices" in face of shocks (Rodrik 1999) – Overcomes disincentive to participate and make effort (Aghion 1998) ↓↓→	– Raises investments in skills – Raises work and entrepreneurial participation rates – Improves willingness to pay taxes (investment) ↓↓ →	– Voice and loyalty – Being in the same boat enhances acceptability – Membership may involve real forms of intra-group redistribution →	– Counteracts corporatism and distributional hold-ups – Standards of fairness and efficiency constrain group demands – Intergroup mobility (exit), disciplines groups ↓
Successful ongoing conflict resolution	– Participation of groups is enhanced – Minimize rent-seeking from corporatism →	– Better adjustment of rules governing entrepreneurship and labor markets – Intelligent ideas more likely to receive support as public policy – Coalitions can form, avoiding chaotic instability →	– Secure groups encourage coalition formation: voice that gets heard (but risk of principal–agent problems) →	– Limits to group power encourage compromise – Exit options, defection, make other coalitions possible, hence dynamically limit principal–agent problems ←

Note: →↓: cumulative and/or one-way causal effect.
→←: two-way interactions and feedbacks.
Source: The authors.

and political elite and poor rural impoverished landless masses afflicted by recurrent droughts. An integrated regional development program for the Northeast, authored in the mid-1950s under the aegis of the Working Group for the Development of the Northeast (GTDN) and later the Superintendency for the Development of the Northeast (SUDENE), placed emphasis on developing its social and economic infrastructure. This was to be accompanied by massive investments to link the Northeast physically and economically to the rest of Brazil, and to install modern social institutions, a market culture, and modern industries. The latter were to be implanted through public investments (nationalized industries and subsidies), on the basis of a strategy of generating backward and forward linkages and hence generating self-propelling development. The development of the Northeast was to accomplish a "civilizing process," extended from the core of Brazilian society and territory, to its periphery (Brazil, 2003; Oliveira, 2003).

Certain forms of economic progress do exist in the region, largely confined to large-scale factories of nationalized firms and to the development of a service economy in the coastal cities. There have also been significant improvements in some indicators, including income, health, and literacy. Nonetheless, in relative terms, the Northeast is just as far behind the rest of Brazil as it was at the beginning of the development push more than forty years ago. Wages in manufacturing are only 55 percent of the Brazilian average, with output per worker at only 48 percent of the Brazilian average. Manufacturing employment has stagnated at less than 16 percent of the Brazilian total, in spite of massive incentives (Lavinas, Garcia, and Barros 2000). The Northeast's share of GDP has fluctuated between 12 and 16 percent of the Brazilian total since the 1970s, and its share of Brazilian exports declined from 20 percent in 1975 to 7 percent in 2001. Overall household income levels and income *per capita* are around half the Brazilian average.[5]

In contrast to the dominant views, our conclusion from a three-year study of the region's low-technology industries is that *economic integration and a certain form of modernization have succeeded*. It is development that has failed. This is because integration has been achieved at the price of importing many of the worst characteristics of Brazilian economic culture

---

[5] Lavinas, *et al.* (1996), in an analysis of national accounts, show that there is a net export of capital from the Northeast to other regions of Brazil, by Brazilian firms implanted in the Northeast. This is yet another sign of the underlying lack of attractiveness of the Northeast: the fact that firms do not practice ongoing capital-augmenting investments, but rather use the region as a source of short-term profits, which are not reinvested in the Northeast.

Table 14.2 *Interactions between community and society*

Factors	Institutionalized behavior	Communitarian forces	Societal forces
Lack of generalized confidence: predation and uncertainty	– Poor interfirm co-ordination – Large-firm dominance disconnected from local networks – Predatory behavior in markets – Regional, low-cost, low-quality markets	– Weak local institutions for promoting generalized trust, confidence in transactions – Highly personalized, nepotistic relationships – High local clientelism – Widespread corruption – Instability in relationships	– National policies and institutions that promote oligopolies – Powerful actors diminish local margin of maneuver – High national clientelism reinforces power of oligopolists – Macroeconomic instability favors bigger firms
Unsatisfactory distributional trade-offs/ arrangements: low effort, misguided effort	– Local entrepreneurs have low ambitions: the playing field is seen as being highly uneven: regional rivalries within Brazil plus no ambition to export – Nonelite cannot get into entrepreneurship because of inequality level – Workers have effort disincentive due to inequality	– Local entrepreneurs seek rents whenever possible: markets incomplete, skewed – Rent "niches" are left overs from dominant national firms – Labor unable to press for upgrading, inclusion, training (extreme inequality)	– Dominant groups seek rents, institutionalize them, especially extremely unequal access to credit and subsidies – Rents reinforce protectionist, inward orientation – Labor dominated by corporatist representation – High level of informality and non-representation – State institutions not strongly organized on the ground

| Ongoing conflict and lack of problem-solving | – Inability to form sustainable developmental coalitions in the region
 – Conflict dominates in face of economic shocks, for all classes: sense that someone else is not sacrificing
 – Firm–worker conflictive relations
 – Conflictive sectional (interregional) relations
 – Low-quality, get-in/get-out strategies because of uncertainty, fear of predation, politics
 – Difficult to get good ideas implemented, accepted, even though their value is widely recognized
 – Extremely conflictive society | – Low sectoral co-operation: networks are fragile, unstable
 – Low firm–worker problem-solving: conflictive and formalistic relations
 – Conflict leads to short-term strategies, unstable and shifting relations between groups
 – Many have good ideas, but nobody builds coalitions to push them
 – Inequality too high at the local level as well | – Policy is interventionist
 – But policy not transparent or stable
 – Depends on power
 – Policies work one at a time, lack medium-term consistency and predictability
 – Winners take all in policy competition, until next round
 – But political alliances shift, so even elite coalitions do not have ability to push strategies in sustainable way
 – No tradition of consensus-seeking |

Source: The authors.

in general – lack of generalized confidence, unworkable distributional arrangements, and ongoing conflict and unstable coalitions. These strong societal features interact with elite clannish behavior, and they block the creation of incentives that would be necessary to generate a vibrant indigenous entrepreneurial economy. Moreover, this grafting of the national economic culture onto the Northeast generates few of the advantages of bigness, concentration, and state-sponsored capitalism that have benefited Southeastern Brazil.

The overwhelming majority of local firms in these Northeast sectors make products that target the lower reaches of their markets, with only occasional forays into medium- and high-quality products.[6] Some firms act as mass production subcontractors or are assembly plants owned by medium-to-large-sized Brazilian firms, mostly from the Southern and Southeast regions. The products of the latter are destined for national markets; by contrast, the products of Northeast firms are destined principally for regional markets; neither category has any significant presence in markets outside of Brazil, with the exception of shoe-producing firms who work for foreign buyers. Though entrepreneurs and managers regularly attend trade shows in the United States and Europe, and a significant percentage are well aware of new product concepts and production technologies, for the most part, their ambitions are limited. Table 14.2 shows the interactions between the community and society that account for this lack of local ambition and the limited local ambitions of national firms, which, in turn, limit developmental success in the Northeast.

14.3   Lack of confidence

There is nothing automatic or universal in the ways that entrepreneurship is carried out; economies vary widely in their collective entrepreneurial levels and habits (Kirzner 1973; Casson 1995). Brazil has a powerful large-firm presence in many sectors, which are "piloted" by the big firms, who exercise critical market power, limit access to distribution, and have

---

[6] We performed site visits, interviews with key actors in both firms and government, in sectors that are amenable to this type of upgrading via learning, but which start out with low barriers to entry and low technological requirements. These sectors include glassware and ceramics, shoes, textiles, food products made with tropical fruits, wood furniture, and certain services (Lavinas and Storper 1999–2002). We conducted additional interviews in the machinery sector and in certain service industry firms, especially courier services. We also interviewed local and state economic development officials and university-based incubators and conducted detailed statistical analyses at the IPEA, in Rio de Janeiro.

technological mastery.[7] These firms also have political access, especially to public credit through the Banco Nacional de Desenvolvimento Economico e Social (BNDES – National Bank for Economic and Social Development), and thus have dramatically more staying power than do small firms, especially in the face of Brazil's endemic macroeconomic instability and the big firms' propensity to exploit rents from public policies that consistently tilt in their favor. Consistent with this, many Brazilian sectors are highly oligopolistic, well beyond what one would expect in a domestic economy of its size. And, unlike South Korea – another "big-firm" developing economy (Amsden 1992) – Brazil exports a very small percentage of its output,[8] but its big firms do earn significant rents in domestic markets.

In spite of this big-firm orientation, Brazil is also a highly entrepreneurial economy; its overall rate of entrepreneurial activity per 100 adults is ranked fifth in the world, just ahead of Ireland and the United States (Reynolds *et al.* 2001). In the West, South, and Southeast of Brazil, there were many examples of such entrepreneurship leading to long-term growth, from small to medium and even large size, especially during the period of rapid development in the 1950s and 1960s; however, Northeastern start-ups were not part of this process, and today they do not follow this growth pattern. Part of this has to do with the phenomenon of being a "latecomer" region in a country with more highly developed regions and firms and of having missed out on the great developmental jump of earlier decades. Northeast firms occasionally, though not frequently, become suppliers to big national firms from other regions. Although this may provide them markets, it does so within the established structure of oligopolistic markets, and so places local firms in positions of submission to large national firms, and it discourages them from striking out on their own. An analogy may help in understanding this. The United

---

[7] Indeed, large-firm presence in Brazil is much greater than in Mexico, and average manufacturing productivity much higher. Part of this has to do with the bigger internal market in Brazil, but this makes it all the more striking that there is little observable benefit to the Brazilian export sector. It also illustrates that the barriers to entry for Northeastern firms are high, because of the way that economies of scale have been developed in many Brazilian manufacturing sectors (see Mulder, Montout, and Lopes (2002) for a Brazil–Mexico comparison).

[8] The dominant view of this in Brazil is that protectionism on the part of the European Union and the United States is to blame for Brazil's poor export performance. It is incontestable that Brazil's main export strength, agricultural commodities, would grow considerably were there not such agricultural protection in Europe and the United States. However, this would do little for Brazil's weakness in manufactured exports, and cannot explain why Brazil has done so much more poorly over the last fifty years than other countries, especially the highly-performing Asian economies (HPAEs), which started out in the same position as Brazil. For a detailed comparative analysis, see Amsden (2001).

States does not do well in many of the industries in which Italy does; it is difficult to imagine US firms engaging in the small-scale, high-quality furniture production which abounds in Italy, because US national supply structures are dominated by large firms. Small firms, when successful, are likely to be bought up in the United States, with their products commercialized on a vast scale and subjected to mass marketing. This is not a problem if there are other areas in which regions can excel. But it is a problem for a region such as the Northeast, because it starts out in a dependent position and does not have the means to enter as an innovator in other markets.

Northeastern SMEs respond to this situation by avoiding competition with the big national firms, but in the wrong way. They orient themselves toward regional markets for the low-quality products that do not interest the national firms. They exploit limited incomplete areas in markets through a calculated risk strategy, but they do not benefit from sufficient optimism or confidence in the economic process to undertake true, market-reshaping innovative entrepreneurship (Knight 1921; Kirzner 1973; Schumpeter 1991; Casson 1995).

Still, these problems cannot be attributed exclusively to the predatory large-firm behavior that is encouraged by these societal forces. The communitarian forces that might, under some circumstances, be able to generate entrepreneurial capabilities capable of innovating in the face of these market structures, do not exist. Some would counter that, in any case, the communitarian forces that support entrepreneurialism never constitute serious competition for oligopolistic firms, but examples such as the post-war experience of the "Third Italy" prove them wrong.[9]

There is thus a clear existence of a problem of society versus community: regional entrepreneurs have low ambitions, not because they lack creativity or knowledge, but because of rational fear of the risks that come from the national (societal) environment, and this lack of generalized confidence is not counterbalanced by the alternative of solid communities that could facilitate co-ordination.

Distributional arrangements: hierarchy and rent extraction

The situation described above is reinforced through distributional arrangements – big and southern versus small and northern firms, and successful rent-seeking by the former group to the exclusion of the

---

[9] In the face of highly oligopolistic firms in Lombardy and the Piedmont, which were favored by the national government in Rome, the firms in the "Third Italy" managed, through local collective action underpinned by generalized confidence, to carve out viable market niches for themselves and came to dominate Italy (and many export markets).

latter. Distributional arrangements also concern the distribution of wage income. The literature on success stories makes a great deal out of the "good" work habits found in those places, as opposed to the bad or "disorganized" labor markets in other places. In the countries that have done well in the kinds of industries we considered in the Northeast, many approaches to shaping labor markets are in evidence. In Italy, the entrepreneur is often a former worker, the family unit remains important in many industries, workers often have strong durable ties to local communities, and local and regional states, in turn, play an important role in labor training (Becattini 1987). In Denmark, family is not especially important, but local ties are, with extensive co-operation in the locality, in the context of a highly regulated national labor market that shapes relations on the shop floor, in the direction of equality and mutual respect (Lorenzon 1999; Lundvall 2002). In Taiwan and Hong Kong, families often own and operate firms, with multi-generational extended families providing the firm's labor and capital resources, to some extent outside normal market circuits (Numazaki 1991).

Brazil does not closely resemble any of these examples, though there are certain features of the Brazilian labor-supply process that have counterparts elsewhere. For example, Brazil has a history of large-scale unionism (like Italy and Korea), a large unionized public sector, and a tradition of corporatism in its labor market (as in France) (Marsden 1999). Labor relations have been fraught with conflict, as in South Korea. Brazil, and especially Northeastern Brazil, however, stands in contrast to all these examples in the key ways its institutional framework generates labor supplies and incentives to work, train, and learn. Most important, in our view, is that South Korea, Taiwan, and Hong Kong all have much lower levels of inequality than does Brazil; in the first two cases, because there were significant land reforms at the beginning of the current industrialization process. Brazil, by contrast, has industrialized against the background of an enormous rural population lacking access to land resources, and hence to the possibility of a satisfactory rural life, along with rapid urbanization and industrialization, and extensive modernization of the agricultural sector. Income inequality is among the highest in the industrialized world. Education is highly uneven, with significant parts of the population lacking literacy or other nonmanual skills or having insufficient levels of them. Moreover, although these are general characteristics of the national labor market and income structure, they are more severe in the Northeast. Recent theories hold that both labor and entrepreneurial effort and participation can be subject to a strong disincentive effect above certain degrees of inequality (Aghion 1998). This is because the probability of getting access to such essential resources as a decent wage or capital (respectively) is extremely low when inequality is extremely high and positionality effects are high.

Brazil also has a strongly formalistic system of labor relations, anchored in huge union federations,[10] modeled after certain European countries; the state is the key intermediating actor between these "social partners" (Marsden 1999). Given the extreme inequalities of Brazil, however, the most frequent outcome of this situation has not been sustained dialog between worker and employer organizations, but a distant and conflict-ridden relationship and a high degree of state paternalism. The paternalistic labor relations system actually interferes with building the communities through which independence and upgrading might one day become possible. Labor is thus largely unable to serve as a force for constructing any putative developmental coalition. Aggravating this situation is the fact that even these rather dismal formal relations apply to only 40 percent of the work force, so that for the other 60 percent straightforward power relations – highly asymmetrical because of a very high rate of informality and extreme abundance of the unskilled – are the rule (Oliveira 2003).

Though schooling has improved somewhat[11] – with higher rates of school attendance and growing literacy – the average poor person in the Northeast has little or no chance of being able to use much more than very modest improvements in formal education, because the skill complementarities they would require are absent in the region (Easterly 2002, chapter 4). The middle classes are, of course, where the strongest incentives for knowledge accumulation and use are present; and yet, as we have seen, these middle-class entrepreneurs, even when they are skilled and knowledgeable, are frustrated at every turn in the road.

Absence of coalitions to solve problems and generate confidence

The various problems described above interact and have cumulative effects, one of which is to limit the formation of coalitions that would boost the developmental potential of the Northeast. The society–community interactions that are present in the Northeast conspire to generate conflict, unstable and shifting coalitions, and hence a lack of capacity for long-term upgrading of industrial performance.

---

[10] As in certain European countries, the Brazilian union federations control big pension funds and administer them, and they pay for big professional staffs via this activity. They are also the privileged negotiators of changes in labor law with their respective legislatures. In some countries, they are constitutionally recognized in these roles (Marsden 1999).

[11] Average years of schooling for Brazil as a whole is six, as compared to four for the Northeast.

The vicious circle of low skills, low wages, high mobility, low trust of workers, and a huge skills gap between management and workers is not just injurious to the social mobility of the less-skilled; it has the wider effect of discouraging firms from training their workers or trying to involve them in a medium-term strategy of quality improvement. Labor is thus not present as an institutional agent in any putative developmental coalitions.

One of the principal areas in which this failure to have problem-solving coalitions is reflected is in the poor export performance of the Brazilian economy. Enhancing export performance obviously depends, in part, on relatively straightforward technical measures: tariff policies; bureaucratic efficiency in import and export regulation, inspection, and transportation; clear and enforceable contracting and payment procedures, aligned with international norms, and so on. Serving external markets, however, also requires co-ordination with those markets, which, in turn, depends on the development of detailed networks of human relations: between domestic producers, trading companies, and external buyers. It requires building up a reputation for on-time production of goods that conform to the prices and qualities desired, and that the co-ordination between producer, transporter, and buyer link the producer successfully to the outside. It requires absorption of information from buyers and from external market "environments" about the evolution of products and confidence on the part of external buyers that producers will be able to keep up with this evolution. Generalized confidence is essential to all these transactional processes. A number of our interviews were disturbing in relation to these criteria. While only a minority of the entrepreneurs interviewed were unaware of these requirements, many more evidenced an attitude of resignation with respect to their capacity to meet them or even with respect to the possibility of developing such capabilities. To transform such an environment would require collective action, but there is a lack of effective developmentalist coalitions that would be capable of doing so.

This is merely a particularly extreme expression of the institutional dynamics of the Brazilian economy as a whole, albeit with certain regional specificities. In this vein, Schmitz (1999) studied industries in the Sinos Valley in the southern state of Rio Grande do Sul, one of the areas of Brazil that has been most successful in industrializing based on SMEs. He showed that developmental coalition-building failed there because firms are reluctant to engage in any kind of horizontal co-operation. Hence, attempts at upgrading production systems through organizations designed to promote more effective marketing through quality standards, respect of delivery times, and consistent use of design information, have all failed.

Things are not like this in all low-tech regions in developing countries, however; the examples of our two clusters in the state of Jalisco, Mexico, provide a counterexample to the Brazilian Northeast, in virtually all respects.

14.4   Two innovative small-firm clusters in Jalisco, Mexico

Like Brazil, Mexico engaged in a significant effort to integrate itself into the global economy during the 1990s. Unlike Brazil, which remained relatively closed, the Mexican economy saw rapid growth in the value of its exports (30 percent of GNP as against 6 percent for Brazil), exporting almost three times as much as Brazil, whose economy is larger than Mexico's. Of course, a principal reason for this development is Mexico's proximity to the United States, its principal trading partner, reinforced via its entry into the North American Free Trade Agreement (NAFTA). But the effects of globalization are wider and deeper than this point might suggest, and some of them – such as the case we are about to analyze – predate NAFTA by many decades.

The region of Guadalajara, including parts of the state of Jalisco and the neighboring state of Michoacán, is home to numerous vibrant clusters of SMEs dedicated to a wide range of goods. In the Mexican economic literature, Guadalajara is known as "the big city of small firms" (Arias 1985). From the colonial period to the present, the entrepreneurship of the region has been reflected in a much greater presence of SMEs than the national average. In the metropolitan area and its hinterlands can be found clusters of SMEs in jewelry, accounting for 60 percent of national output in gold jewelry, and a district specializing in women's shoes, which is second in Mexico only to the much-studied cluster in Léon in the state of Guanajuato. Guadalajara has twice as many firms as the Monterrey metropolitan area. Labor-force statistics show that Jalisco has a far higher proportion of workers without wage income – i.e. workers in family firms – than does the nation as a whole (table 14.3). Tonalá and Tlaquepaque (hereafter, T&T) are of particular interest because of their concentrations of firms engaged in production of low-technology goods – housewares, furniture, ceramic tiles and other artisanal building materials, and glassware – with a very high proportion of output destined for export markets. They are thus comparable to the activities we examined in the Brazilian Northeast.

T&T are successful because each has strong incentives for production and accumulation, which are outcomes of the interactions between community and society, as summarized in table 14.4.

Table 14.3 *Manufacturing activities in the districts*

Selected activities	Economic units[a]			Employment		
	1988	1993	1998	1988	1993	1998
Tlaquepaque						
Total manufacturing	545	979	1,858	7,224	13,961	20,107
Garment, textiles, leather	12	28	71	955	706	1,506
Wood industries and wood products	43	85	211	818	1049	1,837
Mineral nonmetallic product. (except products derived from petroleum and coal)	126	173	419	1,788	1,707	2,650
3812, metal structures including *herreria*	62	120	185	152	899	1,219
3813, metal furniture	8	14	39	62	252	411
Total selected sectors	251	420	925	3,775	4,613	7,623
Tonalá						
Total manufacturing	275	502	2,475	1,428	2,759	10,814
Garment, textiles, leather		21	100		393	801
Wood industries and wood products	10	31	236	29	114	1,204
Mineral nonmetallic product (except products derived from petroleum and coal)	139	151	1,264	750	1,064	5,081
3812, metal structures including *herreria*	25	67	174	59	172	442
3813, metal furniture		6	83		66	500
Total selected sectors	174	276	1,857	838	1,809	8,028
Tonalá and Tlaquepaque						
Selected sectors	425	696	2,782	4,613	6,422	15,651

Detail on production activities in **Tonalá**
Tonalá Census summary[b]

Product	Workshops	%
Clay and ceramics	812	66.9
Stonework	17	1.4
Plaster	93	7.7
Bronze, copper, and brass	32	2.6
Papier mache	85	7.0
Blown glass	43	3.5
Furniture and wood products	42	3.5
Tinware	18	1.5
Ironworks	37	3.1
Various	34	2.8
Total	**1,213**	**100**

Source: INEGI (1988, 1993, 1999).
Notes: [a]The census counts both formal and informal sector firms; however, it is very likely that informal firms are undercounted, because many do not have an official address or are in residential quarters with no indication of being a business.
[b]Casa de Artesanos de Tonalá, *Census of Artisans 1997.*

Table 14.4 Production and accumulation incentives

Incentives	Institutionalized behaviors	Communitarian forces	Societal forces
Socially constructed, localized confidence	– 1200 SMEs in Tonalá. 800–1000 in Tlaquepaque = strong entrepreneurship. Schumpeterian in Tlaquepaque (innovation); Kirznerian in Tonalá (market niches). – Excellent interfirm co-ordination: family firms are subcontractors to medium-sized firms and international marketing agents (like Italian *imprenditori*) – Co-operation helps intermediators promote districts' products to outside, tempers corruption and moral hazards inside – Reputation effects are central – There are limits on predatory, price-exploitative behavior on part of distributors/intermediators – International markets: incentive to keep trying, but also to adapt, refine, innovate products based on local culture/skills/look (the "scarce" asset)	– Entrepreneurs know, identify with each other. – Informal associationalism within district reduces transaction costs and moral hazards – Informal co-operation between producers and intermediators – Most local intermediators are in it for the long run, because they see themselves as part of the community, diminishing attempts to exploit producers – Production-sharing is common – "What produces growth is not the state, but pre-Hispanic culture and "mestizo sincretism" (local bonds prevail)	– Long-time presence of foreigners who link local producers to world markets: reinforces confidence – Local actors in concert with locally involved foreigners: circumvent national oligopolies, avoid corruption – National distributors/intermediators create price pressures on producers – Macroeconomic instability somewhat offset by access to foreign markets, and by commitment to quality – Imported business practices help stabilize the situation, providing incentives to do so – International markets create price and quality incentives and possibility of expansion

Distributional arrangements: hierarchical, but stable, and considered fair: incentives to keep trying	– Local entrepreneurship encouraged and transmitted from owners/artisans to workers and within families – Incentives to work hard because possibility of long-term survival or even "getting ahead" – Even indigenous people have a chance: some village production has become stable and remunerative	– Medium-sized firms (50–60 employees) use family–community system to regulate labor supply and distributional rules – Other firms specialize in consolidation and act as "cultural translators:" define orders, finance, and organize subcontracting – Blurred distinction between workers, entrepreneurs, and families in transmission of skills, bonding to avoid moral hazards – Foreigners who appreciate local culture actually reinforce local bonding	– Local groups have access to local political power, but foreigners have access to markets and information (sometimes they are mixed: there are many couple-based firms where one is Mexican the other non-Mexican) – Thus, there are local–global intermediaries – Pressure from world market is real: foreign buyers seek cheaper imitations in other countries
Dynamic problem-solving, adjustments, responses to crisis, institutional innovations	– Nexus of foreign community, cosmopolitan buyers, and shippers, powerful family–ethnic culture, artisans – Locals have a stake in problem-solving, there is no winner-take-all solution	– Relatively non-antagonistic relations because many entrepreneurs are former workers/artisans – Many different voices, but overlapping networks for expressing voice – Local informal solutions arise in order to circumvent national politics, rules, and bureaucracy, and to temper local corruption, and informal relations are stronger than formal	– Intermediaries have to press for local solutions in terms of price and quality: reality check is strong, but so is creativity to respond. – Coalitions form which do not depend directly on national politics or political brokers – Local formal associations are sometimes captured by national political parties and/or become corrupt

Source: The authors.

Confidence

In the small-firm clusters in T&T, there is strong localized confidence in the sustainability of the local economies. This is not to say that there are not great hardships, including economic cycles, competitive pressures inside and from outside the districts, and even failures of local co-operation, cheating, and corruption. All in all, however, there is a strong sense – supported by experience – that the clusters have staying power and offer conditions under which skill and hard work can pay off. The evidence for such confidence is strong. As the statistics show, T&T have enjoyed steady growth in the number of firms, employment, and exports. In qualitative terms, interviews demonstrate the importance of reputation effects in limiting, though not eliminating, predatory behavior – especially the undercutting of local prices by cheating on product quality or working conditions so much that competitors cannot survive.

One important reason why confidence is renewed is the connection to international markets; they provide a long-term demand level that local or national markets could never sustain: 75 percent of blown glass and 60 percent of ceramics production were exported in the late 1980s (Mercado *et al.* 1989), and this dynamism persists today. Confidence comes from the fact that the districts survived several rounds of being challenged by competitors, and of reinventing themselves to serve foreign markets through better or updated products.

This long-term staying power is a result of ongoing adaptation, the incorporation of national and international artistic influences, and the inclusion of new Mexican and foreign agents into the system. Mexican popular art was saved from oblivion in the 1920s when a major international exhibition of the Mestizo native and colonial art of Mexico was held in Mexico City and Los Angeles, in concert with the publication of *Las Artes Populares en México*, prepared and edited by the well-known Jaliscan muralist, Dr. Atl, a book that created an artistic "canon" for indigenous crafts and established their identity as works of art (Monsivais 1996). T&T capitalized on this revived recognition of the artistic value of their products. Again in the 1950s, they were given a new boost when Jorge Wilmont from Monterrey and Ken Edwards from the United States (Romo Torres 1990) were both attracted by the rich pictoral motifs in local pottery and linked them to foreign buyers. From there, Odilon Avalos from Puebla incorporated blown glass and new techniques of coloring the glass (Álvarez 1969) improved later by Camaraza; Sergio Bustamante drew on the Guadalajara gold jewelry traditions to bring jewelry and paper maché to the districts; new rustic *hacienda* furniture styles arrived via the Alfaro family from Nogales; and Luna and Figueroa subsequently grafted new design forms for urban residents in Mexico and abroad (*Adobe Diseño*); ironwork was later added to the mix (Mercado-Célis 2003), among other numerous contributions. Thus, each time demand shifts (fashions, foreign buyers, chain stores redefine their lines), it is worrisome, but the challenge has been met through artistic and stylistic product innovation.

This confidence is also the result of a very delicate balance between local solidarities, which act as shock absorbers when national and international forces push for change. Entrepreneurs know each other and identify with each other, both in Tonalá, where entrepreneurs have often worked together in firms, or even are members of the same or of linked families, and in Tlaquepaque, where they may emerge out of working for highly esteemed artists or may be members of the artistic community themselves. According to Mercado *et al.* (1989), who classified the workshops into three categories – family, semi-industrial, and industrial – Tonalá's family workshops are on average thirty-three years old and some go back four generations; 54 percent of workers are the owners' children, 18 percent are their wives, and 28 percent are brothers or other family members. The semi-industrialized workshops have an average age of ten years, 80 percent were founded by the current owner, and they employ an average of six workers. In this category one-third of the workers are family members. The industrial workshops average seventeen years and employ thirty-seven workers, with the largest having eighty-seven employees. Family members here work in administrative, management, and supervisory duties, and occasionally design, but not in direct production (Mercado *et al.* 1989). Family members or other workers are often assisted in establishing their own firms and then work as contractors to the workshops where they started out. This system of spin-offs and subcontractors leads to extensive local knowledge-sharing. But knowledge diffusion also comes about through common socialization, a shared culture which incorporates elements of indigenous, Mestizo and colonial aesthetics, as well as through local bridging via intermediaries, between producers and designers, artists and artisans; this is a highly structured "society of communities."

The role of marketing intermediaries is critical in maintaining the community–society balance in T&T. The intermediaries have one foot in the local community and another in the wider network of international markets, trade shows, and clientele. But these intermediaries see themselves as part of the districts. Foreigners came to T&T several decades ago. A small number of people, notably from the United States and Canada, were attracted to the area by its cultural and artistic traditions. They became involved in working with local producers, helping them to reach North American and later, European markets. Later on, this became a two-way street, where they brought back knowledge of markets that permitted local producers to adapt their products to be more suitable to those markets. Over time, this behavior developed beyond a few maverick personalities into a stratum of intermediaries, who are very much analogous to the *imprenditori* found throughout the "Third Italy." Nowadays, they generate business for local producers, putting together the firms necessary to meet a particular order; some represent the districts in international trade shows, while others simply wait for the buyers to come to Jalisco, relying on established reputations. In any case, they bring the discipline of foreign prices and the need to meet foreign quality standards and timing (Mercado-Célis 2003). All is not rosy: there are occasional intermediaries who attempt to exploit the locals; interestingly, most of them are Mexican rather than foreign, seeing the districts as just a way to make products as cheaply as possible. Here, again, there is a radical difference between our Mexican and Brazilian cases: in Brazil, intermediaries are almost always seen as opportunistic rent-earners who raise prices and lower the efficiency of markets.

Ethnic identities are also mobilized as community bonds. Indigenous communities have strong participation in certain regional production chains.[12] There are many towns in Jalisco and Michoacán populated by very small firms, who act as subcontractors to larger firms in the Guadalajara metropolitan area. Although there are latent ethnic tensions, the arrangements are relatively stable, because they are collective in nature. Michoacán is full of towns specialized in distinctive crafts, the best-known of which is Santa Clara de Cobre, a town devoted to the production of copper products. These local communities are, in turn, linked to world markets through the markets of T&T.

Hierarchical, but stable, distributional arrangements

One of the most impressive aspects of T&T is their "buzz," the energy that one senses in being there, from the sheer amount and pace of work being done, from the conversations and exchanges occurring inside firms, on the streets, in front of juice and coffee stands, and on street corners. Yet the buzz does not feel like pressure or exploitation, because the people involved have complex connections, through family, community, and previous work situations.

---

[12] For an analysis of different types of production chains, see Polenske (2001).

This stands in marked contrast to the feeling one gets in so many places we visited in the Northeast of Brazil, which is of slowness and routine, even in the large factories where high output levels are expected of the wage workers. In Mexico, the level of entrepreneurship – in production and marketing – is high because there are reliable long-term payoffs to creating firms. In part, this has to do with the internal and external distributional arrangements of the districts. Internally, as already noted, many firms employ family members or people they know through community or family relationships. This creates a certain flexibility in remuneration, so that when times are good, compensation is made for the sacrifices that occur when times are bad. In addition, family-based firms lower their costs through nonwaged labor. At the same time, this gives individuals possibilities of long-term wealth accumulation that would not be possible were they merely wage laborers. These distributional arrangements are also interethnic to some extent; as noted above, subcontracting extends from districts in Jalisco to certain villages in Michoacán and elsewhere, which are essentially populated by indigenous peoples. This gives them an economic base, which, however subject to the harsh realities of fluctuating markets, is something that they rely on for their independence – a big incentive to keep at it. Societal forces also play a role in the achievement of this delicate distributional balance. Local groups have access to local political power, but foreigners have access to markets: the dialog between the two groups is key to achieving the mix of price–efficiency, quality–efficiency, and sharing out of risks and benefits that creates incentives for everyone to keep trying.

In Tlaquepaque, there are numerous artists and artisans whose products give them international renown. The economic rewards are considerable, but not such as to make others feel they are unattainable; the incentive effect is therefore quite strong. In Tonalá, there are cases of firms growing to have relatively large production runs, mostly by supplying large foreign chains, such as The Pottery Barn or Pier One Imports. Once again, this is a contrast between our Mexican and Brazilian cases: in the Northeast, there is widespread fatalism about the possibility of serving international buyers, even in the shoe industry where an international clientele already exists, because it is taken for granted that Brazilian firms will soon lose out to the Chinese.

Problem-solving and adjustment

Problem-solving is principally informal and "distributed" in nature; there are few formal organizations of local government and producers, and those that have been attempted have more than often failed. For example, the *Instituto de la Artesanía Jalisciense* is a public agency for promoting Jalisco crafts, but in practice it has little role to play in the district. The *Casa de la Artesanía de Jalisco*, a marketing branch of the Instituto, is a rarely visited crafts store somewhere in Guadalajara. Formal industry associations in Guadalajara have also shown weaknesses and internal conflict, notably in the case of the jewelry association, which after recurrent scandals has not been able to generate a mechanism to assure the quality and metal content – gold and silver – in their members' products. There are happy exceptions, an important one of which is the furniture association of Jalisco. After a long period of conflict, it has coalesced into the organizer of the most important furniture trade show in Mexico. But it should equally be noted that formal organizations have the disadvantage of being identifiable by, and hence, subject to the influence of dominant political parties, governments, and public bureaucracies, which generally limit their problem-solving capacities more than they enhance them. Thus, rather than taking the form of formal developmental coalitions, the problem-solving activities of the districts are characterized by discussion between different agents in the system and consequent adjustment in firms.

The key linkage in making this happen is once again the intermediaries, who bring information about markets and products to local producers and take information from local producers to wider markets. This is where the "data" on problems comes from; it is the early-warning system for local producers that problems may be coming, but it is also the early-alert system that they may be on to something good. The information gets distributed because the intermediaries are not producers themselves; they have no incentive to hoard information, but rather in most cases want to diffuse it. But even among firms there are incentives to diffuse, because of the system of production-sharing on the one hand, and on the mixed identities (artisans and owners are often former workers or family members), on the other.

The one area in which formal coalitions are successful is that of urban planning and local development. Tlaquepaque's commercial districts, in conjunction with the local authorities, have secured zoning for the integrated production and sales of crafts, art, and connected services. They have also conserved the architecture and urban amenities of a splendid colonial town, and this image is a key element in the promotion of the district and its products. The place-specific qualities of Tlaquepaque provides them with the symbolic and material infrastructure to create a strong consumer image and attract tourists eager to find high-quality, unique Mexican crafts – and willing to pay for them. Tonalá has used its urban space in a different way, more directly related to local social networks. The *tianguis* secure high-cost scarce urban space for the smallest producers and distributors through the local government. They thus effectively control who can enter the district and where they can locate, but they also prevent the disintegration of the district due to scarcity of space. The contrast to the towns we studied in Northeastern Brazil could not be more marked: workshops there are crowded either into poorly maintained urban areas with crumbling infrastructure or are in isolated, depressing industrial parks with dusty unpaved access roads and effectively no nearby services, and no integration between production, sales, and community life.

More generally, the nexus of design-oriented producers and intermediaries has been effective on a number of occasions in problem-solving. In the 1970s, when times were difficult for the districts, Bustamante[13] achieved better linkage between high-level foreign retailers and producers in Tlaquepaque, allowing the latter to raise average prices and save their businesses. His example was followed by the Preciado family[14] and by Agustín Parra[15] and Rodo Padilla,[16] among others. They concentrated on maintaining high quality, establishing recognizable personal styles, and creating an image associated with their names (a sort of trademark). They did so, in part, by participating in national and international competitions, thus entering the art world. In this way, they pushed up their market value, enabling them to earn profits well above the industry average. In so doing, they had positive spillover effects on other, less well-known, producers, who could raise their prices through the market's association of them with the place and its style. Still, there is a long way to go. Producers complain that there is insufficient institutional incorporation of design. They compare the treatment of design and designers in the Guadalajara area unfavorably to the institutional recognition

[13] Bustamante is an artist and artisan, known for his sculpture and jewelry, which are exhibited around the world. He is also the owner of a chain of galleries which sell his work in Mexico and abroad. A detailed biography and catalog of his work may be found at www.sergiobustamante.com.mx.

[14] The Preciado family is one of the most visible artisan–entrepreneur groups in Tlaquepaque. They produce a wide variety of objects, ranging from wood furniture to decorative products. They export a great deal and are present in many international shows.

[15] Agustín Parra is a painter, sculptor, *retablista* and designer of high-quality furniture and wood sculptures. He is an entrepreneur with production facilities, as well as retail shops in Tlaquepaque and Guadalajara. His work can be seen at www.agustinparra.com.mx.

[16] A specialist in ceramic figures and sculptures based on Mexican folklore, see at: www.rodopadilla.com.

of design in Italy or Catalonia; producers are said to want design without paying for it and without acknowledging it in an institutional sense.

Current challenges are numerous. Cheap imitations of Mexican-style products are fabricated in China. An American consumer can buy a Chinese-imitation *chimenea* for her patio at K-Mart for $60.00, where the real product made in Tlaquepaque will cost five times as much. There are quality differences, but there is no *appellation d'origine contrôlée* to clearly identify the real thing. High-end products are subject to fashion changes and competition from European design-oriented firms. There are ongoing, but informal, attempts to face these challenges and to compose the coalitions that could do so. A key aspect is the production and diffusion of design in the district. New generations of artisans and other agents have backgrounds as professionally trained designers; they are coming to the district and bring new ideas for production, marketing, and organization. At the current time, they have complained of a lack of accurate information on external markets and their changing fashions, and insufficient public and private support for design. All in all, problem-solving exists, but all is not well, and further attention to design upgrading is needed.

14.5   Explaining contrasts in development

Some analysts might be tempted to reduce the differences between the Brazilian and Mexican cases examined here to their different colonial pasts and the social structures inherited from them, much in the same way that some have claimed that the successes of European industrial districts are due to their accretion of social capital over the very long-run (Putnam, Leonardi, and Nanetti 1993). But the cases at hand both share histories of colonization, with the attendant creation of colonial elites and disenfranchised masses. There are important differences, in that in the Northeast slavery was pronounced and institutionalized, and a slave population was imported from Africa, whereas in Jalisco and Michoacán indigenous communities – though strongly affected by the colonial and post-colonial epochs – have survived. Still, in both, strong mestizo cultures were generated; in both, colonial structures were not so different. T&T have benefited from the revaluation of Mexican artistic traditions and from the small-firm industrial structure of the Guadalajara region, while the Northeast has suffered from the devaluation of its artistic traditions and from a long history of industrial policies in Brazil that emphasize large firms, "top-down" policies, and the neglect, if not the active destruction, of communities. Brazilian national policies and societal dynamics have not only neutralized many of the intended positive effects of regional development policy, but have actively created blockages to regional development in the Northeast. In the Mexican case, though national policies and forces have done relatively little good,[17] they have been gotten around in many ways; and Jalisco has benefited from wave after wave of innovative, enthusiastic agents from outside the region, who have had the right ideas at the right time. They have also found fertile ground with which to implant those ideas and make them grow.

It should be clear, then, that societal and communitarian forces are the results of long pasts, but also are constantly evolving; they shape the incentives to act upon current information, market possibilities, and other resources that become available. Much contemporary regional development policy takes the operational level of practices, routines, and institutions – clusters, interfirm relations, best practices, and marketing – as its direct target. Our analysis suggests that while these might be valuable benchmarking exercises, such operational aspects of economies come about only when underlying social forces generate incentives that encourage agents to make them happen. Policy that focuses only on these observable intermediate outcomes of the development process is likely to fail. The kind of policy that is likely to succeed will have not only short-term goals, but long-term structural effects on institutions, in the sense of changing expectations that underlie the co-ordination of economic agents so that different patterns of collective action can emerge.

APPENDIX   BASIC INDICATORS

[17] There have been no significant regional economic development plans for Jalisco state or the Guadalajara region. In the case of Michoacán, a development pole was installed, in the form of a large steel mill and a port (the Las Truchas Project in Lazaro Cardenas), creating an isolated development enclave typical of such, largely failed, experiments. Thus, the regions in question were much less the object of co-ordinated national development policies than was the Northeast of Brazil, with the SUDENE experiment. See footnote 10 for more information on the SUDENE regional development policy in Brazil.

Table 14A.1 *Basic indicators: Mexico, Jalisco, and Michoacán*

	Mexico			Jalisco			Michoacán		
	1980	1990	2000	1980	1990	2000	1980	1990	2000
Firms[a]	131,625	138,835	344,118	9,902	10,204	27,784	5,464	6,996	19,731
Change N of firms		5.5	147.9		3.0	172.3		28.0	182.0
Average firm size[a]	20.5	19	12.3	17.1	17.2	11.7	6.2	8	4.2
% firms less than 10 W	81.2[b]	86.3	90.1	85.1[b]	80.5	87.2[c]	93.2[b]	94.4	96.6[d]
% firms less than 100 W	93.3[a1]	96.2	98	95.7[a1]	97.3	98.5[c]	97.3[c]	99.1	99.6[f]
Per capita income (GDP/pop)	3343.5[x]	4088[e]	5371[f]		4082[e]	5305[f]		2051[e]	2947[f]
PCI as % of national PCI					99.9[g]	98.8		50.2[g]	54.9
% product exported, region						36.8%[h]			7.1%[n]
% product exported, nation		3.97%[ij]	15.71%[i]			9.8%[h1]			0.6%[n]
Exports of goods and services as % of GDP	6.9[k]	12.9%[l]	28.7%[m]						

Notes: W = Workers.

[a] Data for 1980, 1988, 1998: 1980, *XI Censo Industrial*; 1989, *X Censo Económico*; 1999, *XII Censo Económico*.

[a1] % of firms with wage workers, *XI Censo Industrial INEGI*, 1980.

[b] Fewer than twenty-five workers % of firms with wage workers: *XI Censo Industrial INEGI*, 1980

[c] Data for 1998: INEGI, *Anuario estadístico Jalisco*, edición 2000.

[d] Data for 1998: INEGI, *Anuario estadístico Michoacán*, edición 2000.

[e] GDP data for 1993; population data for 1995: GDP, INEGI, *Sistema de Cuentas Nacionales de México*; population data, *Censos de Población y Vivienda*, INEGI.

[f] GDP: INEGI, *Sistema de Cuentas Nacionales de México*; Population data: *Censos de Población y Vivienda*, INEGI.

[g] With data for 1993.

[h] State GDP/state total exports: *Source* SEIJAL with data of BANCOMEXT, at http://seprove.jalisco.gob.mx.

[h1] Total national exports/total state exports: SEIJAL with data of BANCOMEXT, at http://seprove.jalisco.gob.mx.

[i] Manufacturing exports/manufacturing total production value. Manufacturing exports SHCP, Banco de México, Secretaría de Economía e INEGI; production value: 1990: INEGI, SCNM, *Cuentas de Bienes y Servicios, 1988–1999*; Aguascalientes, Ags., Mexico, 2000. 1999–2001: INEGI, SCNM, *Cuentas de Bienes y Servicios, 1996–2001*; Aguascalientes, Ags., Mexico, 2003.

[j] The NAFTA Commision for Labor Co-operation presents 18.3% exports as % of GDP.

[k] GDP data from *World Development Report 1999/2000*; exports data from Banco de México.

[l] Data for 1994: *OECD Main Economic Indicators*, February 1996.

[m] *OECD Main Economic Indicators*, August 2002.

[n] Exports and GDP for 1999: Secretaría de Desarrollo Económico de Michoacán.

[x] GDP for 1980: *OECD Main Economic Indicators*, March 2003.

Table 14A.2 *Basic indicators: Brazil and Northeast*

	Brazil			Northeast		
	1980	1990	2000	1980	1990	2000
Firms[a]	1,088,918	1,428,368	2,238,687	107,555	140,578	288,998
Total Employment[a]	20,492,131	23,198,656	26,216,463	3,134,418	3,670,857	4,374,850
Average firm size[a]	18.8	16.2	11.7	29.1	26.1	15.1
% firms less than 10 W[a]	79.93	81.64	85.01	74.82	76.45	83.32
% firms less than 100 W[a]	97.42	97.86	98.61	95.97	96.59	98.12
Monthly average working income (in minimum wages)[a]	3.68	5.43	5.02	2.87	4.16	3.55
Monthly average salary manufacturing (in minimum wages)[a]	3.96	5.36	4.79	2.77	3.3	2.9
Per capita income (GDP/pop)[b]	3,236	3,116	3,400[c]	1,527	1,744	2,038[c]
PCI as % of national PCI					99.9[b]	98.8
% product exported, region						36.8%[c]
National GDP (billion US$)[a,d]	211	469.3	602.2			
Regional Share – NE/National GDP[d]				14.10[e]	12.86	13.09
% product exported, NE/Total exports[d]				28%	12%	7%
Exports of goods and services as % of GDP						

[a] RAIS (for the 1980s, data refer to 1985).
[b] SUDENE,–US$ 1999.
[c] 1999.
[d] IPEA–IBGE, *Regional Accounts of Brazil*, 1985–2000, micro-data.
[e] 1985.

REFERENCES

Aghion, P., 1998. "Inequality and Economic Growth," in P. Aghion and J. Williamson, *Growth, Inequality and Globalization*, Cambridge: Cambridge University Press: 5–102

Álvarez, J. R., 1969. *Vidrio Soplado: Guadalajara*, Colección Jalisco en el Arte, Guadalajara: Planeación y promoción, SA

Amsden, A. H., 1992. *Asia's Next Giant: South Korea and Late Industrialization*, Oxford: Oxford University Press

2001. *The Rise of the "Rest": Challenges to the West from Late-Industrializing Economies*, Oxford: Oxford University Press

Arias, P., 1985. *Guadalajara la Gran Ciudad de la Pequeña Empresa*, Michoacán, El Colegio de Michoacán

Becattini, G., 1987. *Mercato e Forze Locali*, Bologna: Il Mulino

Brazil, 2003. Ministério da Integração Regional, Secretaria de Políticas de Desenvolvimento Regional, *Bases para a Recriação da SUDENE: Por uma Política de Desenvolvimento Sustentável para o Nordeste*, Brasilia: Ministry of Regional Integration

Casson, M., 1995. *Entrepreneurship and Business Culture*, Aldershot: Edward Elgar

Cohen, S. and G. Fields, 1999. "Social Capital and Capital Gains in Silicon Valley," *California Management Review*, 41(2): 108–130

Easterly, W., 2002. *The Elusive Quest for Growth: Economists' Misadventures in the Tropics*, Cambridge, MA: MIT Press

Gambetta, D. (ed.), 1988. *Trust: Making and Breaking Cooperative Relations*, Oxford: Oxford University Press

Instituto Nacional de Estadistica Geografia e Informatica (INEGI) (Mexico), 1988, 1993, 1990. *Economic Census, 1988, 1993, 1999*, Mexico City: INEGI, at www.inegi.gob.mx, Censo Económico

Kirzner, I., 1973. *Competition and Entrepreneurship*, Chicago: University of Chicago Press

Knight, F., 1921. *Risk, Uncertainty, and Profit*, New York: A. H. Kelley

Lavinas, L., M. Borges Lemos, C. Machado, M. Magina, and C. Rolim, 1996. "Saldo Comercial, Transferências Intergovernamentais e Movimento de Capital Interregional," *Estudos Econômicos*, 26(1): 5–20

Lavinas, L., E. Garcia, and F. Barros, 2000. *Salários e volume de emprego industrial no Nordeste*, Working Paper prepared for research project, Rio de Janeiro: IPEA

Lavinas, L. and M. Storper, 1999–2002. *Trajetórias para a economia do aprendizado: os novos mundos de produção no Nordeste*, Research Reports I, II, and III to the Banco do Nordeste, prepared at IPEA, Rio de Janeiro

Lorenzon, M., 1999. *Localised Learning and Community Capabilities*, Copenhagen: Copenhagen Business School, PhD series, 5.99

Lundvall, B.-Å., 2002. *Innovation, Growth, and Social Cohesion: The Danish Model*, Cheltenham: Edward Elgar

Marsden, D., 1999. *A Theory of Employment Systems*, Oxford: Oxford University Press

Mercado, F. J., A. Tapia, L. Robles, H. C. Sánchez, and A. Cuevas, 1989. *El perfil patológico de los artesanos de Tonalá y Tlaquepaque, Jalisco: Cuadernos*

de Divulgación, segunda época, Guadalajara: Editorial Universidad de Guadalajara
Mercado-Célis, A., 2003. "Tlaquepaque and Tonalá: Small Firms, Economic Practices and the Local Milieu," PhD dissertation, UCLA, Los Angeles
Monsivais, C., 1996. "Las artes populares: hacia la historia de un cannon," in *Arte Popular Mexicano: Cinco siglos*, Mexico City: Colegio de San Idelfonso: 15–28
Mulder, N., S. Montout, and L. Peres Lopes, 2002. "Brazil and Mexico's Manufacturing Performance in International Perspective, 1970–1999," Paris: CEPII Working Paper, 2002–5 at www.cepii.fr
Numazaki, I., 1991. "The Role of Personal Networks in the making of Taiwan's guanxiqiye," in G. Hamilton (ed.), *Business Networks and Economic Development in East and Southeast Asia*, Hong Kong: Hong Kong University Press: 123–191
Oliveira, F. de, 2003. *Critica à razão dualista – O Ornitorrinco*, São Paulo: Boi Tempo
Polenske, K. R., 2001. "Competitive Advantage of Regional Internal and External Supply Chains," in M. Lahr and Ronald Miller (eds.), *Essays in Honor of Benjamin H. Stevens*, Amsterdam: Elsevier: 259–284
Putnam, R., 2000. *Bowling Alone: The Collapse and Revival of American Community*, New York: Simon & Schuster
Putnam, R., R. Leonardi, and R. Y. Nanetti, 1993. *Making Democracy Work*, Princeton, NJ: Princeton University Press
Reynolds, P. D., S. M. Camp, W. D. Bygrave, E. Autio, and M. Hay, 2001. *Global Entrepreneurship Monitor: 2001 Executive Report*, Kansas City, MO: Kauffman Center for Entrepreneurial Leadership at the Ewing Marion Kauffman Foundation
Rodrik, D., 1999. *The New Global Economy and Developing Countries: Making Openness Work*, Washington, DC: Overseas Development Council
Romo Torres, R., 1990. *Dinámica sociocultural de la cerámica de Tonalá*, Cuadernos de difusión científica, 16, Mexico: Universidad de Guadalajara
Saxenian, A., 1994. *Regional Advantage*, Cambridge, MA: Harvard University Press
Schmitz, H., 1999. "Global Competition and Local Co-Operation: Success and Failure in the Sinos Valley, Brazil," *World Development*, 27(9): 1627–1650
Schumpeter, J. A., 1991. *The Economics and Sociology of Capitalism*, ed. Richard Swedberg, Princeton, NJ: Princeton University Press
Storper, M., 2005. "Society, Community and Economic Development," *Studies in Comparative International Development*, 39(4): 30–57
Wade, R., 1990. *Governing the Market: Economic Theory and the Role of Government in East Asian Industrialization*, Princeton, NJ: Princeton University Press

Index